THE SOURCES OF
THE DOCTRINES OF THE
FALL AND ORIGINAL SIN

THE SOURCES OF THE DOCTRINES OF THE FALL AND ORIGINAL SIN

F. R. TENNANT

Introductory by Mary Frances Thelen

Eugene, Oregon

TO MY WIFE

Wipf and Stock Publishers
199 W 8th Ave, Suite 3
Eugene, OR 97401

The Sources of the Doctrines of the Fall and Original Sin
By Tennant, F.R.
ISBN: 1-59244-857-7
Publication date 9/10/2004
Previously published by Cambridge, 1903

CONTENTS.

CHAPTER I.

THE FALL-STORY AND ITS EXEGESIS.
PAGE

Introductory—The Jahvist Document, its date, theological standpoint, style, composition—Exegesis of the narrative of Gen. iii.—Literary criticism of the Fall-story—Oral tradition . . 1

CHAPTER II.

THE ETHNOLOGICAL ORIGIN AND RELATIONS OF THE FALL-STORY.

Present state of comparative study of sacred legend—Elements of Fall-story derived from early religion of nomadic Hebrews—Phoenician parallels—Egyptian parallels—Babylonian parallels—Greek parallels—Iranian parallels—Indian parallels—Conclusion 22

CHAPTER III.

THE PSYCHOLOGICAL ORIGIN OF THE FALL-STORY: ITS RELATION TO HISTORY, ALLEGORY AND MYTH.

Traces of legends about the first man and Paradise in O.T.—Psychological origin of conceptions of the Garden of Eden, a golden age, the trees of Paradise—Fossil conceptions imbedded in Fall-story—Hypothetical reconstruction of early history of Fall-story—The story neither history, nor allegory, nor, in the strict sense, myth 61

CHAPTER IV.

THE PREPARATION IN THE OLD TESTAMENT FOR A DOCTRINE OF THE FALL AND OF ORIGINAL SIN.

PAGE

The use of elements of the Fall-story in the O.T.—Absence in O.T. of any doctrine derived from it—An alternative O.T. source of speculation on the origin of human sinfulness—Growth, in the O.T., of ideas involved in the doctrine of Original Sin—Universality and inherence of sinfulness—The *yezer* . . 89

CHAPTER V.

THE TEACHING OF ECCLESIASTICUS ON SIN AND THE FALL.

Introductory—Place of Ecclus. in Jewish literature—Its teaching as to Sin, the Fall and its consequences, Death 106

CHAPTER VI.

THE PREPARATION FOR THE DOCTRINE OF THE FALL IN ALEXANDRIAN JUDAISM.

The Sibylline Oracles—Wisdom—Philo—The Book of the Secrets of Enoch (Slavonic Enoch)—Note on 3 and 4 Maccabees . 122

CHAPTER VII.

THE FALL AND ORIGINAL SIN IN RABBINICAL LITERATURE.

Date and nature of the Rabbinic literature—Its teaching on man's first estate and fall—The tempter—The Fall-story regarded as symbolically descriptive of a sin of unchastity—Crude notion of inherited corruption derived from Eve—Rabbinic speculation on the introduction of Death—Adam and the race—The doctrine of the *yezer hara* not a doctrine of Original Sin . . . 145

CHAPTER VIII.

THE FALL AND ORIGINAL SIN IN JEWISH PSEUDEPIGRAPHIC LITERATURE.

Origin and characteristics of apocalyptic literature—I. The (Aethiopic) Book of Enoch, (*a*) The groundwork—Its Theodicy grounded on the legend of the Watchers : (*b*) The Similitudes :

Contents

PAGE

(c) Interpolations — II. The Testaments of the Twelve Patriarchs—III. The Book of Jubilees—IV. The Apocalypse of Abraham—V. Pseudo-Philo—Note on The Assumption of Moses, The Psalms of Solomon, The Testament of Abraham—VI. The Books of Adam, (a) The Apocalypse of Moses: (b) The Vita Adae : (c) The Book of Adam and Eve (Malan) or The Conflict of Adam and Eve (Dillmann): (d) The Treasure Cave: (e) The Apocalypse of Adam or The Testament of Adam and Eve : (f) The History of the Creation and of the Transgression of Adam : (g) Fragments of late Adam-literature—VII. The Greek Apocalypse of Baruch 177

CHAPTER IX.

THE FALL AND ORIGINAL SIN IN JEWISH PSEUDEPIGRAPHIC LITERATURE—(*continued*).

VIII. The Book of the Secrets of Enoch (Slavonic Enoch)—Its unique doctrine of Original Sin—IX. The (Syriac) Apocalypse of Baruch—X. 4 Ezra (2 Esdras)—Its relation to the last work and to S. Paul 204

Appendix to Chapter IX.—Incidental Allusions to the Fall in undoubtedly Christian Apocryphal Writings 232

CHAPTER X.

THE GROWTH OF THE DOCTRINE OF THE FALL, AND OF ITS ELEMENTS, IN JEWISH LITERATURE AS A WHOLE.

Usage in Jewish Literature of the Fall-stories of Gen. vi. 1-4 and Gen. iii.—Development of Doctrine from Gen. iii.—Summary of Jewish teaching on Adam in the unfallen state, The Fall and Death, The Tempter, etc. 235

CHAPTER XI.

S. PAUL'S DOCTRINE OF THE FALL.

The endeavour to interpret S. Paul in the light of contemporary Jewish thought—Discussion of Rom. v. 12 ff. and its exegesis—Rom. vii. 7 ff. on the psychological source of sin—1 Cor. xv. 45-50 irrelevant to our subject—Effects of the Fall on Nature—Dicta of S. Paul embody results of previous Jewish speculation 248

CHAPTER XII.

THE DOCTRINES OF THE FALL AND ORIGINAL SIN IN THE FATHERS BEFORE AUGUSTINE.

PAGE

The actual sources of the ecclesiastical doctrine of Original Sin not wholly identical with those of corresponding Jewish teaching—New sources appear in Irenaeus, Origen and Tertullian—The Doctrine of the Fall and Original Sin in I. The Apostolic Fathers—II. The Greek Apologists: Justin Martyr, Tatian, Theophilus of Antioch, Athenagoras—III. Irenaeus—IV. The Early Alexandrines: Clement, Origen 273

CHAPTER XIII.

THE DOCTRINES OF THE FALL AND ORIGINAL SIN IN THE FATHERS BEFORE AUGUSTINE—(*continued*).

V. Methodius, Athanasius and Cyril of Jerusalem—VI. The Cappadocians: Basil, Gregory of Nazianzus, Gregory of Nyssa—VII. The Antiochene School: Chrysostom, Theodore of Mopsuestia—VIII. Tertullian—IX. From Tertullian to Augustine: Cyprian, Hilary, Ambrose—Conclusion . . 307

ADDITIONS AND CORRECTIONS 346

INDEX OF PASSAGES 349
INDEX OF AUTHORS 355
INDEX OF SUBJECTS 360

CHAPTER I.

THE FALL-STORY AND ITS EXEGESIS.

Introductory.

THE starting-point for the historian of the Christian doctrines of the Fall and Original Sin is undoubtedly the narrative contained in the third chapter of the Book of Genesis. S. Paul's teaching as to the connexion of human sin and death with Adam's transgression is but one of the various possible interpretations of this narrative, slowly and tentatively reached after some centuries of Jewish exegesis and reflection. S. Augustine's fuller and more definite doctrine is but a developed form of one of the possible interpretations of the statements of S. Paul, arrived at after the preparation of further centuries of Christian speculation. The record which both the Apostle and the great Father of the West treated as essentially an account of historical fact was for each the ultimate source and foundation of his views with regard to the origin and universality of human sinfulness.

But this Old Testament story implies a previous course of development in theological thought much greater in duration than that by which were subsequently reached, from the biblical narrative as starting-point, the most complex post-Reformation theories of unfallen and fallen human nature. It can no longer be assumed, in the light of knowledge yielded by comparative mythology and the prehistoric sciences, that the third chapter of Genesis supplies us with the record of a revelation of historical fact, divinely given at some definite time, or even with a story whose form and details were wholly the creation of its writer's inspired imagination. It is a record which presents a complicated past history for our investigation. The theologian, then, who would completely trace the history of the doctrine of the Fall, though using the early chapters of Genesis as the fixed point whence to set out, must work backwards from their narrative itself to its mythological sources, and even, as far as possible, to the psychological conditions for the origin of these sources, as well as forwards to the developments and refinements familiar to students of the doctrine as it was expounded by scholastic theology in the period of its most highly perfected elaboration. And indeed it is only thus that he can estimate, from a purely theological standpoint, the validity of the claim which is still commonly made on behalf of this narrative: the claim that, whatever view be taken of its literary nature, it embodies a revelation of actual historical fact which forms the basis of the Christian doctrines of Sin and Redemption.

It is intended, therefore, in the present study of the development of the theory of the origin of human sinfulness involved in the ecclesiastical doctrines of the Fall and of Original Sin, to discuss somewhat fully the scriptural narrative from which those doctrines have been derived. It will be important to ascertain, in so far as it is possible, the meaning which this narrative had for the age in which it received its present form. This can of course only be done by divesting ourselves of all ideas which familiar later developments of thought cause us, perhaps, habitually to read into it; and by translating ourselves, as completely as may be, to the mental standpoint of its writer. And for guidance towards this end it will be necessary to make use of two lines of research. In the first place, it will be essential to recapitulate some of the results which can be said to have been reached, with any high degree of probability, concerning the date and nature of the writing in which the story of the first transgression is contained. Only thus can we attempt to recover its historical background. In the second place, it will be desirable to sift the material yielded by investigations in the fields of comparative religion and race-psychology for any such facts or general principles as may throw light upon the sources and previous history of the elements of which it is composed. The former of these lines of inquiry, together with the exegesis of the narrative as a whole, and its literary criticism, will occupy the present chapter.

The Jahvist Document.

The Paradise-story belongs to that stratum of the hexateuch called the Jahvist or, less happily, the Prophetic document (J). This is believed to draw from more ancient sources than the Elohist document (E), with which it came to be blended. The time at which the Jahvist history was written, and the length of the period occupied by the process of committing its material to writing, have not been ascertained with exactness; they are still matters of speculation. Indeed the data for an accurate determination of its age, as a writing, do not at present exist; there is a complete want of external evidence. Various dates between the limits 900—700 B.C. have been assigned to it, and the mean between these two extremes would perhaps be provisionally adopted by the majority of scholars. More definite statements on the matter, however, in the present condition of knowledge, are unsafe. It is therefore impossible to decide whether the history in which the account of the loss of Paradise is contained was first reduced to writing in the age of the earlier literary prophets or in pre-prophetic times. Inasmuch as it is precarious to ignore the possibility of the coexistence of widely different mental temperaments and theological standpoints at a time of active progress in religious thought; since we are ignorant as to how far the archaic characters of the stories contained in J are due to the fixation of their verbal form in oral transmission, and how far their editor or editors were content to be the servants rather than the masters of their material, which, though merely folk-lore, was doubtless very venerable in their eyes[1], it is not absolutely safe to infer that

---

[1] Several questions dealt with in this discussion of the Fall-story are complicated by our inability always to feel sure exactly how much of what is written represents the real standpoint of the Jahvist compiler, and how much is tradition of hoary antiquity whose perpetuation he desired or tolerated. There can be little doubt that the two motives, of preserving venerable traditions and of adapting them to be the vehicle for the highest Hebrew religion of his time, both strongly influenced the writer.

the Jahvist history, as a written document, was of necessity chronologically earlier than the period of the prophets. On the other hand there are no proofs of the influence of the writing prophets upon J sufficient to compel us to believe that that document could not have existed before the time of Amos or Hosea. On the contrary, it is not difficult to gauge the difference between the Jahvist source and the earliest prophetic books as to position on the scale of advancement in ethical, religious and theological reflection. Measured by such a standard, the Jahvist writing would seem to be decidedly the more primitive.

We may notice first, in illustration of this assertion, the crude naïveté of J's delineation of Jahveh. Jahveh is represented as possessing many purely human characteristics. He walks in the garden to enjoy the cool of the evening; He makes clothes for Adam and Eve; He smells the savour of Noah's sacrifice. He is wiser than men, but His knowledge is limited: He needs to come down to see the tower of Babel, and to ascertain by His own investigation whether the wickedness of Sodom is as great as He has heard. Jahveh is assigned many ethical attributes; but His character is not as yet very perfectly moralised. He apparently misrepresents to Adam and Eve the consequences that would follow from partaking of the tree of knowledge: He is jealous of man's encroachment on His prerogatives of knowledge and immortality. Jahveh is pourtrayed, in fact, in somewhat crudely anthropomorphic manner. And this anthropomorphism is altogether different from that, for example, of Amos, which is a necessary expedient for the description of God as a personal Being; that of the Jahvist narrative is the expression rather of a definite stage of theological thought, beyond which the prophets had advanced. Again, we fail to find in the Jahvist source any disapproval of reverence for 'holy places,' for sacred trees and wells, and similar survivals of Israel's earlier Nature-worship, such as would be vehemently denounced, as if heathenish and unspiritual, by the prophets. To them, much that the narratives of J contain must have been somewhat repulsive. These narratives evince a simplicity in the toleration of ancient morality and religion such as would have been impossible had they been the literary creation of writers thoroughly imbued with the severely ethical and polemically monotheistic ideas which characterise the message of the prophets. Thus the Jahvist history would seem to be approaching, rather than to have attained, the prophetic standpoint. It exhibits, however, much of the moral earnestness of prophecy, as may be seen from its treatment of sin. In the story with which we are especially concerned, for instance, the standpoint of earliest Hebrew moral thought, according to which sin is the breach of human custom, or an involuntary wrong, is left far behind[1]. Sin, in the Paradise-story, is a matter of what we should call the will and the conscience in relation to God, a deliberate transgression of a divine command: and this is the view of the prophets. But there is no reason to assume that we have here an instance of prophetic influence; rather must we postulate that the lofty ideas of the prophets had been developing in the minds of individuals who preceded them. It is also to be observed that the borrowed traditions incorporated into this source are very largely purified from mythological elements. Such foreign stories are modified in *ethos* and adapted to the purpose of the writer's theology. This self-purification of Hebrew religion had doubtless been in process, however, long before the period of the prophets.

Thus, if it is impossible to carry back, with safety, the *writing* of the Jahvist document to a time at all distantly pre-prophetic, it is extremely probable, for the reasons which have just been given, that the narratives contained in it are of much greater antiquity than the document itself, and that they are witnesses to the religious thought of Israel long before the times in which the literary prophets lived. We shall probably not be far wrong if we refer the present literary form of J to a writer who lived somewhere near the threshold of the prophetic age; and if, in our exegesis of it, we endeavour to interpret it from the mental standpoint of that

---

[1] See W. R. Smith, *The Prophets of Israel*, 1895, pp. 102 ff.; Clemen, *Lehre von der Sünde*, 1ᵉʳ Theil, S. 21; Schultz, *O. T. Theology*, E. T.

time, in so far as that standpoint is capable of being recovered[1].

It may be added that the Jahvist record is in all probability to be regarded, so far as it is a collection of elements of folklore and history, as the product of a school of writers. For there are overwhelmingly strong reasons, from the point of view of literary criticism, for believing it to be ultimately of composite authorship, and for regarding it as capable of differentiation into further elements.

Adopting the suggestion of Wellhausen, Budde was the first to point out the existence of different sources in J; and he has been followed, in so far as his main results are concerned, by most other critics. But in spite of being thus incompletely homogeneous in structure, the Jahvist document, when considered in relation even to the Elohistic writing, has generally been held to be a unity distinguished for the most part by a characteristic style and other traits. Its literary style is simple, incisive and vivid; and the artistic merit of some of its stories, which present a highly finished picture by means of a few entirely concrete touches, is of the highest order. The account of the temptation and transgression in Eden is often said, from this point of view, to be a pearl of Hebrew literature.

The conciseness and skilful construction of some of these stories has suggested to several of the ablest scholars that they owe the form in which they appear in our written records to gradual perfection whilst being orally transmitted. In this case, the literary criticism which has emphasised minute differences of style between the various strata of the hexateuch, and has attempted "to get some coherent conception of the authors from their works[2]," has overreached itself. And indeed the reaction against such criticism has already set in. In Prof. Gunkel's recent commentary on Genesis[3], which

---

[1] J's deep knowledge of human nature and its moral capacities, his extensive ethnological information, and other qualities, point towards a date bordering on that of the earlier prophets. See McCurdy, *History, Prophecy and the Monuments*, vol. III. chap. iii.

[2] *Critical Review*, XII. i. p. 5.

[3] A work to which, perhaps, even before this point, indebtedness should have been acknowledged.

represents the tendency of methods of research which will probably be further used in the immediate future, the symbols J, E etc. are indeed retained; but they cease to represent individual writers or composers: they stand rather for collections of *oral* tradition, for the work of guilds rather than of single persons. But reactions proverbially go to extremes; and however large may have been the part played by oral reciters of the *sagas* of Genesis in giving them dramatic form, and however great the reverence of collectors for the venerable material which tradition yielded, there are obvious proofs that those who finally embodied it in the written record which we inherit dealt freely with it in respect of expurgation and adaptation to a moral and religious purpose, and therefore stamped upon it the impress of their respective individualities. Moreover some at least of the stories of J, besides sharing in common the marks of a single purpose and the traits of one and the same literary style, suggest the master hand of uncommon genius; they reveal an art which cannot safely be ascribed to successive casual improvements of a floating popular poem, but which receives a more natural explanation in the view which sober criticism has long scientifically upheld: the view, namely, that the final *literary* form of these stories is due in the main to the artistic genius of a moulder of tradition[1].

The existence in oral tradition of the narratives which are woven, in the Jahvist document, into a continuous history, will call for notice at a later page. Meanwhile, it is hoped that the foregoing account of the writing in which the Fall-story is enshrined, brief as it has of necessity been, may suffice to show that, when the materials of this story were taking their present form, Hebrew religion was of a comparatively primitive kind, and Hebrew theology, as distinguished from the mythology which preceded it, was in a scarcely more than nascent state. These considerations should make us cautious lest we attribute to the narrative, didactic though it was intended to be, a doctrinal significance deeper than its writer knew, and

[1] There are now and again verbal coincidences between the several narratives of J which would seem to be best explained by this theory. Cf. *e.g.* Gen. iii. 16 and iv. 7; iii. 17 and iv. 11; iii. 9 and iv. 9.

ignore the possibility that much of the rich theological suggestiveness which it bears for us was undesigned. To its marvellous artistic merit, and to its having been taken, rightly or wrongly, to treat, with all its characteristic vigour, of a deep problem in which mankind have for ages been profoundly interested, must largely be attributed, no doubt, the influence, exceptional not only for Old Testament lore but for literature in general, which it has exerted upon the thought of so many centuries, and the fact that so many generations, and indeed so many great philosophers, have read in it their own reflections and ideas[1].

Exegesis of the narrative of Gen. III.

Regarding the Paradise-story as a single connected narrative embodying one or several particular didactic purposes, and postponing for the present the questions of its composite nature and of the past history of the materials of which it is composed, we may now proceed to the exegesis of the story as it stands. We have to endeavour, that is, to ascertain what was the meaning which its *literary* author, the individual who gave to it its present written form, intended to convey to contemporaries of the early prophetic or the pre-prophetic period. It is from the standpoint of that age, in so far as we can recover it, that the Jahvist narrative must be read. Consequently it is necessary for the present to ignore the lingering reminiscences of still earlier meaning and association which portions of the passage undoubtedly

---

[1] *e.g.* Kant, Herder, Hegel, Schiller.

For a full treatment of the questions discussed above, for authority for the statements made, and for many of the inferences drawn from them, the student is referred to the following works: Carpenter and Harford-Battersby, *The Hexateuch*, vol. I. 1900; Addis, *Documents of the Hexateuch*; Spurrell, *Notes on the text of Genesis*, 2nd ed.; Holzinger, *Einleitung in den Hexateuch*, and *Genesis*; Montefiore, *Hibbert Lectures*, 1892; Gunkel, *Genesis*; W. R. Smith, *Religion of the Semites* and *Prophets of Israel*; Budde, *Urgeschichte*; Kittel, *History of the Hebrews*, E. T.; Worcester, *The Book of Genesis in the light of modern.knowledge*; Arts. *Genesis, Hexateuch*, etc., in Hastings' *Dictionary of the Bible* and *Encyclopaedia Biblica*. Opposed views may be found in Green, *Unity of Genesis*. For an attempt to reproduce the idiom and style of Gen. iii. by literal translation, see Duff, *O. Test. Theology*, vol. II. The translations of Lenormant into French, and of Kautzsch into German, may be found useful.

contain, and to concentrate attention solely upon the implications which its compiler himself intended to convey; and it is equally essential to avoid the opposite extreme of unhistorical interpretation already mentioned, the natural tendency to find in the story the reflections of far later ages. It will be desirable therefore, at the outset, to lay aside any ready-made views or doctrines which we have been wont to associate with its contents, and which inevitably transmit their colour to its statements; remembering that what New Testament or patristic writers understood from it only enables us to estimate what it meant to them, not what it implied to its compiler or to the generation to which it was addressed.

Of these two errors, the former has frequently been committed by students of folk-lore and comparative mythology, who, disregarding the facts supplied by history and literary criticism, have discussed the Fall-story as if it were on a level with the crudest of heathen mythology or symbolism, and have regarded it as intended to convey a meaning which could only have been associated at all with the much more primitive ideas whence possibly the imagery of the story was at first derived, but which only survive in the existing narrative as lingering echoes; ideas which, in their entirety and their original significance, were incapable of being inculcated in the work of a writer belonging to such a period as we assign to the Jahvist document. It is the opposite anachronism to this, however, which calls for more emphatic notice here; for it is this which vitiates the traditional exegesis of the third chapter of Genesis. This exegesis is less an exposition of the real meaning of the narrative than an imposition upon it of subsequently developed teaching. According to the interpretation which hitherto has generally been adopted, the story is primarily an account of a fall of the human race in its first parents; it is not merely an account of the historical entrance of sin into the world but also an explanation of the origin and universality of sinfulness throughout mankind.

There is no hint, however, in the passage itself, of Adam's moral condition being fundamentally altered by his act of disobedience. The only allusion to the original estate of our first parents, attributing to them absence of shame at the fact that they were naked, of itself implies no more than that they shared the ignorance of childhood, or that they did not possess even the most elementary characteristics of civilisation. Indeed, in the following chapter the same history describes the beginnings of the rudest arts. The narrative, too, connects the awakening of shame not with sense of guilt, but with acquisition of knowledge due to the magical virtues of the tree. And the changes brought about through the punishment of the transgression are physical: the ills of human life. There is no implication that Adam originally differed from any other man as regards capacity for integrity or for intercourse with God, or that his 'nature' was perverted by his act of disobedience. The idea that his sin was the source of the sinfulness of succeeding generations, or in any way an explanation of it, is altogether absent from the narrative; and, so far as we can gather from the Old Testament, it was foreign to the thought of the prophetic, not to speak of the pre-prophetic, age. For though the Jahvist source undoubtedly emphasises the seriousness and the general diffusion of sin[1], it yet has no adequate sense of the *absolute* universality of sin, such as was attained in later ages[2]. Nor is there room for the inference that it assigns to Adam's fall any deteriorating influence upon the free self-determination of his posterity. Cain's sin is by no means thus explained; but the whole of his guilt and responsibility is thrown upon the sinner himself. Sin is personified and compared to a ravenous beast lurking for its prey; but Cain is told that 'he ought to rule over it[3].' If sinfulness

[1] Gen. iv., vi. 5—8, 12, viii. 21, ix. 20—27, xi. 1—9.
[2] Gen. vi. 5 ff., 12, viii. 21 speak of sin as being universally spread, but only at a particular time. Abel is regarded as well-pleasing to God, and Noah as righteous before Him; therefore the representation of 'all flesh' as having 'corrupted its way,' and of man as such that 'every imagination of the thoughts of his heart was only evil continually,' cannot, without inconsistency, be interpreted as if it were an absolute statement about all mankind from the beginning onwards.
[3] Gen. iv. 7 (R.V. *margin*). This translation makes much better sense than that adopted in the text, and embodies what was apparently the recognised interpretation of the synagogue (*Siphre* 82 b; *Jerus. Targum*). The *Targum of Onkelos* misses the meaning here. See, on this passage, Loisy, *Revue d'histoire et de littérature relig.*, I. 335 ff.; Spurrell, *Notes on the Heb. Text of Genesis.* Sin is

is traced to an 'evil imagination,' it is not ascribed to what we call the evil 'nature,' of the individual heart. We are here very far even from the Jewish doctrine of the *yezer hara*. Finally, if the Jahvist compiler has intended, in his account of the beginnings of human history, to sketch the development of sin in the world, which may well be the case, it must be observed that the first transgression is not only not treated as different in import from others, as if it were the most momentous catastrophe, but simply as the first of a series whose members are arranged in ascending order of magnitude: the disobedience of the first parents, the fratricide of their son, the increased bloodthirstiness of Lamech, the general corruption calling for the deluge[1].

It is to be concluded then, from exegetical grounds alone, that the history contained in Gen. iii. was not intended by its ultimate compiler to supply an explanation of the cause of universal sinfulness. The most that it offers is an account of Sin's actual beginning. Mankind's capacity for sin from the first is assumed. Later Hebrew literature, as will be seen, supports this conclusion by strongly suggesting that, at the period in which J was produced, the time was not ripe for such advanced reflection. The Jahvist writer must be said to have had no doctrine of a fall of the race in Adam as the cause of the moral evil of Adam's posterity.

It is indeed open to question whether the narrative under consideration was intended *primarily* as a description of the entrance of sin into the world, rather than as an explanation of the ills of life, which are here, as in many ancient legends, associated with the striving after knowledge and civilisation. Perhaps, after all, its chief moral is that human evils are the consequence of sin[2]. Man's hard lot is indeed traced to *sin*;

personified and viewed as masc., according to this interpretation. The Heb., however, leaves the R.V. (text) rendering possible.

[1] The general depravity which brought upon the race the visitation of the deluge is expressly assigned by J to another cause (Gen. vi. 1—4, probably a more original Hebrew account of the entrance of sin into the world; see below, chs. viii., x.). Increased sinfulness is associated with increased scope for indulgence of passion consequent upon increased progress in the arts.

[2] Rothe regarded it as an account of the origin of death rather than of sin. See Dorner, *System of Christ. doctrine*, E.T., III. p. 13, n. 5. For other views see Clemen, *Lehre von der Sünde*, S. 151 ff.

Adam and Eve consciously transgress a divine command, and Eve admits that she has been 'beguiled.' But though the story thus assumes the character of a history of the first sin, it may be doubted whether it does so in a manner other than secondary and, to some extent, incidental. The writer has certainly imparted a moral tone to his material which it possibly altogether lacked in an earlier state; yet, if we are to judge from the structure of his skilfully told drama, his interest centres rather on the physical evils of life than on the moral cause to which they are attributed. It is the introduction of these ills that forms the climax to which his account of the transgression leads. This point is, however, very difficult to decide. For the story is really complex, and deals simultaneously with several questions which seem to have perplexed primitive thought; and no help towards a decision is supplied by the surrounding context, which deals with several aspects of human development. But it is much less to the point to answer this question than to raise it; the only useful purpose served in either case being a protest against the hasty assumption that the passage should be regarded exclusively, or even pre-eminently, as a Fall-story. There would seem to be much reason for associating it with the class of stories called culture-legends, and for considering it as part of a history of the growth of civilisation regarded on its religious side. And this brings us to the question: what was the nature of the act in which the transgression consisted?—a question which in turn depends on the interpretation to be given to 'the tree of the knowledge of good and evil.'

Wellhausen[1] made a new departure in the exegesis of Gen. iii. when he repudiated the view that the eating of the forbidden tree of knowledge was intended to represent the means by which man acquired moral determination, the awakening of conscience, or the knowledge of the difference between virtue and sin. The knowledge which the narrator understands Adam and Eve to have thus obtained, and for

---

[1] *Prolegomena*, 2te Ausg., 1. S. 315 ff. Clemen thinks that Wellhausen here unconsciously follows von Hofmann, and refers to that writer's *Schriftbeweis*, 2te Ausg., S. 475 ff.

the acquisition of which they were punished, Wellhausen urges, could not possibly be moral knowledge. The possession of this is already presupposed in that the narrative represents the man and woman as understanding beforehand the difference between obedience and disobedience; and God could hardly be regarded by the writer as wishing to withhold knowledge of this kind from man. It is, on the contrary, general knowledge, or cleverness, which is here prohibited, and which man is represented as anxious to possess: knowledge which, in the highest sense, belongs only to God, and in appropriating which man is regarded as exceeding the limits of his nature, as encroaching upon divine prerogatives, and as making himself independent of and equal to God. It is the knowledge of the secrets of the world, the knowledge which is power, and which, at the same time, involves a break with the state of nature. Wellhausen also seeks to justify this conclusion by pointing out that the primary sense of the Hebrew words for 'good' and 'evil' is 'beneficial' and 'hurtful'; and it is in this sense that he considers them to be used in the present passage.

In criticising this treatment of the story of the loss of Paradise, Budde[1] attempted to evade the difficulty that, if the tree was the means by which man's moral judgment or self-determination was to be acquired, God must be here represented as unwilling for man to rise above the non-moral level of the brutes. This writer maintains that the name of the tree of the knowledge of good and evil signifies that man was destined in any case to learn by it what was morally good and evil; for, whether he obeyed or transgressed the command concerning it, he would equally attain to such knowledge, and in the former case would have done so without violating the will of God. Dillmann would similarly explain the meaning of the tree of knowledge[2]. Smend, however, has shown that there are insuperable objections against such an interpretation[3]. As he points out, Adam and

---

[1] *Urgeschichte*, S. 65 ff.   [2] *Genesis*, 6te Aufl., S. 46.
[3] *Alt-Test. Religionsgeschichte*, 1893, S. 120. The few pages to be found here on the contents of Gen. ii., iii., form a valuable piece of literature on the subject.

Eve are represented as being expelled from Eden not because they had *wrongly* acquired the knowledge of good and evil, but because they had come to possess it at all. This knowledge has made them so dangerous to Jahveh, Who says 'the man is become as one of us,' that if they now obtained the further divine prerogative of immortality His unique majesty and superiority would be threatened. Therefore are they driven out of Paradise and deprived of access to the tree of life. The knowledge imparted by the tree, then, could scarcely be the discernment of moral good and evil; this could not make its human possessor a dangerous rival to the Deity. The knowledge, moreover, was forbidden *absolutely*; and analogy with the tree of life requires that it could only be acquired by the actual eating of the forbidden fruit, not at all by the moral discipline involved in resisting the temptation to partake of it[1]. We do not hesitate to conclude, therefore, that the knowledge of good and evil spoken of in this narrative is, as Wellhausen maintained, the knowledge which makes man more or less the lord of Nature, the wisdom which can turn natural forces to human use[2]. Thus the Paradise-story attempts to connect the painful elements of human life with the thirst for progress in knowledge and culture, and at the same time, in harmony with nascent Hebrew ethical religion, identifies the transition from ignorance to intelligence, just because it, in turn, has been connected with the introduction of physical evils, with a transition from innocence to guilt. That this reading of the narrative involves the representation of Jahveh as hostile to man's intellectual development is no difficulty. Such an idea is in keeping with the rudimentary theology of the age to which, in its earlier, oral, forms, at least, the narrative belongs. For Jahveh is not, for ancient Hebrew writers,

---

[1] With this agrees the earliest known Jewish interpretation of the tree and its action, in the *Book of Enoch*, xxxii. 3. See below, ch. viii.

[2] Gunkel, in his recent commentary on Genesis, takes the transgression to be the half conscious sin of children, and the transition which resulted to be that from the ignorance of childhood to the rationality of maturer age. This would seem to be a distinct retrogression from the illuminating and consistent interpretation of Wellhausen, Smend and others, which one is glad to find to be also adopted in at least one Art. (*Knowledge*) in Hastings' *Dictionary of the Bible*.

so far exalted above man as to be omniscient in the sense of knowing without the need of learning[1], or to be superior to the necessity of safeguarding His supremacy against numbers[2], or strength and longevity[3], as well as against the knowledge which is especially said to confer on man 'likeness to God[4].' The original meaning of the story, or of one strand of its intertwined component elements, undoubtedly reveals itself in the verse[5] which assigns dread, within the divine circle, of man's becoming a rival power as the reason for the expulsion from Paradise, and therefore for the prohibition of the tree of knowledge.

The narrator evidently assumes without question the justice of the divine resentment; he acquiesces in the punishment of the sinners, and attributes to Adam and Eve the same culpable intention as that of the builders of the tower of Babel. Their act bespoke a wrong independence of God, Who had prepared the world and Paradise especially for man, and Who would have continued to insure man's happiness had he not overstepped the limits within which, according to the thought of a remote age, mankind's development was conceived as intended to proceed. It is difficult, however, on account of the surviving traces of more primitive thought[6], to catch here with certainty the note of one who writes or compiles, as it would seem, from the verge of the prophetic point of view. But the idea of Jahveh's strong resentment of any form of human exaltation against Himself, or of encroachment upon His divine prerogatives, is conspicuous in many Old Testament writings, according to which pride and self-reliant defiance constitute the essence of sin[7]. If Jahveh's resentment of man's progress in knowledge

---

[1] Cf. above, p. 4.   [2] Gen. xi. 6—8.
[3] *Ibid.* vi. 3. R.V. *margin*.   [4] *Ibid.* iii. 5, 22.
[5] *Ibid.* iii. 22, a verse which escaped editorial purgation of its polytheistic implications.
[6] Thus in iii. 22, Jahveh admits that the serpent's assertion as to the virtues of the tree was true and no lie; and His own threat as to the consequence of eating, on the other hand, was not fulfilled. Did an older version directly impute a benevolent deception to Jahveh? See also below, p. 72 f.
[7] Cf. the incidents of Israel's asking for a king, 1 Sam. viii. 6, and David's numbering of the people, 2 Sam. xxiv.; and see, in the prophetic books, Hos. viii.

seems to us an impossible thought to attribute to the writer of Genesis iii., we must bear in mind, in addition to the crudity of his theology, and the existence, elsewhere in the Old Testament, of ideas which present some approach to that which we are inclined to think objectionable, the fact that the writer was probably almost as much the servant as the master of the substance of his venerable traditions. Moreover, it has seemed to some authorities that what he thus derived, to some extent, ultimately from foreign sources in order to furnish a 'history of origins,' he hardly assimilated, in all respects, to his own thought[1].

Literary Criticism of the Fall-story.

It has already been stated that, in the opinion of some of the best critics, the Jahvist document is composite in literary

---

3, 4, x. 13, xii. 8, 14; Isai. ii. 7—22, iii. 1—4, x. 13 ff., xiv. 12 ff., xxii. 7—11, xxxvii. 24; also (later) Ezek. xxviii. The idea that there are secret things that God alone possesses the right to know, appears in Deut. xxix. 29. That wisdom is 'hid from the eyes of all living,' is taught in Job xxviii. 21. The conception of lofty things being in antagonism to God occurs also in Job xxi. 22, xxxviii. 15; Isai. x. 33 (see Toy, *Crit. Commentary on Proverbs*, p. 128). Hebrew thought on this point had therefore at least some resemblance to that of the Greeks embodied in the Prometheus legend. It may be added that the folk-lore of a much later age attributed man's knowledge of various arts and sciences to devilish agencies, as is evident from the groundwork of the *Book of Enoch* (see below, chap. viii.).

[1] Smend, *op. cit.*, S. 121-2, observes that the pessimistic tone of the conclusion of Gen. iii., and the deep rupture which it describes as existing betwixt God and man, is forgotten when the writer passes on to the history of the patriarchal time. Gunkel (*op. cit.*, S. 29), however, demurs to the inference that the pessimistic view may not have been equally characteristic of Hebrew thought.

Though the primitive myths which underlie the Paradise-story were doubtless largely foreign in origin, we need not have recourse to the supposition of incomplete assimilation or 'Hebraisation' in order to explain the apparent inconsistency, just alluded to, in its portraiture of Jahveh. It is true that Jahveh is now conceived in it as an Elohim-Being who resents human knowledge of certain things as an encroachment on the divine sphere, and now as the beneficent Power who prepared the world for man, and created him to enjoy an easy and pleasant life in the divine garden. We have, in this portraiture, elements in common with the characters of both the Kronos and the Zeus of Hesiod. But, as pointed out above, there is something remotely resembling envy clinging to the character of Jahveh in O. T. writings later than J. This fact is sufficient to explain the implications of Gen. iii., and to show that there is foundation in early Hebrew thought for both the qualities of character there attributed to Jahveh.

structure. Indeed in its story of Paradise and the temptation there appear signs of compilation from more than one written source, or of editorial interpolations. Inasmuch as the nearly contemporary Elohist document refers by name to previously existing books[1], it is *a priori* probable that earlier *writings* were also used in the compilation of J. A close study of the document, and indeed of that portion of it with which we are especially concerned, goes far to prove this supposition inductively. It will be unnecessary to enter here with any degree of fulness into the literary-critical problems which the Jahvist narrative of Gen. ii—iii. presents[2]. It will be sufficient to mention such provisional results of the close scrutiny to which the record has been subjected as are probable in themselves and relevant to the purpose in hand, passing by the more elaborate attempts to assign minute shreds of the dissected narrative to particular sources and, above all, conjecturally to rewrite the text, as somewhat arbitrary, and decidedly less trustworthy than ingenious and bold.

The first nineteen verses of Chap. iii. are admitted with almost complete unanimity to be a practically homogeneous literary composition. The account which they present of the temptation, sin and punishment of Adam and Eve is a self-consistent whole: a story methodically and skilfully told with hardly a superfluous word: the outcome of creative or adaptative reflection upon traditional material, and very possibly welded, to some extent, into its present form during the process of oral transmission. The 20th verse, however, which offers somewhat irrelevantly and abruptly an etymological explanation of the name Eve (*Havvah*), such as would be more in place in Chap. iv., is generally suspected of being

---

[1] The Book of the Wars of Jahveh (Num. xxi. 14, but this passage is obscure, see *Academy*, Oct. 22, 1892), and the Book of Jasher (or the Upright) (Josh. x. 13, 2 Sam. i. 18). These books are likely to date from about David's reign.

[2] For a fuller treatment see Budde, *Urgeschichte*; Holzinger, *Einleitung in den Hexateuch*, and *Genesis*; Gunkel, *Genesis* (*Nowack's Hand-Kommentar zum A.T.*, 1901); Schrader, *Studien zur Kritik u. Erklärung der bibl. Urgeschichte*, S. 119 ff. (which maintains the unity of authorship of the history of chaps. ii. and iii.); Carpenter and Harford-Battersby, *Hexateuch*, vols. I. and II. (*in loc.*).

an addition from a different source, or a redactor's interpolation. There is also considerable doubt as to whether the last three verses of Chap. iii. do not contain fragments detached from at least one other source than that which supplies the main portion of the narrative[1]. Budde, followed by Holzinger, Stade, Gunkel and many others, regards the passages mentioning a tree of life as interpolations foreign to the main thread of the story, which only refers (iii. 3) to one tree 'in the midst of the garden[2].' Again, the expulsion from Eden seems, in vv. 23 and 24, to be narrated twice; and a similar reduplication has been thought to exist in the description of the planting of Eden in Chap. ii., implying the use of varying traditions. Finally, the verses in that chapter (10—14) which describe the four rivers of Paradise have generally been regarded as an addition of later date[3].

[1] Gunkel (*Genesis*, S. 23) makes suggestive but venturesome conjectures with regard to some of these supposed fragments. The source which yields ii. 8, 9, and perhaps iii. 21, 22, and the allusion in iii. 24 to the 'flame of a sword,' would appear to him to be more mythological than that from which the main part of the story is drawn. This writer's division of J into sub-sources differs from that of Budde.

[2] For his reasons, some of which are strong, see *Urgeschichte*, S. 46 ff., or Holzinger, *Genesis*, S. 26 and 41. Inasmuch as in both Chaps. ii. and iii. one tree only is forbidden, though from iii. 22 the tree of life ought equally to be prohibited, because, once tasted, it would have conferred immortality and made man, in that sense, 'equal to God,' it seems possible that the tree of life was inserted in ch. ii. (the construction of ii. 9 *b* is awkward and remarkable; see Kautzsch and Socin, *Genesis*, and on the opposite side Driver, *Hebraica*, 1885, p. 33) to prepare the way for iii. 22, which is possibly derived from a different written source than that which supplies iii. 1—19. It is sometimes held, on the other hand (see Addis, *op. cit., in loc.*; Worcester, *op. cit.*; Kuenen, *Theol. Tijdschrift*, xviii. 136; Cheyne, *Encycl. Bibl.*, Art. *Paradise*), that the passages which mention the tree of life represent an older version; that the tree of knowledge, said to be more distinctly Hebrew, replaced it in the later source used by the writer of ch. iii. and that its name was interpolated in ch. ii. Cf. also Loisy, *Revue d'histoire et de littérature religieuses*, i. 225 ff.

[3] It will be obvious that the arguments for the existence in this narrative of fragments of at least one more written source than the principal are based not upon alleged differences of style, but upon apparent repetitions, discontinuities, and even discrepancies. It would be difficult, *e.g.*, to believe that the three various statements as to the position of Eden relatively to the writer's home, in ii. 8, 11—14 and iii. 24, could have been originally penned by the same hand.

It may be mentioned here that Budde, *op. cit.*, S. 83, and Robertson Smith (*Religion of the Semites*, 1894, p. 307, n. 2) regard the words in ii. 15, 'to dress it ahd to keep it,' as a later addition inconsistent with the punishment mentioned in iii. 17—19. Possibly the whole verse should be assigned to the same source as that from which the four preceding verses are taken. Gunkel (*Gen., in loc.*)

We may provisionally accept these results of criticism without admitting that they are all so indisputably grounded as to compel conviction. It can indeed hardly be doubted that they contain some truth. In that case we have evidence of the existence, probable enough in itself, of several varying written forms of the Paradise-story, from which the complete Jahvist account was ultimately compiled.

It is probable that the writing of continuous national history began, with the Hebrews, about the time of David or Solomon[1], perhaps a century or so before the compilation of the Jahvist document. During this interval there was scope for numerous recensions of the first written collections of folk-lore to have been produced, embodying variants of the several legends and incorporating additions derived from living oral tradition by successive compilers. The work of the final editor of J, like that of the redactor who united it with E, would probably consist less in the collection of oral material at first hand than in the more purely literary process of blending and rewriting the different narratives of his predecessors, adapting them to his own purpose and point of view, and impressing upon the material thus worked up the thought of the generation or the circle which he represented, or, it may be, the results of his own reflection. This, however, is but probable conjecture. The time is perhaps yet distant when we shall be able to define the relation of the 'author' of our narrative to his work[2].

banishes ii. 8, but only the word 'Eden' in *v.* 15. According to this writer's criticism, there would be no mention in the main narrative of the name Eden. According to the emendation of Budde and Robertson Smith (cf. Loisy, *op. cit.*), man would not be represented as intended for agricultural labour, before the act of disobedience, even in so small a degree as would be implied in the keeping of a garden of fruit-trees.

[1] See *Encyclopaedia Bibl.*, Art. *Historical Literature*; McCurdy, *op. cit.*, vol. III. chap. iii.

[2] By way of illustrating the variety of possibilities which present themselves, the following sentence may be quoted from an Art. by Prof. Toy in the *Journal of Bibl. Literature*, x. p. 1 : "The author may be an editor who has retouched the less perfect work of a predecessor; or he or some earlier writer may have gathered material from several sources, and combined different narratives into one story ; or various traditions, growing up under diverse conditions, may have coalesced ; or the present narrative may be the result of several or of all these processes—the final redactor, for example, may have made selections from narratives, already worked over by tradition and by the pen, and treated them in his own way for a particular purpose.

It may further be borne in mind that the connected narrative commencing at Chap. ii. 4 *b* and continuing through Chap. iii. is also complex in another sense than in that which has been mentioned. In addition to the literary-critical problem which has just been discussed, there is an archaeological problem, more closely associated with the inquiries to which the two succeeding chapters are to be devoted. Besides including, as we have seen to be probable, extracts from more than one history dealing with similar subject-matter, the passage Gen. ii. 4 *b*—iii. also comprises different legendary narratives dealing with different subjects. Most critics recognise the presence of a Creation-story and a Paradise-story; and the latter of these would in turn seem to betray signs of being compounded of two elements[1] quite different in their purport.

These elements, in the prehistoric time when traditions were only transmitted orally, were once probably independent and unconnected units. In the Jahvist document these originally independent entities have been welded into a continuous history; yet not so perfectly as to obliterate discrepancies. It is these several "sagas," each a whole in itself, as Gunkel has recently insisted[2], that are to be considered as the ultimate units of which Genesis is made up, rather than the written sub-sources J_1, J_2, etc., which have been laid under contribution in its literary compilation. If the writers of the primaeval history may have done much in the way of purging, adapting, arranging and blending their material, they took little or no part, in all probability, in the creation of its substance and imagery. This was rather the work

---

[1] For details see Toy, *op. cit.*, p. 12, and Gunkel, *op. cit.* S. 21—24. Such a theory seems necessary to account for some of the discrepancies which commentators have observed in the narrative. Clemen (*Lehre von der Sünde*) thinks that a Hebrew sin-story became afterwards modified into, or welded with, a culture-legend, giving the present narrative.

[2] *Op. cit.*, S. xix. The introduction to this commentary, perhaps the most important on Genesis in existence, contains much that is indispensable to the future student. Its author, in calling attention to the probable long continuance of much of the contents of Genesis in the state of oral tradition, makes an important advance in the science of criticism for which several investigators had already recognised that the time was ripe. In more than one passage free use has here been made of Prof. Gunkel's Introduction.

of the people collectively. When the stories came to be
for the first time reduced to writing they were already of
high antiquity; they had existed as unwritten folk-lore for
many generations, and different elements in them are perhaps
of very different age. It was during this period of oral transmission that the variants of the myths arose, of whose existence we have some evidence in Genesis itself and in other
parts of the Old Testament. Distortion, embellishment and
elimination, due to the inherent impossibility of oral tradition
to keep itself pure and unaltered, and also deliberate adaptation to changed circumstances of life and diverse stages of
religious development, must inevitably have affected the form
of the folk-lore of the Hebrews during the interval between
their settlement in Canaan and the commencement of a
national literature after the establishment of the kingdom.
The purification of this folk-lore from nature-myth and polytheistic association, largely accomplished in the Jahvist source
though still leaving room for further expurgation and refine-
ment in the Priestly Code, belongs, perhaps, mostly to the
beginning of the literary period. Grosser elements may have
been eliminated, of course, whilst the narratives were still
handed down by word of mouth ; the process, doubtless, was
gradual. Myths originally relating to profane subjects may
have already come, in prehistoric times, to embody a religious
motive. Independent explanations of the origin of different
things would become welded into a single complex story.
Touches of native colouring would inevitably here and there
replace details in an exotic myth ; whilst elements derived
from foreign sources would become permanently incorporated
in traditions of purely Hebrew origin. From such general
considerations as these with regard to the possible or probable
history of Hebrew legends during the pre-literary age, it may
be inferred that the thorough analysis of any one of them,
and the tracing of its several elements to their ultimate
sources, must form, in the present state of our knowledge, a
problem not admitting of complete solution. The subjects
discussed in the present and the succeeding chapter are
matters upon which an enormous amount has been written
but about which very little is certainly known.

CHAPTER II.

THE ETHNOLOGICAL ORIGIN AND RELATIONS OF THE FALL-STORY.

IT is the purpose of the present chapter to commence inquiry into the previous history of the contents of the Jahvist narrative of the Fall, by collecting from the field of comparative religion such evidence as there may be of connexion between it and the corresponding legends of other peoples.

It is an easy matter to find, in the literature of ancient nations or in the traditions of modern uncivilised races, stories in some degree parallel to, or containing elements in common with, the Hebrew account of the first man and his fall. But to assign the true cause for such similarities in particular cases is, in the present state of knowledge, for the most part far beyond our power. To determine how much of the similarity is due to actual borrowing on one side or the other, and on which; how much to inheritance from a common stock of traditions; how much to the psychological unity of mankind, to the fact, that is, that human thought, on the same level of culture, proceeds to a great extent in accordance with the same psychological laws and evolves more or less similar products; and, finally, how much to mere coincidence: this is a task for which our generation is not equipped. Before we are able to trace relations of actual dependence, except in the case of a few points of detail, great advances in the collection and, more especially, in the critical sifting of material must be made. At the present time there is an insufficiency of data accessible to the theologian to guarantee much valuable

CH. II] *Ethnological Origin and Relations, etc.* 23

progress. We have to remain content, for the most part, with merely laying the parallels side by side, and with stating the various conjectures to which their study has given rise. Perhaps the whole important question of the relationship of Hebrew 'origins' to the myths of other races, Semitic and Aryan, will continue in its present unsatisfactory condition until the *joint* labours of specialists in the various branches of Semitic and Aryan ancient literature respectively will supply a sufficiency of material, historically and critically sifted, to warrant trustworthy conclusions. Of course future explorations may supply knowledge which will considerably modify our present provisional views. We expect further light not only from Babylonia, which has been but partially explored, but also from Phoenicia, where excavation may scarcely be said to have been begun. And with this confident hope within us it is easy to believe that advancing knowledge will render some of our present conjectures worthless. As a recent author has said: one who writes now on the results of comparative study of cosmological and other legends " is writing on the sand with a rising tide."

It is only possible here to endeavour to present to the student, as systematically as the nature of the subject will allow, such results of the labours of investigators in various departments of comparative religion as are generally known in regard to the connexion of the Hebrew Fall-story with the folk-lore of other nations. In doing so, it will be easy to enable him to realise that, though resort to the specialist in each department of research concerned is quite essential, it is necessary to remember that the inevitable "preoccupied aloofness" of each from the fields of other specialists will frequently render authoritative expressions of opinion misleading until they have been checked and qualified by similar pronouncements from those whose studies have lain in another department of ancient literature. The student of cuneiform writings is apt to explain Hebrew legends by exclusive reference to Babylonian parallels; the expert in oriental studies usually over-emphasises the similarities presented by Iranian literature, to the neglect of those which appear in Semitic records; the specialist in the accessible traces of

Semitic thought, recoverable from the early religion of Arabia and of the nations most closely akin in relationship and culture to the nomadic Hebrews themselves, sometimes writes in forgetfulness of the close bond, possibly amounting to literary dependence, between Israel and highly-civilised Assyria: and thus particular problems are apt to be presented, even by the most competent authorities, as much less complex than they really are.

Elements derived from the early religion of nomadic Israel and kindred peoples.

The early religion, and indeed the early history, of Israel are unfortunately wrapped in uncertainty and obscurity. There is no doubt that the ancestors of the heterogeneous people which eventually settled in Canaan were for a long period pastoral and nomadic tribes[1]. And inasmuch as the native traditions of all races are strongly coloured by the circumstances of their life, this fact should supply a test as to whether certain elements in the early biblical narratives were earlier or later than the settlement in Canaan. We know from the account in Genesis of patriarchal times that the Hebrews, long after they had become an agricultural people, had lively remembrances of the conditions of their former nomadic life. The question must be raised, therefore, whether the story of Paradise, of the temptation and transgression of Adam and Eve, contains elements which can be regarded as native products of the common thought of the Hebrews at this early stage of their history. It is not perhaps very profitable to attempt to decide on general or *a priori* grounds what forms of speculation were possible, and what were not, to a relatively uncivilised pastoral people such as the Israelites are generally supposed to have been previously to their absorption of Canaanitish culture. Of course it is impossible to believe that they then possessed such a story as the narrative of the Fall in the form in which it occurs in Gen. iii. On the other hand it is impossible to

[1] For a concise account of the successive Semitic immigrations into W. Asia from Arabia see *Der Alte Orient*, 1ᵉʳ Jahrgang (Leipzig, 1900), S. 1 ff.

believe that they did not possess myths or legends of some kind; and, perhaps, amongst them, conceptions which in more developed or more modified form are woven into that portion of the Jahvist history. Whether this was actually the case only becomes a subject for possible investigation when we identify Israel, as we well may at so remotely ancient a time, with the Semitic races to which it was most nearly akin.

But we cannot pursue this inquiry far on account of the paucity of the information at our disposal. If the Edomites, Ammonites, Moabites and Aramaeans possessed any legends or myths relating to the beginnings of human history and comparable to those contained in the early chapters of Genesis, they have perished. Of the traditions of the pre-Mohammedan Arabs, also, extremely little has been allowed to remain; and amongst that little there seems to be no trace of a story analogous to that of Gen. iii. The South Arabians in particular, who, as they practised an elaborate cult, presumably had a much more highly developed mythology than the Bedouins of Central Arabia, have bequeathed to us nothing but inscriptions from which we can learn scarcely more than the names of their gods and fragments of ceremonial[1]. This is the more unfortunate because, had fuller information from this source been forthcoming, it would have thrown more important light on the more primitive beliefs of the Hebrews than most of that which has been obtained from Babylonia, whose religious literature supplies us chiefly with an extremely elaborate mythology, artificially systematised in the interests of politics and priestcraft.

The possible traces of nomadic Hebrew, or of undifferentiated Semitic, tradition in the Paradise-story may be briefly mentioned here; the fuller discussion of some of them belongs more properly to the succeeding chapter.

It is not until we arrive at the 20th verse of Gen. iii., that we meet with the proper name Eve. The verse, as has already been observed, is suspected, though not proved, to

---

[1] For some account of these inscriptions, and of the early history of the Arabs in so far as it is known, see Weber, *Arabien vor dem Islam* (*Der Alte Orient*, 3ter Jahrg.).

26 *The Ethnological Origin and* [CHAP.

be a later addition. In any case the verse is by no means an essential part of the narrative to which it is attached. The meaning of Eve (*Ḥavvah*) is extremely uncertain. If the word be more than 'a Hebraised form of a name in a non-Hebraic story[1],' there are other possibilities than that suggested by Robertson Smith[2], who saw in the word a phonetic variation of *hayy*, a group of female kinship. Taken in connexion with Gen. ii. 24 ("therefore shall a man leave his father and his mother, and shall cleave unto his wife: and they twain shall be one flesh"), with Jacob's marriages, and other incidents of Old Testament history which appear to refer to what is called *beena* marriage, this verse has seemed to some scholars to contain an allusion to the primitive institution of 'mother-descent' or matriarchate, and therefore a reminiscence of the distant past. The suggestion, however, has not been very generally received[3].

The site of Eden has been assigned sometimes to Arabia, where, as is now fairly generally agreed, was once the common

---

[1] *Encycl. Bibl.*, I. Art. *Adam and Eve.*
[2] *Kinship and Marriage*, p. 177. According to other views, the word means (*a*) 'living creature'; (*b*) 'life'—a fem. abstract—see, *e.g.*, Baethgen, *Beiträge zu Semit. Rel. Geschichte*, 1888, S. 148 Anm.; (*c*) 'serpent,' see Wellhausen, *Proleg.*, 1895, S. 313; *Compos. des Hex.*, 1889, S. 343; *Reste Arab. Heidentums*, 1897, S. 154; Nöldeke, *Z. D. M. G.*, xlii. 487; *Encycl. Bibl.*, *loc. cit.* Most of these references and the following facts have been kindly supplied by Mr N. McLean, of Christ's College. In Arabic, *ḥayya* means (i) 'living creature,' (ii) 'serpent.' Syriac uses a closely related form for (i), but for 'serpent' apparently uses a derivative of the same root, and for the first *y* substitutes the kindred letter *w*. In Ethiopic an entirely different word, *arewē*, combines the same two meanings. The meaning 'serpent,' in Arabic and Syriac, may be *derived* from that of 'living creature.' In this case Wellhausen and Nöldeke's interpretation of 'Eve' would seem more improbable. To these statements it may be added that the above suggestion, of the derivation of the meaning 'serpent' from that of 'living creature,' is one which comparative mythology strongly confirms. On the other hand, many facts are explained (see Wellhausen) by identifying Eve with serpent. For instance, it is stated that Ethiopian legend places a serpent at the head of the human race as its ancestor. On Jastrow's view that the serpent of Gen. is an etymological confusion for Eve, see below, pp. 41, 43.
[3] For criticism of it see Hastings' *Dict. of the Bible*, Art. *Marriage*. Cf. Jastrow in *Amer. Journal of Semit. Languages*, XV. No. 4, p. 207. Barton, in his *Sketch of Semit. Origins*, tells us that *beena* marriage was common to many Semitic races; that matriarchate, however, in the light of recent investigation, turns out to have been limited to a few races under special conditions: and he adds (p. 41), "the whole subject merits a new examination."

II] *Relations of the Fall-story* 27

home of the Semitic peoples. Glaser has argued, on geographical and other grounds, that the account of the situation of Paradise given in Gen. ii. 10—14 was intended to locate it in that country[1]. But the identity of the river Pishon and the situation of Havilah are questions of great uncertainty; and most authorities hold opinions opposed to this, as will presently be seen.

The reference in Gen. iii. 22 to the plurality of Elohim-beings is a survival of the old Nature-religion common to Israel, before and immediately after its entrance into Canaan, and kindred Semitic races. Such reminiscences are not uncommon in the Jahvist record; and if this document, as is widely maintained, emanated from Judah, it may be pertinent to the inquiry with which we are here concerned to bear in mind that the Southern kingdom was not so thoroughly leavened with Canaanitish influences as the Northern; that it was affected by intercourse with Arab and other nomadic tribes, and was more tenacious of pre-Mosaic traditions.

The conception of the Paradise itself, and of its planting by Jahveh, has been regarded by Robertson Smith as belonging to the same circle of ideas as the oldest forms of the Semitic conception of the 'Baal-land,' a favoured spot, or oasis, such as would seem to be planted and watered by the hand of the local god, the giver of its fertility. The idea of a divinely planted *garden* would be a development, bound up with the growth of agricultural society, of the more primitive idea of the god's special home on earth[2]. Such a conception as the garden would be impossible to nomadic tribes, and would seem to be derived, like the Baal-worship with which it is associated, from the agricultural Northern Semites.

It is not to be confounded with that of the *himâ*[3] of central

---

[1] *Skizze der Geschichte u. Geographie Arabiens*, II. S. 317—357. Sprenger, and also Hommel (*Die Alt-Israel. Ueberlieferung*, S. 314 ff.), have maintained a similar view. In a recent work, *Fünf Neue Arab. Landschaftsnamen im A. Testament*, Prof. König combats Hommel's view.

[2] *Religion of the Semites*, 1889, pp. 98, 106. Gunkel, *Genesis, in loc.*, holds the similar view that the Jahvist account of Paradise is a description of an oasis in the desert. See also Barton's view mentioned below, p. 71.

[3] The word *himâ* is derived from a root signifying 'protect,' and denotes an enclosed piece of land upon which it was usually forbidden to fell trees, to hunt

Arabia, which is based on the idea of *taboo* rather than on that of property, though, like the garden, a development of the idea of a divine abode. The garden of Eden is a divine homestead rather than a sanctuary; it is the conception of an agricultural, not a nomadic, state of society, but in all probability it is nevertheless only the development, carried out at a later time, of the transplanted conception of the fertile haunt of the divine beings of the original Semite.

The tempter of the Paradise-story may well be a native conception, a survival of the primitive Hebrew animism on which the Jewish demonology is based, and perhaps also of the totemism of which traces occur in the Old Testament. "The demoniac character of the serpent in the garden of Eden is unmistakable; the serpent is not a mere temporary disguise of Satan, otherwise its punishment would be meaningless. The practice of serpent charming, repeatedly referred to in the Old Testament, is also connected with the demoniac character of the creature[1]." The *jinn* of the Arabs and other Semites, often closely associated with the serpent, would seem to embody a similar conception to that which underlies early Semitic magic. The *jinn* of some trees are said to take the form of the serpent[2], and the facts that, in the story of the temptation of Eve, the serpent is regarded as clever rather than

game or to shed blood. Such holy places were sometimes associated with the graves of heroes by the Arabs, as well as assigned to the gods. They were frequently well-watered and fertile tracts, and were originally regarded as haunts of divine beings or *jinn*. The animals and vegetation upon them were considered as instinct with divine life. They were the most ancient sanctuaries. See Robertson Smith, *Religion of the Semites*, lect. IV.; Goldziher, *Muhammedanische Studien*, I. S. 235 ff.; Wellhausen, *Reste Arab. Heidentums*, S. 101 ff.; Holzinger, *Genesis, in loc.*, has suggested that the ḥimā is the root idea of Paradise; this is impossible, but the ḥimā and Paradise are probably divergent developments of the Baal-land or oasis.

According to Kremer, *Die Süd-Arab. Sagen*, S. 19, the ancient Arabs seem to have had a tradition of original giant inhabitants, ruled over by Seddâd, who built 'the earthly Paradise.' But this was an enchanted city, and therefore the tradition is of late origin.

[1] Robertson Smith, *op. cit.*, 1889, pp. 423-4; 1894, p. 442.

[2] *Op. cit.*, 1889, p. 113, and references there. The same work may be consulted for further facts about the *jinn*. See also Nöldeke, *Zeitschr. für Völker-Psychologie*, 1860, S. 412 ff., for interesting information on the serpent-*jinn* of early Arabia.

II] *Relations of the Fall-story* 29

evil, and is closely connected with the tree of knowledge, also point towards the most primitive Semitic demonology, or animism, and possibly magic, as the source of the figure which, in the Jahvist narrative, leads the first parents to their fall. It would certainly seem most probable in the present state of our knowledge that this element in the Fall-story will receive its genetic explanation in a survival of such extremely primitive Semitic thought[1].

The tree of the knowledge of good and evil is the element of the Paradise-story to which it has hitherto been most difficult to adduce any parallel. Robertson Smith expressed the view that it was a conception common to the Northern Semites, but seems to have left us no information as to its derivation and significance. It has been compared to the oracle-trees mentioned in the Book of Judges and elsewhere in the Old Testament, which certainly were an element in early Semitic superstition[2]. But unlike such trees, the one in question communicates its virtue only through being eaten. If it be a creation of the writer of the Jahvist story, as some have thought, or an interpolation of his into a legend which had hitherto only spoken of a tree of life, its function may possibly have been suggested to him by the familiar oracle-tree, whilst its mode of action may have been assimilated to that of the tree already figuring in his tradition. A more probable derivation is discussed below[3].

[1] For an interesting corroborative suggestion see the remarks on the curse of the serpent in Hastings' *Dict. of the Bible*, Art. *Demon* (i. p. 590 n.), and the quotation there given from Doughty's *Arabia Deserta*. See also Baudissin, *Semit. Religionsgeschichte*. Jastrow (*Amer. Journal of Semit. Languages*, xv. No. 4, p. 209) conjectures that the serpent of Gen. iii. is an addition to the original story, due to the confusion of the Hebrew names for serpent and Eve. See above, p. 26. It does not read, however, as Cheyne has remarked, like an afterthought.

One looks forward with interest to the Art. on *Serpent* in the *Encycl. Bibl.*, in the hope that it may contain some matter, hitherto unpublished, from the pen of the late W. R. Smith.

Further discussion of the Fall-story in the light of primitive 'common Semitic' ideas will be found in the following chapter.

[2] Lenormant, *Les Origines de l'histoire*, 1880, i. p. 86 f., states that the pre-Mohammedan Arabs and the ancient Phœnicians possessed similar trees. See also Arts. in Bible Dictionaries on *Magic, Divination*, etc.; Baudissin, *op. cit.*, II. S. 227.

[3] Barton's view: see ch. iii.

It may be concluded from what has so far been said that, though there are at least some traces of extremely ancient Semitic conceptions, going back to remotely prehistoric times, in the details of the Fall-story[1], there is no evidence at all that it was possessed by the Hebrews in its entirety before their entrance into Canaan. There are no signs that the narrative, in its existing form and with its present didactic import, was a native product of nomadic Israel; and some of its elements seem certainly to have been derived from a people of settled agricultural life[2].

[1] It will be seen at a later page in this chapter, and also in the next, that there is a considerable amount of evidence, of more than one kind, pointing to the conclusion that, though the didactic implications of the story were a result of Hebraisation of borrowed material, its basis consists mainly of tradition which, by no means the creation of civilised Babylonia, originally bore a very different significance, and could arise only in an extremely primitive state of society.

[2] The curse of the ground for Adam's sake (Gen. iii. 17) is not necessarily to be understood, as has been thought by Goldziher and others, to be the expression of the nomad's contempt for agriculture. The fact that the Paradise-story takes it for granted that man was intended to be an agriculturist from the first (Gen. ii. 5, 15), is a proof that its aetiological signification was conceived, and impressed upon the narrative, after nomadic life had become a thing of the past. It is true, as we have seen above, that some critics have been inclined to regard these references to the keeping and tilling of the garden as an interpolation contrary to the spirit of the Jahvist writing. This would seem perhaps a little unnecessary; for the light and easy work which appears to be implied in such an occupation need not be identified with the field-labour whose toilsomeness resulted from man's sin. But in any case the allusion to agriculture as the lot of man in his present state, and as a toil whose laboriousness, at any rate, calls for explanation, is a proof that this element in the story, if not the gist of the story as a whole, was received by the Hebrews from the people who taught them agricultural pursuits in Canaan, or else was invented by themselves subsequently to their occupation of that country. Presupposing, as it does, the conditions of civilised life, the story can hardly have been brought from the desert. As to which of the alternatives just mentioned is the more probable, it is precarious to argue further merely from the allusion to agricultural labour. In some parts of Palestine such an occupation was easy; in other parts it was hard, and the land is spoken of (Numb. xiii. 32) as one "that eateth up the inhabitants thereof." There is no doubt that the earlier prophets represent the happy and peaceful national future to which they look forward as an age of agricultural life (Amos ix. 13, Hos. xiv. 7, Isai. ii. 4), and it is certain that the fact that such pursuits had been learned from the foreigner had been forgotten (Isai. xxviii. 26 ff.), so that agriculture had come to be looked upon as a divine institution. Yet Israel perfectly well remembered its nomadic and pastoral days, as we see from the narratives of Cain and Abraham. Some have therefore concluded that we have,

Relations of the Fall-story

Now there is no doubt that after their settlement west of the Jordan, and the change of life consequent thereupon, the Israelites derived most of their civilisation, arts and culture from the Canaanitish peoples with whom they were brought into so intimate relationship. We know, too, how easily, after the settlement, Hebrew religion absorbed into itself elements of the lower religions of these kindred races. It is highly probable, then, that the Israelites largely imbibed the traditions current among the Canaanites and used them in reconstructing the 'history of origins' which we find in Genesis. But there is reason to believe that the legends and folk-lore thus rendered accessible to the Hebrews would be made up of very mixed elements. Phoenician culture and religion had already been influenced by centuries of close connexion with Egypt, and by intercourse with Assyria, long before the Israelite immigration into Canaan[1]. Babylonian mythology was therefore within reach some centuries before Israel's literary activity began, and it is most probable that such Babylonian influence as is traceable in the narratives of the Jahvist source was derived at this period[2].

But the Phoenicians and Canaanites were a medium

in the Fall-story, an example of unassimilated borrowing. Others have deduced the same conclusion from the pessimistic view which the story takes of agricultural labour, and remark that Egypt or Babylon, with their arduous irrigation work, would seem to be the natural home of such an outlook. Such arguments, however, lose sight of personal idiosyncrasy and temperament, as well as of variety in the conditions of life in different districts of one country. Alongside of the passages referred to above, we must put the allusions to agricultural labour as a heavy burden; *e.g.* 1 Sam. viii. 12, Isai. lxi. 5, Zech. xiii. 5, Ecclus. vi. 19. In this connexion the verse Ecclus. vii. 15 is interesting, as we there get the two aspects placed side by side:
"Hate not laborious work;
Neither husbandry, which the Most High hath ordained (created)."

[1] See Benzinger, *Hebräische Archäologie*, S. 66-7. The Tel-el-Amarna tablets (c. 1400 B.C.), which contain letters addressed by governors in Phoenicia, Syria and Palestine to the king of Egypt, show that the diplomatic language in these countries was Babylonian. Inasmuch as some of the tablets contain mythical legends they show also that the literature, as well as the language, of Babylonia was current at least in Egypt. King, *The Babylonian Religion*, p. 118 ff.; see also *Der Alte Orient*, 1er Jahrg. S. 37 ff.

[2] This view seems to be now established. For its exposition and vindication see Gunkel, *Schöpfung u. Chaos*, 1895, S. 146—155, and Zimmern, *Bibl. und Babyl. Urgeschichte*, in *Der Alte Orient*, 2ter Jahrg. S. 71-88, 107-8.

through which other influences than those of Egypt and Babylonia may have reached the Hebrews in the centuries immediately preceding the writing of their earliest history. Both Phoenicia and Babylonia had intercourse with Persia; and interchange of culture and mythology between Phoenicia and Greece goes back, perhaps, to the pre-Homeric age[1]. It is, of course, a very remote possibility that at this early date influences from these sources were received, in the slightest degree, by the Hebrews. But the bare possibility is worth recording, even if no practical results are to be traced thereto.

In discussing the points of similarity between the biblical Fall-story and kindred legendary traditions of other ancient nations, it will be essential to bear in mind that, as to the traditions of Phoenicia and other Canaanitish peoples, which it would be of the first importance to us to know, we are almost altogether ignorant; whilst provisional conclusions formed from Babylonian parallels may at any time be modified or reversed by further discoveries.

Phoenician Parallels.

The Jahvist account of the beginnings of human culture contained in Gen. iii. and iv. certainly seems to have affinities with the fragments of ancient Phoenician folk-lore handed down, probably in much distorted form, by Philo Byblus and preserved by Eusebius[2]. In one of these fragments a being, Aeon, who would seem to correspond to Eve, is said to have discovered the use of the fruit of trees for food[3]. The first clothing is said to have been invented later, and to have consisted of the skins of animals. Its use is expressly associated with the origin of animal sacrifice. These ideas would seem

[1] Preller, *Griechische Mythologie*, 1872, I. S. 8.
[2] *Praep. Evang.* Lib. I. c. x. The Phoenician account of the earliest stages of civilisation has points of agreement with Gen. iv. which have suggested identity of origin for the two histories. It is at least possible that the Phoenician stories are based on Genesis. See Renan, *Mémoires de l'Académie des Inscriptions*, XXIII. part ii., p. 259.
[3] Εἶτά φησι γεγενῆσθαι ἐκ τοῦ Κολπία ἀνέμου, καὶ γυναικὸς αὐτοῦ Βάαν, τοῦτο δὲ νύκτα ἑρμηνεύειν, Αἰῶνα καὶ Πρωτόγονον θνητοὺς ἄνδρας, οὕτω καλουμένους. Εὑρεῖν δὲ τὸν Αἰῶνα τὴν ἀπὸ τῶν δένδρων τροφήν.

to be vestiges of a myth of a golden age of fruit-eating which possibly arose, like the corresponding Greek tradition, out of sacrificial ritual, and of whose existence among the ancient Phoenicians there is other evidence[1]. This tradition appears to be known to the Jahvist compiler, and has been considered by some to be implied in Isai. xi. 6 ff. We meet with a belief in a golden age also in Egyptian mythology[2], which was laid under contribution by the Phoenician cosmogony described by Philo Byblus.

These fragments of Phoenician legend do not carry us far; they imply, what might have been guessed without them, that similar subjects to those discussed in the early narratives of Genesis occupied Phoenician thought, and were dealt with in a similar way. But they supply us with no parallel to the Fall-story[3].

The absence of information as to indisputably ancient Phoenician legend is most deplorable to the student of the sources and origin of the Hebrew Fall-story. For if we can dimly conjecture the probable objects and conceptions in which the primitive legend underlying this story took its rise, and can trace, in such Babylonian literature as we possess, the existence of ideas and associations of ideas which throw light upon the development and modification of such legend on Babylonian soil, we have to remember that it was almost certainly in a form modified by Phoenician influences that Babylonian lore was received by the Hebrews on their entrance into Canaan. Moreover there are elements, not only in the teaching, but also in the original mythical material, of the story, such as its apparent implication of something like

[1] On this point see W. R. Smith, *op. cit.* Lect. viii., especially p. 288 ff. (ed. 1889).
[2] See below, p. 34.
[3] Lenormant alleges evidence that the Phoenicians possessed a story similar in nature to that of Gen. iii., *op. cit.*, 1. p. 93; cf. Renan's paper referred to above, p. 32; but not much can be built from these data. Fergusson, *Tree and Serpent Worship*, 1873, p. 11, states that representations of a serpent coiled round a tree occur on Phoenician coins; the very fact that they occur on coins makes it improbable that they allude to the figures of the Fall-story. The analogy between elements in this narrative, and the legend of the garden of the Hesperides, which Lenormant (*op. cit.*) asserts to be incontestably of Phoenician origin, is discussed below, p. 53 f.

a golden age, to which the cuneiform literature supplies nothing parallel. There is therefore a most important link missing in the chain of development connecting the Jahvist story with its conjectured prehistoric and animistic basis[1]: a link which a survey of such knowledge and speculation as has been accumulated on the subject would lead one to suppose to be essential to the reconstruction of the history of this interesting tradition. The deficiency of Phoenician legendary literature such as might throw light upon the Paradise-story in the stage of its development which immediately preceded its Hebraisation, should in itself make us cautious in accepting, as a complete key or parallel, any of the various legends from Babylonia or elsewhere which have been thought to have supplied the material of the Jahvist writer's story.

Egyptian Parallels.

There are one or two parallels to portions of the Jahvist history of origins in the mythology of Egypt. The conception of man's creation out of clay is one of them. Ptah is said to have modelled man with his own hands, and Khnûmû to have formed him on a potter's table[2]. Another is the belief in a golden age under Râ. "Certain expressions used by Egyptian writers are in themselves sufficient to show that the first generations of men were supposed to have lived in a state of happiness and perfection[3]." 'The times of Râ' was apparently a common expression for an ideal age. But whilst this was a popular and indigenous legend, there were nevertheless Egyptians who, "on the contrary, affirmed that their ancestors were born as so many brutes, unprovided with the most essential arts of gentle life. They knew nothing of articulate speech, and expressed themselves by cries only, like other animals, until the day when Thot taught them both speech and writing[4]." This latter tradition closely resembles the Chaldaean legend preserved by Berosus, according to

---

[1] See next chapter.
[2] Maspero, *Dawn of Civilisation*, S. P. C. K. 3rd ed. p. 156.
[3] *Ibid.* p. 158, n. 3; Lenormant, *op. cit.*, I. p. 58.
[4] Maspero, *op. cit.*, p. 158.

II] *Relations of the Fall-story* 35

which the first men lived after the manner of beasts until Oannes taught them better[1]. It is by no means necessary to suppose, however, that the Jahvist creation story, or the Paradise narrative, was indebted to Egyptian influences. Creation of man from the clay or dust is an idea which occurred spontaneously to many nations, as for instance the Babylonians[2]; and the same of course is true as to the belief in a paradisaic age.

There is evidence of the worship, in ancient Egypt, of both the palm tree and of the serpent[3], but there has been no connexion established between these objects of veneration and the imagery of the Fall-story. Wiedemann[4] alludes to the cult of a tree at Heliopolis whence the phoenix arose, and on whose foliage "Thoth, or else Safekht, the goddess of learning, inscribed the name of the king, who by this act was endowed with immortal life." This association of a tree of life with the goddess of learning is of interest as possibly implying the same connexion of ideas as some would detect in Gen. iii.; but of course there is no parallel to the Fall-story.

In spite, therefore, of the close relations of Israel with Egypt implied in the story of the bondage, there seem to be no definite traces of Egyptian influences on Hebrew thought and institutions[5]; and there are probably no indications of developed Egyptian mythology having been absorbed by Israel.

Our attention has recently been called, however, to the existence in hieroglyphic Egyptian of the elements of a story similar to what Prof. Barton, in his recent *Sketch of Semitic Origins*[6], takes to have been the germ of the Hebrew narrative

[1] *Ibid.*, p. 546. Cf. also Greek traditions, pp. 52, 53, below.
[2] See below, p. 39.
[3] Maspero, *op. cit.*, p. 121.
[4] *Religion of the ancient Egyptians*, 1897, pp. 156, 157. Wiedemann adds: "it is however a curious fact that the palm, a tree otherwise so intimately associated with Egyptian thought and feeling, may be said to have no place in this cult." This is of interest in connexion with what is said below of Barton's theory of the tree of knowledge. Massey, *Natural Genesis*, I. 382, states that Thot is elsewhere associated with the palm, but gives no reference.
[5] Renouf, *Hibbert Lectures*, p. 243 f. "It may be confidently asserted that neither Hebrews nor Greeks borrowed any of their ideas from Egypt."
[6] See below, p. 69 ff.

of Paradise and the Fall, in extremely ancient times. Prof. Barton tells us that he derived this information from Prof. W. Max Müller, to whose forthcoming work the student will therefore look forward with eagerness. Through the kindness of this latter scholar the present writer is enabled to state that no complete story analogous to the narrative of the Fall is to be found in ancient Egyptian literature, but that scattered allusions exist which show that almost all its elements, the serpent, the rivers and trees of Paradise, and the idea that death was due to the ancestress of woman, were known in the earliest Egyptian religion. If this should be proved to be the case, a most interesting problem will be presented to the student of the sources of the Fall-story; but speculation on the matter will not be profitable before the publication of Prof. W. Max Müller's work.

Babylonian Parallels.

It is universally admitted that some of the early narratives of Genesis, to whatever stratum of the hexateuch they belong, show obvious traces of indebtedness to Babylonian tradition. The borrowing, however, is by no means either wholesale or always direct. The differences between the Hebrew stories and those supplied by Babylonian literature are perhaps even more striking than the resemblances. This fact, and also the tenacity of the hold which some of the narratives containing borrowed elements took upon the thought of Israel, point rather to indirect derivation[1]. It has already been stated that the Canaanites were the medium through which such influences could easily be accessible to the Hebrews. It remains to enumerate the possible cases of adopted Babylonian tradition, or of 'undivided Semitic' conceptions which reached the Hebrews from Babylonian soil, and bear the signs of Babylonian local colouring.

The Jahvist account of Paradise stands in very close connexion with what is commonly spoken of as a Jahvist account of the Creation. Some writers, regarding Gen. ii. 4 *b* ff. as

---

[1] Cf. M. Jastrow, in *Jewish Quart. Review*, July 1901.

a practically complete Creation-story[1], have argued that it implies the existence of quite different climatic conditions in the place of its origin than those exhibited in Gen. i., which are certainly Babylonian, and such as point to a barren wilderness as, *e.g.*, the Syro-Arabian desert. If this view be correct, the narrative can hardly be said to be an account of the making of the world. A creation-story must begin further back than with an existing solid world, even if its imagery be drawn from scenes of desert life. It is, however, both possible and natural to regard the narrative, with its abrupt commencement, as a fragment whose beginning has been cut off to avoid repetition of previous subject-matter. Indeed instances of verbal similarity between it and Babylonian writings have been pointed out which have suggested, though perhaps not very convincingly, that it is a mutilated borrowed story[2]. The phenomena which it implies, as another writer has observed, are such as would be witnessed by the first colonists of Babylonia on the occasion of the yearly inundations of the Euphrates and Tigris, before these were controlled by a system of irrigation-channels.

Again, the description of the site of Eden in Chap. ii. 10—14 is generally considered to be an interpolation of Babylonian origin, reproducing Babylonian words in Hebraised form[3]. And even when these doubtful verses have been eliminated there remain suggestions that the tradition is of foreign origin[4]. Parallels to the description of the garden of

---

[1] As, *e.g.*, Gunkel, *op. cit.*; Zimmern, in *Der Alte Orient*, 2ter Jahrg. S. 88 ff.; Worcester, *op. cit.*

[2] There are correspondences in structure and phraseology, though these cannot be pressed, with an Accadian Creation-account published by Pinches in *Journ. Roy. Asiat. Soc.* 1891. See also Jastrow, *Religion of Babylonia and Assyria*, p. 444 ff.; *Encycl. Bibl.* art. *Creation*, 16 and 20. Gen. ii. 5 resembles the line "'no reed grew and no tree was formed,'" though hardly sufficiently to establish interdependence. The 'mist' of ii. 6 should rather be 'flood,' according to some authorities, which would appear to rise 'from the earth.' The Babylonian story goes on to speak of man being made by Marduk with the help of the potter-goddess Aruru (evidently out of clay), then of the creation of the animals, 'parks and forests,' and of cities.

[3] See *e.g.* Schrader, *Cuneiform Transcriptions and the O.T.*, ed. 2, vol. 1. p. 26 ff.

[4] The name 'Eden' and the location of the garden in 'the East.' Edin was the name given to the 'plain' of Babylonia (Sayce). See also *Encycl. Bibl.* Art. *Garden*.

38 *The Ethnological Origin and* [CHAP.

Eden can also be adduced from Babylonian legend. In the epic of Gilgamesh, Parnapishtim, who is the Noah of a Babylonian deluge-story, finds favour with the gods, and having been, with his wife, made immortal, is caused by Bel "to dwell afar off at the mouth (or confluence) of the rivers." This place Jensen would regard as the Babylonian earthly Paradise and the original of the Hebrew Eden[1]. The streams, according to Haupt, are the Euphrates, the Tigris, and two others which formerly emptied themselves independently into the Persian Gulf. Others see in the ancient town of Eridu, situated near the confluence of the Euphrates and Tigris, the prototype of the biblical Eden. This was a sanctuary of the gods, 'the centre of the earth,' where was a grove into which 'no man hath entered' and containing a famous oracle-tree, a sacred palm 'with a root of bright lapis[2].' The isle of the blessed was rather an Elysium than an Olympus or Paradise; but just as these two conceptions coalesce in the mythologies of Greece and Egypt[3], so did they also in that of the Babylonians. Indeed Jeremias adduces strong evidence to show that the 'island of the blessed' at the confluence or mouth of the rivers was very closely connected with Eridu. He also states that the magical virtues of Eridu play a conspicuous part in the Babylonian mantic literature, and that here Adapa[4] was created by Ea. Further, with this Babylonian Paradise were connected the food and water of life, the equivalents of the Greek ambrosia and nectar[5].

[1] *Kosmologie der Babylonier*, S. 212 ff.; 507 ff. See also Jastrow, *op. cit.*, p. 505 ff. Here we have a supernatural place containing magical trees and waters (healing plant obtained and lost by Gilgamesh, the spring which cures him of his leprosy), and guarded by supernatural beings (the scorpion-men, comparable to the cherubim of Paradise).

[2] See Hastings' *Dict. of the Bible*, Art. *Babylonia*; Hogarth, *Authority and Archaeology*, p. 19 ff.; also below, *Additions and Corrections*.

[3] Lincke, quoted by Jeremias, *Bab.-Assyr. Vorstellungen*, S. 93, mentions an Egyptian 'isle of the blessed' in the fields of peace where the gods dwelt and ate of the tree of life.

[4] See below, p. 45.

[5] Jeremias, in *Der Alte Orient*, 1ter Jahrg. S. 91–98, on *Hölle u. Paradies bei den Babyloniern*.

Gunkel (*op. cit.*) and Zimmern (*Der Alte Orient*, 2ter Jahrg. S. 90 ff.) see in Ezek. xlvii. and Rev. xxii. allusions to an older form of Paradise legend, in which Paradise was in heaven and the river of life was as prominent a feature as the tree.

Perhaps the most remarkable Babylonian source of ideas and imagery analogous to those of the biblical narratives of Adam and his fall is the Eabani legend, which is interwoven with that of the hero Izdubar or Gilgamesh. This epic is in all probability one of the most ancient stories in existence; at least this may be said of the part of it which deals with Eabani, a figure that has evidently come down from hoary antiquity. As Prof. Jastrow says, who has devoted a very thorough study to this legend, and made many suggestions with regard to it which at least are of the greatest interest, Eabani was used as a suitable person to whom to attach traditions relating to the primitive state of man; and the description of him belongs to quite a different period of culture from that of Gilgamesh with which it came to be associated[1]. In the Gilgamesh epic Eabani does not represent the first man; he enters upon a world already populated. This, however, does not preclude the possibility of his having originally been a Babylonian Adam; and the fact that he never was so regarded would be no obstacle in the way of the Hebrew Adam being derived from him. He is said to have been created in order to rival and to combat the hero Gilgamesh, and in the manner of his creation we come upon the first conspicuous resemblance between him and the biblical first man. For he was made by the goddess Aruru out of a piece of clay, as the man of the Paradise narrative was made by Jahveh from the dust of the earth. He is represented as being as it were half man and half beast, naked and hairy, living in a savage state, perfectly at home amongst the animals, with whom he eats and drinks and sports. The purpose assigned to his creation in the epic is frustrated by Gilgamesh sending to him a sacred prostitute, Ukhat, to ensnare him[2]. She entices him, 'unabashed,' from the beasts to herself:

---

[1] See this author's paper on *Adam and Eve in Babylonian Literature*, in the *Amer. Journal of Semitic Languages*, vol. xv. No. 4.

[2] This refers to the Ishtar worship to which Herodotus alludes, prevalent in Babylonia as in other Semitic countries; cf. Gen. xxxviii. 21; Deut. xxiii. 17. The word Ukhat means priestess of Ishtar (A. Jeremias).

40   *The Ethnological Origin and*   [CHAP.

"Lofty art thou, Eabani, like to a god.
Why dost thou lie with the beasts?
Come, I will bring thee to walled Uruk.
　　　　*　　*　　*　　*　　*
He yields and obeys her command.
In the wisdom of his heart he recognised a companion[1]."

Eabani abandons the society of the beasts for the more suitable mate who 'is brought to him,' and who is the means of rousing him to a sense of his superiority to them. The two then proceed to Uruk, "the symbol of civilised existence." At this point the tablet is defective, though there appears to be an allusion to festive garments, and, further on, a description of a grove which "reminds one forcibly of the garden of Eden," and into which Eabani is introduced for a habitation[2].

Now, as Jastrow points out, the Jahvist narrative represents Adam as living at first in very close connexion with the animals about him; Jahveh's motive in bringing them to him to be 'named' may imply that he might possibly have been expected to find a companion amongst them[3]. The idea that Adam at first satisfied his desire upon them, like Eabani in the Gilgamesh legend (according to Jastrow's reading of it), may possibly be an old Hebrew tradition, as it appears in rabbinical haggada[4]; and many writers have suggested reasons for believing that, behind the association of the tree of knowledge with the beginnings of culture, there lay originally that of the origin of human passion[5]. Jastrow further maintains that the expression for 'assigning names' to the animals in Gen. ii. is a euphemism for what the Gilgamesh legend more plainly says of Eabani's relation to them; and if this be the

---

[1] The translation is from Jastrow, *Religion of Babylonia and Assyria*, p. 477 ff. In the paper above referred to the writer adopts Haupt's rendering of the first line, "thou wilt be like a god." Cf. Gen. iii. 5.

[2] Jastrow, *op. cit.*, pp. 479, 481.

[3] This thought has also occurred to Stade (*Zeitschrift für A. T. Wissenschaft*, 1897, S. 210), to Gunkel (*Genesis*, S. 9), and Worcester (*op. cit.*).

[4] Eisenmenger, *Entdecktes Judenthum*, I. 371 ff.
In Hershon's *Genesis with a talmudical Commentary*, p. 63, it is stated that R. Elieser taught (*Jebamoth*, 63 a) that Adam had tried to find a connubial partner among all cattle and living creatures, but was only suited when he got Eve.

[5] See below, ch. iii.

case, the parallel with Genesis becomes still more striking[1]. He also believes that the expressions "brought her unto" the man (Gen. ii. 22) and "knowledge of good and evil" (Gen. ii. 9) are similar euphemisms, the former of these phrases being identical with the usual expression "come in unto"; and he interprets Gen. ii. 24 in a similar sense, in relation with Adam's leaving the animals to cleave to his wife, instead of as an allusion to the institution of matriarchate. The elimination of the serpent from the original Fall-story, as a late etymological confusion and a doublet for Eve, a conjecture which we have already had occasion to mention, makes the narrative of Genesis still more closely resemble the legend of Eabani. That the objectionable features of the original Paradise-story, as Jastrow reconstructs it, which the Jahvist writer purges away and hints at only by veiled expressions, were not remote from the life of the early Hebrews, is to be inferred from such passages as Levit. xviii. 23 and xx. 15, 16 (cf. *Beresch. rabba*, on Gen. ii. 16 and 24, and legends mentioned in Chaps. VII—IX. of this work). It remains to add that Eabani is stated, later on in the epic, to have 'become dust[2],' and to have cursed Ukhat for having 'brought death' upon him[3].

Hitherto in this account of the Eabani legend we have followed the interpretation of it given by Prof. Jastrow. Dr Worcester, in his book on Genesis, gives independently a similar reading of its more essential features. This writer also sees in it an account of a being who becomes truly human through association with woman instead of with the beasts; a being tempted from his contented animal life and plunged by her into the toils and struggles which beset the state of civilisation: a being, therefore, closely comparable with the Adam of the Jahvist writing.

[1] This is rendered questionable by the possibility that we have here an allusion to the wisdom which, in some ancient traditions, was ascribed to the first man. Cf. below, p. 61 f. Jastrow, however, regards his explanation as the only one capable of throwing light upon this curious act of naming the animals, which he says is meaningless unless 'to name' means something more than to name. Barton, *op. cit.*, follows Jastrow.
[2] Jastrow, *op. cit.*, p. 490.
[3] *Ibid.* p. 511.

It remains to be seen how far the very plausible argument thus given by Prof. Jastrow for the dependence of the Jahvist account of our first parents on the legend of Eabani will stand the test of expert scrutiny. It must be mentioned that Maspero and others had previously read this Babylonian legend differently. Maspero[1] sees in Eabani a satyr or half-beast, and takes the story to imply that he had influence over the animals till he became incontinent; then the beasts fled from him, whereupon he was filled with fear. He adds that Eabani is said to have possessed intelligence "which embraced all things past and future," which hardly suits Jastrow's interpretation. This writer also translates the lines quoted above so that they do not necessarily suggest the relation with the beasts which Jastrow's rendering directly attributes to Eabani[2]. One feels, in fact, on reading the Izdubar epic as it is translated and interpreted by other scholars, that the plausibility of Jastrow's argument depends somewhat on certain features being minimised and certain others being perhaps a little over-pressed. A. Jeremias[3] regards Eabani as a kind of Priapus, a god of gardens and fields, and representative of unbridled lust; and King[4] disputes the grounds of Jastrow's identifications. One cannot therefore receive it as finally agreed that the Eabani legend supplied the basis for the Jahvist narrative of Adam and Eve, much as the suggestion seems to have to commend it, and likely enough as it is in view of the fact that the deluge-stories of Genesis are undoubtedly mainly of Babylonian origin and one such story is contained in the complex epic of Gilgamesh in which the Eabani legend is also imbedded[5].

[1] *Dawn of Civilisation*, ed. 3, p. 576.
[2] *loc. cit.* In this respect other translators agree.
[3] *op. cit.*, S. 83, *Anmerk.* Cf. Hommel, Art. *Babylonia* in Hastings' *Dict. of the Bible*. A. Jeremias, *Izdubar-Nimrod*, S. 46., *Anm.* 16, notes that Eabani is called 'man of Ninib,' *i.e.* peasant or man of fields.
[4] *Babylonian Religion*, p. 113.
[5] A work on this subject has been announced as forthcoming by Prof. Jastrow.

The fact that the Eabani legend testifies to the actual existence, in remotely ancient Semitic folk-lore, of conceptions and associations of ideas which have been supposed on independent evidence (see next chapter) to lie at the root of the original legend which was developed by subsequent reflection into the Fall-story, is very noteworthy, whatever criticisms some of the coincidences in detail, asserted

From these descriptions of man's origin and primitive state, and possibly, also, of his enticement from animal to civilised life, we turn to examine such other Babylonian parallels as have been adduced to the story of the Fall itself. The attempt to connect the serpent of Gen. iii. with Tiâmat, the female personification of the primaeval watery waste, so prominent in some of the Babylonian creation-myths, and generally represented in the form of a dragon, may very safely be neglected, and indeed is now generally abandoned. Except that Tiâmat was called 'the enemy of the gods' and was overcome by Marduk, she has nothing in common with the tempter in the Paradise-story. It is true the Babylonian dragon or serpent was also called 'serpent of darkness' and 'wicked serpent[1],' but it is extremely improbable that the tempter of Genesis was originally intended to be pre-eminently an evil power; the narrative rather suggests that, if he were ever more than a demoniac animal or kind of *jinn*, he was a power beneficent to man. Tiâmat, however, is a being which we can hardly suppose to be the original, however remote, of the subtly persuasive figure of Genesis; she was a terrible monster, and reappears in the Old Testament writings as Rahab and Leviathan, the principle of chaos, the enemy of God and man[2].

by Prof. Jastrow, may require. Of course there is much in the Fall-story, even after its 'prophetic' teaching has been removed from it, which finds no parallel in the Eabani legend. The suppression of the serpent, to which Jastrow is led in order to establish closer identity, seems to us arbitrary ; especially since reading Barton's instructive treatment of the subject, which, by the way, absorbs and agrees with, as well as supplements, the knowledge, if it be wholly knowledge, brought to light by Jastrow's interesting investigation.

It may be mentioned that a work has recently been published by Dieckmann entitled *Das Gilgamis-Epos in seiner Bedeutung für Bibel und Babel*; the writer has not had access to it.

[1] Sayce, *Chald. Account of Genesis.*
[2] Gunkel, *Schöpfung u. Chaos*, S. 383, considers Tiâmat, however, to be the original of the 'old serpent' of Rev. xii. 9, a conception resulting from the blending of the old chaos-serpent (so frequently alluded to in the later books of the O.T.) after its meaning had become forgotten, with the serpent of Gen. iii., which is quite a different conception. This view is supported by the presence of other Babylonian imagery in the context, else other alternatives would be deserving of attention. Thus, Pherecydes of Syros is said by Eusebius (*Praep. Ev.* I. x.) to have derived his 'old Ophion' from Phoenician mythology; post-exilic Jewish Satanology and doctrine of fallen angels, or Zoroastrian influence, would also supply an explanation of the expression.

There is more justification for the view which sees in the Babylonian god Ea the possible original of the tempter[1]. Ea was god of the waters under the earth; and as they were regarded as the source of wisdom, he came also to be the god of culture and knowledge. He is the Oannes of Berosus, who rose out of the Persian Gulf and taught men the beginnings of civilisation: the 'intelligent fish,' the 'lord of understanding.' We find him represented as especially the god of humanity, always beneficent towards man, whom he befriends, as, for instance, during the deluge, against Bel. His name has been supposed to be connected with the Arabic *hayya*[2], and he is naturally easy to associate with the three figures of the serpent, the tree of life and the tree of knowledge[3].

This association is still further confirmed when we learn that Ea is called "the god of life," and is represented as applying the fertilising male cone of the palm to the palm tree[4]. There was a sacred tree, presumably of this kind, at Eridu[5]; and Eridu was Ea's city. As Barton has suggested, the artificial cultivation of the date-palm, which seems to be associated with the earliest Semitic civilisation, may have been brought by the colonists of Babylonia to Eridu, and in consequence of the connexion of this tree with Semitic agricultural progress on the one hand, and with Ea as god of life on the other, wisdom and culture came also to be ascribed to this deity.

But, as in the case of other details of the Fall-story, the serpent probably supplies us, not with a case of direct borrowing, whether of Tiâmat or of Ea, but with a natural

[1] Cf. Sir H. Rawlinson, *Herodotus*, ed. 1, 1. p. 600, where the suggestion was perhaps first made. Lenormant (*op. cit.*, 1. p. 106 n.) and Gunkel (*Genesis*, S. 34) seem favourably inclined to this view, which is also widely accepted by writers on mythology.

[2] See above, p. 26, n. 2.

[3] For these assertions see, besides Rawlinson, Jastrow, *op. cit.*, and de la Saussaye, *Science of Religion*, E.T. p. 484. Cf. also Maspero, *Dawn of Civilisation*, 3rd ed., p. 546.

[4] Barton, *op. cit.*, refers to Lenormant (*op. cit.*, 1. 232) on this point, and to an unpublished cylinder in the Brit. Museum alluded to by Prof. Sayce in his *Hibbert Lectures*, p. 133.

[5] See above, p. 38. Pinches, *The O. Testament in the light of the hist. records of Assyria etc.*, pp. 72 ff., gives reasons for believing the tree compared to 'white lapis' to have been the vine.

Hebrew or Canaanitish development of a root-conception common to many mythologies. The facts stated above, p. 28 f., are perhaps more to the point than these instances of similar conceptions and combinations of ideas in kindred but foreign folk-lore.

The only Babylonian writing in which we have evidence of Ea's performing a definite act for mankind analogous to that ascribed in the present form of the Paradise-narrative to the serpent (though possibly the *rôle* of the tempter was very different originally, as will presently be seen) is the Adapa legend[1]; and in this story he is the creator of man and also, indirectly, the means by which Adapa is prevented from obtaining immortality. This purpose he effects, too, by a deception; but it is of a kind the converse of that of the Hebrew serpent-tempter, and somewhat resembles the deception contained in the threat attributed to Jahveh in Genesis, "in the day that thou eatest thereof thou shalt surely die[2]." Adapa is handed over by Ea, for punishment, to Anu and other gods. He is warned by Ea to refuse, on entering into their presence, the 'food of life' and 'water of life' which will be offered him. Adapa is thus allowed entrance into heaven, and is consequently permitted by Ea to obtain the knowledge of the 'secrets of heaven and earth,' which it is not ordinarily permitted to mortals to behold. Anu and the gods then agree to confer immortality upon him, and the food and water of life are accordingly offered to him. They are refused, as Ea advised; and, thus deceived, Adapa forfeits the virtues which they would have conveyed.

[1] This comes from Tel-el-Amarna and is therefore, in the written form, as early as the 15th cent. B.C. The legend embodies a tradition somewhat similar in nature to that of Eabani incorporated in the Gilgamesh epic. Adapa is called the 'seed of mankind' (Hommel), and is a representative mortal man. For the best statement, perhaps, of the relation of this story to that of Gen. iii., see Zimmern in *Der Alte Orient*, 2ter Jahrg. S. 91 ff. Prof. Sayce's identification of Adapa with Adama has not met with general acceptance.

[2] See also Jastrow's comments on this story, *op. cit.*, p. 550 ff., where an English rendering of Zimmern's German translation (for which, in turn, see appendix to Gunkel's *Schöpfung u. Chaos*) will also be found.

In many respects the Babylonian Ea is the parallel of Jahveh in the Fall-story, rather than of the serpent. If the original story related to the conferring, by means of the tree of knowledge, of a gift on mankind which was not the object of divine prohibition (see next chapter), the parallel would be very much stronger.

This is obviously no Fall-story, but it contains much that unquestionably resembles certain details in the Jahvist representation of the relations between Adam and God. The legend is concerned with man's possibility of acquiring immortality and likeness to the gods, one of the root ideas underlying the Bible story of Paradise in its present form. It is not an exact parallel: the knowledge which Adam sought in opposition to Jahveh's will was freely granted to Adapa, though in the case of both stories immortality was lost through deception by a supernatural being.

Important conceptions are common to the two narratives; the divergence lies in the fact that they are differently combined. Of course the mode in which Hebrew writers used Babylonian material in other cases prepares one not to expect a complete appropriation of the qualities and deeds of one individual, such as Ea in the present instance, and the attribution of them in totality to the character or action of the corresponding person, such as either Jahveh or the serpent-tempter[1]. Nor does the Jahvist writer devote his borrowed material to a purpose corresponding to that which it served in its original setting. His Abel-story, for instance, is supposed to deal with the sons of the first man; yet it presupposes a populated world, and therefore originally served a purpose altogether different from that to which he puts it. The same kind of thing has been done with the Eabani and Adapa legends if they have really contributed any of the conceptions met with in the biblical account of Adam.

Another point of detail in which some writers have seen a resemblance to Gen. iii. is the statement that Ea, when warning Adapa against the acceptance of the food of the gods, tells him to receive the garment they will offer. This has been compared to Jahveh's gift of the coats of skins to Adam and Eve on their attaining to forbidden knowledge. It is, however, precarious to attach much significance to this coincidence; it is probably one of 'letter' only, and entirely superficial.

---

[1] Thus Parnapishtim in the Gilgamesh epic has traits in common with Adam, Noah, Enoch and (according to one authority) Lot: Gilgamesh is believed to have suggested both Nimrod and Samson.

II]   *Relations of the Fall-story*   47

It would seem that in the Babylonian traditions so far referred to it is immortality rather than knowledge that is mankind's great quest, and which is forbidden by the gods. Knowledge, in several myths, seems to be freely given rather than grudged; its acquisition by man was not associated, so far as our fragmentary knowledge of Babylonian literature goes, with any undue self-exaltation or any fall. There is one legend, however, that of Zu the storm-bird god, in which Prof. Sayce sees a meaning very closely akin to that of Prometheus, and therefore the implication that knowledge was brought to mankind against the will of the gods. A tablet exists which yields part of a story of a being Zu who desires to be Bel and, dreaming that he is the father of the gods, protector of heaven and earth, steals the tablets of destiny with which he flees away. He is proclaimed an outcast, and Anu is urged to pursue him. There is nothing in this story to imply that Zu committed the theft for the benefit of mankind; but another inscription tells of the flight to the mountains of a god Lugal-turda, who was transformed into the likeness of a bird. This Zu-bird is the deified storm-cloud, and originally, Prof. Sayce believes, was an Accadian totem conception which passed into a god in the Semitic period. Zu was the presiding deity of the town of Marad and was worshiped throughout Babylonia. From these facts it is inferred that Zu was regarded as the bringer of the lightning from the gods to men, giving them the knowledge of fire and the power of reading the future in the flashes of the storm: that, in fact, he stole the secret wisdom and communicated it to man, and was therefore doomed to suffer[1]. The coincidences between these combined legends and that of Prometheus, if it be granted that the latter is a development into legend of a lightning-myth[2], are certainly striking and suggestive of the inferences which Prof. Sayce has drawn. Still it is obvious that certain links in the chain of evidence that Zu is the equivalent of Prometheus are supplied rather by assuming the analogy which it is sought to prove than by necessary

---

[1] Sayce, *Chald. Account of Genesis*, chap. vii.; *Hibbert Lectures*, p. 295 ff.
[2] As is so ingeniously maintained by Kuhn in his essay *Die Herabkunft des Feuers und des Göttertranks*.

implications of the statements of the Babylonian texts. That Zu was worshipped by men, for instance, is no proof that he stole the tablets on man's behalf. For our purpose, however, it is sufficient to remark that the legend affords no parallel to the Fall-story except in the implication that the gods resented man's acquisition of divine knowledge; and this, as has been said, is the most doubtful feature in the interpretation of it just examined.

The Etana legend has sometimes been appealed to as evidence that ideas similar to those taught by the Paradise-story were common to Babylon. Etana, a hero who desires to obtain something which will mitigate the pains of parturition for his wife, is tempted by the eagle to ascend with him to the heavenly regions. Both of them are cast down to the lower world, apparently as a punishment for presumption, and both subsequently encounter death. But Etana is not a representative of the human race; and if he were, the story would better illustrate that of the tower of Babel than that of the expulsion from Paradise.

Other alleged analogies may be briefly discussed. The incident of the hero's loss of the health-plant, in the Gilgamesh legend, which was snatched from him by a serpent, can hardly be cited as a parallel to the loss of access to the tree of life in Gen. iii. It is introduced apparently as a mere accident. The supposed narrative of a fall, very similar in nature to that of Adam and Eve, through eating the 'asnan fruit' in the garden of the gods, contained in a mutilated Creation-tablet, proved, as is now well known, to be an account of a feast of the gods and not of a human fall[1]. The celebrated representation, upon a seal, of two figures seated near a tree, behind one of whom a serpent stands, certainly suggests at first sight the scene described in Gen. iii. But one of the figures is horned, and therefore, say some authorities, divine: it is impossible to say whether the figures are not of the same sex: the one is not handing the fruit to

---

[1] Boscawen's translation appeared in the *Babylonian and Oriental Record*, 1890, and is quoted in Ryle's *Early Narratives of Genesis*, p. 40. For the true rendering see Jastrow, *op. cit.*, p. 424, or the translations of Delitzsch and Zimmern.

II] *Relations of the Fall-story* 49

the other, and they are both seated. The meaning of the picture is therefore possibly something totally different from that which was at first supposed[1]. The serpent, moreover, was a symbol of very varied signification in Babylon.

It may be safely concluded, then, that we possess no Babylonian parallel to the Hebrew Fall-story[2]. That individual conceptions embodied in it, such as that of the divine resentment of human encroachments, or of a garden of the gods, or of a tree of life[3], are common to Babylonian religion, is of course as true as it is natural; but such ideas were the common property of most ancient nations. The evidence is strong that the account of Paradise contained in Gen. ii. is partly derived from Babylonian material, and that the basis of the story had much in common with the Eabani legend, which, from its antiquity, is perhaps rather to be considered as Semitic than exclusively Babylonian. Here, however, the proof of interdependence ends. There is no parallel, as yet, in Babylonian literature, to the didactic element of our narrative which constitutes it essentially a Fall-story. It is sometimes urged that the sense of sin and of need for forgiveness evinced by the Babylonians almost demands the existence among them of a tradition of a Fall[4]. To this it may

---

[1] There are similar seal-representations in which, though some of the features of that above described are reproduced, there is no reason to suspect any allusion to the Fall. See Schrader, *op. cit.*, i. 38; this writer's opinion is shared by Baudissin and most authorities.

F. Delitzsch, in a recent pamphlet, *Babel und Bibel*, S. 37, still adheres to the opinion that the seal mentioned above represents the Fall-story. Prof. E. König's pamphlet, *Bibel und Babel*, one of a number evoked by Delitzsch's essay, maintains the more usual negative or sceptical attitude. König (S. 23, 24) sums up expert opinion when he says: "Eine Erzählung über die erste Verletzung menschlicher Pietät—also eine Parallele zu Gen. iii., 1 ff.—ist bis jetzt in der Keilschriftliteratur nicht gefunden worden."

[2] See *Additions and Corrections* at the end of this volume.

[3] We read of a 'plant of life' in the legend of Gilgamesh, 'food of life' and 'drink of life' in that of Adapa, and a 'plant of birth' in that of Etana; also of the sacred tree, apparently a 'world-tree' like Ygdrasil, and an oracle-tree; at Eridu. The cedar, used for healing and also for soothsaying, and the date, used for wine, were sacred with the Babylonians. See Sayce, *Hibbert Lectures*, p. 240 ff.; Lenormant, *op. cit.*, etc.

[4] Hommel, Art. *Babylonia* in Hastings' *Dict. of the Bible*; F. Delitzsch, *Wo lag das Paradies?* S. 45.

be replied that an intense feeling of personal sin can exist apart from any doctrine of a Fall, and that the penitence expressed in the Babylonian psalms does not so much bespeak an abiding consciousness of inherent sinfulness as the occasional conviction that sin was the necessary reason or cause for a particular personal calamity or divine visitation. The penitential psalms of Babylonia contain no allusion to such conceptions as are involved in a developed doctrine of a fall of the race, and the implication that human nature is corrupted. Moreover the sense of sin which they reveal is much less inward than that of the Hebrew psalmist.

Further, it is to be noticed that the cuneiform literature has as yet supplied no trace of a Babylonian belief in a golden age. It cannot of course be concluded that no such tradition existed, as our records of Babylonian beliefs are but fragmentary; indeed it is almost incredible that the Babylonians did not possess such a legend[1]. But the fact that no such tradition has come down to us is noteworthy in connexion with the similar absence of a Fall-story.

In so far as negative evidence can aid in the establishment of any positive conclusion, we may say that the absence in Babylonian literature of a Fall-story in the strict sense, that is to say of a legend accounting not so much for the loss of Paradise, or for the association of troubles with civilisation, as for the introduction of sin into the world, tends to confirm the opinion that the Paradise-story did not become a Fall-story, even to the limited extent to which it is to be regarded as one at all[2], until it was remodelled by the Hebrew people, and perhaps mainly by the Jahvist compiler, in the interests of the theology, and in relation to the sin-consciousness, of an age bordering upon that of literary prophecy. Babylonia,

[1] There is evidence that the ancient Babylonians observed the feast of Sacaea; see Athenaeus, *Deip.* XIV. 639 c., and *Records of the Past*, new series, II. pp. 83, 84, references which have been very kindly furnished by Prof. Sayce. Now Frazer (*Golden Bough*, 2nd ed. III. 150) connects the Sacaea with the Saturnalia, which in turn is said to have been popularly based elsewhere on the tradition of a golden age (p. 138). It is not proved, however, that such festivals grew out of that tradition, nor, therefore, that the Sacaea necessarily implies the belief, in Babylonia, in a golden age.

[2] See above, p. 12.

however, already throws abundance of light on the ideas, and the vestiges of earlier associations, which are embodied in the picturesque details of the narrative. It was probably on Babylonian soil that an animistic and crude legend, whose earliest implications were similar to some of those which Jastrow and others have discovered in the story of Eabani[1], developed into a culture-legend, Semitic in imagery, but akin to Aryan speculation from a similar level of civilisation in its *ethos*; a legend which, after modification at the hands of the Canaanites who had obtained it from Babylonia, was taken up by the Hebrews, and made the vehicle of ideas about Jahveh and the beginnings of human culture, and subsidiarily, though of set purpose, of teaching as to the entrance into the world of human sin.

Greek Parallels.

It is a remarkable fact that the most striking parallel which can be found to the teaching of the Hebrew Fall-story as a whole, if the exegesis of it here adopted be correct, is derived from an Aryan source. This, however, may merely be due to the imperfection of the Semitic record; or, with greater probability, to similarity of thought and feeling between the Jahvist compiler and the Greek people with regard to the relation of the Deity to human culture. Extant Semitic traditions serve, as we have seen, to throw considerable light on the origin, and the development in meaning, of the imagery with which the history of the Fall is clothed. Indeed we may regard its figures and underlying conceptions, for the most part, as common property, in some form, of several Semitic nations. But such sources fail to supply us with any explanation of some of the ruling ideas, or the *ethos*, of the narrative, which certain writers have believed to be foreign to the Hebrew mind.

It is the myths of ancient Greece which reveal with least uncertainty a vein of thought similar to that disclosed by the

---

[1] Such crude legendary elements may perhaps go back to the age in which Semites and Hamites had a common home. The facts stated above, p. 36, on the authority of Prof. W. Max Müller of Philadelphia, point to this conclusion, and are confirmed by the work of Prof. Barton to which reference has been made.

exegesis of the Fall-story of Genesis which was maintained in Chapter I. Allowing for the difference between the Hebrew conception of God's nature and disposition towards man and that of Greek thought even as represented in Aeschylus, there is a great similarity between the teaching of the legend of Prometheus and that of the acquisition of knowledge through the eating of the forbidden fruit. Both contain the idea that the ills of human life are a punishment for man's overstepping the limits of the sphere assigned to him: both regard human knowledge and culture as something requiring to be wrenched from a deity jealous of human encroachments, and whose acquisition was mediated by a superhuman being: both imply that human inventiveness or desire for material advancement can scarcely be distinguished from arrogant independence or defiance, and see in ὕβρις the primal sin[1].

The story of Prometheus as the fire-stealer, which is considered by some to be more ancient than that of his deception of Zeus in the matter of the sacrifice, though not embodying the original *rôle* of Prometheus[2], is closely associated in Hesiod with the once independent legend of Pandora. This latter story agrees with Genesis in making woman, or feminine curiosity, mediately the source of human evils[3]. Pandora is

[1] The same moral is perhaps taught by the fable of the Aloades; see Preller, *Griech. Mythologie*, 4te Aufl. S. 103.

The Prometheus myth, or myths, for it appears to be a fusion of different stories of different date, is to be found in its popular form in Hesiod, *Works and Days*, 40 ff.; *Theog.* 506 ff. The attitude of Aeschylus towards the legend is impossible to determine with certainty as we have but the middle third of his trilogy. If the last part contained a vindication of Zeus, as is probable, he would have done for the old folk-story, to some extent, what the Jahvist writer or his predecessors did for the original myth which they Hebraised.

[2] Preller, *op. cit.*, S. 95 ff.

This view is of course opposed to the ingenious philological speculations of Kuhn (*Mythol. Studien*, Bd. 1.).

[3] It is interesting to note that two features of the Hebrew Fall-story common to Greek mythology, viz. the agency of woman in the cause of evil and the acquisition of knowledge as the means of temptation to it, appear also in the legend of the Sirens. When these address Odysseus they sing: "For none hath ever driven by this way in his black ship, till he hath heard from our lips the voice sweet as the honeycomb, and hath had joy thereof and *gone on his way the wiser*. For lo, *we know all things*, all the travail that in wide Troy-land the Argives and Trojans bare by the gods' designs, yea and *we know all that shall hereafter be upon the fruitful earth.*" *Odyssey*, XII. 184 ff.

a Greek Eve, and her story, before being used for didactic purposes, implied that the first woman, unlike men who were generally regarded as autochthonous, was the handiwork of the gods. Her later creation forms another parallel with the Jahvist history[1].

The Prometheus-legend was never used to account for the loss of the golden age; indeed Aeschylus makes the state of man, previous to his benefactor's intervention, to have been almost bestial. But we find in Hesiod a tradition of the golden age of Kronos which has certain features in common with the history of the first man in Genesis, and which have been considered to have had a similar, but independent, origin.

It remains to mention that in the garden of the Hesperides we have a picture of a home of the gods where Earth produced her choicest gifts and which contained a tree analogous to the tree of life. The tree was committed to the guardianship of a dragon, and its fruit was stolen by Herakles. This story is undoubtedly at bottom a solar myth depicting the conquest of the night by day, but which became in course of time complicated with accretions and fraught with new associations. Whether it has anything in common with the Paradise-story other than its conception of the garden of the gods and its tree bearing golden apples, is extremely improbable. Ladon, the guardian of the fruit, has quite a different function from that of the serpent-tempter who gives it away; and Herakles has no counterpart in the Hebrew narrative. It is too often imagined that every mythological combination of a tree and a serpent implies a kindred legend to that which forms the basis of the history of Adam and Eve. In the present instance the connexion was maintained by so high an authority as Lenormant, who asserts, moreover, that the myth is indisputably of Phoenician origin[2]. According to this writer, the story of Herakles and Ladon would be practically another Prometheus-legend, and one wearing much of the outward

---

[1] Cf. Gomperz, *Greek Thinkers*, E. T. I. 37: "Once more we are astounded at the similarity of mythical invention obtaining among the most diverse peoples, and one almost involuntarily recalls the allied Hebraic story of Eve—the mother of all life—and the ominous consequences of her sinful curiosity."

[2] *op. cit.*, I. pp. 94, 95 n.

form of the Fall-story. The really essential features of the latter history seem, however, to be wholly wanting from the Hesperides legend, and the resemblances, with the exception of the scenery, to be entirely outward, superficial and incidental[1].

Such similarities of thought as have been mentioned between the Jahvist Fall-story and the myths of Greece require, of course, some explanation. That possibilities for early interchange of legendary traditions, through the medium of Phoenicia, between Canaan and Greece existed, we have already stated. But that Greek influences actually penetrated to the Southern Kingdom, whence the Jahvist document is now generally supposed to have been produced, is a theory improbable in itself, and one to which we are by no means compelled to resort for an explanation of the facts before us. We have seen reason, and shall soon find further reasons, for believing that the present *ethos* of the Bible narrative of the fall of Adam and Eve was impressed upon ancient Semitic traditions possessing an altogether different meaning, and was the creation of Hebrew religious thought if not of the Jahvist compiler. And it may easily be the case that similar ideas about the origin of human evils, and the attitude of Deity to human self-advancement in its non-religious aspect, occurred to minds as different in character as those of Greek and Hebrew, when thinking on the same subject-matter from somewhat similar planes of culture and ethical reflection. The 'psychological unity' of man, in the same circumstances, is obviously in this case an available, a natural, and a sufficient, explanation of the phenomena.

Iranian Parallels.

In the oldest portion of the Avesta, the Gâthâs, written in archaic Iranian resembling the Vedic Sanskrit, we find a reference to a being named Yima, who is identical with Yama of the Vedas, and belongs to the 'undivided Aryan'

---

[1] Even the meaning of the golden apples has been variously interpreted; see, *e.g.*, Art. *Hesperides* in *Encycl. Brit.*, and Cox, *Aryan Mythylogy*, II. 10, 38.

period before Indians and Iranians were separate peoples[1]. It is doubtful whether in that period Yima or Yama denoted the first man. He is called in the Avesta 'the son of Vîvanghat' (Vedic, Vivasvant), whom some consider to have then played that rôle[2], and also receives the epithet 'shining,' which confirms the supposition that he was a mythical solar hero before he came to be an earthly king[3]. In the Vendidâd[4] and other portions of the Avesta later than the Gâthâs, Yima is certainly not the first man, but rather a first king and promoter of civilisation, whose reign was a kind of golden age in which there was 'no envy made by the daevas[5],' no disease nor death, and man and flocks increased so that the earth had to be made larger[6]. He is also the Noah of a story which cannot be called a deluge-legend, but which is closely akin to one[7]. This Yima, however, fell into sin. He possessed the 'glory,' we read, till his 'lie,' when he began to delight in falsehood[8]. The nature of his lie is not stated, but Firdûsi (10th century) says that he pretended to be a god. The more ancient passage of the Avesta, to which allusion has already been made, is also generally supposed to contain a reference to a fall of Yima such as would be connected with the introduction of flesh-eating. But the passage is one as to the translation of which oriental scholars do not agree, and which, in the judgment of Tiele, contains no such implication[9].

[1] See Spiegel, *Eran. Alterthumskunde,* I. 439; Windischmann, *Zoroast. Studien,* S. 20. The passage in question is *Yasna* xxxii. 7-8.
[2] Oldenberg, *Religion des Veda,* S. 275. In the Avesta Vîvanghat is the first mortal who prepared the haoma, and in the Vedas the first sacrificer, to whom fire was brought from heaven by Agni. Lenormant, *op. cit.,* I. 68 and Darmesteter, *Ormuzd et Ahriman,* p. 74, consider that Yima stood at first for the first man.
[3] *Sacred Books of the East* (henceforth denoted *S. B. E.*), XXIII. 60. These translations have been generally used here.
[4] *Fargard* II.
[5] *Yasna* IX. ; *Yast* XV.
[6] Old age and death are represented as reigning before Yima's time, *Yast* IX.
[7] Darmesteter, Spiegel, Kohut and other authorities believe this story to be due to Chaldaean or Hebrew influence.
[8] *Yast* XIX. 34 ; cf. *Yast* V. 25-31.
[9] A translation furnished by the Rev. J. H. Moulton, to whom the author is greatly indebted for generous aid in supplying some facts relative to Iranian literature, interprets *Yasna* XXXII. 8 thus: "Of these sinners Yima the son of Vîvanghat was famed to be, who, wishing to please our people, devoured cow's

56   *The Ethnological Origin and*   [CHAP.

If the opinion of the majority be adopted, and this passage be allowed to associate Yima with a fall from a primitive state of vegetarianism to one of flesh-eating, the whole of what we are told of him does not supply a story which can be at all compared with that of Gen. iii. Yima is not tempted to evil by the 'fiendish serpent,' Azhi Dahâka[1], but only falls under his power after he has sinned. There is surely no need

flesh." Spiegel renders the verse : "Zu diesen Bösen sprach Yima der Sohn des Vîvanghat, der uns Menschen gelehrt hat das Fleisch in Stücken zu essen." Tiele (*Geschichte der Religion im Alterthum*, Bd. II., 1te Hälfte, S. 90–91) considers that the rendering 'sinners' in this passage is grammatically impossible, and construes the verse : "Of this punishment had Vîvanghat's son Yima heard, who (therefore) taught men to give to us a share of the flesh, when themselves eating." [Von dieser Strafe hatte V.'s Sohn Yima gehört, der (deshalb) die Menschen unterwies, selbst essend einen Teil des Fleisches uns (zu geben).] Spiegel states that he knows no myths according to which Yima taught men to eat flesh, but adds : "Doch wird demselben die Einrichtung verschiedener Festlichkeiten zugeschrieben, mit welchen Gastmähler verbunden waren."

Ch. de Harlez translates the passage : "C'est par ces châtiments qu'est connu Yima, le fils de Vivanhâs, qui voulut enseigner aux mortels à manger des chairs dépecées"; and he adds "Il èst difficile de ne pas voir ici une allusion à la déchéance de Yima et à son supplice."

Darmesteter (*Annales du Musée Guimet*, Tome XXI. pp. 238–9) renders the passage: "Ces pécheurs avaient pourtant entendu Yima, fils de Vîvanhat, qui enseigna aux hommes de nous donner une part de la viande qu'ils mangent." He adds : "On serait tenté de traduire, 'qui *réjouit* les hommes en nous donnant une part de la viande qu'il mange,'" and states this to represent the opinion of Dînkart. Darmesteter also remarks : "La paraphrase de Dînkart est très obscure : elle semble indiquer qu'il ne faut pas gaspiller et jeter la viande, ni tuer inutilement, mais seulement pour son besoin et celui de ses serviteurs."

Mills (*S. B. E.* XXXI.) gives the following translation : "Of these wretched beings Yima Vîvangusha was famed to be; he who, desiring to content our men, was eating kine's flesh in its pieces."

Dr E. W. West has very kindly furnished the author with a literal rendering of the Pahlavi version of the passage: "Of those demons, a malicious sinner heard Yima, him who *was* son of Vîvanhas, by whom *it was* explained to men (thus) : 'He eats the meat of our people in portions (equally greedy with the lapfuls and armfuls of mankind).'" The Pahlavi translator tries to explain the Avesta text as literally as possible, so far as his experience permits, and introduces several explanatory clauses in further illustration of his meaning. This version, says Dr West, was probably written A.D. 226–240, but afterwards revised about 531–579. It may be considered as the best authority we have for the meaning of the Avesta text; but the version as a whole is said to be by no means absolutely trustworthy.

[1] This is a mythical person corresponding to the Vedic Vritra, the storm-cloud snake. It would seem that the legend of Azhi and Yima grew out of a solar myth. Weber, *Ind. Studien*, III. S. 416 ff.

to speculate on the very remote possibility of the Hebrew story being suggested by this source or borrowed from it[1].

The mystic drink Haoma (Soma of the Vedas), corresponding in properties to those of the tree of life, and perhaps also to those of the tree of knowledge[2], need not be appealed to as the source of those conceptions in the biblical narrative after what has been said of corresponding, and still more closely analogous, figures in the more kindred Semitic traditions[3].

On passing from the Avesta to the Bundahesch, we find parallels to the early narratives of Genesis somewhat more suggestive of possible interdependence. The Bundahesch, however, was not written till about the 9th century A.D.; and though it largely drew from ancient tradition and embodied matter contained in lost Avestan writings, it was also enriched with comments after the manner of Jewish haggada, so that it is not always easy to discriminate with certainty its really ancient elements. Some of its legends are developments of ancient Iranian lore, but much new oral material accumulated during the Sassanian period; and before it was reduced to writing there was abundant opportunity for intercourse between Persians and Jews[4]. It would

---

[1] Horn considers the sin of Yima to be a late addition to his history and due to Hebrew influence. Spiegel, here as in other cases, believed in a Semitic origin (*Eran. Alterthumskunde*, I. S. 446 ff.), as to the *possibility* of which other authorities agree. But there is no serious evidence of contact with Hebrew thought till a much later time than that of the composition of J. There appears to have been too great a readiness on the part of many scholars to assume that analogies, often distant and superficial, are necessarily due exclusively to direct influence of one nation on another. Before such a view can be safely adopted, the history and chronology involved, and the possible means of inter-communication, need to be much more minutely investigated than has usually been the case.

[2] The haoma was, like the soma (*Rig Veda*, X. 97. 17), king of healing plants. It 'kept death away' (*S. B. E.* XXIII. p. 20). It was supposed to give victory in battle (*Yast* XIV. 57), and 'brilliant offspring' to women (*Yasna* IX. 22); and even to bestow wisdom and knowledge also (*ibid.*).

[3] On traces of a tradition of a Paradise in the Avesta, with its trees, see Windischmann, *op. cit.*

[4] See Kohut, *Jewish Quart. Review*, III. 231 ff. Cheyne, Art. *Deluge* in *Encycl. Bibl.*, like Kohut and others, thinks the Persians borrowed from Hebrew traditions. This would seem to be *prima facie* as likely as the converse relation in the case of the narratives of P; in the case of those of J, whose antiquity is beyond question, it is infinitely more probable. On the other hand there are

be extremely difficult, in case of actual borrowing, to decide on which side the debt lay; but perhaps too much has sometimes been made of the alleged points of resemblance. In this relatively late work we read of a first man and woman, Maschya and Maschiana, who sprang from the seed of the dead Gayomard, a being who may be compared to the 'celestial Adam' of the Talmud or the 'generic man' of Philo[1]. The first truly human pair are said to have at first acknowledged Ormuzd as creator; then their minds became corrupted and they exclaimed that the earth had been made by Ahriman[2], under whose power they passed. The story continues with an account of how they then began to use animal food, first milk and then the flesh of a sheep which they roasted; how they clothed themselves in skins, fashioned implements, and made themselves a shelter. We are next told that they fought with one another. After 50 years they were 'moved to desire'; they ate their first children and afterwards had others[3]. It is noticeable that we have here the notion of a gradual fall of the first representatives of the human race closely associated, if not identified, with the transition to flesh-eating and progress in culture, and that the story has points in common with Gen. iii. and iv.[4] But the stories, for all their points of resemblance, are widely different; and if their general meaning may be the outcome of independent speculation on the same subject, the details may easily be coincidences, especially as they are not so closely

strong reasons for believing that many of the legends connected with demons, the trees of Paradise, and Adam, which are met with in pseudepigraphical and Jewish literature, were in part borrowed from Persia and elsewhere.

[1] Firdûsi makes Gayomard, like Yima in the Avesta, a first king and teacher of civilisation.

[2] This false speech is said to have been uttered 'through the will of the demons,' *S. B. E.* v. p. 52.

[3] *S. B. E.* v. p. 52 ff. Spiegel, *op. cit.*, I. p. 508 ff. Kohut, *J. Q. R.* II. 223 ff.

[4] Lajard, *Culte de Mithra*, p. 59 ff., hints at the possibility of the borrowing of this story from Gen. The story does not occur in the Avesta, but Lajard (p. 60) asserts that it must have been originally included therein because allusions to it occur in the Yasts of Tîr and Mithra. Lajard relies here on the translations of Anquetil du Perron (see his *Zend-Avesta*, Tome II. p. 189 and p. 214); but in Darmesteter's rendering (*S. B. E.* XXIII. p. 96 and p. 132) the name Maschya vanishes and the sense is different.

II] *Relations of the Fall-story* 59

similar as to absolutely demand the hypothesis of borrowing. The Bundahesch also tells of Ahriman leaping to earth in the shape of a serpent to spoil the creatures of Ormuzd[1]. It speaks also of Al Burz as a kind of Eden with mystic rivers[2]. Its account of the dealings of Jem (Yima) with the demons, according to which he took a demon to wife and gave his sister to a demon, from which unions sprang apes and bears, seems to have certainly been derived from, or to have suggested, the extremely similar fancies met with in Jewish literature[3].

Indian Parallels.

The Vedas yield no fall-story. Yama, ultimately identical with the Iranian Yima, is god of the underworld. Some, however, have seen in the story of the incest of Yama and his sister Yami, in the tenth book of the Rig Veda, the implication that these figures corresponded to Adam and Eve[4]. Max Müller regarded the story as a myth of the dawn. In any case there is no parallel here to the Hebrew Fall-story.

Mention must be made of a story told in Hardwick's *Christ and other Masters*[5], and sometimes repeated by writers on the Fall-narrative as if it were a genuine parallel from Hindu tradition. The first man (Manu Swáyambhuva) is identified with Brahma, who, thus humanised, is tempted by Siva. Siva drops from heaven a blossom of the sacred fig, which was "regarded as the tree of knowledge" (bódhidruma). Brahma thinks this will make him immortal; he gathers it and, intoxicated with this fancy, thinks himself divine. Then the god appears in majesty, curses him and banishes him from Brahmapattana to an abyss of degradation. It is added that Brahma's ambitious hopes were instigated by his wife.

The tree here spoken of is the well-known tree of Buddha, under which he received his enlightenment. The story is of very late date, and embodies no ancient Hindu tradition.

[1] *S. B. E.* v. p. 17. This idea may be the source of the Jewish identification of Satan with the serpent of Gen. iii.   [2] *op. cit.*, p. 34.
[3] Spiegel, I. S. 527; cf. Eisenmenger, *Entdecktes Judenthum*, II. 412 ff.
[4] See *e.g.* Phillips, *The Teaching of the Vedas*.
[5] Part II., p. 135 ff. (1855).

According to high authorities in oriental studies there is much in Hardwick's work which, like this story, is of no value as an illustration of ancient Hindu thought.

* * * * * *

The general impression left upon the reader by a consideration of the details presented in the foregoing pages will probably be somewhat as follows: that the material is too scanty to enable us to reconstruct Israel's religious state and legendary possessions, with any degree of completeness, previously to the nation's entrance into Canaan: that the elements of which the framework or imagery of the narrative of the first sin is composed belonged to the legendary lore more or less common to Semitic races generally: that the didactic import of the story as a whole was due to pre-prophetic or prophetic Hebrew thought, which treated its traditional material in some respects conservatively, in other respects with drastic rigour and unfettered licence: that our conclusions suffer in finality from our ignorance of Phoenician legend, which may possibly have been influenced by communication with ancient Greece[1]: that the parallels supplied by Aryan tradition are better explained, for the most part, by the hypothesis of independent though psychologically similar origin: that the possibilities of actual borrowing have probably often been unduly magnified: and that, in the present state of knowledge, it is impossible to form a conclusion as to the ethnological sources of the Fall-story to which finality can attach. The material at our disposal is also too fragmentary to be considered representative[2].

[1] It is generally believed that the Phoenicians were rather receptive of external influences than apt to impress their thought on other civilised nations.

[2] The more important literature on the subjects discussed in this chapter has for the most part been referred to in the notes. The indispensable foundation is Lenormant's *Les Origines de l'histoire*, which is very trustworthy for facts but is perhaps now somewhat old and contains some uncritical inferences. Dillmann's *New Commentary on Genesis*, vol. I. (E.T.), is also rich in facts and references. But the works of specialists in *each* branch of ancient literature must be compared, else the student will be led astray.

Since the above chapter was written new works on Babylonian religion by Prof. Sayce and T. G. Pinches have been announced. For information supplied by that of the latter author the reader has already been referred to *Additions and Corrections* at the end of this volume.

CHAPTER III.

THE PSYCHOLOGICAL ORIGIN OF THE FALL-STORY: ITS RELATION TO HISTORY, ALLEGORY AND MYTH.

IT has already been found necessary to allude to the legendary or, as they are usually called, mythological substrata which underlie the narrative of Gen. ii. and iii., and which reveal themselves in it in spite of their having been for the most part refined away in the interests of an increasingly ethical and monotheistic religion. External evidence is supplied by the Old Testament that such traditions concerning Paradise and the first man, more mythological in character, though not necessarily, for that reason, more ancient[1], than that embodied in Genesis, were handed down at a considerably later date.

Thus in Job xv. 7 ff.[2], there is an obvious allusion to a legend that the first man was a kind of demigod, created before the hills, who had access to the council of God[3] and acquired extraordinary knowledge of the mysteries of the

---
[1] This is Gunkel's view, but it cannot be adopted unquestioningly; for legendary allusions in post-exilic books may indicate late borrowing of Babylonian and other folk-lore, induced by closer contact with foreign influences. There is evidence of renewed interest in mythology after the exile.

[2] R.V. "*Art thou the first man that was born? Or wast thou brought forth before the hills? Dost thou hearken in the council of God? And dost thou restrain wisdom to thyself?*" ('*didst thou steal wisdom for thyself?*' Hoffmann, Gunkel, etc.). See Delitzsch, *Job*, E.T. I. 251 ff. Gunkel (*Schöpfung u. Chaos*, S. 148; *Genesis*, S. 29 f.) assumes perhaps too confidently that we have in these last words a reference to the fall of Adam.

[3] Cf. Jer. xxiii. 18.

world[1]. Some scholars translate the verb, rendered in our version 'restrain,' by 'steal'; but this is a possible, rather than a necessary, rendering. If it could be adopted with certainty, we should possess in this passage a tradition having something in common with Gen. iii., and a strong confirmation of the view maintained above, after Wellhausen, that the sin which caused man's expulsion from Paradise consisted in the illegitimate or forbidden acquisition of wisdom. The *ethos* of either story would then be very similar to that of the Prometheus legend. This view possesses great attractiveness; but it must be admitted that the writer may have only intended to imply that the first man acquired his wonderful knowledge through his privilege of access to the council of God. In any case he knew of a legend which endowed the first man with semi-divine attributes: a feature which the Jahvist writer, if he was acquainted with it, did not admit into his history. It seems, however, unlikely that the legend which is used by the author of Job xv. had any connexion with the mythical material utilised by the writer of Gen. iii. The view that the first man was a being endowed with extraordinary privileges and excellences, the view reproduced in Job and, as we shall presently see, in Ezekiel, would seem to belong to an altogether different cycle of legend from that which represented him, like the Jahvist narrative, as emerging from the natural, and perhaps almost animal, state and attaining to a knowledge and culture which were expressly denied him by his Maker. If the Adam of Genesis was conceived after the model of an Eabani, he had no identity with a figure resembling, in some respects, the personification of Wisdom and, in others, the most splendid of oriental monarchs. The latter kind of legend, too, would seem to represent a higher level of culture and a later mode of thought than that embodied in our Paradise-story, which was probably derived from very remote antiquity. Certainly it was this post-exilic

---

[1] Cf. the personified Wisdom of Prov. viii. 22 ff., esp. vv. 22, 25. Toy (*Crit. Comm. on Prov.* p. xxix), disagreeing with Ewald, Davidson and Budde, will allow no allusion in Job xv. 7 to the description of Wisdom contained in these verses. Budde (*Handkommentar zum A.T.*, *Hiob*, S. 77-8) sees only a reference to Wisdom, and none to a 'first man.'

representation of the first man, rather than that of the Jahvist narratives, which was chosen for elaboration in later Jewish literature, whether of the apocalyptic or the rabbinical class[1].

Again, in Ezek. xxviii. we find what is undoubtedly an account of an expulsion from Eden applied in a figurative manner to the downfall of the king of Tyre. The legend of which use is here made possibly implies that the version of the story in Genesis is a recension of a fuller, richer and more mythological narration, in which the garden of Eden was associated with a mountain of God[2].' The text of the passage is unfortunately very corrupt, so that its exegesis is difficult; and no confidence can be placed in conjectural attempts at its amendment. The king of Tyre is figuratively compared to a legendary being who lived in the garden of God, whose clothing was adorned with precious stones, and who, in consequence of proud self-exaltation, was expelled from the divine abode. The passage probably implies, further, that this being, like the prince who is compared or identified with him, was of preeminent physical beauty and wisdom. Whether he was the first man[3], or an angel[4], or a 'son of Elohim[5],' is not definitely stated in the context, but the first of these alternatives would seem to be the most probable[6]. There is therefore some doubt as to how far this legend used by Ezekiel is to be regarded as identical with that which underlies the Fall-story; but the passage leaves no room for

---

[1] The later Jewish speculation on the first man certainly appears to have been largely directed by foreign influences. Amongst these, Persian legend probably played a considerable part. See Kohut on Parsic and Jewish legends of the first man, *J. Q. R.* III. 231 ff.

[2] Such is Gunkel's opinion. See his *Genesis* for an account of Hebrew and Jewish conceptions of Paradise. On Ezek. xxviii. see the Commentaries, on that prophet, of Cornill (S. 360), Keil (E.T., in loc.), Bertholet; also Art. *Cherub*, *Encycl. Bibl.*

In Ezek. xxxi. we find 'the Assyrian' compared to a tree envied by "all the trees of Eden, that were in the garden of God" for its surpassing excellence. The Eden of Ezekiel reminds us very forcibly of the Mountain of Masu in the Gilgamesh epic (A. Jeremias, *Izdubar-Nimrod*, S. 28-30), where was a tree bearing 'costly stones' as its fruit. Cf. Ezek. xxviii. 14, 16.

[3] Keil, Gunkel, Kraetzschmar (*Ezechiel*, in Nowack's *Handkomm. zum A.T.*).
[4] Cornill.   [5] Cheyne.
[6] The splendid clothing attributed to him may be the state-dress of one of the sons of Elohim (Cheyne), or, equally well, that which ancient tradition sometimes assigns to the first man; see the Targums on Gen. iii.

64   *The Psychological Origin*   [CHAP.

uncertainty as to the existence, in the prophet's time, of oral tradition about Paradise and its guardian cherubim more mythological and, it may possibly be, more ancient than the Jahvist recension.

With the witness supplied by these two Old Testament passages to the actual existence amongst the Hebrew traditions either of ancient variants of the Paradise-story or of alternative stories, we may the more confidently examine the narrative more closely than was attempted in the preceding chapter for indications of the character which its material previously bore.

We may begin with the idea of the garden of Eden. In the Jahvist history this is represented as the home of the first human beings, prepared for them by the benevolent care of God. Such an anthropocentric view of the garden is surely not primitive or original. It may well be one of the marks of the treatment which the more ancient conception of Paradise received at the hands of the generations represented by the Jahvist school, or of generations anterior to that time. It is the product of relatively well-developed Jahvism, and marks an advance in the direction of ethical monotheism upon the conception which it replaced. This earlier conception is not completely refined away in our narrative. Eden has evidently been the 'home' of Jahveh on earth, where He enjoys the cool of the evening ; its two trees, not to speak yet of their probable signification at a still earlier time, impart qualities which belong of right only to Deity, and which, if analogy with Aryan mythology at a corresponding stage of development be relevant, may perhaps have been regarded as the food of Jahveh and the divine beings associated with Him, who are definitely referred to in Gen. iii. 22. In the variant of the story which is used in Ezek. xxviii. it is spoken of as the 'garden of God[1]' and is associated with a 'mountain of God[2].'

---

[1] Cf. Gen. iv. 16, xiii. 10; Isai. li. 3; Ezek. xxxi. 8, etc. The references in the prophets to the garden of Eden (see also Ezek. xxxvi. 35; Joel ii. 3) show that this element of the Paradise-story was familiar in Hebrew tradition. The expressions 'tree of life,' 'fountain of life,' 'water of life,' occurring in Prov., Pss. etc., and the allusions in Ps. xlvi. 4, Isai. xiv. 13 (eschatological) are also based on conceptions embodied in, if not derived from, this legend.

[2] See the commentaries of Dillmann and Gunkel.

The idea of a permanent earthly abode of the gods is common to (agricultural) Semitic and (relatively advanced) Aryan religions, and indeed is one which must inevitably arise in the development of religious thought. The transition from it to that of a Paradise for man and of a golden age is an easy step in mythological logic. The gods' land supplied the colouring for an earthly Paradise[1], just as the lost earthly Paradise supplied imagery for the Jewish and Christian descriptions of heaven.

The psychological origin of the idea of 'a golden age' at the beginning of human history, common to so many peoples, is by no means difficult to explain. It is so universal a tendency of the individual to optimise his distant past that one can easily see the psychological necessity of such a conception of human history to man when he has arrived at a certain stage of reflective thought and speculation[2]. Widening experience of life brings to most men more disappointments of hopes and prepossessions than unexpected joys; and, by a very natural transference, we are inclined to interpret our expanding knowledge of the evil of the world by concluding that the world is growing old. When middle age looks back regretfully at departed youth; or when Rousseau urges a 'return to Nature' and the mediaevalist calls the times of darkest ignorance and superstition the 'ages of faith,' the same subjective psychological process is involved as led half-civilised man to dream of a simpler and happier world long before his time. And if it is knowledge which begets the consciousness of evil, widening experience which discloses more and more of life's ills; above all, if the ever-growing acquisitions of 'social heredity' and the ever-increasing requirements of progressive civilisation impose more and more demands upon the

[1] See Usener, *Religionsgeschichtliche Untersuchungen*, Theil 3, S. 182 ff.

[2] Cf. W. R. Smith, *Rel. of Semites*, 1894, p. 303: The idea of a golden age "is the natural result of psychological laws which apply equally to the memory of individuals and the memory of nations"; and Maspero, *The Dawn of Civilisation*, S. P. C. K. 3rd ed. p. 160: "It is an illusion common to all peoples; as their insatiable thirst for happiness is never assuaged by the present, they fall back upon the remotest past in search of an age when that supreme felicity which is only known to them as an ideal was actually enjoyed by their ancestors."

individual will, and a greater break with the state of nature; what is more natural than to conclude that acquisition of knowledge is responsible for increased capacity for human evils, and to deduce that some elements, at least, in human self-advancement were resented by the gods? It would be surprising indeed if no such legends as the Fall-story and its partial analogues had grown up in the infancy of philosophical speculation. That they are, in some form or other, as we have seen, so widely spread, requires no further explanation than that the conditions for their origin have been everywhere the same. It was as true in early ages as it is to-day that "he who increaseth knowledge increaseth sorrow."

The two trees of the garden are obviously still looked upon by the writer of Gen. ii. and iii. as having acted in a magical way and as endowed with divine energies. They impart their virtues when their fruit is eaten[1]. It has already been seen that similar legendary conceptions are to be found throughout ancient Aryan and Semitic mythologies; and perhaps light may be thrown upon their origin and their most primitive meaning by an examination of the folk-lore of races which have retained in tradition the myths which belonged to them when in a state of religious and intellectual infancy. Indeed a large amount of evidence has been collected, though it needs to be subjected to rigorous criticism before one can venture to make use of it, to show that the root-idea associated with such magical trees is that of reproduction of life. And there have not been wanting, from antiquity to the present time, those who have suspected such an implication to have been originally embodied in the Fall-story, before the idea of immortality or of progress in culture superseded it. Comparative mythology, of course, affords numerous instances of the transference of a symbol associated with one circle of ideas to quite another such circle, according to change of circumstances or advance in civilisation and religious development. And if the story of Paradise,

---

[1] We find the same idea in the groundwork of the *Book of Enoch*, dating probably from the 2nd century B.C. See below, Chap. VIII.

as has been seen to be most probable, was derived from Phoenicia or Canaan, where phallic worship flourished and was closely associated, both in theory and practice, with agricultural life, it is by no means impossible that this story, even when first received thence by the Hebrew people, possessed a significance in some way connected with the ideas upon which phallic religion is based[1]. Some writers have seen in the selection of the use of clothing as the example of the application of the knowledge acquired through 'the opening of the eyes,' though apt enough in itself as an illustration of the beginnings of civilisation, a trace of such primitive meaning in the story; especially as this advance is expressly associated with the awakening of the feeling of shame. If the knowledge bestowed by the tree was originally identified with the consciousness of sex or the origin of passion, there is, it is argued, a natural reason for the choice of this particular example of the effects of partaking of the fruit of the tree of knowledge, and possibly for the presence in Gen. iii. of a verse which otherwise seems out of place[2]. It is to be observed that, in a later period, literature which drew upon ancient legendary tradition, but which at the same time fancifully embellished it, hints at an interpretation of the story which would regard the first sin as connected with sexual desire[3]. Comparative mythology is also not unfavourable to this conjecture, which, moreover, would associate the original function of the tree of knowledge very closely with that of the tree of life, and harmonise with the suggestion, which has been advanced for more than one reason, and by students who have approached the subject from the point of view of diverse branches of study, that the one of these

[1] On the close connection which exists in the primitive human mind between the plant world and man as regards fertility and life-giving power, see Frazer, *Golden Bough*, 2nd ed. vol II. pp. 204 ff. The association of Ishtar worship etc. with agricultural life seems to be based on this confusion.

[2] Gunkel offers the conjecture that Gen. iii. 20 (often thought to be an interpolated fragment from a variant of the story), which implies that Eve had conceived before the expulsion from Eden, is derived from a source which regarded the tree of knowledge as having the significance alluded to above; *Genesis*, S. 23.

[3] See below, Chaps. VII–X. Cf. Jastrow's derivation of the Paradise-story from the Eabani legend, mentioned in the preceding chapter.

trees is fundamentally a reduplication of the other. Trees were certainly symbolical, in Phoenicia, Arabia, and elsewhere, of the earth's productiveness[1], and had a close connexion with Ishtar-worship, which there is reason to believe to have been common to Semitic races generally. They are asserted to have frequently been phallic symbols of some kind or other, and Movers[2] states that this was the case in Phoenicia. This author's assertions with regard to phallicism have, many of them, been disputed; and doubtless, like many other statements made by the numerous writers on folk-lore and ancient symbolism who read phallicism almost everywhere, and see in it "the key to all mythologies," they require careful sifting. But there is growing empirical evidence, and also increasing volume of reasons deduced from the consideration of early man from the evolutionary point of view, for the belief that ideas connected with the phenomena of propagation in the organic world and in the human species largely moulded the early religious conceptions of mankind at a certain stage of his mental development.

We have to distinguish, however, between the present purport and purpose of the Paradise-story, intended by the Jahvist compiler, and those of the various previous forms of the narrative, or of its component elements, which students of early human culture think they can partially trace. Increasing knowledge of the modes of thought of remote times, and of the immensely long development implied in such civilisation and theology as existed in Israel in the prophetic age, has shown us how easy it is to commit great anachronisms when we endeavour to throw light on a myth or legend, coming to us from within the historical period, by means of conceptions culled from folk-lore without reference to the stage of development which such tradition represents. The problem of ascertaining the probable previous history of the conceptions underlying the story of the Fall has been

[1] W. R. Smith, *Prophets of Israel*, p. 411. The haoma tree of the Avesta (see p. 57) and Bundahesch imparted health, generative power, immortality, and also wisdom, thus combining the qualities of the two trees of Gen. ii., iii.

[2] *Die Phoenizier.*

revealed to be one of infinitely greater complexity than was formerly thought. Earlier methods of investigation have become obsolete; and earlier solutions were far too easy.

It is an anachronism, for instance, to interpret the story of the Fall as embodying ideas of the class to which we have just alluded in connexion with it, *except as fossils*. The Jahvist writer certainly did not wish to teach that the first sin (a conception which he was perhaps the first to introdnce into the narrative, or which, at least, could not in his day be of any great antiquity) consisted in forbidden marriage-relations between Adam and Eve to which Eve was instigated by the serpent; the tree of life, according to his usage, conveyed immortality, and the tree of knowledge an opening of the eyes to more than what is actually stated, inasmuch as he represents the acquired wisdom as dangerous to Jahveh. The connexion of these trees with the ideas of sex-knowledge was an association of thought belonging perhaps to his legendary material at an earlier period, and from which he intended to clear his narrative. This association was only read into the story again when his meaning had been lost, and the utter absence of capacity for historical exegesis made it impossible for commentators to recover it. Nor was Gen. iii. intended as a protest against current or previous Canaanitish phallic rites[1]; this would again imply that the story had no connexion with the problems of immortality and civilisation, and was of the nature of an allegory, whose homiletic purport was concealed with very unnecessary skill.

A more scientific attempt to penetrate beyond what we may call the ninth century meaning and value of the Fall-story, by a study of the significance of sacred trees in primitive Semitic thought, will be found in the work of Prof. Barton to which reference has already been made[2].

---

[1] As is maintained by Cobb, *Origines Judaicae*; cf. Donaldson, *Jashar*, pp. 41 ff.; Trumbull, *The Threshold Covenant*, p. 437 etc. Similarly Fergusson, *Tree and Serpent Worship*, 1873, p. 7, regards the story as polemic against an earlier Hebrew serpent worship.

On the relation of Hebrew prophecy to Ashtoreth worship, see Barton, *Journal of Bibl. literature*, x. 73 ff.

[2] *A sketch of Semitic Origins*; see esp. Chaps. ii., iii.

This writer starts from the fact that the date-palm was closely connected with earliest Semitic life and husbandry. It appears to have been much cultivated at an extremely ancient period; and the fact that, for fruit-bearing, it requires a considerable amount of artificial aid in effecting its fertilisation, may be supposed to have led to its being looked upon as a reflex of man's own primitive social life[1]. This cultivation of the palm being also the means of his agricultural progress, the early Semite would be likely enough to attribute his knowledge to the tree; especially, on account of the fact previously mentioned, would he connect with it his knowledge of sex and procreation. This circumstance, together with the fact that at such a time sexual irregularity was prevalent amongst Semites, as indeed probably among mankind generally at a similar stage of development, would doubtless make a deep impression upon early religious ideas and practices. There is no doubt that, in the animistic and totemistic stage, man regarded trees as animate, as having perceptions and passions like himself. And, indeed, so deeply does this mode of thought influence many savage races at the present day, that mutual sex-relations between the human race and the animal and vegetable kingdoms are believed in and acted upon[2]. Thus Barton regards the date-palm, significant on account of its dioecious nature and its extensive usefulness and cultivation, as the prototype of the tree of knowledge. The tree of life he supposes to be a later conception, which only arose with the dawning desire for future life; but of course the conception of trees of life or food of life existed before that of immortality. The tree of knowledge, however, would thus be identical with the sacred tree which figures largely in Babylonian religion. Its prohibition to man is to be regarded as introduced when the original meaning of the tree had been changed so as to suggest only the means by which man arrived at culture or practical wisdom, a process whose

---

[1] It is noteworthy that in the earliest Jewish interpretation of the tree of life that is extant, *The Book of Enoch*, Chaps. xxiv., xxv., its fruit is said to resemble the dates of a palm. This *may be* a tradition of hoary antiquity.

[2] See the pages of Frazer's *The Golden Bough* just referred to.

successive stages are associated by the Jahvist writer with the descendants of Cain, and apparently with sin as their consequence if not their cause. Barton believes that before the progress of man from a state of kinship with the animals to a state of incipient mastery over nature came to be looked upon as a punishable offence bringing death and other physical evils in its train (a connexion of thought discoverable in the ancient Eabani legend as well as in the Paradise-story), both civilisation and the sexual relation were regarded as blessings permitted by Jahveh (or Ea, or other corresponding deities), the latter of which things was especially commended by the example of the sacred tree in the divine homestead, and offered to man by the friendly half-divine serpent. According to this writer, then, the basis of the story of Paradise and the Fall is supplied by the contemplation of the phenomena of the primitive Semite's Arabian oasis. This was the haunt of his god; and it became identified with a garden when Arabia was exchanged for Babylonia. Its water and trees were visible representations of deities. The trees of the oasis were palms, the main feature in whose life-history was suggestive of those human relations which necessarily loomed very large in the life of uncivilised man.

In a note to p. 118 of his work Prof. Barton adds: "My friend, Prof. W. Max Müller, tells me that the whole Paradise-story of Genesis, which, as we have seen, reflects primitive Semitic ideas, has a parallel in the hieroglyphic Egyptian"; and this he explains as due to the fact that institutions proved for Arabia were born in N. Africa[1].

The serpent is introduced, in the Paradise-story, simply as a speaking animal, cleverer than the other beasts of the

[1] For Prof. W. Max Müller's information on this point, kindly supplied to the present writer, see last chapter, p. 36.

It must be borne in mind, of course, that Prof. Barton's interesting book is a pioneering work, and one which to some extent breaks new ground. His speculations are used here tentatively, therefore, and are not to be regarded as altogether possessing finality.

In his first chapter this writer deals with the theories as to the situation of 'the cradle of the Semites,' and concludes in favour of the view that though Arabia was the specific home whence they spread, yet N. Africa was the primitive seat of the Hamito-Semitic race.

field[1]. But it is quite plain from the narrative itself that he only became the creeping animal known to us in consequence of punishment for his temptation of Eve[2]. And it is strongly suggested that he had originally been regarded as more than a beast endowed with erect posture, power of speech, and exceptional sagacity. He was even more than the ordinary jinn or demoniac animal. He is acquainted with the real nature and potency of the forbidden tree, "and speaks as if he were on terms of intimacy with the divine circle"; "as if he were in a position to say exactly what the Deity knew[3]." He attributes misrepresentation to Jahveh, and the truth of the charge is practically admitted in the words, "Behold the man is become as one of us to know good and evil[4]," and in the failure of the threat of instant death to take effect[5]. This certainly seems to point to a more primitive story in which the serpent was a supernatural being, higher than man; a legendary story, in fact, the mythology of which has paled and almost been extinguished. Whether the serpent was represented in such an earlier tradition Prometheus-like, as the friend of man, who revealed to him the source of divinely forbidden wisdom; or whether, as Barton has suggested, he was a half-divine animal which offered to man the gift of the knowledge of sex, a gift which the primitive Semitic mind did not, and could not, conceive as divinely forbidden, we cannot say. Such conjectures can be collected and compared; but in the present state of our knowledge, certainly, they can no more be established than they can lightly be dismissed. It is overwhelmingly probable, however, that the *rôle* of tempter was assigned to the serpent only when the legendary basis of the story, whatever may have been its earlier significance, was utilised to explain the existence of

---

[1] Josephus seems to have seriously believed in the power of animals to speak. *The Book of Jubilees*, which he perhaps follows, teaches that all the animals spoke before the Fall; but this reads more like an afterthought than the naïve statement of Gen. iii.

[2] This was afterwards explicitly taught by the Rabbis; see p. 152.

[3] Toy, *op. cit.*, p. 13.

[4] Gen. iii. 22.

[5] This is usually explained as implying an act of mercy on the part of Jahveh; but there is no more evidence for this view than for the other.

human ills and to bid us see their cause in sin. This use of the serpent was only possible to a nation which had acquired a relatively high ethical conception of God, and to a writer who was prepared to attribute man's loss of Paradise, if not his attainment of self-reliant wisdom, to a sin demanding punishment. In this attribution to the serpent of a hostility to Jahveh, a tendency culminating much later in his identification with Satan, we therefore see an example of the way in which the Jahvist writer, or the Hebrew folk, impressed upon borrowed or inherited legend the mark of their increasingly ethical religion.

Facts have already been adduced to show that the Arabian oasis probably furnished both the scenery of the Paradise-story, which has survived, and its original significance, which has been lost and which we can only tentatively endeavour to recover. The oasis, to a society still influenced by animistic and totemistic modes of thought, was a place in which gods, animals and men formed one social circle. A speaking serpent, possessing more than human knowledge, would be a perfectly natural denizen of such a home. And it would seem that it is to such a source, and not to any phenomenon or abstract conception symbolised by the serpent[1] in mytho-

[1] The subjects of serpent-symbolism and serpent-worship are too vast to be entered upon here, especially as they form one of the favourite resorts of dilettantism, and but little that is of scientific value has been written upon them. The facts are so numerous and various that the mutually inconsistent theories intended to generalise them seem equally plausible and equally impossible. The serpent, in different mythologies, and even in the myths of the same people, symbolises many ideas; and it is as yet premature, if not wholly arbitrary and fanciful, to attempt to trace these to a common root. Thus one of the most primitive and fundamental uses of the figure of the serpent (or dragon) is its symbolisation of the lightning, the storm-cloud or chaos generally, the supposed enemies of the sun, withholding its blessings from man. This symbol, derived from solar mythology, is common to the most ancient Aryan (Vedic) as well as to Semitic thought, and is found somewhat frequently in poetical passages of the O.T.; probably it is a Babylonian element, naturalised at an early date and underlying the Creation story of Gen. i. Such Nature-symbolism, or mythology proper, will not, however, account for all serpent-imagery. Another group of ideas akin to one another, with which the serpent is associated, are those of life, ancestry, generation, health, healing, immortality. Again we have the serpent representing cleverness and wisdom, and connected with mantic practices; and finally it is often the earth-dwelling, autochthonous animal, the natural guardian of earth's treasures. Each of these ideas has been exclusively associated with the tempter of Gen. iii. It is obvious,

74   *The Psychological Origin*   [CHAP.

logy proper or in the folk-lore of partially civilised peoples, that we are to turn, if we would seek for the most probable origin of the details and scenery of the Fall-story. We are then presented with conceptions suggested by such natural objects as the early Semite was most familiar with. And if the facts hitherto collected, admittedly too scanty to be as yet gathered into a final induction or theory of the history of the Paradise-legend from the creation of its germ in remotely ancient Semite society to the time of the Jahvist document, may be knit together, for the modest purpose of giving them temporary arrangement and of inviting the criticism by which knowledge of such a subject can alone be furthered, into a working hypothesis of which conjecture largely forms the connecting tissue, the following view may be suggested.

While the Semites were still in their common Arabian home, or even in their supposed Hamito-Semitic cradle, while animism and totemism were their natural and inevitable modes of thought, their religion and science centred largely round the double association of the palm-tree, connecting the origin of knowledge of sex with that of the first steps in civilisation arising out of husbandry. This view, most clearly formulated in the recent work of Prof. Barton, and having some basis at least in fact, is confirmed by the fragments of Hamite tradition soon to be published by Prof. W. Max Müller, as well as by the Eabani legend, which carries us back to an extremely ancient date and primitive stage of thought and culture, and in which we meet with a similar association of

from what has been said, that such associations could only attach to the serpent at all in a stage of development of the story prior to that on which it entered when incorporated into the Jahvist history. It will be clear also that some at least of these significations could never have belonged to the serpent of the Paradise-story; perhaps all but one or two are wide of the mark and none of them is relevant.

On the subject of serpent-symbolism the student may refer to the following works, whence he will find fuller references to the literature: Baudissin, *Semit. Religionsgeschichte* I.; Goldziher, *Mythos bei den Hebräern*; Fergusson, *Tree and Serpent Worship*; Cobb, *Origines Judaicae*; Keary, *Primitive Belief*; Wake, *Serpent Worship*; Cox, *Aryan Mythology*, II. 114; Mähly, *Die Schlange im Mythus*; Squiers, *Serpent Symbolism*; Jennings, *Phallicism*; Forlong, *River of Life*; Massey, *The Natural Genesis*. Most of these works must be read, however, with great caution, and with a healthy scepticism as to the finality of any of their generalisations on the subject here in question.

III]   *of the Fall-story*   75

ideas. A legend embodying these conceptions would be carried to Babylonia, and, undergoing modification in terms of Babylonian civilisation and advancement in religious thought, would seem to have become closely connected with Ea and Eridu. The scenery of the desert oasis would be exchanged for that of a garden of the gods. The tree of life would gather associations with health and healing, sustenance and immortality, over and above (and perhaps increasingly to the exclusion of) its earliest association with the phenomena of reproduction.

Knowledge, of whatever kind (and we have seen that the date-palm and the god Ea of Eridu were associated with both knowledge of sex and practical wisdom), would continue to be regarded as divinely permitted or divinely given: so much may be gathered, we have found, from Babylonian myths. With legends of this nature, referring indirectly to human origins, would come to be associated the dream, arising everywhere spontaneously in the mind of man, of a previous age of simplicity of life and immunity from the trouble necessarily incidental to widening experience and increasing culture. The home of the gods became the primitive abode of man. The geography of the earthly Paradise, embodied afterwards in the Hebrew story, became fixed in the Babylonian tradition. And such a composite legend was naturalised in Canaan during the millennium preceding the Israelitish immigration. Modified again, we may suppose, according to the bent of Canaanitish thought and tradition, the legend, amongst many others, became now the property of the Hebrews, who doubtless would still possess, as a heritage from the distant past, conceptions similar to those of the older forms of the now essentially Babylonian story. The Jahvist compiler, probably aided by other scribes before him, collects such folk-lore. He deliberately attempts a somewhat systematic history of origins: of man, of sex, of primitive life, of beginnings of culture and of the ills and toils of human existence, of the entrance and growth of sin. In common with others of his time, he is painfully conscious of the dark side of human self-advancement, and is charged with the Hebrew feeling that many human ambitions are arrogant encroachments on the unique rights and prerogatives of Jahveh. He feels strongly too about sin and the misery it has caused. Somewhat naturally, and with an insight which was deep if not wholly clear, he takes the old legend of the origin of man's knowledge, now both a culture-myth and a Paradise-story, and makes it also serve the purpose of accounting for the introduction of human sin. Thus there emerges, for the first time, a " Fall-story." This writer is conservative of the externals of his venerable tradition ; he is zealously reformatory, though, fortunately for the archaeologist, not wholly successful, in stripping it of its previous heathenism and its coarser significance ; he is earnestly religious in making it minister to the interests of the Jahvism of his time. Hence the present form of the story : its composite nature, its conflicting standpoints, its didactic meaning, its abiding worth.

* * * * * *

Much, of course, of the contents of this chapter is matter of conjecture. The purpose of what has been written, however, has not been to attempt to establish conclusions as to the details with which the chapter has been concerned. On the contrary, the aim has rather been to show, in many cases, their individual uncertainty. It has rather been intended to strengthen the general evidence, external and internal, that the Fall-story was the result of the perfectly natural and necessary processes of human speculative thought working upon material of legendary nature partly derived in turn from mythology, and also to indicate the psychological conditions under which its conceptions must be supposed to have arisen. The story as a whole may be compared to a quarry in which several strata of different antiquity, with their characteristic organic remains, are at once exposed to view : or, more aptly, to a cave into which the relics of such different strata have been swept. Though the detailed history of its growth can perhaps never be recovered, the general course and conditions of its construction, it is hoped, have been made clear. The general results to which these three chapters have led may be summed up thus : the Fall-story contains elements of various degrees of antiquity, which were the natural products of human thought at relatively early stages of its development; it is a fusion of aetiological legends embodying conceptions which arose in the animistic stage of the evolution of religion; it states the results of early reflection on matters pertaining to the beginnings of human life; and it was intended by the writer or editor as the equivalent of history which, at his time, was not clearly distinguished from products of the imagination. It breathes, however, the spirit of Hebrew religion as it was passing into ethical monotheism.

* * * * * *

While proceeding to discuss the import and the consequences of the view of the origin and nature of the Fall-story to which the foregoing investigation has led, it will be well briefly to examine the other two modes of interpreting it which have generally found favour in the past.

The narrative has been taken, both in ancient and modern times, to be a literal statement of historical truth. Passing by the modes of defence of this position adopted by early Western Fathers and Reformation divines, it will suffice to notice the basis upon which it has been supported by more recent scholars. The fact, which the modern science of comparative religion has brought to light, that somewhat similar stories to those of the opening chapters of Genesis occur widely scattered through the literary remains of ancient nations, appeared to many investigators in this field to find its best explanation in the view that such stories were corrupted forms of a genuine tradition handed down from the very beginning of human history; which tradition, in its pure and true form, was enshrined in the pages of the Hebrew Scriptures. The great scholar Lenormant was, for instance, of this opinion; though one can scarcely believe that, had he lived a little later, he would have been able to retain such a position[1]. It is now

---

[1] For an elaborate defence of this same view, marshalling a great array of scientific facts in a somewhat unscientific spirit, see a fairly recent work, Zöckler's *Urstand des Menschen*. Several great geologists, *e.g.* Sir J. W. Dawson, have also supplied facts and reasoning with a view to upholding the historical truth of the narratives; which attempts, detached from the main line of scientific testimony, have been utilised in the interests of the traditional opinion in several theological treatises.

78   The Psychological Origin   [CHAP.

generally abandoned by archaeologists and theologians alike[1]. Indeed, if man is evolved from a non-human ancestry, if his reason, language, morals and religion are the product of gradual development, if his antiquity is what geology asserts it to be, and his earliest condition, as human, that to which several sciences now strongly point, it is quite impossible to entertain at all the view that the Fall-story, and the legends kindred to it, embody any genuine tradition once common to the race, or, therefore, any scientific or historical truth. This supposition would logically necessitate the theory of the special creation of man, and that of an original or primitive revelation. All that we know of prehistoric man, derived from many and varied sources and many independent methods of empirical investigation, renders the view that such a tradition could be true or, if true, could have been handed down to historical times, altogether untenable[2]. It must therefore be considered as utterly unfaithful to the cumulative and conclusive results of modern study, still to seek for even a kernel of historical truth, and a basis for a theological doctrine of human nature, in such a narrative as the Fall-story of the Book of Genesis[3].

[1] It still lives, however, in Germany as well as in England: as, *e.g.*, in some Arts. in Hauck's *Real Encyclopädie*.

[2] For the same conclusion see Dillman, *Genesis* I., E.T. vol. I. p. 99, on the subject. It is impossible to substantiate here the assertions made in the text; the task would require several chapters. The following references will, however, enable the student unfamiliar with the sciences involved to find access to the chief results that are relevant, and to make himself acquainted with the methods of investigation and reasoning by which they have been reached. Darwin, *Origin of Species, Descent of Man*; Romanes, *Darwin and After-Darwin*, vol. I.; *Mental Evolution in Man*; Lubbock, *Origin of Civilisation*; Tylor, *Primitive Culture* and *Early History of Mankind*; A. Lang, *Making of Religion, Myth Ritual and Religion*; Keane, *Ethnology*; Clodd, *Story of Primitive Man*; P. Kropotkin, *XIXth Cent.*, March, 1896; Mackenzie, *Manual of Ethics*; Réville, *History of Religions*, pp. 35-64 (on impossibility of primitive revelation or tradition). For views opposed in various respects to those embodied in the foregoing works, the student may consult the writings of Max Müller on Mythology and Religion, and of Dr Fairbairn and Sir J. W. Dawson. Prof. Orr gives references which are relevant in his *Christian view of God and the World*, but the natural science of this work must be received in some cases with great caution, inasmuch as it one-sidedly represents the opinion of the minority in the scientific world.

[3] The untenability of the doctrines of the Fall and of Original Sin, whose history is being examined in the present work, has been fully discussed from the point of

We pass to an altogether different question when we ask whether the Jahvist writer himself understood his account of the loss of Paradise to be history. And it is a question which it is not easy definitely to answer. The narrative has here been discussed on the supposition that it was compiled out of folk-lore, and was probably regarded by its author or literary editor, if not as history, at any rate as a working substitute for history. It occurs in a context which certainly was intended to supply information as to the origin of things, and a record of the earliest doings of mankind. But it seems natural to believe that in its writer's day it was somewhat difficult to estimate the difference between imaginative poetry, especially if venerable as tradition, and an account of actual fact. To ask whether, in introducing into his story of the distant past the magical trees and the speaking serpent, not as extraordinary marvels[1] but as belonging to the natural course of things, the writer was conscious of their legendary and fictitious nature[2], or whether he intended them to be regarded as historical realities, is perhaps to commit oneself to a wrong statement of the question at issue. These alternatives were not so clearly differentiated in the Jahvist's day as they are in ours. We are rather dealing with an age in which the line between the natural and the supernatural, and that between legend and history, were only vaguely drawn. The thought of that time was scarcely troubled with the distinction between what was possible and what impossible. If Josephus could take the details of this story as historical, and if Mohammed "would not eat lizards because he fancied them to be the offspring of a metamorphosed clan of Israelites[3]," we need scarcely wonder at a writer of about the 9th century B.C. seriously describing the Paradisaic age in terms of mythical conceptions, and offering his traditional narrative as the equivalent of history.

view of natural science and philosophy in the author's Hulsean Lectures on *The Origin and Propagation of Sin*, Camb. Univ. Press, 1902.

[1] As seems to be the case in the account of Balaam's ass.
[2] As Schultz (*O.T. Theology*) and Cheyne (*Encycl. Bibl.* Art. *Adam and Eve*) believe.
[3] W. R. Smith.

If this view of the writer's own attitude towards his literary production be adopted, the main evidence for its truth being perhaps the comparatively easy way in which the narrative may be expounded in the light of it, the possibility that the story was originally intended for allegory is necessarily excluded. It has often been held that the narrative of the Fall is a symbolic description of the origin of sin in general, in the individual as well as in the race, whose essential truth is assured by the inspiration of the sacred book in which it finds a place. One of the representatives of this view in modern times best known to English readers is S. T. Coleridge, whose discussion of the Fall and of Original Sin in the *Aids to Reflection*, largely following Kant's use of the Bible story in the interests of his theory of radical evil, is based on the supposition that Adam was intended to be the representative of all his successors. Coleridge tells us that it was his own deliberate and conscientious conviction that the proofs of allegorical interpretation having been the intention of the inspired writer or compiler of the book of Genesis "lie on the face of the narrative itself[1]."

This view, however, has been almost entirely abandoned; at least by theologians. Exegesis alone renders it untenable. The narrative supplies its own proof that, even supposing it was not to be taken perfectly literally, it was not intended for an allegory. The curse of the serpent, condemning it and its seed after it (the serpent race), to creep upon the ground and eat the dust, of necessity implies that the writer had in mind a real animal; not the personification of a 'principle of evil' which introduced sin into the human world 'from without,' still less a symbol of the seductive power of temptation, or of the lower nature, after the later manner of Philo and other allegorical interpreters. And if the serpent cannot stand here for an allegorical symbol, the same must needs be said of the tree of knowledge; for it plainly belongs to the same circle of ideas, and must have a similar signification. We have indeed already seen that the semi-allegorical interpretation which

---

[1] *Aids to Reflection*, end of note to 7th reflection on Aphorism cviii.; ed. Fenby, 1896, p. 229.

makes the forbidden tree the indirect means whereby moral self-determination might be, rightly or wrongly, acquired, is exegetically impossible. Another argument which is fatal to the view that the Fall-story was intended as an allegorical representation of the origin of sin in a universal sense is supplied by the fact that the narrative appears in, and indeed is essentially interwoven with, a context which plainly professes to supply information as to the beginnings of human history. Whatever be the didactic value of the story, it could not have been inserted where it is if its purpose were merely homiletic or psychological, and if it treated of temptation and sin in general rather than of the history of the first parents of the race[1]. And, finally, it may well be doubted whether allegory of so abstract a nature as would pertain to this story, if it were allegory at all, was historically possible to the Jahvist writer. The imagery which is in any degree of an allegorical nature in pre-exilic writings is of a very much more elementary character, rather to be described as fable or parable when it is more than simple personification or metaphor[2]. To look for complex allegory, therefore, in Gen. iii. is to commit an anachronism. Indeed, were allegory a literary method of the eighth or ninth century B.C., it is far removed from the naïve

[1] It may be added here that in fable and allegory the imagery is invented in order to express dramatically the didactic purpose; in the Fall-story the lessons are obviously superimposed upon the pre-existing material, and have probably been the cause of its free manipulation.

[2] Hosea's representation of the tribe of Ephraim as a man, and the comparison of Jahveh's relation with Israel to that of human marriage, belong to the simplest type of imagery. Similar are the representations of Israel as a vineyard (Ps. lxxx.), or as a harlot (Ezek. xvi.), and the comparisons of the king of Tyre to a mythical inhabitant, or 'the Assyrian' to a tree, of Eden (Ezek. xxviii. and xxxi.); more complex are Ezek. xvi. and some of this prophet's 'parables,' *e.g.* xvii. 2–10: but all these are examples rather of allegorical imagery than of allegory. The fables of Judges ix. 8 ff., 2 Kings xiv. 9–10, and the parables of 2 Sam. xii. 1–6 and Isai. v. 1–7, are not at all of the nature of the Philonic allegory asserted to be intended in Gen. iii. All these images represent one concrete thing by another concrete thing; there is no personification of an abstraction and embodiment of a general concept in a fitting material symbol. There is in fact no allegory proper in the Old Test. Not that any hard objective distinction can be drawn between the meanings of words of such elastic signification as symbol, fable, parable, allegory, etc.; but there is a great difference between O.T. literary imagery, in all its forms, and Philo's usage of the Fall-story, where real allegory appears.

concreteness which forms one great charm of the Jahvist's style.

Explanation more or less allegorical still finds its place, to ome extent, even in modern scientific commentaries. Reuss regards the story as a psychological and ethical myth treating of a daily occurrence, a general and symbolic description suitable to all particular sins : that is, an allegory. Dillmann opposes this view ; but while denying that the narrative can possibly embody a true tradition, denies also that its writer intended it for history. In his opinion, it is related to the myths of other nations, but is to be distinguished from them by an essential difference. The peculiar relation of Israel to God involves that the story contains actual truths about man's nature (Wahrheiten, richtige Gedanken)[1].

The same assertion is involved in the designations 'revelation-myth,' 'religious myth,' 'inspired myth' which have been applied to it by various writers. Such a judgment, which cannot be derived inductively from the narrative itself, but is based upon a particular theory of inspiration deduced from certain doctrines, or from a survey of Old Testament literature as a whole, we are not now concerned to dispute, inasmuch as the problems which at present form the subject of our investigation are purely exegetical, historical and scientific. But if such assertions and designations are intended to perpetuate the supposition that the third chapter of Genesis is "a combination of history and sacred symbolism[2]," or to imply that its inspiration guarantees for it any scientific or historical truth about human nature other than that which is contained in its very simple psychology of so complex a thing as temptation, then the drift of all that has been said in this and the preceding chapters may be summed up in their repudiation.

There has already been occasion to use the term myth, which there has long been a growing tendency to apply to the story of the Fall. But this narrative is not a myth. If the allegory is too late a product with which to identify the story, the myth, in any of the stricter acceptations of the term,

---

[1] *Genesis*, 6te Auflage, S. 43.
[2] Martensen, *Dogmatics*, E.T. 1866, p. 155.

is much too early a one. Elements in the imagery of the narrative, *e.g.* the garden of Jahveh, the magical trees, the serpent, of course belong to the realm of what has generally been called the mythological; certainly they are legendary. These conceptions were "produced by the unconscious play of plastic fancy," and are, as the preceding chapter was intended to show, entirely on an equality with heathen mythical figures or ideas. And in so far as its imagery is of this nature (and we have seen reason to conjecture that its motive was once more crude than it is now), the narrative can be said to be mythological. But still the story as a whole is not a myth. There is no one name, as a recent writer has remarked, by which it can be adequately described. It is, we repeat, an equivalent for history dating from a time when fact and fancy were not sharply differentiated; and if this were all, it might be called an 'aetiological myth': but it is something more. The Fall-story is an attempt at philosophy, and an attempt of a different kind from that which is sometimes the purpose of the mere myth. It still uses mythological objects, in place of inaccessible historical facts, for the concrete presentation of its teaching; but in its theological and ethical implications, which, after all, constitute its abiding worth, it has emancipated itself from the characteristics of primitive mythological speculation, and deserves a place amongst the earliest attempts at theological philosophy[1].

The term myth, the application of which to the Fall-story as a whole we cannot justify, is one of elastic usage and indefinite signification. Some writers on comparative mythology have endeavoured to restrict its use exclusively to what

[1] Inasmuch as philosophy, science and theology all originate in mythology, and the point at which each of them emerges from that condition is difficult to define, we are dealing here with a question of degree rather than of kind.

The Fall-story has been called a 'genetic fiction' (Redslob, *Der Schöpfungs-Apolog*, 1846), and has been compared with the numerous O.T. narratives invented to account for existing customs, etc.; *e.g.* the stories of the shrinking of Jacob's thigh, of the institution of the Sabbath, of the meaning of the rainbow, etc. Genesis is rich in such genetic fictions, and the narrative Gen. ii. 4—iii. is full of them. The term is perhaps better than 'aetiological myth,' but it rather suggests the immediate creation of a literary author than the elaboration of existing legend or folk-lore for a didactic purpose.

is often called the nature-myth. It is in fact asserted by certain writers that everything mythological in the broader sense is derived from nature myth; this, however, is not allowed by other schools, and is an unwarrantable position.

The nature-myth in its simplest form has been defined as the verbal expression of the effects wrought on the human mind by natural objects and processes[1]. It came into being with the use of language. It is a symbolic description of natural phenomena in terms of man's experience and personality: a primitive metaphor due to the attribution of one's own consciousness to inanimate or impersonal objects. To explain, is to trace the unknown back to the known; and primitive man could only explain unknown Nature in terms of himself, his will, passions, interests and common acts, the matters of his most immediate and vivid experience. Mythology, in this sense, is a form of mental activity through which developing human intelligence must inevitably pass; it is a necessary stage in mankind's intellectual growth. It formed the first common-sense view of the world. It was the only way in which the results of intercommunication of primitive thought between an individual and his fellows could be expressed.

According to those who see in animism one of the widest generalisations with regard to early human thought, dream-images played a very considerable part in moulding man's conception of the universe. Hence came the peopling of Nature with spiritual beings similar to the soul which was supposed to live, during sleep, independently of the body. Thus a quasi-personal agency is attached to objects; gods are placed behind phenomena. Moreover primitive thought had not arrived at a clear distinction between the inorganic and the organic, or between the organic and the human worlds. "The poet ignores the scientific knowledge of Nature when he describes a river or a tree: the savage does not ignore it, for he never had it[2]." The mythical mode of

[1] Goldziher, *Mythos bei den Hebräern*.
[2] Stout, *Psychology*, vol. II.; cf. Höffding, *Psychology*, E.T. In connexion with these pages the student may be referred to Schultze, *Psychologie der Naturvölker*, 1900.

describing Nature, assisted by conceptions derived from animism, would be the source, as has already been said, of science, philosophy and theology, if not religion. And the theist believes, for reasons of a philosophical and theological nature, that while human thought was on this low plane and was distantly groping after religious truth, the natural process of its progress was already guided by the Supreme Reason immanent in that of man. This 'revelation,' no longer conceivable, in the light of modern knowledge, as a communication from a wholly transcendent God acting from without, addressed itself to, and necessarily expressed itself in terms of, such mythical modes of thought as we have just stated to have once been characteristic of mankind's mental life[1]. We cannot base our faith in such divine guidance on an empirical study of the early narratives contained in our sacred records. Of themselves, these yield no such assurance; they only do so when interpreted in the light of a generalisation from Old Testament studies collectively, made under the guidance of previously and independently formed theological beliefs. Still the records serve to illustrate the belief that God's self-manifestation, though no longer to be regarded as what was called a 'primitive revelation,' was already active when mankind inevitably thought and spoke in terms of 'myth.'

In later stages of the development of thought, when increased intercommunication between subjects had rendered human knowledge more objective (a process of which our natural science is but the continuation), its anthropomorphism was reduced, and myths therefore gradually became less mythological. They came to deal with what was in part objectively, instead of what was merely subjectively, true. Thus grew up the product which some would exclude from the connotation of the term myth, the aetiological, or the philosophical, myth[2]. If Kuhn's derivation of Prometheus

[1] To avoid repetition of what has been said elsewhere the author may be allowed to refer to pp. 141 ff. of *The Origin and Propagation of Sin*.
[2] Thus nature-myth frequently passed into cosmogony. The numerous references in the O.T. to the figures Rahab, Leviathan, etc., are allusions to the old Babylonian nature-myth of Tiâmat which underlies the cosmogony of Gen. i.

from *pramantha* be correct, the development of the Greek legend from the ancient Aryan nature-myth furnishes an admirable illustration of this process. Similarly the myth proper developed into the legend, and instead of merely embodying man's primitive thought about natural phenomena, began to differentiate into what passed for knowledge about the self, the world and God. As religion became more and more monotheistic among the Hebrews, the tendency to banish mythology of Nature increased proportionately. Mythical, or, to speak more correctly, legendary figures persist in the story of Paradise; but myth has here made the transition into intended history, and the conceptions which belong to mythology or to legend are entirely subservient to moral and theological purpose.

Besides the sense of the word 'myth' already mentioned (nature-myth), to which one school of writers seeks to restrict it, there are others in which it is commonly used. There are not only legendary productions which are developments of nature myths, such as cosmogonies and some culture-myths, but also the class called etymological myths, and many culture-myths and cult-myths which cannot wholly be traced to this particular origin. These would be included in such a definition of myth as is given, for instance, by Réville[1]: "The myth is either the description of a natural phenomenon considered as the exponent of a divine drama, or else the incorporation of a moral idea in a dramatic narrative. In both cases, that which is permanent or frequent in nature and in humanity is brought together into one event accomplished once and for all, and the drama, although invented, is looked upon as real[2]."

See, especially, Gunkel's *Schöpfung und Chaos*. Some think the deluge stories, in which the world is so rich, to be founded upon nature-myth; but this is very doubtful.

[1] *Prolegomena of the History of Religions*, E.T. p. 111.

[2] Of quite distinct nature from the myth proper, which results from the natural play of primitive intelligence, is much of the fanciful literary fiction which we meet with, for instance, in later Jewish writings, apocalyptic and rabbinical; also the gnostic 'mythology' which consists largely in the personification of abstract conceptions. Such relatively modern examples of what is sometimes loosely called 'mythology' are not specimens of thought natural and necessary to

We conclude then, that the Fall-story is not a myth in any of the senses to which modern scientific usage restricts that term; it can only be called mythological in the sense that it embodies, in a fossil state, legendary or mythological matter. It has no similarity, either, to a Platonic myth, or to an allegory. But it is possible to make two statements with regard to the biblical narrative of which we have now completed the investigation, each of which has been asserted with regard to true mythology. Firstly, the explanation of the story ought to be nothing but its history[1]. Allegorical interpretations of it, to quote words used by Robertson Smith in reference to myths, "are the falsest of false guides as to the original meaning" of the story. And secondly, the narrative, like a proper myth, "is the history of its authors, not of its subjects[2]." It records some stages of developing theological speculation: it tells us nothing of the human nature we inherit, or of the history of the first parents of our race.

The bearing of the conclusion thus reached, with regard to the nature of the Fall-story, upon the 'inspiration' of the Scripture of which it forms a part, cannot here be fully discussed. The view most likely to be adopted by those who agree only in part with the opinion expressed in the latter portion of this chapter will be such as was put forward by the late Prof. Hort. After stating his disbelief in the historical character of the biblical account of the Fall, this scholar said: "But the early chapters of Genesis remain a divinely appointed parable or apologue setting forth important practical truths on subjects which, as a matter of history, lie outside our present ken. Whether or not the corrupted state of human nature was preceded in temporal sequence by an incorrupt state, this is the most vivid and natural way of exhibiting the truth that in God's primary purpose man was

the age which produced it, but exhibit a literary phenomenon comparable with what, in the sphere of biology, is termed degeneration. It will be needless to add that the myths of Plato, to allude to another literary product which has received the name of myth, have nothing in common with myths in the modern scientific sense, nor again with a narrative such as that of Genesis iii. They are a conscious resort to poetic imagination where philosophy has failed to help.

[1] De la Saussaye, *Manual of the science of religion*, E. T. 1891, pp. 222-3, etc.
[2] Tylor, *Primitive Culture*, 1891, I. p. 416.

incorrupt, so that the evil in him should be regarded as having a secondary or adventitious character. Ideal antecedence is, as it were, pictured in temporal antecedence[1]." In the light of the probable past history of the Fall-story, and according to the view that its writer intended it as equivalent to history, this mode of regarding the narrative, as an ideal picture, cannot exactly be adopted here. If it could, a more or less definite view as to wherein lay its ' inspiration ' would lie close at hand. It would seem, however, to the present writer that the inspiration of the story is a little further to seek; and it may be added that the time for defining what ought to be meant by predicating inspiration of such a narrative has not yet come. Certainly, what man has thought about his race and about his God, even when such thought is embodied in the Bible, cannot, without further inquiry, be put down as what God has revealed to man. The problem is by no means so simple. For the present, whilst resolutely declining to interpret the Old Testament narrative by any *a priori* theory of inspiration whatever, we may seek to prepare for a future definition, to be made in the light of *inductively* established facts about the passage of Scripture here in question.

* * * * * *

The reader who is curious to study what may be called theosophical explanations of the Fall-story is referred to the writings of Jacob Böhme, Baader and Steffens. Space cannot be found here for an account of the eccentricities of modern speculation on the subject.

[1] *Life and Letters*, vol. II. p. 329.

CHAPTER IV.

THE PREPARATION IN THE OLD TESTAMENT FOR A DOCTRINE OF THE FALL AND OF ORIGINAL SIN.

It has been made evident by the general tendency, as well as by certain details, of the subject-matter of the preceding chapters on the Paradise-story, that any such doctrines as that of a fall of the race in Adam, or that of a corruption of human nature and of hereditary transmission of its sinful bias, are not contained in it. They were not intended to be conveyed either by the original traditions on which the narrative is based, or by the literary product which is the outcome of the elaboration and reconstruction received by these legendary traditions at the hands of the compiler of the Jahvist document. It is now necessary to investigate the rise and development of these doctrines which later theology so closely associated with the story of Paradise and the sin of Adam. In the first place we shall need to inquire whether the Fall-story of Genesis was used in later Old Testament writings, and, if so, to what extent and in what manner. Allusion must then be made to another ancient piece of Hebrew folk-lore imbedded in Genesis, which, from about the Maccabean age, was commonly utilised in connexion with speculation on the origin of human sin. Finally, it will be necessary to trace the growth, in the canonical books of the Old Testament, of certain conceptions connected with sin and involved in the doctrines with whose history we are here concerned. This will be to sketch, in some of its aspects, the growth of

Old Testament teaching with regard to sin. The doctrine of sin in its completeness, however, includes more than the present work takes upon itself to investigate, and its general treatment will therefore not be undertaken. Indeed this is all the more unnecessary now that we possess a work upon the subject by Dr Clemen[1], and that the English reader has been furnished with a useful and concise article dealing with the Old Testament doctrine of sin, from the pen of Canon Bernard[2].

The use of the Fall-story in the Old Testament.

It has frequently been remarked that the later books of the Old Testament are practically wanting in references to the 'history of origins' contained in the early chapters of Genesis. The Fall-story as a whole, its didactic meaning and its quasi-history of the beginnings of human sin, seem never to be alluded to, unless the passage of Ezekiel discussed in the preceding chapter is directly based upon the narrative of Gen. ii—iii. This is perhaps less probable than that the prophet drew from a variant of the Genesis story, less purged of its original legendary character or else more highly embellished with foreign additions. Nevertheless we have here a reference to the story which, still floating in oral tradition, perhaps, in Ezekiel's day, had been used by the Jahvist writer as the basis of his history. The doctrinal use, if we may use the expression, of this tradition by Ezekiel, so far as connexion with our subject is concerned, is, however, absolutely *nil.*

For the rest, we only find in the Old Testament the isolated occurrence of conceptions which also appear in Genesis as individual details of the imagery of the Paradise narrative; and such references, on account of their fragmentary nature, are wholly unimportant. They probably imply that the legendary notions of a garden of Jahveh, a

---

[1] *Die Lehre von der Sünde*, Theil I.
[2] Art. *Sin*, in vol. IV. of Hastings' *Dictionary of the Bible.*

tree of life, and kindred conceptions[1], were living in Hebrew tradition, rather than point to literary borrowing from the Jahvist history; and they throw no light on the question whether any theological use was made of the Fall-story as a whole.

It is thus extremely doubtful whether there is any allusion in the whole of the Old Testament to the story of Paradise and the Fall as that story is told in Genesis, though there are indications of remembrance of the legendary traditions utilised in the narrative. The reference contained in Ezek. xxviii. is the only one to which probability attaches. There is certainly no didactic use made of the subject-matter of the Fall-story with regard to human sinfulness and its origin. This fact is not what might have been expected; and it has been variously accounted for. The silence of the Old Testament as to the Fall, especially the silence of the Wisdom-literature, is strange; because, though the prophets were more concerned with the practical treatment of sin than with its

---

[1] Possible allusions to Adam's transgression occur in Job xxxi. 33, "If like Adam I covered my transgressions," and Hos. vi. 7, "But they like Adam have transgressed the covenant." But though these renderings have found place in the text of the R.V., and that of the former verse at least is still sometimes maintained to be the more natural (see, *e.g.*, Gibson's *Commentary on Job, in loc.*), the alternatives given in the margin of the R.V., in which for the proper name Adam is substituted 'man' or 'men,' are now generally adopted: see Schultz, *O. Test. Theology*; Clemen, *op. cit.*; Hastings, *op. cit.*, Art. *Fall*, etc.

It is noteworthy that the allusions to the garden of Eden (Ezek. xxviii. 13, xxxi. 8, 9, Isai. li. 3) belong to the prophets of the captivity: Joel ii. 3 is perhaps an exception, though it may be post-exilic.

The phrase 'tree of life' (Prov. iii. 18, xi. 30, xiii. 12) is possibly derived from the legendary conception embodied in Gen. ii—iii., and surviving in traditional lore, as well as its equivalent 'fountain of life' (Prov. x. 11, xiii. 14, xiv. 27). These again are post-exilic passages. The fact that in Prov. the 'fountain of life' is found as a synonym for the 'tree of life' makes it less probable that the latter term was a definite loan from Gen.

Other passages, such as Job xxxiv. 15, Ps. xc. 3, Eccles. xii. 7, which speak of man's returning to dust, and Isai. lxv. 25, Mic. vii. 17, which allude to the serpent eating the dust, need not be supposed to have been suggested by the language of Genesis. The former expression needs no literary precedent to account for it, and the idea of the dust being the serpent's food must have been a common popular belief to have found a place in the Fall-narrative at all. Eccles. vii. 29, "God made man upright; but they have sought out many inventions" is hardly an allusion to the Fall. Psalm lxxxii. 7 is no longer appealed to as containing a reference to Genesis. Isai. xliii. 27 refers not to Adam but to Jacob.

theoretical explanation, and were occupied with national rather than with universal questions, some of the sapiential books deal, to a certain extent, with problems of a nature bordering on the philosophical. That of theodicy is handled from various points of view in some of these writings; and in Job, a work in which the popular view that physical evils result wholly from sin is repudiated, and in which the question of the source of human sinfulness once or twice suggests itself, a reference to Gen. iii. would by no means have been irrelevant, especially if any well-known doctrinal views had as yet been derived from that chapter. The argument from silence is, doubtless, generally precarious; but the question is forcibly suggested whether at the time, whatever that was, in which the book of Job was written, any inference from the Fall-story, at all resembling that drawn by a later age, was authoritatively or widely taught.

The question why a doctrine of human sinfulness as somehow associated with the fall of Adam was not thus utilised or referred to by late Old Testament writers is distinct from, though connected with, the question: how is it that the contents of Gen. ii—iii., apart from any interpretation of them, are so scantily alluded to in later books? Both of these questions would be summarily answered if, with F. Delitzsch[1] and others, we could regard the Jahvist, as well as the Priestly, document as post-exilic. This, however, is impossible. So far as the Prophetic books are concerned, we need not be surprised at the omission. Their writers looked to the future rather than to the past; in the past for its own sake, especially in the past before the exodus, they had but little interest. And, as we have already observed, the prophets were national seers, not world-philosophers. We do not expect to find in them anything like a theological system. But, before the latest of them had passed away, the horizon of Hebrew thought had been vastly widened. Theological philosophy had developed greatly between the ages represented by the Jahvist history and the Book of Job. The silence of the sapiential and poetic literature, therefore, needs to be accounted for.

[1] *Wo lag das Paradies?*

It has sometimes been suggested that an explanation of the absence of allusions, in the later canonical books, to the Hebrew *Urgeschichte* in general is to be sought in the fact that it was known to be of foreign origin, and that it had not really been assimilated to Hebrew thought.

This, however, does not appear to be a satisfactory explanation. In the first place the narratives of Genesis were not wholly, nor directly, nor abruptly, borrowed. There are many reasons for believing them to have been gradually absorbed and Hebraised; and they might easily have come to be regarded, therefore, as immemorially Hebrew, like the agricultural pursuits learned through the selfsame medium. And further, there are frequent allusions, both in poetic and prophetic books, to the mythical figures of Rahab, Leviathan, etc., which are admittedly of Babylonian origin.

Possibly the difficulty receives its best explanation in the reflection that the narratives of Genesis would not be likely to exert much influence on Hebrew thought before the canonisation of the pentateuch. Certainly in the Book of Job the creation of the world is incidentally imaged, and the first man is alluded to, without any recognition of Genesis as the sole source of authoritative information on such subjects. The date of this work, however, is too uncertain to warrant the secure assumption that it was written after the pentateuch had acquired canonical authority. If this was not the case; if, for instance, it was written before or during the captivity; it ceases to be extraordinary that the book should not refer to, or be guided by, the Jahvist 'history of origins.' And this is perhaps, after all, the only book in which such omission really calls for notice. If the later date assigned by many critics to the Book of Job be justified, the question we have raised is still unsolved; for the early history of Genesis must then have been both taught and reverenced. In any case the fact remains that the Old Testament supplies no trace of the existence, among the sacred writers, of any *interpretation* of the Fall-story comparable to the later doctrine of the Fall.

It has occasionally been assumed that some such doctrinal inference *must* have been drawn by later Old Testament writers, notwithstanding their silence on the subject, in order to account for the depth and earnestness of their sense of sin. This assumption cannot be sanctioned. It savours of the error of attributing an association of ideas which we, with our doctrinal legacy inherited from distant centuries, require to make an effort in order to dissolve, to an age in which, so far as the scanty evidence seems to indicate, this association had not yet been effected. We shall presently see reason to believe that, very possibly, such a doctrine of the Fall as post-exilic Jewish theology came to acquire was arrived at independently of the narrative of Gen. ii—iii., and, instead of being deduced from those chapters, was read back into them. But the presupposition of a Fall-doctrine, *i.e.* a doctrine affirming the moral state and capacities of every individual to have been affected by a corruption of the nature which he inherits from his first parent, is certainly not logically a requisite for a deep sense of sin, or for a belief in the empirical universality of sinfulness amongst mankind.

It is to be concluded, therefore, that the Old Testament books of later date than the Jahvist document supply no evidence of a doctrine of the Fall having been extracted out of Genesis. And whilst this by no means proves that such a doctrine or idea could not, or did not, exist, in ages subsequent to the recognition of the authority of the Jahvist writing, yet, taken in connexion with what has already been said with regard to the exegesis of the narrative of Genesis ii—iii., and with the results of the investigation undertaken in the remainder of the present chapter, this negative evidence points somewhat strongly towards a negative conclusion.

* * * * * *

An alternative Old Testament source of speculation on the origin of human sinfulness.

With the question whether the Paradise-story of Genesis was intended by its compiler, or taken by later Old Testament writers, to supply an explanation of human depravity, is connected that of the nature and meaning of the story given (by J, as is usually believed) in Gen. vi. 1–4, which now

IV] *for a doctrine of the Fall* 95

stands in close union with the Jahvist deluge-story, and for which it was evidently intended by the compiler to afford a preparation or introduction. For this curious legend of the Nephilim has been considered by many modern critics to be parallel in meaning to Gen. iii., and to supply an alternative hamartigeny or explanation of the origin and universality of sin[1].

The linguistic difficulties of the narrative in question are so great, the attempts hitherto made to restore the corrupted text are so wanting in agreement and in objectivity, and the story itself is so sadly mutilated a fragment, that it is easily possible to dogmatise too freely on its signification. A few statements, however, may be collected with regard to it to which a high degree of probability appears to attach.

The story, both from its archaic language and its naïvely legendary nature, seems to have been taken over from a lower form of faith[2], and in fact to have been originally intended to explain the existence of the giants, heroes (cf. Izdubar), or demigods, which many ancient races place as a connecting link between divine and human beings, and by which they express their belief in the divine ancestry of mankind. Similar legends are common to Semite mythology, and there is evidence of their existence amongst the Babylonians, Phoenicians[3] and Arabs[4]. Perhaps the present mutilated condition of the story is due to the fact that the Jahvist compiler found much in it that was too repulsive for his taste and too

---

[1] Budde, *Urgeschichte*; Wellhausen, *Prolegomena*, E.T. p. 307 n.; Schultz, *O.T. Theology*, E.T. vol. I. p. 30, etc. Clemen (*op. cit.*) thinks that if this story was intended to account for human sin, Gen. iii. could not have been so intended by the same compiler.

[2] W. R. Smith, *Religion of the Semites*, ed. 2, p. 446, where it is suggested that it was a local legend derived from Mount Hermon. The descent of the watchers is associated with Mount Hermon in apocalyptic literature.

[3] See esp. Dillmann, *Genesis*, E.T. vol. I. p. 23 ff., where the following quotation from Philo Byblus (Eusebius, *Praep. Evang.* I. x. 6) is given, which illustrates the assertion in the narrative of Genesis with regard to marriage relations between gods and mortals: ἀπὸ μητέρων δὲ, φησὶν, ἐχρημάτιζον τῶν τότε γυναικῶν ἀναίδην μισγομένων οἷς ἂν ἐντύχοιεν.

[4] W. R. Smith, *op. cit.*, p. 50.

On the Semitic belief in the kinship of gods and men, see Barton in *Journal of Bibl. Literature*, XV. 168 ff.

unsuitable for his use. Though he has preserved for us the connexion of the story with the origin of the Nephilim, well known to ancient Israelitish folk-lore, and has not wholly purified it, any more than he did the Fall-story, from its legendary and polytheistic implications, he has rather used it to account for the universal wickedness of mankind, upon which the deluge was held to be (as in Babylonian tradition) a divine visitation. If, in its earlier form, the legend had as much to do with the history of the sons of Elohim as with mortals, the Jahvist writer uses it exclusively in the latter connexion. He says nothing of a fall of angels, and does not imply that the conduct of these Elohim-beings was wicked. From its position in the Jahvist history, this story would certainly seem to have been incorporated with the purpose of explaining the visitation of the deluge, and therefore of assigning a reason for the general depravity of man at that particular period. In this case it would appear that the Jahvist compiler himself did not intend to teach in Gen. iii. that the sin of Adam and Eve concerned any but themselves, in the sense that it altered human nature for the worse or made human sin more easy. And it is partly because of this inference that the passage calls for mention in the present chapter. It remains to be added that not only does the story, in the context in which it has been placed, bear upon its face, more clearly than does that of Gen. iii.[1], the pretention to furnish the cause of human sinfulness and of its ubiquitous diffusion, but the earlier Jewish apocalyptic literature attached more importance to it in this connexion than to the story of the loss of Paradise[2].

* * * * * *

[1] It may be observed that the *ethos* of the legend is similar to that of Gen. iii. Man has become, through relations with the sons of Elohim, too powerful for Jahveh to endure: therefore the duration of his life is shortened. Cf. Stave, *Einfluss des Parsismus auf das Judenthum*, where it is said that this story teaches that man might have had eternal life if he had not, through false self-advancement, overstepped the limits assigned to him.

[2] For the subsequent usage of this narrative in apocalyptic writings, see Chaps. VIII. and IX.

The doctrine of the fall of angels alluded to in more than one New Testament book, may either have been deduced from Gen. vi. 1–4, or have been a survival

Growth, in the Old Testament, of ideas embodied in the doctrine of Original Sin.

The impression which has already been forced upon us that the doctrinal interpretation of the Fall-story of Genesis only commenced long after the narrative had been reduced to written form, will perhaps be further confirmed by a glance at the development of certain ideas with regard to human sinfulness which prepared the way for the view that Adam's transgression affected his descendants far more profoundly than by causing their exclusion from the Paradise which he himself at first enjoyed. We shall see that these ideas, which are collectively implied or involved in the doctrines of the Fall and of Original Sin, exhibit a gradual growth in the writings of the Old Testament, and a growth which nowhere appears to be moulded by, or to be avowedly connected with, a doctrinal interpretation of the story of Paradise.

It may be mentioned at the outset that already in the Jahvist document itself we meet with conceptions of sin which form necessary constituents of the doctrines whose early history this volume endeavours to trace. We find, in the first place, sin personified as a power or agency external to man; thus in Gen. iv. 7, a passage which has already been noticed, sin is spoken of as 'couching at the door' (of the heart?) like a ravenous beast. It is also taught, of course, that sin is the cause of the sufferings of life: not only is this the main burden of the narrative of the third chapter of Genesis, but it is implied elsewhere also, as, *e.g.*, in the history of the Deluge. Sin, again, is regarded not only as the isolated act, but as a state: the state of sinful habit due to the fact, which the Jahvist history often illustrates, that one sin leads on naturally to other sins. But more than this: we also meet in the Jahvist document with the idea that man possesses an evil disposition; and one of the two passages in which this doctrine

in modified form of the same ancient legend, or have been afterwards read into this passage though suggested by Isai. xxiv. 21 (see Davis, *Genesis and Semitic Tradition*, p. 103): but most probably it was mainly derived through apocalyptic literature from foreign sources.

is expressed implies that such an evil inclination is partly due to the constitution which man received at the hand of his Maker. For if in Gen. vi. 5 it is said that "the Lord saw that the wickedness of man was great in the earth, and that every imagination (*yezer*) of the thoughts of his heart was only evil continually," implying that the race freely brought upon itself, and deserved, the terrible punishment of the Deluge, it is nevertheless implied, when in Gen. viii. 21 "the imagination (*yezer*) of man's heart" is declared to be "evil from his youth," that the possession by man of such a propensity towards sin was regarded by Jahveh as a ground for His showing mercy and compassion, and for His refraining from afterwards visiting the world with a similar destruction. These passages just quoted from the Jahvist history are the more interesting because in them lies the source of the later doctrine of the evil inclination (*yezer hara*), whose development it will be needful subsequently to trace. Meanwhile they are only appealed to as evidence that even at so early a period as that of the Jahvist writer the conception of an inherent bias to evil, if not of an evil nature, had already taken shape. But it must be observed that no hint is expressed as to the cause of this bias to sin which is regarded as ingrained in man from his youth. At least there is certainly no warrant supplied for the view that the evil imagination was a consequence of Adam's sin entailed upon his children, or even that it was transmitted by physical descent. Oehler's assertion[1], that this evil inclination is to be taken as a consequence of the Fall, has no justification whatever from the Jahvist history. Such sinfulness as is there ascribed to men is neither, to use Schultz's expression, "a hereditary doom" nor something characteristic of man's *fleshly* constitution. Save for the slight hint in Gen. viii. 21 that the inclination to evil is not wholly a matter of man's choice, sin, with the Jahvist writer, is always a voluntary act or a habit resulting from such acts.

Finally, the Jahvist document teaches something like the universality of this state of sinfulness. But it is scarcely the absolute universality which would follow from the Fall-story

---

[1] *O.T. Theology*, Eng. Tr., vol. I. p. 235.

if it were to be interpreted in the light of the doctrine of Original Sin. In fact there is no reason to assume that, in the verses where this idea is found (the same that have already been quoted, Gen. vi. 5 and viii. 21), the assertion of the universality of sin has a wider application than to the particular time to which the historian is referring : the Jahvist writing, as a whole, seems, on the contrary, to preclude any other inference[1].

A recent writer[2] has seen in "the prevalent feeling that the nation rather than the individual was the subject of sin " a probable preparation " for the thought of all mankind being involved in the guilt and penalty of Adam and Eve, when religious thought came to reflect on the relation to God of mankind generally, and not merely of Israel." This may perhaps be the case, notwithstanding the fact that this sense of solidarity, or, rather, this deficient sense of individuality, was characteristic of a stage of thought which, at the time when the national horizon was being exchanged for the universal, and speculation as to the cause of human sinfulness was probably commencing, was being replaced by the more individualistic conception of the connexion between sin and guilt developed by Jeremiah and Ezekiel[3]. The idea of sin as common to the family or to the people to which the single sinner belonged is, of course, rather a survival of a relatively primitive and crude morality than an onward development of the conception of sinfulness. The completely individual personality emerges late, and only gradually, in the process of human thought. Instances of this notion of community, or solidarity, in sin occur in passages such as Gen. ix. 25, xx. 9, xxvi. 10; Exod. xx. 5, xxxiv. 7; 2 Sam. iii. 29, xxi. 5 ff.; 1 Kings ii. 33, xvii. 1; 2 Kings v. 27; and the notion by no means disappears when insistence on the responsibilities and rights of the individual begins to find expression after the exile[4]. Dr Clemen thinks that the idea of "common sin" which occurs in the prophetic writings

---

[1] See above, p. 10.
[2] Canon Bernard, Art. *Sin*, in Hastings' *Dictionary of the Bible*.
[3] See Jer. xxxi. 29, 30; Ezek. xviii. 2-4.
[4] Signs of this tendency appear in Gen. xviii. 23, xix. 15; Exod. xxxii. 33.

is somewhat different from this earlier deficiency of moral discrimination; he seems to see in it an inference from the belief that all physical evil is of the nature of a punishment, and takes it to imply that an individual's sin which has brought ruin upon a community must be attributed to this community as well as to the particular offender, else the community could not have been subjected to the punishment. But it is difficult to read this implication into most of the passages which he collects in order to illustrate the prophetic use of the idea of common sin[1].

It is therefore hard to agree with this writer's assertion that the prophets "no longer believe in the imputation of others' sins." There are certainly passages which point to the existence, in the prophets, of this attitude of mind[2]; but it is as yet only struggling against the dead weight of opposed tradition. We shall see later that in Jewish literature of a subsequent period the justice of imputation of others' sins, or of community in punishment, was accepted side by side with the individualistic conception of guilt and responsibility.

The narrative of the Fall does not, of course, teach the imputation of Adam's guilt any more than the corruption, through his transgression, of the nature derived from him by his posterity. It merely implies that the physical evils which he brought upon himself as punishments were also visited upon his descendants. In this respect the story represents a more advanced stage of ethical reflection than many other passages in the earlier portions of the Old Testament. Not that these definitely teach imputation of guilt, which as a formulated belief is of comparatively modern origin; they simply fall short of an adequate conception of guilt, due to deficient moral feeling with regard to sin.

The conceptions of sin as absolutely universal, and as ingrained in man, conceptions which we have seen to be approached, though not fully reached, in the Jahvist history,

---

[1] *Op. cit.* S. 46. Some of these passages may be mentioned : Hos. i. 4; Isai. vii. 17, xiv. 21 ; Obad. 10 ; Jer. xiv. 20, xv. 4, xxii. 28, 30, xxvi. 15, xxxii. 18; Lam. v. 7 ; Deut. v. 9.

[2] Besides the verses in Jer. and Ezek. referred to above, see Amos ix. 8, and cf. the retrospective passages Deut. vii. 10, xxiv. 16 ; 2 Kings xiv. 6.

attained to full development in the later Old Testament books. A very important step was thus taken in the way of preparation for a thorough-going doctrine of inherited sinfulness of nature. There is a great difference between the Jahvist compiler's treatment of sin, serious as it is, and such as we meet with in the Book of Job or in certain of the Psalms. It needed the work of the prophets to make men realise more fully the moral character of God: it required the sufferings of the exile, and the introspectiveness which they fostered, to deepen the personal sense of sinfulness, before the content of sin came to include the thoughts, the desires and emotions; before sin could be looked upon as a disorder of the whole being inherent in a man from his birth; and before it could be adequately apprehended that there is none on earth that is truly sinless in the sight of God.

The following are the passages of the Old Testament which most strongly emphasise the universality of sin: "Shall mortal man be just before God? Shall a man be pure before his Maker?"; "Who can bring a clean thing out of an unclean[1]? Not one"; "How then can a man be just with God? Or how can he be clean that is born of a woman?" Job iv. 17 (R.V. margin), xiv. 4, xxv. 4. "Who can say, I have made my heart clean, I am pure from my sin?" Prov. xx. 9. "For there is no man that sinneth not," 1 Kings viii. 46, 2 Chron. vi. 36. "For there is not a righteous man upon earth that doeth good and sinneth not," Eccl. vii. 20. "If thou, Lord, shouldest mark iniquities, O Lord, who shall stand?"; "For in thy sight shall no man living be justified," Pss. cxxx. 3, cxliii. 2.

Allusions to sin as inherent in man from birth occur in the following passages, in addition to some of the verses just cited: "What is man that he should be clean? And he which is born of a woman, that he should be righteous? Behold, he putteth no trust in his holy ones; yea, the heavens are not clean in his sight," Job xv. 14, 15. "Behold, I was shapen in iniquity; and in sin did my mother conceive me," Ps. li. 5. Without assuming that the writer of the passage last

---

[1] Some scholars consider this sentence to be a gloss. See, *e.g.*, Loisy, *L'Enseignement Biblique*, 1892, p. 113, n. 6; Art. *Job* in *Encyclopaedia Biblica*.

quoted taught that the mode of origin of his existence was evil, it is evidently implied that man inherits a tainted nature. The idea of sinfulness as an ingrained state, though not necessarily as inherent from birth, occurs also in Jer. xvii. 9, "The heart is deceitful above all things, and it is desperately sick: who can know it¹?"

Such passages supply abundant evidence that, before the later Old Testament books were written, there was a deep sense among the Hebrews of sin as both absolutely universal in the race and all-pervading in the individual's human nature. But this inherent sinfulness, often spoken of in terms which are inapplicable to acquired sinful habit, is nowhere definitely traced to its cause or source. Some of the language quoted above in reference to it seems to imply that it was regarded as hereditary.² But beyond this implication we cannot pierce. It can certainly be said that this sinfulness is nowhere traced to Adam and the effects of his fall upon human nature collectively. Nor is there the smallest reason for suspecting that any such view lay tacitly behind the assertions of man's proneness to evil from his birth. A different explanation is suggested more than once by the language of the Book of Job for the sinfulness of human nature on which it insists so strongly³. It is that of the creaturely weakness, the natural infirmity, of a being such as man, attaching to him in virtue of his finiteness and temporariness. This frailty of mankind, of which Job frequently speaks, and in which he sees a claim upon God's compassion rather than a provocation of His wrath, seems to be regarded as belonging to man as such, to man as he was made by God. The writer looks upon human nature as corrupt, but not corrupted; and the corruption is appealed to as an apology for his actual

---

¹ Ps. lviii. 3 is poetic hyperbole, and not an instance to be added here. Nor is Isai. xlviii. 8 : "transgressor from the womb" probably refers to Gen. xxv. 26; cf. Hos. xii. 3.

² The explicit belief of later generations in the heredity of sinfulness derived from Adam might be moulded on Isai. xliii. 27, 28, "Thy *first father* sinned... therefore...I will make Jacob a curse, and Israel a reviling." Of course these words do not refer to Adam.

³ We cannot agree with Clemen (*op. cit.*), in holding that the sinfulness asserted in the passages cited above from this book is actual, and not inborn, sin.

sinfulness. That which is born of flesh is flesh, and flesh is essentially weak; as man is born to trouble, so also is he born to imperfection. Indeed the angels of heaven, as created and finite beings, are imperfect and unclean.

At this point a few words may be said with regard to the further use in the Old Testament of the conception of the *yezer*, which has already been met with in the Jahvist document. There is but a slight development towards the rabbinical doctrine of the evil inclination to be traced within the pages of the Old Testament itself; but the one step of advance which appears to have been made is worthy of notice. The phrases of Gen. vi. 5 and viii. 21 are merely repeated or cited in 1 Chron. xxviii. 9 and xxix. 18; that is to say, 'imagination' (*yezer*) is qualified by the words 'of the thoughts' or 'of the thoughts of the heart.' But in Deut. xxxi. 21 we find the 'imagination' spoken of absolutely, or without such modifying amplification as is supplied by the words 'of the thoughts.' Dr Porter[1], whose statements are here reproduced, has also referred to Isai. xxvi. 3 as a probable example of this same usage of *yezer*, in the sense of the disposition or mind. In Ps. ciii. 14, he adds, the word may mean 'frame,' as the second clause suggests, but the context points to a wider sense, 'nature,' as Wellhausen has rendered it. The word thus seems to have gained, in Old Testament times, a certain independence, as meaning the nature or disposition of man; and this nature could perhaps be regarded either "as something which God made or as something which man works."

In Psalm li. the inherited tendency to sin to which the writer confesses is not appealed to in a sense bordering upon that of excuse or plea for compassion, but rather as an aggravation of personal uncleanness and personal guilt[2]. But here again there is no implication of a belief in the fallen, as distinguished from the sinful, condition of human nature. Sin is apparently conceived as a hereditary taint, and, so far,

---

[1] *Biblical and Semitic Studies*, by members of Yale University, 1901, p. 109.
[2] Whether the Psalmist writes of himself, or as a representative Israelite giving voice to a national confession, is of no importance here; in any case he expresses the conception of inherited and inherent sinfulness as the root of actual sin.

as 'original' sin; but not in the sense that mankind shares in the sin, or the consequences of the sin, of its first parent. The origin of sinfulness, in the last resort, is left unexplained in the Old Testament.

The degree in which the ecclesiastical doctrines of the Fall and of Original Sin are approached within the pages of the Old Testament (excluding, of course, the Apocrypha), may now be concisely defined. There is no evidence that any connexion between human sinfulness and Adam's transgression had as yet occurred at all to the Hebrew mind. That the 'divine image' was lost at the Fall is contrary to the implications, if not to express statements, of the Old Testament[1]. It is more than doubtful whether death was as yet regarded as caused by Adam's sin[2]. The serpent is not identified, apparently, with Satan; though Satan already serves as an expedient for removing from God the responsibility for human evil which early Hebrew writers did not shrink from imputing to Him. So much with regard to the use of the Fall-story itself. As for conceptions which are essential to that deep sense of pervading sinfulness of which the doctrines of the Fall and of Original Sin may be taken to be the mature expression, we have seen that, before the Old Testament was completed, Jewish thought had arrived at the truth of the absolute universality of human sinfulness, and had come to regard it as a state which was inherent in man and received by him at birth as part of the nature he inherits; that no cause for such uncleanness or corruption, where it is regarded as prior to habit established by voluntary acts, is definitely assigned, though the writer of Job, at least, seems to

[1] What exactly is meant in the Priestly Code (Gen. i. 26, 27, v. 1, 3, ix. 6) by 'the image of God' is uncertain; probably no more than writers such as Ben Sira or Pseudo-Solomon seem to have associated with the phrase. In Ecclus. xvii. 1 ff., the image of God would appear to be identical with supremacy over the beasts and with rationality; the Book of Wisdom asserts these properties of man, though not expressly in connexion with the divine image (ix. 2, 3; cf. Ps. viii. 6), which, in ii. 23, it associates with immortality of the soul. It is not until we come to the apocalyptic books and the rabbinic writings that the image of God is taken to include more remarkable endowments; and the identification of it with moral excellences was due to Christian teachers.

[2] See below, p. 117 f.

have seen its source in the necessary and normal infirmity which pertains to the finite creature. The identification of this inherent tendency to sin with a corruption of human nature wrought once and for all by Adam, and *thence* naturally engendered in his posterity, alone is wanting of the constituent elements whose union is essential to the later doctrine of the Fall. The increasing sense of individual moral personality, which is conspicuous in certain later books of the Old Testament, is a tendency which might be supposed to make against the acquisition of such a doctrine of solidarity in a 'first father' of the race, or in the effects of his transgression; but indirectly it aided the formation of such a view, by adding point to the individual's sense of personal sin, and so fertilising the soil in which the doctrine of hereditary acquired corruption has its root.

CHAPTER V.

THE TEACHING OF ECCLESIASTICUS ON SIN AND THE FALL.

Introductory

THE last chapter was largely concerned with the question, whether there are signs, in the books included within the Old Testament canon, of any exegetical use of the Fall-story such as would imply that this narrative was held by any Old Testament writer to be an authoritative source of a doctrine of human nature and human sinfulness. So far as the evidence went, it was seen to point to the conclusion that the narrative of Paradise, though undoubtedly taught and reverenced as part of the 'first canon,' did not as yet exert any influence upon the development of the doctrine of sin in what are called Old Testament times. We have now to pass on to later Jewish writings which found no place in the canon.

This literature may conveniently be divided, for our purpose, into three classes: (i) Alexandrian, (ii) Rabbinical, and (iii) Pseudepigraphic. These groups of writings will subsequently be examined in the order mentioned above, which is also the order of increasing importance in respect of similarity of spirit to that of the first Christian writers, and of influence upon the earliest Christian thought.

But before we discuss the development of the doctrine of the Fall as it is traceable in these three classes of literature, another early non-canonical Jewish book calls for full consideration, in virtue of its representing a definite stage in the transition from the Old Testament to the New Testament,

CH. V] *The teaching of Ecclesiasticus* 107

on the one hand, and also to two of the three classes of literature which have just been enumerated, on the other.

This is the book Ecclesiasticus, or the Wisdom of Ben Sira; and its examination will occupy the remainder of the present chapter.

Ecclesiasticus.

The book Ecclesiasticus occupies a place of considerable importance in the history of Jewish thought, and especially in the history of the doctrine of the Fall, notwithstanding the fact that its treatment of this subject is relatively slight and only incidental. There are two reasons for regarding the writing as thus important to the student of the growth of the doctrine of the Fall. In the first place, we derive from it the most ancient extant reference, for anything like doctrinal purposes, to the narrative of Genesis relating to the first sin and its consequences for mankind. Ecclesiasticus, in fact, presents us with the first appearance of a partial exegesis of that story[1]. In the second place, the book has an interesting relation, as has already been stated, both to the Old Testament, on the one hand, and to the Jewish literature which is to be dealt with in the succeeding chapters. The Wisdom of Ben Sira, in fact, is a most valuable, and a unique connecting-link. It has indeed no affinity, and no connexion of any kind, with the pseudepigraphic writings; although these must have already begun to be current in Ben Sira's day. And excluding this kind of literature, of which we certainly possess little, if we can be sure that we possess any, that is of similar antiquity to the book Ecclesiasticus, the latter work is the only one which unquestionably reflects light upon the Palestinian thought of its time concerning the origin of sin and death in Adam. The Talmud and Targums perhaps imply that exegesis was actively pursued as early as Ben Sira's day, and may possibly contain, in spite of all the loss which attended their compilation, teaching that was then current. But such teaching cannot be isolated from the

[1] It will be seen in Chap. VIII. that the groundwork of the *Book of Enoch*, probably older than Ecclus., alludes to the story of Adam's fall; but it extracts no general *doctrine* of sin from it.

accretions of later periods. The sayings in that part of *Pirke Aboth*, even, which deals with cosmological and philosophical rather than with moral questions, are anonymous. And this fact of the uniqueness of the witness of Ecclesiasticus to the Palestinian thought of its time, on the subject with which we are concerned, remains true whether the book be regarded as a product of the later half of the second century B.C., which is the view now generally adopted in England and in Germany, or whether, as is occasionally maintained, it dates from the end or the middle of the third: whether it be a work contemporary with Ecclesiastes, or even with Wisdom, or, as is more probable, with neither.

As regards the relation of Ecclesiasticus to the Old Testament, it may be considered as a continuation of that element in it which is usually known as the Wisdom-literature. Ben Sira fully respects the authority and inspiration of the books which first came to be recognised as canonical, especially the Law. His exceedingly numerous quotations from the Scriptures confirm his grandson's statement that he had 'much given himself' to their study. Fritzsche, indeed, speaks of him as a pure Old Testament type[1]. And such a designation for him, as a man, requires but slight qualification to be appropriate to him as an author. "The literary ambition of that age did not, as the Wisdom of Ben Sira clearly shows, presume either to write Scripture or even to add to it; it was content with studying the inspired documents of the past, interpreting them and imitating them[2]." This, however, does not preclude the writer's venturing to supplement the Wisdom-literature, whose canonicity was not fixed in his day. Still, except with regard to matters of practical wisdom and morals, he does not allow himself much liberty of thought, though he was probably conscious of the inadequacy of his inherited theology to solve all the problems which presented themselves to his highly educated and observant mind. Ben Sira is preeminently conservative. He disparages ventures of speculative thought in contrast

---

[1] *Kurzgefasstes exeget. Handbuch zu den Apokryphen* (1859), Bd. v., S. xxxiii.
[2] Dr Schechter, in his and Dr Taylor's *Wisdom of Ben Sira*, 1899, p. 32.

v] *on Sin and the Fall* 109

with reliance upon authority[1]; and he claims to be a collector, at least as much as an original thinker, with regard to the practical instructions which represent the main purpose of his book[2].

For these reasons Ben Sira is to be regarded as a reliable exponent of such theological teaching as was orthodox in his day, and therefore as a useful guide to the views of his time, at least in the circle to which he belonged.

To define that circle, in so far as is possible, is to sketch the relations of the author of Ecclesiasticus to the later standpoint of each of the kinds of Jewish literature about to be discussed.

Ben Sira, says a recent writer, "seems to have been a Palestinian sage, a philosophical observer of life, an ardent Israelite and devoted lover of the Torah, but probably neither a priest nor a *sofer* (scribe), unless that term be understood in a very wide sense. He had too wide a circle of interests to be easily identified with either of those classes, though he was in close relation with them both[3]." He gives great prominence to the Law, but he is far removed from the later Pharisee. And if he "wrote like a rabbi[4]," the statement must be taken to imply that he manifests, in a very elementary degree, the tendencies of thought and method which characterised the later writers of the Talmud, rather than that he exhibits them in their maturity. The element of haggada[5] introduced into his work is comparatively slight;

---

[1] iii. 21–24.
[2] xxxiii. 16.
Some authorities have considered B. Sira to be by no means an original writer, and have regarded his work as but a compilation from already existing sources: *e.g.* Bretschneider, *Liber Jesu Siracidae Graece*; Ewald, *Geschichte des Volks Israel*, IV. 342 ff.; Ryssel, Kautzsch's *Apokryphen und Pseudepigraphen*, I. 239. Schürer (see last reference) maintains the opposite view, with most other writers.
[3] Prof. Toy, Art. *Ecclesiasticus* in *Encyclopaedia Biblica*.
[4] Schechter, *op. cit.*, p. 32.
[5] Some readers may perhaps desire a definition of this term, frequently to be used in later chapters; the following one is therefore supplied from an article in the *Jew. Quart. Review*, IV., by Bacher: haggada is "the exegetical elaboration of the contents of a verse, the evolution of new ideas based upon the interpretation of the biblical text." See further, note 1, p. 145.

110 *The teaching of Ecclesiasticus* [CHAP.

his exegesis freely adapts, but does not venture much beyond, the words of Scripture. Ben Sira represents the common root whence were afterwards differentiated the standpoints of the Pharisaic rabbi and of the Sadducee; and perhaps there is some approach to that of the Alexandrian school. For though he betrays no trace of Alexandrian influence[1], and has no interest in Greek philosophical thought, he shows signs of having absorbed general Hellenic culture, and his horizon is by no means limited by his native Scriptures[2].

Thus Ben Sira neither breaks with the traditional religion of the past nor adopts any considerable doctrinal innovations from without. The direct contact of his country, at a previous time, with Persia, appears to have produced no effect upon his thought. Indeed he is peculiarly chary of beliefs in a future life, and in angels and demons; and, if a particular passage in his book has been correctly interpreted by certain authorities, he appears to adopt an attitude which is protestant, if not rationalistic, towards the new development in doctrine which would regard Satan as the personal tempter of man[3].

It will be obvious, for the reasons which have now been given, that the book Ecclesiasticus occupies a position of very considerable importance for the student of the growth of Jewish doctrine, representing, as it does, a period from which we have few literary remains. It has therefore been thought worth while to sketch its historical background here with some fulness, although the amount of light which the book

---

[1] The signs of Alexandrian influence formerly adduced by Gfrörer, Dähne, etc., are now generally regarded as based upon faulty interpretation; see Drummond, *Philo Judaeus*, vol. I.

[2] Cf. Montefiore, *Hibbert Lectures*, pp. 380 ff.; Nestle, Art. *Sirach* in Hastings' *Dict. of the Bible*; Toy, *loc. cit.*, especially the remarks which this writer makes on the personified wisdom of Ecclus. The more direct Hellenic influences which have been said by some to be traceable in this book have sometimes been regarded as due to its translator; see Edersheim in the *Speaker's Commentary on Ecclus.*; Bois, *Les Origines de la Philosophie Judéo-Alexandrine*, p. 172; Herriot, *Philon le Juif.* One such supposed instance of Hellenising by the younger B. Sira has been disproved since the recovery of the Hebrew fragments: see Tyler, *Jew. Quart. Review*, Apr. 1900, pp. 555 ff.

[3] See below, p. 115.

actually throws upon the problems of sin and evil is not relatively large.

Ben Sira's teaching as to Sin.

Ben Sira's view of sin in general does not involve the deeper and more inward conceptions which have been described as existing in some of the later canonical writings of the Old Testament: *e.g.* Job, Ps. li., and such passages in the prophets as Jer. xxxi. 33, Ezek. xxxvi. 26. Sin consists, according to him, in the breach of explicit law rather than in an inward disposition expressed by the aims and affections of the man[1]. His recognition of the universality of sin, again, finds no deeper expression than that "all are worthy of punishment[2]." Sin is not conceived as an inherent spiritual disease clinging to man from his birth; and it is scarcely regarded as an external power. Such 'moral solidarity' as he incidentally predicates of the race consists only in the punishableness of the children for their parents' sins[3], and in the influence of example[4]. Ben Sira's attitude generally speaking is individualistic: and he magnifies personal freedom and responsibility, as will be seen from certain passages presently to be discussed. These facts lead us not to expect in Ecclesiasticus a very thorough-going doctrine of the Fall, so far as moral consequences are concerned. *A priori* considerations, however, must not prejudice the empirical examination of the statement, such as it is, which deals directly with the point in question.

This statement is to be found in xxv. 24[5], which affords a convenient starting-point for the study of Ben Sira's views as to the historical origin of sin[6]. So long as only the Greek and Syriac versions were accessible, two interpretations of

[1] But cf. the doctrine of the *yezer*, below, p. 114 ff.
[2] viii. 5.
[3] xxiii. 24, xlvii. 20.
[4] xli. 5. This passage *might* mean more, but there is no reason to believe that it does.
[5] Verses are quoted according to the English Revised Version of the Apocrypha
[6] ἀπὸ γυναικὸς ἀρχὴ ἁμαρτίας,
καὶ δι' αὐτὴν ἀποθνήσκομεν πάντες.

this verse were equally possible, owing to the ambiguity of ἀρχή, which elsewhere in the book (*e.g.* x. 12, 13) undoubtedly bears the sense of 'cause' in addition to its primary meaning of 'beginning.' For this reason Bruch was led to think that the former sense was predominant here, unless indeed Ben Sira had not distinguished the two alternatives in his own mind. Bretschneider[1] translated ἀρχή by *causa* for other reasons. Edersheim, on the contrary, guided by the Syriac, which he translates 'from the woman began sins[2],' concluded that the Hebrew had the equivalent of that rendering and denied the implication in this verse of any doctrine approaching that of Original Sin. Fritzsche[3] adopted the same interpretation, believing that the original for ἀρχή did not contain the sense of *causa* or *origo*. Quite recently the original Hebrew of the passage has been recovered[4], and the word represented by ἀρχή proves to be *teḥillah*, not *rēshīth*; 'beginning' is therefore to have a predominantly temporal sense. Still it has to be borne in mind that when, in the second clause of the verse, the writer passes to the thought of death, to the relation of Eve's sin to our universal mortality, a causal connexion is distinctly asserted. The use of *teḥillah* in the former clause does not perhaps, in itself, preclude the thought of such connexion, in the case of sin also, having presented itself to Ben Sira's mind; but it certainly does not suggest any such connexion. This verse may still be pronounced ambiguous as a guide to its writer's teaching on the introduction of general sinfulness, and its meaning must be sought by comparison with other passages. It would indeed be venturing further than was his wont beyond the letter of the scriptural narrative which he had in his mind, and also stating a deeper view of the first transgression than we should naturally have expected, if Ben Sira intended to imply here that Eve's transgression was the cause or source of human sinfulness. If one presses the literal meaning of the former clause of the

---

[1] *Op. cit., in loc.*
[2] *Speaker's Commentary, in loc.*
[3] *Op. cit., in loc.*
[4] See *Jew. Quart. Review*, April, 1900. It is assumed here that the recovered Hebrew is not a retranslation.

verse so that an antithesis is produced between ἀρχή and δι' αὐτήν, one does but extract a doctrinal result thoroughly in keeping with what later Jewish literature, most akin to Ecclesiasticus, would lead us naturally to expect.

Fortunately we can resort to a more objective method of deciding this question than by reliance on such considerations as these, relevant though they may be. It may legitimately be argued that the doctrine which would be implied in xxv. 24 a, if ἀχρή bore the sense of causal origin, is precluded by the sense of other passages of Ecclesiasticus, which contain an incompatible theory of the source of human sinfulness.

These are the passages in which the word *yezer* was used, or has been alleged to have been used, by Ben Sira. On this account alone they are important for the study of the history of the Jewish doctrine of sin.

Of these passages we may first consider xvii. 1 ff. The writer speaks here of man's creation by God, his mortality, and his endowment with the divine image, with which dominion over the animals is either identified or closely associated. He then adds[1]: "counsel...gave he them to understand withal," and continues with the statement that man was endowed with the knowledge of wisdom, of good and evil, and received a law of life and an everlasting covenant, together with a warning against unrighteousness. The word 'counsel' (διαβούλιον), as Prof. Margoliouth and Dr Taylor[2] maintain, is probably not the equivalent here of *yezer*, but represents a verb (created), which indeed appears in the Syriac. We cannot therefore assume that Ben Sira is speaking of man's original endowment with a *yezer* or inclination; but the general drift of the whole passage is certainly difficult to reconcile with the view that Eve's transgression was the cause of universal human sinfulness. Undiminished freedom, responsibility, and capacity for righteousness, seem rather to be distinctly attributed to the first and the succeeding generations of mankind.

The passage in which the original existence of the word

---

[1] xvii. 6. The R.V. is followed here, which omits several verses.
[2] *Sayings of the Jewish Fathers*, ed. 2, pp. 148, 152.

114   *The teaching of Ecclesiasticus*   [CHAP.

yezer was first suspected is xv. 14 f.[1]; and the conjecture of Edersheim and others that this term was the equivalent of διαβούλιον has been verified. The passage is contained in the Cambridge fragments published by Dr Schechter and Dr Taylor, in whose work the following translation of the Hebrew of verse 14 is given:

"For (?) God created man from the beginning;
And put him into the hand of him that would spoil him;
And gave him into the hand of his inclination[2]."

Edersheim[3] and Ryssel[4] both assert that Ben Sira used *yezer* here in its earlier (biblical) sense of disposition or mind, and not in its later application to either the good or the evil impulse in man. Prof. Margoliouth[5] believes that in Ecclesiasticus *yezer* is used in its "technical sense"; but what is its technical sense is not made plain. The relation of B. Sira's general conception of the *yezer* to those implied in the biblical and rabbinical uses of it respectively is a matter of considerable importance, and must be discovered by an examination of the various passages in which the word occurs. In the

[1] xv. 14   αὐτὸς ἐξ ἀρχῆς ἐποίησεν ἄνθρωπον,
              καὶ ἀφῆκεν αὐτὸν ἐν χειρὶ διαβουλίου αὐτοῦ.
    15   ἐὰν θέλῃς, συντηρήσεις ἐντολάς,
              καὶ πίστιν ποιῆσαι εὐδοκίας.

[2] Dr Schechter suggests that the third clause of this verse, which appears in the Greek, is a doublet of the second, which is represented by the Syriac (p. 51). I. Abrahams considers these doublets, which are frequent in the Cairo fragments, to be distinct ancient recensions of the Heb. (*Jew. Quart. Review*, Oct. 1899, p. 175; cf. the opinion of the Rev. G. Margoliouth, p. 2 of the same number). He thinks, however, that some of them are due to B. Sira himself, and result from his imitation of Prov. (cf. Tyler, *J. Q. R.* April 1900, p. 555 ff.). M. Lévi, who supports (or supported?) the view that the recovered Heb. is a retranslation, considers them to be corresponding renderings of the Greek and Syriac. Dr Schechter (*J. Q. R.* April 1900, p. 459) also has important remarks upon the subject.

Dr Porter, *op. cit.* p. 138, writing on this verse, says: "If the 2nd and 3rd lines ...are doublets, the Gk decides in favour of the 3rd as more original; since the 2nd line is wanting in the Gk, we should not, perhaps, put weight upon the personification of the *yezer* which it implies. It is quite possible, however, that the line was omitted by the translator, or by later Christian scribes, as suggesting too much intention on the part of God that man should fall into sin."

[3] *Speaker's Commentary on Ecclus.*, *in loc.*
[4] Kautzsch's *Apokryphen und Pseudepigraphen*, *in loc.*
[5] *Expositor*, 4th Series, I. 297 ff.

v]   on Sin and the Fall   115

verse at present before us the *yezer* is a disposition implanted in man by God, from which, evidently, there proceeds the solicitation to sin. It is therefore spoken of as man's spoiler. It is something, however, which man is not compelled to follow; the commandments of God may be kept in spite of it, and no one can say "my transgression was of God[1]." It is not identical with free-will, and διαβούλιον is an inaccurate rendering of its sense; it is rather one of two alternative powers—the other emerges in another passage—between which man's free-will has to choose for the determination of his conduct. This would seem to imply considerable development towards the rabbinical conception of the *yezer hara*.

In xxi. 27 the evil inclination seems to be in the writer's mind, where he says "When the ungodly curseth Satan he curseth his own soul[2]." If this translation be correct, the *yezer* may possibly have been already identified by contemporary scribes with Satan; and Ben Sira, resenting this innovation in doctrine, may here perhaps be rationalising Satan into the *yezer* and denying his existence as a personal tempter. But however this may be, and whatever the exact stage to which the doctrine of the *yezer* may have been carried in Ben Sira's day, this verse may be appealed to in favour of

[1] vv. 15, 11; see the whole context.
[2] LXX. ἐν τῷ καταρᾶσθαι ἀσεβῆ τὸν σατανᾶ αὐτὸς καταρᾶται τὴν ἑαυτοῦ ψυχήν. The Syriac, according to Lagarde's critically edited text, runs thus: 'when the fool curseth him that did not sin against him he is cursing his own soul.' Mr J. H. A. Hart informs me that a very slight alteration here would give 'him that made him to sin' instead of 'him that did not sin against him,' and thus emends the text. The sense then becomes similar to that of the Greek. Edersheim (*in loc.*) believed that the Syriac avoided the plain meaning by a paraphrase; Ryssel (*in loc.*) objects to seeing a motive in the Syriac, and thinks the Greek has a wrong translation, embodying more advanced thought. Of the older authorities, Bretschneider translated τὸν σατανᾶ by the word *calumniator*, which Fritzsche rejected, at the same time not accepting 'Satan.' The latter rendering was defended by Edersheim, and Cheyne inclines to it, quoting as a parallel in meaning Ps. xxxvi. 1, R.V. margin (*Expositor*, series XI., p. 346). The Heb. of the verse, if it should be recovered, would be interesting.

See Taylor, *op. cit.*, p. 147, note 20, for a quotation from Maimonides on the (later) identity of the evil inclination, the adversary (Satan), and the angel of death; also, p. 130, where it is stated that the *yezer* is called 'enemy,' amongst other names, in *Sukkah*, 52 a—b. Edersheim also refers to *Baba Bathra*, 16 a, for the identification of Satan with the evil *yezer*.

116 *The teaching of Ecclesiasticus* [CHAP.

the main contention with which the present investigation is concerned; namely, it emphasises man's responsibility for his own sin, and so far militates against the view that Ben Sira held any doctrine approaching that of original sin. In xxi. 11 (LXX.) occurs the sentence, ὁ φυλάσσων νόμον κατακρατεῖ τοῦ ἐννοήματος αὐτοῦ. The Syriac, however, reads: "he that keepeth the law constrains (oppresses) his *yezer.*" This most probably represents the original, which has not yet been recovered. In that case, "it is unmistakably the so-called rabbinical sense of the term (*yezer*) that meets us here[1]." The idea of the torah as given for an antidote to the evil inclination occurs somewhat frequently in rabbinical literature, as does also the expression 'constrains' or 'masters his *yezer*.'

There remains another passage whose original probably contained the word *yezer*. In xxxvii. 3 a, we read: "O evil inclination (ἐνθύμημα, probably =*yezer*), why wast thou created?" (ἐνεκτίσθης for ἐνεκυλίσθης, by following Syr. and Lat.). The Greek gives a better text here than the Syriac, which reads: "Enemy and evil, to what end were they created?"

These passages have been collected together because they show that, whether or not Ben Sira knew of a doctrine of two *yezers*[2], or of the evil imagination as personified into an external power, he certainly believed an evil disposition to have been inherent in man from the first, and regarded this inclination, which the individual can still coerce by free-will and devotion to the law, as the source of his sinfulness. But so far from any signs of Ben Sira considering this evil nature to have been derived from our first parents' sin, more than one passage which has been mentioned above distinctly implies

---

[1] Porter, *op. cit.*, p. 141.
On the same page Dr Porter discusses the meaning of *yezer* in xxvii. 6, where it had not been suspected. He inclines to the view that the word means there what it does in the passages previously discussed. The Syriac of xvii. 31 (see below, p. 117, n. 2) also contains *yezer*, but its existence in the Hebrew is doubtful.

[2] Analogy with the *Testament of Aser* (I. and V.) and similar passages has suggested the tacit implication of the two *yezers* in Ecclus. xxxiii. 14, 15, taken together with the preceding context. This, however, is only a conjecture. Ben Sira invariably speaks of man as possessing but one inclination, identified with evil.

that he held it to have been originally implanted in man by God[1].

We therefore conclude that Ben Sira was the precursor of the talmudic teaching as to the Fall rather than that of the more serious pseudepigraphic literature of the first century A.D. Although he holds that sin entered into the world as an actuality in Eve's transgression, and also recognises that all men are sinners (viii. 5) and are descended from Adam (xvii. 1), he nevertheless implies that the Fall brought no moral incapacity in its train, no inherited corruption of nature, to diminish man's power of self-determination. If any excuse is offered for human depravity, it is that of our natural and essential frailty referred to in xvii. 30—32[2] and elsewhere; and its ultimate source, or rather its ground in so far as man's will is excepted, is God, not Adam's self-perversion[3].

Ben Sira's teaching as to the introduction of death.

Before we examine the few passages in Ecclesiasticus which deal with the subject of man's mortality, it will be well to glance at the Old Testament teaching on the point.

If it be assumed that the compiler of Gen. ii.—iii. intended to teach that man, so long as he did not sin, possessed the capacity for deathless existence, it is difficult to decide whether he must be taken to imply that human death is a

---

[1] Inasmuch as B. Sira regards man as perfectly enabled to master his *yezer*, he can logically shift the responsibility for sin from God; see xv. 11 ff.

[2] The meaning of the last two of these verses, in the Greek, would seem to be: "Even the sun darkens itself—the brightest thing in the world; how much more, then, frail man!" But the text is corrupt, and the writer's meaning doubtful. The Syriac has (v. 31) "When the sun passeth away from the day, also (*i.e.* then) there cometh darkness: so is the son of man that does not tame his nature (*yezer*), for he is flesh and blood." This rendering was kindly supplied by Mr Hart, who states, however, that the Syriac scarcely gives a translation here.

[3] It is noteworthy that Eve is stated in xxv. 24 to have been the first sinner. Not only does this faithful following of the letter of Gen. make it less likely that B. Sira held any theological doctrine of Original Sin, such as later attached itself exclusively to Adam, but this important verse is only introduced casually; the context shows that the emphasis is laid, not on the introduction of sin and death, but on woman.

punishment for the transgression of Adam and Eve falling not only upon them but also upon their posterity, and that man was originally intended to be immortal; or whether he held man to be mortal by nature, in virtue of his material frame (dust), and originally capable, through access to the tree of life while innocent, of indefinitely prolonging his existence, and in this sense attaining to immortality. Both these views might be said to imply that man was endowed with 'conditional immortality'; and, practically, they are identical. To attribute the latter of them to the compiler of Gen. ii—iii. would involve the supposition that constant recourse would be had to the tree of life to maintain existence, and that this tree was not at first forbidden. The verse iii. 22, however, seems to imply that once to partake of the fruit of the tree of life would confer immortality upon man; and in this case the former of the interpretations seems preferable. A third view of the meaning of these chapters is possible; viz. that according to which man was made essentially mortal, and died in accordance with the course of nature, though perhaps prematurely on account of his sin. The meaning of the story, on this particular point, is not perfectly clear; and considering the non-homogeneity of the narrative, that is to say the surviving echoes of earlier implication which, superimposed like overtones, obscure the fundamental note of the Jahvist's meaning, this is not unnatural. It is the last named view to which the exegesis of these chapters given above in Chap. I. naturally leads. It would seem that death is presupposed, in Gen. iii. 19 (" for dust thou art, etc."), to be a natural consequence of man's earthly origin; in other words, death was decreed for man from the first. Gen. ii. 17 cannot, without violence, be made to contain anything but an unfulfilled threat; removal from access to the tree of life does but make unconditionally necessary what before there was only a supernatural means of avoiding[1]. The verse iii. 22 distinctly implies that immortality was never intended for man at all, and that Jahveh, in removing

[1] And if the tree of life alone stood in the earliest narrative, or if the original tree shared the properties of both that of life and that of knowledge, this road to immortality was originally regarded as closed by divine command.

man from the possibility of acquiring it, was protecting Himself, rather than punishing His creature. The present writer is thus in agreement, as to the teaching of Genesis with regard to death, with the view expressed by Prof. Charles[1]. And the doctrine thus attributed to Genesis is generally admitted to be that of the Old Testament as a whole. Death is treated everywhere as the inevitable outcome of natural human limitations. Psalmists sometimes speak of premature death, never of death in itself, as being a punishment; it is shortness of life, rather than liability to death, which is, in the Old Testament, the wages of sin. In the Talmud and the pseudepigraphic books various opinions as to the cause of death are found; these will be mentioned, however, in their place.

It may be assumed, then, that there is no indication of the view that death is a consequence of our first parents' sin in Hebrew literature of earlier date than Ecclesiasticus; and the teaching of this book must now be examined.

The only perfectly explicit and unambiguous statement on the question is that contained in xxv. 24, a verse which has already been examined for its doctrine of the introduction of sin. The words καὶ δι' αὐτὴν ἀποθνήσκομεν πάντες directly assert the sin of Eve to have been the *cause* of death to the race. It is true that the death here spoken of has been said to be *mors religiosa* as opposed to *mors naturalis*[2]; but this opinion was surely suggested rather by the supposed contradiction[3] between this verse and those about to be discussed than by the contents of the verse itself.

An important passage for the estimation of Ben Sira's teaching with regard to death is xiv. 17 b: ἡ γὰρ διαθήκη ἀπ' αἰῶνος θανάτῳ ἀποθανῇ. An ambiguity arises here in consequence of the possibility of assigning to ἡ διαθήκη ἀπ' αἰῶνος either of two meanings: (1) an original, predetermined, divine appointment of death to man as belonging to his essential nature, or (2) the decree proclaimed to Adam and Eve, whereby death was threatened and denounced as a

---

[1] *The Apocalypse of Baruch*, XXIII. 4, note.
[2] Rähiger, *Ethice librorum apocr. Vet. Test.*
[3] First asserted by Bretschneider, *Liber Jesu Siracidae Graece*, in loc.

consequence of their transgression. Some writers have considered the former of these meanings to be alone admissible, although ἀπ' αἰῶνος is commonly used in the sense of 'from the beginning' (of the race) or 'from of old' (cf. xvii. 12; xliv. 2, 18; Gen. vi. 4; Tob. iv. 12 &c.). But the original Hebrew of this passage, contained in the Cambridge fragments, has the common phrase *ḥōḳ 'ōlām* ('perpetual decree'), which perhaps describes a law of empirical observation equally well as a decree announced by authority. In any case it would be perfectly applicable to the pronouncement to Adam and Eve that disobedience would be punished by death; and the obvious reference to Gen. ii. 17 (lit. 'expiring they shall expire,' an alteration of 'dying thou shalt die'), makes this interpretation overwhelmingly preferable. It would thus seem more probable that in this passage the writer is attributing human death to the disobedience of our first parents than that he regards it as in accordance with the foreordained counsel of God. The latter doctrine is indeed found exceptionally in ancient rabbinical writings[1], and *might* have been held by Ben Sira; but the context does not favour the view that it is intended here. Nor is any such teaching *necessarily* contained in the opening verses of chap. xvii. The whole passage presumably deals with matters of human history, and therefore a reference to God's original counsel is not to be expected.

The verse xl. 11 has also been regarded as implying the doctrine that man was originally intended to be mortal. But it may quite as easily allude to the state of things which actually holds as to one which might have been originally determined. The context here is not such as to lead us to expect a universal proposition so much as the statement of an empirical fact; and in any case the passage would seem to have too little of the nature of a doctrinal assertion to form the basis of an argument[2].

It is thus doubtful whether, as some writers have thought[3], we are to see two doctrines as to the introduction of death

---

[1] See Edersheim, *Life and Times*, &c., I. p. 166.
[2] xli. 3 is similarly ambiguous.
[3] *e.g.* Prof. Charles, *loc. cit.*

in Ecclesiasticus. The passages which have been taken to imply the view that man was originally intended to be mortal are scarcely conclusive, on account of their ambiguity. But it is by no means impossible that Ben Sira gives expression to divergent views. Whether he entirely breaks with the traditional Old Testament view or not, there is no doubt that xxv. 24 furnishes the first appearance of such an exegesis of Gen. iii. as finds in it an account of a Fall attended with universal consequences for the race, other than exclusion from Paradise. Ben Sira supplies evidence that, in his day at least, the way was being prepared for such an interpretation of the Paradise-story as eventually led to the doctrine of Original Sin. The result here reached is that the author of Ecclesiasticus taught that death was a consequence of the sin of the first parents of the race; and that, whilst seeing in this transgression the first of the series of human sins, he suspected no causal connexion between the first and the succeeding members of that series. In the literally rendered words of xxv. 24, the Fall was the *cause* of death, but only the *beginning* of sin.

NOTE. The Book of Tobit, which, though probably not written in Palestine, and containing a developed demonology somewhat suggestive of Persian influences, has much in common in its thought and ethical teaching with Ecclus., may be referred to as strongly emphasising the doctrine, illustrated of course in other Jewish writings, that all evil is due to sin (iii. 1—6: xiv. 4 ff., 15). The existence of this belief would aid the growth of a doctrine of the Fall.

CHAPTER VI.

THE PREPARATION FOR THE DOCTRINE OF THE FALL IN ALEXANDRIAN JUDAISM.

THE literature of Alexandrian Judaism[1], or such of it, at least, as was theological in nature, owed its distinctive character to the fact that it was intended to bring the teaching of the Old Testament into harmony with Greek philosophy, and to present that teaching so as to commend it to men of Hellenic culture. We should therefore expect its treatment of the problem of the origin of human sin and death to show signs of Hellenic influence and to contain elements not represented in the writings of Palestinian Jews. Alexandrian-Jewish literature did not, perhaps, exert much influence upon the teaching of the Rabbis of the mishnic and talmudic periods, though it contributed somewhat to the shaping of subsequent Christian speculation concerning the fall of man.

The Sibylline Oracles.

It is probable that, through the unfortunate loss of part of Book III. of the Sibylline Oracles, we have been accidentally deprived of a glimpse at the ideas of an Egyptian Jew, practically contemporary with the Palestinian Ben Sira, with regard to the scriptural narrative of the fall of man. For the date of this book of the Oracles, or of at least the greater

---

[1] On the general features of this literature see Schürer, *Jewish People*, E. T. Div. ii. vol. III.; Drummond, *Philo Judaeus*, vol. I. ; Art. *Alexandria* in Hastings' *Dict. of the Bible*; Bois, *Sur les origines de la Philosophie Judéo-Alexandrine* ; Herriot, *Philon le Juif*; also the older work of Dähne.

part of it, is generally regarded as known with certainty, and to be about the middle of the second century B.C. Its opening, which appears to be missing, probably dealt with the history of the early chapters of Genesis.

In their present state the Sibylline Oracles are but very distantly concerned with our subject. The fragments preserved in Theophilus, *ad Autol.* II. 36, called in the editions Books I. and II., emphasise the infirmity of the physical nature of man. The flesh is unable to see and know God; error in life, such as idolatry, is due to ignorance, but ignorance is in turn due to a fault in the will. Neither man's sensibility nor his understanding, therefore, is the source of his evil desires and his frailty.

The date of the composition of these fragments is not so definitely assignable as that of Book III.; but if they should be the prooemium to that book, which is possible, we cannot but regret all the more the loss of the author's comments on the biblical account of the first transgression.

[The fragments of Aristobulus, who is called, by writers who believe in the genuineness of those fragments, the founder of the Judaeo-Alexandrian philosophy, preserved in Eusebius, *Praep. Evang.* VIII. 10 and XIII. 12, contain no allusion to the origin of sin or of death.]

The Book of Wisdom.

The question of the exact date and the authorship of the Book of Wisdom is probably insoluble. There are very strong grounds, however, for believing it to be not only independent of the writings of Philo, but also prior to them. Like the earlier Palestinian work of Ben Sira, the Book of Wisdom closely follows the Old Testament and uses it as its own theological basis. But its interpretation of Scripture is influenced by its author's eclectic use of the teaching of several schools of Greek Philosophy.

This is seen, for instance, in his view of the origin of death. If his doctrine is here rightly understood, Pseudo-Solomon nowhere states definitely that *physical* death is the consequence of Adam's sin; on the contrary, his Platonic conception of the soul and its relation to the body makes it probable that he did not regard the mortality of mankind as an anomaly to be accounted for by introduction from without. His teaching in this respect is identical with that of Philo. It is true that the writer of Wisdom maintains that death was not the original purpose of God for man (i. 13), but that it entered into the world by 'the envy of the devil' (ii. 23). The death, however, of which Pseudo-Solomon thus speaks is certainly ethical death, or, in the language of later theology, 'second death.' In his opening chapters, he is attacking the practical consequences of the Epicurean doctrine of the mortality of the soul for the good and the bad alike. He argues that it is only the wicked who actually perish; the righteous, after they have 'seemed to die,' really enjoy a blessed immortality. Some writers have taken various figurative hyperbolisms of Pseudo-Solomon (*e.g.* i. 11 ἀναιρεῖ ψυχήν, iii. 16 ἀφανισθήσεται, iv. 19, v. 14) too literally, and have seen in them assertions of the physical annihilation of the wicked. This view is precluded by the fact that elsewhere consciousness, memory and fear are ascribed to these souls after their death or destruction. The death, then, which the devil is said to have brought into the world, is primarily, if not entirely, ethical death. The question remains whether 'death' for the writer of the Book of Wisdom may *include* physical death. In the passage ii. 23, 24[1], it seems impossible that physical death can be present to the writer's thought. The foregoing context and the antithesis with iii. 1 ff. require θάνατος to be used exclusively of spiritual or second death; the deprivation, that is, of a blessed immortality. Whether it is similarly excluded in the remaining passage (i. 12 ff.[2]) is

---

[1] R.V. "Because God created man for incorruption, and made him an image of his own proper being; But by the envy of the devil death entered into the world, and they that are his portion make trial thereof."

[2]   i 12 μὴ ζηλοῦτε θάνατον ἐν πλάνῃ ζωῆς ὑμῶν,
        μηδὲ ἐπισπᾶσθε ὄλεθρον ἔργοις χειρῶν ὑμῶν·
  12 *a* ὅτι ὁ θεὸς θάνατον οὐκ ἐποίησεν,
     b οὐδὲ τέρπεται ἐπ' ἀπωλείᾳ ζώντων·
  13 *a* ἔκτισεν γὰρ εἰς τὸ εἶναι τὰ πάντα,
     b καὶ σωτήριοι αἱ γενέσεις τοῦ κόσμου,
     c καὶ οὐκ ἔστιν ἐν αὐταῖς φάρμακον ὀλέθρου.

a question more difficult to decide. In this place also, as has already been observed, the writer is dealing with the final death of the wicked soul. The thought of physical death is not therefore directly relevant to his purpose. But the first three clauses of the fourteenth verse seem to make it necessary to assume that he has so far relaxed concentration upon his ruling idea as to have introduced parenthetically, so to speak, that of bodily mortality in a subsidiary degree.

From 13 *b* it may be inferred that τὰ πάντα in 14 *a* is at least as comprehensive as the world of animate beings, and from 14 *b* that it is not more so. Hence εἶναι is equivalent to ζῆν, unless, by a further extension of the writer's tendency to endow physical concepts with an ethical sense, it is to be regarded as the opposite to *male perire*[1] rather than *perire*, so that the first three clauses of the verse amount to no more than an expansion of the thought of Gen. i. 31, "and God saw everything that He had made, and, behold, it was very good." In any case it can only be physical life with which Pseudo-Solomon regards creatures other than man to be endowed; indeed, in ii. 23, he makes man's conditional endowment with spiritual immortality to be identical with the creation in God's image ascribed to him in the Old Testament, and therefore to be the feature distinguishing him from the rest of the creation. It is by no means necessary to assume that the author of Wisdom, in such passages as these, must needs have been confronted with all the consequences of his statements, or have been careful clearly and accurately to expound his thought, or even have been absolutely consistent with himself. Nevertheless, there seems to be no sufficient reason, in this case, to assume that in i. 14 he is making any assertion which would conflict with the statement made in ii. 23. If this be so, all that the passage need be taken to mean is something such as this: just as God appointed to man a destiny of happy immortality and did not Himself ordain the eternal death by which that destiny is forfeited; so the world of lower created things was endowed with the power to perpetuate and maintain itself, each thing enjoying its natural span, without any inherent element of destruction to disturb the

---

[1] Osiander, quoted by Grimm, *op. cit.*, S. 62.

Creator's original appointment. It would seem that any other explanation of this verse involves the necessity of charging Pseudo-Solomon with serious confusion and looseness of thought; a charge which has indeed been made by more than one commentator, but perhaps a little hastily[1].

If the view here adopted be correct, the timely and natural death of living things is regarded in this passage as involved in their original constitution, and as consistent with their having been created εἰς τὸ εἶναι. So far as the lower creatures are concerned, the ultimate cause of physical death is therefore attributed to God. No direct statement is afforded us of the author's belief with regard to the case of man. But if it be legitimate to form an opinion at all as to his position, the balance of probability favours the supposition that he held that man too was intended to be mortal, and that physical death was no introduction of the devil or consequence of Adam's sin. For, in the first place, this view would be the more consistent with that which has been deduced above with regard to the case of the lower creatures; secondly, the belief might more easily than the opposite view be derived from Genesis[2]; and, lastly, the author's philosophical opinions about the soul and its relation to the body would go far to prevent him from regarding physical death as an anomaly to be accounted for[3].

Physical or bodily death is, of course, assumed as the

[1] Grimm dismisses a view akin to that advocated above in the following words: "Wollte man endlich mit *Lyran.* τὸ εἶναι von dem Bestand und der Erhaltung der *Gattungen* verstehen, so würde der Satz keine Anwendung auf die Menschheit erleiden, bei welcher es sich kraft des Zusammenhangs um das Fortleben der *Einzelnen* handelt." But it is difficult to see how this verse could in any case be introduced otherwise than as an illustration of the general principle that the creation, as it left the hand of God, did not contain within itself the germ of its own destruction. The verse is valid as an illustration, and was hardly intended to be a complete analogy or a major premiss.

[2] See above, p. 117 ff.

[3] Pseudo-Solomon believed in the preexistence of the soul (viii. 19, 20), in its constituting the real self (cf. xv. 11), in its immortality (iii. 1—4), and in its being, during this life, 'weighed down by a corruptible body' (ix. 15; cf. iv. 10—14). Hence it is probable that he would regard physical death, consisting in the separation of immortal soul and perishable body, as a good thing, and indeed part of God's original design for man, rather than as an evil introduced from without.

inevitable lot of all, and in vii. 1 its inheritance from Adam is definitely stated; but there is no hint that it is a consequence of Adam's sin.

The interesting question whether the writer of Wisdom regarded the natural world as marred by the Fall, and subjected to vanity in consequence of it, must be decided by the exegesis of this same verse. Perhaps the only becoming attitude towards the question is one of scepticism. Had the verse run (i. 14) "and the generative powers of the world *were* healthsome, and there *was* no poison of destruction in them," the inference would have been suggested that Pseudo-Solomon regarded the course of the world as no longer what it was intended to be. But in 14 c he uses ἔστιν; εἰσίν is therefore to be supplied in the preceding clause. Either, then, he is describing the organic world as it actually is, in which case he does not recognise a cosmical effect of human sin, but regards "Nature, red in tooth and claw" as Nature according to God's appointment; or else he is representing it as it essentially and ideally *is*, but as it actually only *was*. The latter meaning seems to be equally possible as the former, for, as Grimm points out[1], ἐν αὐταῖς may be construed either by *unter ihnen* or by *in ihnen*, i.e. in their essence; it would imply that, if there is an element of imperfection in the world, it is accidental and not essential to its course. Instead of attempting to decide between the two alternatives, one may perhaps venture to doubt whether they presented themselves to Pseudo-Solomon's thought[2].

It may be taken as quite possible, then, for all that is said in the Book of Wisdom to the contrary, that its writer did not regard the bodily mortality of man as introduced by the sin of our first parents and the initiative of the devil; and that he did not embrace, if he was aware of, the idea which we meet with in St Paul, and in other Jewish writers, of a frustration of the original destiny of Nature resulting from the same cause. No more definite statements than these, perhaps, can be hazarded with reasonable certainty.

[1] *Op. cit.*, S. 62—63.
[2] On the notion that the Fall affected Nature, a belief which had grown up before Pseudo-Solomon's time, see below, Chaps. VII–X.

Returning now to the doctrine of ii. 24, that spiritual or eternal death entered into the human world through the envy of the devil, we are at once struck with the writer's advance upon Old Testament history. It has generally been assumed that his teaching is based upon the narrative of Gen. iii. and refers to that context, the devil being identified with the serpent of Paradise; and it has frequently been stated that we meet here with the earliest instance of that identification[1]. The truth of the last assertion depends upon the date of the *Apocalypse of Abraham*, which as yet remains uncertain, and perhaps of that of other pseudepigrapha to be mentioned in a later chapter. It is most probable that the devil is here identified with the serpent of the Paradise-story, though this has been questioned[2]. But the ascription of envy to him as his motive in ruining man suggests that we here have a fusion of the legend of the fallen angels who corrupted the world in the age of the deluge with the story of the loss of Paradise,—a legend which will subsequently call for detailed notice. The 'developments' of Old Testament teaching contained in this passage are derived from traditions elaborated in Jewish

---

[1] The assertion of Grätz (*Geschichte der Juden*, III. S. 444), that Wisd. ii. 24 is a Christian interpolation, has perhaps never been taken seriously.

[2] When M. Bois (*op. cit.* pp. 296, 297) questions this, and sees in the devil (ch. ii. 24) rather the instigator of Cain than the tempter of Eve, or at any rate the equal possibility of either identification, he would seem to overlook the fact that Genesis mentions or assumes no such instigator in the former case; and that the context here requires 'death' to be used in such a sense that it is only applicable to the wicked. When he sees, in x. 1, 2, the implication that "le péché d'Adam a été sans importance grâce à l'intervention de la Sagesse," and asserts "Le premier pécheur de marque et de portée que cite Pseudo-Salomon dans sa revue historique, c'est Caïn," he would seem to be confounding Adam's personal repentance (generally supposed to be meant by Wisdom's 'deliverance' of him 'out of his transgression') with innocuousness of his sin to his descendants, which is what Pseudo-Solomon must be taken to have affirmed before the above conclusion could be drawn. That Adam's sin is passed over very lightly in this passage (ch. x.) is both true and noteworthy; and it is probable that when (v. 4) the deluge is represented as having been caused by Cain, the writer has in view the legend based on Gen. vi. 1—4, which he interpreted as referring to the Cainites, and which, there is reason to believe, had been, until his day, the starting-point for a theory as to the cause of the universality of sin upon earth. But when M. Bois adds that Cain "est mis en antithèse avec le juste Adam," he seems to be venturing further than is legitimate in expounding Pseudo-Solomon's meaning.

literature earlier than the Book of Wisdom. The pronounced (relative) dualism implied in its conception of Satan is, moreover, an advance upon previous Alexandrian thought[1]. Finally, the writer's treatment of the serpent is widely different from that of Philo, by whom it is allegorised into a symbol for temptation arising from the sensuous nature (ἡδονή)[2], and in whose system a personification of what is called 'the principle of evil' finds no place[3].

It only remains now to inquire whether the Book of Wisdom contains any teaching which might be regarded as an anticipation of the later doctrine of original sin; any hint of transmitted sinfulness of nature derived from the fall of the first parents of the race. The question does not involve lengthy discussion, inasmuch as the few passages which have any bearing upon it are not obscure.

In viii. 20 Solomon is represented as having entered into a 'body undefiled' in consequence of the 'goodness' of his soul in its previous state of existence (μᾶλλον δὲ ἀγαθὸς ὢν ἦλθον εἰς σῶμα ἀμίαντον). Though his body was admittedly derived from Adam by natural descent, and inherited the mortal nature common to all men (vii. 1), it was nevertheless 'undefiled' when his soul was first united with it. The force of the word ἀμίαντον is not diminished by the fact that the writer professed the spiritualism characteristic of the Alexandrian school; for he nowhere teaches that the body, or that

---

[1] See Zeller, *Philosophie der Griechen*, 2 Aufl. III. 2.
The identification of Satan with the serpent of Gen. may be accounted for, like the earlier stages in the growth of the conception of Satan, as a natural development of Hebrew demonology determined by the needs of increasingly active speculation on theodicy. It is but a small step from the rôle assigned to Satan in 1 Chron. xxi. 1. But this particular development, and indeed the later stages of Satanology in general, may also have been aided by the stimulus of contact with the more highly elaborated beliefs of Persia. See Stave, *Einfluss des Parsismus auf das Judenthum*, S. 246 ff. That Ahriman took the form of a serpent is a tradition—one knows not of what antiquity—found in the Bundahesch (see S. B. E. v. 17).
[2] *De Mundi Opif.* 56.
[3] Dähne (*Alex.-Jüd. Religionsphilosophie*, II. S. 172) supposed διάβολος here to refer to the serpent as interpreted by Philo, and not to the personal Satan. But (1) φθόνῳ διαβόλου would then be meaningless; (2) the conception of Satan as a personal tempter of man was known long before the time of Pseudo-Solomon.

matter in general, is essentially or actively evil. If any conclusion be drawn, therefore, from the verse in question, it must be that Pseudo-Solomon knew of no doctrine of an inherent and necessary sinfulness propagated by descent from Adam[1]. Yet though the idea of a universal taint of sin, derived from the Fall, is excluded, that of an inborn and hereditary sinful tendency in particular peoples is not foreign to the Book of Wisdom. The justification for this statement is not to be sought in x. 4, where a causal connection is asserted between Cain's crime and the deluge; because the evil influence of Cain upon his posterity, dwelt upon in other writings of this time, might result solely from force of example and intercourse[2], and does not require the presupposition of inherited viciousness of character. Its proof is rather to be derived from xii. 10, 11[3], where inborn and transmitted corruption, caused by the cursing of their ancestor by Noah[4], is unmistakeably attributed to the Canaanites. A commentator has seen in this verse an 'adumbration' of the doctrine of Original Sin[5]. It would be more accurate to say a 'preparation for it.' The possibility, and indeed the actuality, of transmission of a depraved nature by physical descent is plainly asserted; but the one essential feature of the doctrine of Original Sin, derivation of a universal taint from Adam's transgression, is altogether wanting. The Book of Wisdom shows us, in fact, all the collected materials for the elaboration of the doctrine; the introduction from without of evil and

---

[1] In agreement with this conclusion are the facts (1) that in x. 1 Adam's transgression is mentioned without a hint of entailed effects, and, in so far as it concerned himself at least, as remediable; (2) that man's natural frailty is admitted, as well as the necessity of divine assistance for the acquisition of wisdom (viii. 21), though no allusion is made to inborn universal sinfulness in order to account for it.

[2] Josephus actually adopts this view (*Antt.* I. 2, 2).

[3] οὐκ ἀγνοῶν ὅτι πονηρὰ ἡ γένεσις αὐτῶν
καὶ ἔμφυτος ἡ κακία αὐτῶν,
καὶ ὅτι οὐ μὴ ἀλλαγῇ ὁ λογισμὸς αὐτῶν εἰς τὸν αἰῶνα,
σπέρμα γὰρ ἦν κατηραμένον ἀπ' ἀρχῆς.

The phrase ἔμφυτος κακία is noteworthy. φύσει in xiii. 1 seems simply to mean 'unassisted by Wisdom.' See below, p. 144.

[4] Gen. ix. 25.

[5] Deane, *The Book of Wisdom, in loc.*

(spiritual) death, the transgression of 'the protoplast,' the local actuality of transmitted viciousness, the universal frailty of the race; the data all are here: but they are not yet elaborated into a single generalisation.

Philo.

The mingling of biblical exegesis with Greek philosophy, of which the Wisdom of Solomon and the *Book of the Secrets of Enoch* furnish examples, is developed in Philo into an elaborate system of apologetics. But when we speak of Philo's work as a system we do not imply that it presents us with a systematic and unified body of theology. In the first place, though its object is to present to the educated Greek mind an apology for Mosaism, it is almost as much concerned with psychology and ethics as with theology proper; and in the second place, it is a collection of very heterogeneous, and often inconsistent, elements, entirely lacking the unity of a theological system in the true sense of that term. Of course the instrument by which Philo adapts the teaching of the Scriptures, in whose divine inspiration he devoutly believed, to Hellenic thought, is the method of allegorical interpretation: a method which lay ready to hand, inasmuch as it had previously been used both by the Greek philosopher and the Jewish exegete. That this apologetic expedient should be needed in attempting a rational justification of the biblical history, is itself a matter of interest. It implies that the literal interpretation of the early scriptural narratives was now as impossible to the philosophically educated Alexandrian Jew as that of Greek mythology had become, long before, to Xenophanes or Plato. In Philo's exposition, what was originally intended for history is very largely resolved into figurative psychology; and it is not always easy to estimate how far the events described in the Book of Genesis were regarded by him as in any way actual, over and above their repesenting, in a symbolical manner, universal processes in the life of the human soul.

We may feel certain, however, that Philo attaches historical reality to Adam, and does not mean the account which Genesis gives of him to be taken solely as a description of the 'masculine element' of man's mind. His treatment of the story of the Fall, therefore, has an anthropological, as well as a psychological, interest for us. This story is expanded and embellished by Philo after the manner of the Palestinian haggadist. Indeed Philo used the exegetical methods of the rabbinical schools as well as that which he made peculiarly his own, and was well acquainted with the traditions of the recognised interpreters of the Law.

Philo's general anthropology need only be reviewed here in so far as it is necessary to the understanding of his lines of teaching with regard to the origin and universality of human sinfulness.

Man's soul is held to consist of two constituents, a rational and an irrational part. Of these, the latter is earthly in origin, and mortal like the body. The higher element ($νοῦς$) was also earthly and mortal in the first man until God breathed into him the breath of life, when it became rational and immortal, an image of God, and in fact an emanation ($ἀπόσπασμα$) from Him. This divine element in the rational part of the soul is therefore pre-existent; indeed it belongs to the class of incorporeal beings which people the air, some of which have descended to earth and assumed a bodily nature. Philo does not reconcile his doctrine of emanation, which he considered to have been taught by Moses in Gen. i., with that of the pre-existence of the soul as an incorporeal being, and its descent into the body, which he derives from Plato and reads into Mosaism (Gen. vi. 1–4). As regards the cause of the descent of souls, which he identifies with the demons of philosophers and the angels of Moses[1], he vacillates. In *De Plant. Noe*, 4[2], part of the choir of souls are assigned to human bodies apparently in accordance with a universal

---

[1] *De Gigant.* 2, etc.

[2] τὰς μὲν γὰρ εἰσκρίνεσθαι λόγος ἔχει σώμασι θνητοῖς καὶ κατά τινας ὡρισμένας περιόδους ἀπαλλάττεσθαι πάλιν, τὰς δὲ θειοτέρας κατασκευῆς λαχούσας ἅπαντος ἀλογεῖν τοῦ γῆς χωρίου, ἀνωτάτω δ' εἶναι πρὸς αὐτῷ τῷ αἰθέρι τὰς καθαρωτάτας....

[Cohn and Wendland's text has been used in citations.]

In *De Confus. Ling.* 17, the souls of the wisest and best men, such as Abraham, are also represented as having come to earth in a manner, and for a purpose, to which no blame attaches.

cosmic law as in the *Timaeus* (42 ff.); but in *De Somn.*[1] and *De Gigant.* 3, such souls voluntarily descended because they were filled with a sensuous longing for the corporeal state, implying something of the nature of a fall while yet pure spirits, as in the *Phaedrus*. One thus expects in Philo a theory of a fall of all souls in a previous state of existence. But here his vacillation becomes confusion. He not only remains silent as to how purely spiritual beings, whose impeccability he definitely asserts elsewhere[2], could become ensnared and entangled with the things of sense; but, after speaking of evil angels as if they were a class of souls which had sinned, he abruptly tells us that these are wicked men who have 'assumed the name of angels[3].' Nevertheless Philo nearly always treats the soul as pre-existent and as not at home in the corruptible body. His teaching, or rather one side of it, implies and demands a pre-mundane fall; but he stops short of definitely propounding such a doctrine as was later developed, within the Christian Church, by Origen.

We turn now to his treatment of the story of the sin of Adam and its consequences. In the first place we have to set forth Philo's teaching as to man's original estate, the constitution and qualities of unfallen Adam.

(*a*) The scriptural statement that man was made in the image of God is of fundamental importance for Philo. But it is curiously elaborated in his hands. The similitude between man and his Maker is only affirmed with regard to the mind[4]. It is not asserted of the actual or natural first man, but of the generic man[5] (a conceptual abstraction or a Platonic 'idea' of mankind), and, still more exclusively, only of the 'true' or 'heavenly' man, the pure νοῦς, free from any admixture of sense. This true, or heavenly, man is again

---

[1] τούτων τῶν ψυχῶν, αἱ μὲν κατίασιν ἐνδεθησόμεναι σώμασι θνητοῖς, ὅσαι προσγειότατοι καὶ φιλοσώματοι.

[2] *De Confus. Ling.* 35: κακίας δὲ ἀμέτοχοι μέν εἰσιν οὗτοι, τὸν ἀκήρατον καὶ εὐδαίμονα κλῆρον ἐξ ἀρχῆς λαχοῦσαι καὶ τῷ συμφορῶν ἀνηνύτων οὐκ ἐνδεθεῖσαι χωρίῳ, σώματι....

[3] *De Gigant.* 4: οὗτοί εἰσιν οἱ πονηροί, τὸ ἀγγέλων ὄνομα ὑποδυόμενοι....

[4] *De Mundi Opificio*, 23.

[5] *Ibid.* 46.

an ideal or thought, and is said to be an image, not directly of God, but of His word or shadow[1], the archetype of creation, and the instrument (ὄργανον) by which creation was produced. Thus the actual Adam only bears the divine image 'after a manner[2],' or, as is more often asserted, not at all. We may notice, by the way, that Adam is said to have been at first without the νοῦς which, as we have seen, Philo identifies with the 'breath of life' imparted to him by the Creator, so that the doctrine of the pre-existence of the soul is for the time lost sight of. Philo indeed finds it hard to serve two masters. He is now and again led, by his concern to be faithful to Moses, into forgetfulness that he is at the same time a disciple of Plato; but more frequently his Hebrew mode of thought gives place before his preference for the Greek.

(*b*) With regard to the physical excellence of Adam's unfallen state, Philo speaks much in the strain of Palestinian haggada, and is a witness to the existence in Alexandria of many of the fancies met with in the talmudic writings. The tendency to exalt Adam and his first estate, a tendency developed very strongly from this time onwards in Jewish, and afterwards in Christian, literature, had already manifested itself in earlier writings; and it appears to some extent in Philo. Thus, at the moment of his appearance, the first man found all the requisites of life prepared for him[3]. Physically, he was perfect; being superior to all his descendants as regards beauty[4], and endowed with gigantic stature[5]. He had converse with incorporeal beings, higher than himself, with whom he associated in a state of happiness[6]. He was free from all disease and affliction[7]; possessed extraordinary powers of perception[8], so as to be able to perceive 'the natures, essences and operations which exist in heaven'; and was in enjoyment of the most perfect human bliss[9].

---

[1] *Leg. Alleg.* III. 31; *Quis rer. div. haer.* 48; *Quaest. et sol. in Gen.* I. 4.
[2] οὗ τρόπον τινὰ γενόμενος εἰκών... (Mangey, II. 440); *De Nobilit.* 3.
[3] *De Mundi Opif.* 26.   [4] *Ibid.* 47.
[5] *Quaest. et sol. in Gen.* I. 32.
[6] *De Mundi Opif.* 50.   [7] *Ibid.* 52.
[8] *Ibid.* 52; *Quaest. et sol. in Gen.* I. 32.
[9] *Ibid.*

(c) When we come to examine Philo's teaching with regard to Adam's *moral* condition before his transgression, we find that extremely little is said upon the matter. In this respect he made no advance upon Rabbinism. Such passages as seem to bear upon the point speak of Adam in the allegorical and psychological sense; that is to say, as a symbol for $νοῦς$ as distinguished from $αἴσθησις$. If they imply anything at all of actual history, it would only be that, before his transgression, the first man was morally neutral, a mixed being, neither good nor bad, existing in a state described as $μέσος$ or $γυμνός$[1]. When the means of education into a state of virtuousness were offered to him, the good and the evil course being presented as alternatives to his choice, he fell from his state of innocence[2].

But if Philo says little, directly, of the original state of the first individual man, he has much to say with regard to the essential moral nature of man in general, as determined by the constitution which he has received at the hand of his Maker; and this, of course, amounts to the same thing. His teaching in this connexion is, in the main, in agreement with that of orthodox Judaism. It will be shown presently that he did not hold any such view of the fall of Adam as would attribute to it the cause of the sinful tendency of his descendants.

(d) Nor does he regard physical death as the inherited consequence of Adam's sin in Paradise; in other words, immortality, except of the higher part of the soul, was not implied in the original or unfallen state of the first earth-born man. As to his body and the irrational part of his soul, man is 'mortal by nature[3],' and related to the rest of the physical world. Since bodily existence is not a good, physical death is not an evil, thing[4]. The death which Adam brought upon himself was ethical; it was the death of 'the soul buried in evil,' and consisted rather in the firmer union, than in the

---

[1] See *Leg. Alleg.* I. 30, II. 15, 16; *Quaest. et sol. in Gen.* I. 39, 40.
[2] *De Nobilit.* 3, etc.
[3] *De Mundi Opif.* 46 and 51; *De Abrahamo*, 11.
[4] *Quaest. et sol. in Gen.* I. 76: quod nec sensibilis ista vita bona est, neque mors mala.

separation, of soul and body. Physical death is therefore, as we should expect in Philo's system, the necessary consequence of corporeality, and can only be a result of a fall if that fall occurred in a previous life and be identified with the soul's embodiment. Such death, therefore, is no anomaly in the world-order. The good do not really die[1] and the wicked are dead even while they live[2].

The only consequences which Philo attributes to Adam's sin are, therefore, the toils and labours, the loss of the untroubled and happy life in Eden, spoken of in the narrative of Genesis[3].

(*e*) In his account of the first transgression itself, Philo usually interprets the serpent to be a figure for sensuous pleasure. That 'the old poisonous and earth-born reptile' spoke with a human voice is not a 'fabulous invention' but shadows forth an allegorical truth[4]. That the serpent approaches the woman, who then addresses the man, represents the appeal of pleasure to the senses prior to the influence of the senses over the reason[5]. Such an interpretation of the narrative implies that human sin originated solely within man himself as constituted by his Maker. Unlike Pseudo-Solomon, Philo nowhere introduces the doctrine of a personal tempter; in the passage *Quaest. et sol. in Gen.* I. 36 the words *diabolus in ore serpentis* of the translation given in Aucher's edition are an unhappy interpolation, and do not occur in the Armenian version.

It remains now to unfold Philo's views with regard to man's natural constitution and the source of his sinfulness.

---

[1] *Quaest. et sol. in Gen.* I. 16. Cf. the teaching of *Wisdom*, above; and see also *Leg. Alleg.* I. 33.

[2] *Quaest. et sol. in Gen.* I. 16, 56; III. 9.

[3] *De Mundi Opif.* 60. Cf. *De Nobilit.* 3 (here mortality is regarded as a result of Adam's sin, but the word is ambiguous in meaning, as will be seen from the context).

[4] *De Mundi Opif.* 56. Cf. *Leg. Alleg.* II. 18, 26; III. 23. *De Agricult.* 22; *Quaest. et sol. in Gen.* I. 31, etc.

Josephus, for all his dependence on Philo, here adopts the literal view, which is also taken in the *Book of Jubilees*, which, possibly, he knew and followed.

[5] In thus making the Fall-story an allegorical account of the general origin of the individual's sin, Philo is perhaps followed by S. Paul in Rom. vii. 9–11.

We have seen that, according to one line of his thought, man's bodily or phenomenal nature is due to the yielding of his soul, in a previous and purely spiritual existence, to the attractions of the sensible world. For any disabilities consequent upon such a change, the soul would of course be entirely responsible. But though Philo starts to establish such a doctrine of man, we have seen that he abruptly abandons the attempt, probably because he shrank from attributing moral evil to pure spirits. He falls back, for his predominant doctrine, upon the Mosaic view of man's origin, according to which both the soul and the body are the direct creation of God. But while he does so he is sorely hampered by his ineradicable belief that phenomenality is the source of moral evil; and he is always most anxious to avoid the implication that evil is ultimately traceable to God. He would have been spared much trouble and confusion if he could have clearly distinguished between the supposition that corporeality or phenomenality supplies the possibility for evil and the idea that such corporeality involves the necessity of evil.

This, however, he was unable wholly to do; and we consequently find our exposition of his views again rendered difficult by his vacillation. Thus, in some passages, it is implied that the bodily nature of man inevitably involves sin[1]. The fall of Adam and Eve is in fact said to be a necessary outcome of the instability which inheres in things material[2]. But such writing is quite exceptional. Philo's normal and predominant teaching is that the body is that part of man to which sin attaches only in the sense that it is an impediment to the reason and to the pursuit of wisdom, and indeed is to be regarded as a prison or a tomb; sin has nevertheless its real seat in the mind or reason[3]. Irrational

---

[1] *De Vita Mosis*, III. 17: ὅτι παντὶ γεννητῷ...συμφυὲς τὸ ἁμαρτάνειν. *De Profug.* 12: ...τὸ κακίας σύμβολον, ἣν ἀεὶ δεῖ ζῆν ἐν τῷ θνητῷ γένει παρ' ἀνθρώποις. *Quaest. et sol. in Gen.* I. 43: Initium praevaricandi peccandique in legem facit imperfecta et prava (natura) femina. See also *Leg. Alleg.* III. 14.

[2] *De Mundi Opif.* 53: Ἐπεὶ δ' οὐδὲν τῶν ἐν γενέσει βέβαιον, τροπὰς δὲ καὶ μεταβολὰς ἀναγκαίως τὰ θνητὰ δέχεται, ἐχρῆν καὶ τὸν πρῶτον ἄνθρωπον ἀπολαῦσαί τινος κακοπραγίας.

[3] *Quaest. et sol. in Gen.* I. 13; II. 12, 18.

Philo teaches that the passions are "bastards and strangers to the mind and

creatures are incapable of wickedness for the very reason that they are irrational¹. Even the senses *can* be pure². Man, in fact, according to the general tenour of Philo's anthropology, is a mixed creature, between good and evil. And even this seems to necessitate, sometimes, the ascription of his creation only in part to God. Man's mixed nature implies a plurality of workers in his making³, which is accordingly attributed in part to celestial powers, apparently angels.

Philo's representation of man's nature as 'mixed' embodies practically the same idea as was intended to be conveyed by the rabbinical doctrine of the two inclinations. This doctrine is not, of course, to be found in his writings; nor have we been able to find there any certain proof that the *yezer* doctrine as Ben Sira knew it was adopted by the Alexandrian. But as *yezer* had no Greek equivalent, and no uniform Greek rendering, the use of the word is naturally obscure⁴ and the presence of the doctrine associated with it is consequently difficult to trace in Alexandrian literature. Philo sometimes attributes the responsibility for the mixed composition of human nature to God⁵. This is in keeping with the *yezer*

---

spring from the flesh in which they have been rooted" (*Quis rer. div. haer.* 54), and (*ibid.* 55) calls them τὰ σύμφυτα κακὰ τοῦ γένους ἡμῶν. In the same context he writes: Ἀνάγκη γὰρ θνητὸν ὄντα τῷ τῶν παθῶν ἔθνει πιεσθῆναι. But if pressed, he would doubtless deny that the passions were anything more than the occasions and instruments, as distinguished from the cause proper (the will or reason), of sin. The same would apply to S. Paul who speaks of 'sinful passions'; and indeed the language of theology down to the present day has been invariably beset with a similar ambiguity and inaccuracy arising from its not having occasion to interrogate itself as to what, precisely, its meaning was.

¹ *De Confus. Ling.* 35; *De Mundi Opif.* 24.
² *Quod deterius* etc. 47.
³ *De Mundi Opif.* 24; *De Confus. Ling.* 35; *De Profug.* 13, 14; *De Nom. Mut.* 4. The idea was possibly suggested to Philo by the *Timaeus* (41), as Drummond says; but it was a common Jewish interpretation of Gen. i. 26; see below, p. 149.

When such difficulties as are mentioned above in the text are not before Philo's mind he can emphatically assert that man was made by God alone, as in *De Nobilit.* 3.

⁴ See Porter, *op. cit.*, pp. 137, 145.
⁵ *De Inebriet.* 2; *Quis rer. div. haer.* 55. Cf. *Leg. Alleg.* III. 23: εὑρήσεις τὸν θεὸν πεποιηκότα φύσεις ἐξ ἑαυτῶν ἐπιλήπτους τε καὶ ὑπαιτίους ἐν ψυχῇ καὶ ἐν πᾶσι σπουδαίας καὶ ἐπαινετάς.

doctrine; but it involves rather more inconsistency in Philo than in Ben Sira and Palestinian writers generally, because of his very frequent and emphatic insistence on the fact that God is in no way the author or cause of evil[1]: a principle which he maintains in such a way as logically to lapse into dualism. Consistently with such aversion to refer evil to God, he also banishes evil from the neighbourhood of heaven[2].

But whether Philo teaches that God, or celestial powers, or man himself is responsible for human sin, is a matter whose importance for our purpose is subsidiary to that of the question whether he held that those who came after Adam inherited from him a nature in which the evil tendency was strengthened by his great transgression. We find no trace of such a doctrine in any of Philo's writings. As an explanation of the universality of sinfulness, or of the fact that the race is by nature inclined to evil both voluntary and involuntary[3], it would indeed be superfluous after what is implied in his allegorical and psychological interpretation of the Fall, and his doctrine of the mixed nature of man, with its inherent necessity of imperfection, if not of sin. On the other hand there is evidence that he held the opposite view.

Adam's sin is apparently regarded as venial or unimportant in comparison with Cain's[4]. Birth from Adam was still 'noble,' and more excellent than that of any succeeding generation[5]. Humanity started afresh after the deluge, all evil being purged out of the earth[6]; and Noah himself was equal in honour to the first man, nay, to the true or ideal incorporeal man[7]. Though we find Ham spoken of as 'the beginning of misery' to his posterity[8], and the heredity of

---

[1] *e.g.* in *De decem orac.* 33; *Quaest. et sol. in Gen.* I. 78, 89, 100; *De Cherub.*: μόνον ἀγαθῶν ἐστὶν ὁ θεὸς αἴτιος, κακοῦ δὲ οὐδενὸς παράπαν.
[2] *De Mundi Opif.* 60; *Leg. Alleg.* I. 18; *De Profug.* 12, 14.
[3] *De Profug.* 19.
[4] *Quaest. et sol. in Gen.* I. 81. The author of *Wisdom* (chap. x.; see above, p. 128) also passes lightly over Adam's sin and makes much of that of Cain.
[5] *De Nobilit.* 3.
[6] *Quaest. et sol. in Gen.* II. 47.
[7] *Ibid.* 56, but see *De Nobilit.* 3, with which this passage is inconsistent.
[8] *De Nobilit.* 3. For the expression cf. 'beginning of nobleness,' said of Tamar, *ibid.* 6.

moral qualities asserted[1], we discover no recognition, expressed or implied, that Adam was, in a causal sense, the beginning of sin or misery to his descendants. The wicked nature of mankind, which is sometimes spoken of[2], is in no case traced to the sin of the first parents of the race, even though sin is inborn in every man[3]. Though perfect virtue is practically unattainable by anyone endowed with our nature[4], and no mortal, if he live but for a single day, is free from defilement[5], yet man's freedom is unimpaired[6]; and so also is such ability as he ever possessed to follow wisdom and procure release from wickedness and sorrow[7]. Indeed all men are at first neutral, and, before the reason is developed, lie on the border between virtue and vice[8]. They thus resemble Adam in his original state of shamelessness: a state expressly attributed by Philo to the soul of an infant, which has no share in either virtue or vice[9], and even to that of a child during the first seven years of its life, which then has a pure nature comparable to a *tabula rasa*[10]. Thus a bent towards evil is developed anew in every individual by contact with the evil world. Philo might therefore perfectly well say with the writer of the *Apocalypse of Baruch*, that 'every man is the Adam of his own soul.' It is true, as we have seen above, that Philo regarded the founder of the race as superior in many excellences to any of his posterity, and speaks of a gradually increasing deterioration of the race. But these qualities are physical only; and the very figures by which he

[1] *De Confus. Ling.* 26. There is a close similarity between Philo's position and that of the author of *Wisdom*; both mention heredity of moral qualities but both stop far short of the doctrine of original sin.

[2] *De Confus. Ling.* 17; *De Vita Mosis*, I. 33.

[3] *De Vita Mosis*, III. 17: παντὶ γεννητῷ κἂν σπουδαῖον ᾖ, παρόσον ἦλθεν εἰς γένεσιν, συμφυὲς τὸ ἁμαρτάνειν ἐστίν. Cf. *Wisdom* XII. 10, ἔμφυτος ἡ κακία; 3 Mac. iii. 22, σύμφυτος κακοήθεια.

[4] *De Nom. Mut.* 6; *De Poenit.* 1; *De Sacr. Abelis et Caini*, 33, concluding sentence.

[5] *De Nom. Mut.* 6.

[6] *Quod Deus immut.* 10.

[7] *Quaest. et sol. in Gen.* I. 87. Cf. *Leg. Alleg.* III. 47.

[8] *De Praem. et poen.* 11. This is the view of many Palestinian Rabbis, with whom Philo's doctrine has much in common.

[9] *Leg. Alleg.* II. 14.

[10] *Quis rer. div. haer.* 59. Cf. *De Cong. quaer. erud.* 15.

seeks to illustrate and explain his meaning are such as to show that he in no way implies that the degeneracy is due to an inherited moral taint or infirmity[1]. It will have been made obvious that the writings of Philo contain much in common with the Book of Wisdom with reference to ideas preparatory to the doctrines of the Fall and Original Sin. Platonic influences have probably been responsible for the absence, both in Wisdom and in Philo, of the doctrine which was now prevalent amongst one group of Jewish writers, that death, or at least premature death, was a transmitted consequence of Adam's sin. In this respect these Alexandrian writings represent a tendency away from the doctrine of the Fall, as compared with other Jewish literature. On the other hand they have formulated with greater explicitness, perhaps, the idea of the *heredity* of evil propensities[2]. They never connect this idea with effects of Adam's transgression; but they doubtless prepared the way for such a connexion in later times. Another tendency which specially characterises Alexandrian thought, shown by Pseudo-Solomon, Philo, the author of *The Secrets of Enoch* and, according to Drummond[3], by Aristobulus who preceded them all, is that of insistence on not referring evil at all to God. Palestinian Jewish writings generally refer the origin of evil mediately to God; and though they sometimes repudiate any such direct ascription of responsibility for Adam's sin to God, they seem nevertheless to be, on the whole, distinctly less sensitive than the Alexandrians in shrinking from the consequences involved. Philo, of course, shows his characteristic vacillation on this point; but there can be no doubt that, though he now and again lapses, he earnestly strives to represent Mosaism as ascribing absolutely no share in the evil of the world to its Creator. Indeed he seems only to escape from dualism by his inconsistency; and this dualistic

---

[1] *De Mundi Opif.* 49. Later generations are compared to inferior copies of sculptors' or painters' works, and to the iron rings suspended in series from a magnet, in which the strength of attraction diminishes in proportion to the distance from the supporting magnet.

[2] See below, p. 144.

[3] *Philo Judaeus*, I. 253. Some critics regard the fragments of Aristobulus as not genuine.

tendency, noticeable also in the Book of Wisdom, constitutes another characteristic of the Alexandrian school.

In conclusion, what was said of the relation of Wisdom to the doctrine of the Fall, applies without exception to the writings of Philo. The component ideas of the doctrine are all to be found, more or less highly elaborated. But they as yet await gathering together into a single generalisation[1].

The Book of the Secrets of Enoch (Slavonic Enoch).

The teaching of this book with regard to the Fall will be fully discussed in one of the chapters on pseudepigraphic literature, to which class this work of course belongs. But as the book is certainly strongly influenced by Hellenic ideas, and was in all probability written in Egypt, its relation to Alexandrian thought may be briefly dealt with here.

The writer of the *Slavonic Book of Enoch*, in some of his teaching as to man and the consequences of the Fall, is rather the Jewish apocalyptist than the Alexandrian eclectic. Thus, following Ecclesiasticus, by which he seems to have been considerably influenced, he differs from Pseudo-Solomon and Philo in definitely ascribing physical death to the sin of Adam and Eve. In xxx. 16 we read: "And I appointed death on account of his sin"; and, a little further on, "by his wife death came." It will be seen later that the book, in its present form, contains a definite implication of the doctrines of the Fall and of inherited sinfulness. In these respects this pseudepigraph is out of relation with the Alexandrian litera-

---

[1] *Literature on Philo's anthropology.*

The earlier works of Gfrörer (*Philo und die Alexand. Theosophie*) and Dähne (*Geschicht. Darstellung der Jüd.-Alex. Religionsphilosophie*) are written from pronounced standpoints now generally abandoned. The best works of more recent date are Zeller's *Philosophie der Griechen*, III. ii., Siegfried's *Philo von Alexandria*, and the much fuller *Philo Judaeus* of J. Drummond. Schürer has a brief and less accurate summary of Philo's teaching in his *History of the Jewish People*, and there is a short account of it in Edersheim's Art. on Philo in Smith and Wace's *Dictionary of Christian Biography*. The works, referred to in this chapter, of Nicolas and Bois may also be mentioned; and a valuable discussion of some elements in Philo's anthropology will be found in Weinstein's *Zur Genesis der Agada*, Theil II.

VI]   *in Alexandrian Judaism*   143

ture which has been previously reviewed. But it shows a tendency towards the Platonic identification of evil with ignorance, and in this sense is more Greek than the prooemium of the *Sibylline Oracles*, or the Book of Wisdom. This theory of evil is closely associated, in Plato, with that philosopher's doctrine of the soul's pre-existence; a belief which is shared by the writer of *The Secrets of Enoch*[1]. If the soul was originally good, its capacity for evil is naturally attributed by such writers to the limitations of the bodily nature. Some implication such as this must lie behind the author's language in xxx. 16, where God says to Adam: " I knew his nature, he did not know his nature. Therefore his ignorance is a woe to him that he should sin...." The ignorance here attributed to Adam is not ignorance of good and evil, as to which he is already supposed to have been enlightened, but of his own nature with its good and evil inclinations[2]. In xxxi. 7 God is represented as cursing the devil, after his seduction of Eve, 'for his ignorance,' as if the devil's envy and malignity were also ultimately due to want of knowledge. We obviously have, in these passages, a Platonic doctrine superimposed somewhat incongruously upon the current Jewish teaching with regard to original aptitude for sin. The rest of the anthropological doctrine of this book has more marked affinities with Palestinian writings presently to be examined.

[1] xxiii. 5. Note, however, that Bonwetsch translates differently; he has: "alle Seelen sind *bereitet* vor der Welt" (Porter invites reference to Dalman's *Die Worte Jesu*, S. 104 ff., 245 ff.), where Morfill renders: "every soul was *created eternally* before the foundation of the world." Porter, *op. cit.*, p. 154 ff., disputes many of Charles' inferences as to the Hellenising tendencies of this apocalypse, but does not seem to the present writer entirely to remove all traces of such Greek influence.

[2] So Charles (*Book of the Secrets of Enoch*, Morfill and Charles, *in loc.*); also Taylor, *Sayings of the Jewish Fathers*, 2nd ed. p. 151. Cf., however, Porter, *op. cit.*, p. 156.

In xxx. 15 we read of Adam being endowed with freedom of will, and having been originally shown "the two ways, the light and darkness, the good and the evil." This doctrine of the 'two ways,' so far as meaning is concerned, is obviously related with that of the two *yezers*, by which it was afterwards generally replaced in Jewish literature.

It must certainly be admitted that, on the whole, the view of sin taken by this book is more Jewish than Greek.

NOTE. 3 and 4 Maccabees, which should probably be included under Alexandrian-Jewish literature, do not supply us with much that is relevant to the history of the doctrine of Original Sin. In 3 Mac. iii. 22, we meet with the phrase σύμφυτος κακοήθεια, which, taken with the kindred expressions ἔμφυτος κακία of Wisd. xii. 10, and συμφυὲς τὸ ἁμαρτάνειν ἐστίν of Philo, implies that the notion of *inborn* sinful tendency had taken definite shape and was familiarly known amongst Alexandrian-Jewish writers.

In 4. Mac. xviii. 7-8, there is an allusion to a curious Jewish interpretation of the temptation of Eve, which will call for notice in subsequent chapters; but there seems to be no evidence for the existence there of an approach to the doctrine of orignal sin. The writer is largely a Stoic in his ethics. He regards man's inclinations and passions as implanted in him by God (ii. 21), yet placed under the august rule of the understanding. Wickedness cannot be extirpated, but reason can prevent it from overwhelming us (iii. 4); for reason is not the extirpator but the conqueror of inclination. The book seems to teach that we have an inward bias to evil in virtue of our being endowed with passions; but such 'original sin' as this we owe to God, and certainly not to Adam.

CHAPTER VII.

THE FALL AND ORIGINAL SIN IN RABBINICAL LITERATURE.

THE source of information with regard to Jewish opinion which is to be examined in the present chapter is that which, in contrast with the more popular apocalyptic writings, may be called scholastic, orthodox, official and, in one sense, authoritative. It consists of the Targums, Talmud and Midrashim; or, rather, of the haggadic elements in these various departments of rabbinic literature[1]. These writings are generally believed to embody teaching which was current, in oral form, in rabbinical schools for two centuries or more before it began to be reduced to writing. It may therefore be of some value as a source of light upon the teaching of the Synagogue at the beginning of the Christian era.

There were perhaps rabbinical schools in the third century B.C., and Targums in the second[2]; certainly there was "a

---

[1] It may be explained here that the *Targums* are paraphrases, more or less enlarged, of the Old Testament Scriptures. The *Mishna* is a codification of law, intended to supplement and explain the Mosaic law from which it was developed; it practically consists of the results of the discussion of the Rabbis between A.D. 70 and 200 (the *Tannaim*), about the latter of which dates the bulk of it is generally believed to have been written down. The further discussions to which the *Mishna* gave rise amongst the *Amoraim*, or post-mishnic Rabbis, and the explanations and additions which were thus accumulated, make up the bulk of the *Gemara* or *Talmud*. The *Midrashim* are a collection of commentaries on the Scriptures.

The *haggadic* elements of these various works are personal sayings, of the nature of exposition or illustration, and often purely imaginative; while the *halachic* elements, on the contrary, were more fixed and more authoritative. For fuller and more precise information see Edersheim, *Life and Times of the Messiah*, Schürer's *History of the Jewish People*, and similar works.

[2] Zunz, *Gottesdienst. Vorträge der Juden*, 1° Aufl. S. 62 f.

talmud before *the* talmud," and mishna before that of the third Christian century. But it is impossible wholly to distinguish what of ancient Jewish tradition has thus survived among the accretions of later times, or always to be certain that its original meaning has been preserved[1]. Very much that will be quoted here from these writings is doubtless but individual opinion and not ancient tradition at all. Probably much of the older theological opinion, too, was lost in the process of compilation[2]. It is not always possible to be sure of the chronology of sayings which are expressly attributed in the Talmud and Midrashim to individual Rabbis; and very many sayings are quoted anonymously. Until we have advanced many steps in the higher criticism of the rabbinic literature[3] we may be wholly wrong, as Professor Stanton insists[4], in attributing views occurring in the Talmud to remote antiquity. Meanwhile, more caution must certainly be exercised than has been used, in the case of many writers, in relying on post-talmudic Jewish writings as exponents of ancient teaching, or on citations from rabbinic literature found in works of scholars, Jewish or Christian, of the modern period. Alleged citations have sometimes been found to be spurious, and unverified references have occasionally perpetuated error[5].

And if it is thus impossible to rely, without critical inquiry, upon the antiquity of any given saying, view or

[1] Much of the same mythological material in which the pseudepigraphic writings often abound occurs in rabbinical literature, and no doubt a large proportion of this is ancient tradition. There is some truth, perhaps, in the remark: "The rabbinical stories are anything but arbitrary inventions; they are echoes of primeval memories only refused entrance into the Bible by the compilers of the Canon" (Braun, *Naturgeschichte der Sage*, I. 127); but it is only part of the truth, especially if 'primeval' be taken literally.

[2] See Schechter, *J.Q.R.* VI., on Rabbinical Theology, and also IV. pp. 456–7.

[3] On the lines, *e.g.*, of Bacher's valuable works, *Die Agada der Tannaiten*, and *Die Agada der Palästin. Amoräer*.

[4] *The Jewish and the Christian Messiah*, p. 30.

[5] We have been warned, for instance, against Raymund Martin and Schoettgen by Jennings and Lowe. Schiller-Szinessy accuses Martin of forgery. See *Journal of Philology*, vol. XVI. No. 31, p. 130 ff.

Post-talmudic Jewish writers, and doubtless many of the talmudic period, were influenced by contact with Christianity. From the revival of rabbinism onwards there was controversy between the Synagogue and the Church.

doctrine, to be met with in rabbinic literature, it is still less possible, from the very nature of that literature, to derive from it any consistent or coherent body of theological doctrine. The writings in question consist, as has already been said, of tradition and individual opinion dating from different centuries. The doctrine which they contain is wholly wanting in system, classification and dogmatic definition. Great liberty of thought obtained amongst the Rabbis whose teaching is recorded; and consequently we meet with discordant views on particular points, as well as with an abundance of antitheses, due to the emphasis now of this, and now of that, side of a question, at whose reconciliation no attempt is made because the need of such a thing was scarcely felt. It is no wonder then that, as M. Montefiore has said[1], rabbinic literature "needs for its intelligent employment one who has been steeped in it from his youth." And if an unintelligent employment of this literature is to be entirely avoided here, it can only be by making use of the previous labours of acknowledged experts in the field, and that with caution. For a summary of the statements of Rabbis on the subject of Adam's first estate, the Fall and its consequences, Weber's *Jüdische Theologie* has been used to a considerable extent, though by no means exclusively. This work, which has for a considerable number of years been relied upon by many scholars, as the chief source of trustworthy information with regard to rabbinical theology, though almost indispensable and certainly of great value to students who have themselves given no special study to that branch of learning, does not, however, always use its sources quite satisfactorily. Its statements with regard to the rabbinical doctrine of the *yezers*, for example, some of which have been incorporated without verification into numerous theological treatises, are in several respects misleading. It is unfortunate, also, that this learned work cites its illustrative passages indiscriminately from sources of very different date; that it seldom supplies the name of the particular Rabbi to whom the saying in question is assigned; and that it affords, as a rule, no information as

[1] *Hibbert Lectures*, p. 467.

148   *The Fall and Original Sin*   [CHAP.

to which of several varying opinions, if any, was the more generally accepted. Such shortcomings will probably have thrust themselves upon the notice of most students who have had recourse to this mine of rabbinical learning; and those who have verified its references will perhaps have sometimes found that it occasionally expresses the general sense of a passage in words which partially misrepresent it[1].

It is the haggadic elements of the rabbinical literature which have to be searched for teaching as to the Fall and its consequences. Haggada is defined by Bacher as the "exegetical elaboration of the contents of a verse, the evolution of new ideas based upon the interpretation of the biblical text." It may perhaps be described as 'manipulation' of Scripture. Ideas are often reached by the imagination, or by the comparison and blending of the teaching of one passage with that of others; and the result is then 'deduced' from some particular verse. The fancifulness of some of the rabbinical statements is thus to be explained by the curious methods by which they were arrived at.

It will not be necessary to reproduce here so exhaustive a collection of passages from the rabbinic writings, in illustration of their theological treatment of the Fall, as has been attempted in the case of the Alexandrian and pseudepigraphic literature. Such a collection is already accessible to the student in the works of the various authorities whose labours have here been utilised. It will be sufficient to summarise such teaching as is relevant to our purpose, and to select, from the various sources available, the passages which best lend themselves to its illustration.

Following the Old Testament, Jewish theology taught that man was made in the image of God. The simple

---

[1] It may be mentioned that the chief authorities which have here been relied upon, in addition to Weber, are Edersheim, Taylor, Hamburger, Schechter, Ginzberg, Montefiore, Bacher, Hershon and Porter. Wünsche's German translation of the Talmud and of part of the Midrashim has been used. The author also gratefully acknowledges personal help from Dr Schechter. The future student will be furnished with most valuable aid in the English translation of the Babylonian Talmud by Dr Rodkinson, of which some thirteen volumes are already published, though the present writer has not had access to them; and in the *Jewish Encyclopaedia*, three volumes only of which have at present appeared.

scriptural statement is, however, developed in various ways. The Targums of Onkelos and Pseudo-Jonathan[1] witness to the maintenance of the biblical doctrine, as also does the haggada of the Amoraim, and of Akiba[2]; but already in the Jerusalem Targum (Jerus. II.) it is taught : " And the Word of the Lord created man in His likeness, in the likeness of the presence of the Lord He created him[3]." Similarly the Targum of Pseudo-Jonathan (Jerus. I.) interprets the words "Let us make man in our image" as referring to God and the angels who ministered to Him[4]. Thus the original Hebrew doctrine tended to be weakened into that of creation after the image of the angels. Again, we meet in the midrash, as in the writings of Philo, with the distinction between a celestial Adam, made in the image of God, and the earthly Adam[5].

It is unnecessary to endeavour to ascertain precisely how much was intended to be meant by the expression 'image of God' in rabbinic literature, inasmuch as the Fall is not stated to have caused the image to be lost. We pass on, therefore, to observe next, that the tendency to magnify Adam into a super-human being, which some authorities consider to be due to the influence of Chaldaean and Iranian mythology, and which is also observable in Philo and the pseudepigraphic writings, is well marked in the midrash and Talmud. Passages expressing the belief that the first man was endowed with extraordinary stature (he is frequently said to have filled the world), with physical beauty, with surpassing wisdom, with a brilliancy which eclipsed that of the sun, with a heavenly light which enabled him to see the

[1] See Etheridge, *The Targums of the Pentateuch*, pp. 37, 160.
[2] See Bacher, *Die Agada der Pal. Amoräer*, Bd. II. S. 485, and *Die Agada der Tannaiter*, Bd. I. S. 286.
[3] On Gen. i. 27.
[4] Cf. *Pirke Aboth*, III. 14, where Akiba speaks of man as created 'after an image.'
[5] See Taylor, *Sayings of the Jewish Fathers*, 2nd ed. p. 56; Ginzberg on Adam Kadmon in *Jewish Encyclopaedia*.
This distinction was retained in later literature : *e.g. Zohar*, III. 48 b; and (Hamburger) *Idra Rabba*, 144 a. The midrash adopted also the idea that the first man was androgynous, an interpretation of Gen. possibly suggested to Philo by Plato.

whole world, with immortality, and with a ministration of angels, have been collected by Weber[1]. To the statements there made it may be added that Adam was sometimes said to be the father of all arts and inventions[2]. Many of these fancies are common to pseudepigraphic and gnostic literature, and are probably pre-Christian in antiquity and largely foreign in origin. The Jewish-heathen idea of Adam's superhuman wisdom passed over into the Christian Church, as well as into heretical sects; and having received the sanction of several fathers, such as S. Augustine, and of Aquinas and other schoolmen, it became the germ of very elaborate developments at the hands of post-Reformation divines[3].

Many of the physical excellences thus attributed to the first man were lost at his fall[4]. Of Adam's moral endowments at the first, and of the effect of his transgression upon them, something will be said later. It may be further stated at this point, however, that cosmic effects are now and again attributed to the fall of man by the Rabbis. The earth and the heavenly bodies lost their brightness[5]; death came upon

---

[1] *op. cit.*, S. 214, 15. See also Bacher, *Agada d. Amoräer*, I. S. 156, II. S. 50, etc.

[2] *Bereschith Rabba*, cc. 17 and 24. This midrash, according to Zunz, dates from the 6th cent. and preserves old Palestinian traditions.

In *Tanchuma* the saying given above is attributed to R. Eleazer b. Pedath. Similarly R. Simon is reported to have said that "So long as Adam was devoted to his Maker, wisdom and power, counsel and insight were his" (Bacher, *Amoräer*, Bd. II. S. 465). R. Jehuda b. Simon taught that Adam, in his original estate, was allowed to see all future generations, with their wise and learned; (*op. cit.*, III. S. 173-4); and R. Jose asserted that God imparted knowledge to Adam by revelation, so that he was enabled to generate fire by rubbing two stones together (*Pesachim*, 54 a).

[3] In *Clem. Homilies*, II. 18, we read: "Our father (Adam) was ignorant of nothing."

For Aquinas' teaching, see *Summa*, pars I. 94. Bishop South's famous sermon is the best known instance of the fancifully exaggerated post-Reformation teaching, but Bishop Bull goes nearly as far (*Works*, II. p. 349).

[4] See Weber, *op. cit.*, S. 222.

It should be noted, however, that among these the removal of the Shekinah from earth was only by one stage—it was removed further by six successive human sins—and that not permanently, according to *Beresch. Rabba*, c. 19 (on Gen. iii. 8): and in the same place it is said that the reduction of Adam's height to 100 ells (R. Ibo) was the act of Adam himself when he hid from God after his sin.

[5] *Beresch. Rabba*, c. 12. Cf. *Zohar*, III. 83 b.

all creatures, as well as upon the human race¹; the brutes no longer showed awe for man nor were obedient to him²; the course of the planets was changed³; "as soon as the first man sinned everything became perverted and will no more return to order until the Messiah comes⁴." In these details rabbinical speculation is practically identical with that of the apocalyptic writers.

The paradisaic life of the first parents, with its freedom from pain and its outward splendour, is represented by the Rabbis, as in some of the pseudepigraphic books⁵, to have been of extremely short duration—only a few hours. If this opinion prevailed—and ancient speculation seems to have tended to make the period before the Fall very short⁶—the rabbinic statements referred to by Weber⁷, to the effect that the unfallen state was one of peace and untroubled joy, during which man was unhurt by evil spirits, cannot count for much. But we encounter here individual fancies rather than a body of traditional and harmonious doctrine.

Adam's repentance, of which we hear much in at least the post-Christian portion of pseudepigraphic literature, seems also to have been emphasised by several Rabbis of the second century⁸.

The temptation in Eden is treated by the Rabbis very

---

¹ *Beresch. Rabba*, c. 19. The reason here assigned is that Eve gave the animals the forbidden fruit. The phoenix alone did not eat of it.
² *ibid.* c. 25.
³ *ibid.* c. 10. ⁴ *ibid.* cc. 12, 14.
⁵ *e.g.* 'A' recension of *The Secrets of Enoch*, XXXII. 1.
⁶ *Aboth di R. Nathan*, c. 1; cf. *Sanhedr.* 38 b; *Beresch. Rabba*, c. 94. Weber gives references to *Beresch. Rabba*, c. 18, 22, and the much later work *Yalkut Schim., Beresch.* 25. The same view appears in several of the *Adam Books*. In the *Book of Jubilees* the life in Paradise is said to have lasted 7 years: so also Syncellus taught. Josephus puts its duration as at least several days; cf. John Damasc. *De orth. fide*, II. 10, Augustine, *De Civit.* XX. 26, Gregory (Great), *Dial.* IV. 1; these authorities are followed by Pererius and Ussher. R. Ammi (*Beresch. Rabba*, 11.), Irenaeus, Ephrem, Epiphanius, some scholastics, and perhaps Luther, fix upon one day as its limit. Apparently solitary in his wisdom among ancient writers, Eusebius (*Chron.* I. 16, 4, ed. Mai.) said no one could tell anything about it.
⁷ S. 213.
⁸ Kohler, Art. *Adam* in the *Jewish Encyclopaedia*, gives the following references: *Erubin*, 18 b; *Aboda Zara*, 8 a; *Aboth di R. Nathan*, 1.

much in the same way as that with which we shall become accustomed in studying the apocalyptic writings; the details are in many cases common to both streams of Palestinian literature, and may therefore be supposed to be so far derived from common ancient sources—" pre-talmudic haggada."

As in Josephus and the *Book of Jubilees*, the tempter is sometimes spoken of simply as the serpent, which is then represented as somewhat more than a speaking reptile, at least before the curse. Thus R. Hoschaia[1] said that the serpent was double-horned, upright like a stick, and stood on feet[2]. In other passages the serpent is regarded merely as the instrument of Satan or Samael, as will be seen from citations about to be given. The motive of envy is generally assigned as the reason for the tempter's determination to ruin the first parents of the race. Whatever may have been the form of the legend on which the statement of the Book of Wisdom is based, that "by the envy of the devil death entered into the world," there were several versions of it current amongst the Rabbis of the early centuries A.D., as amongst the Jewish apocalyptic writers. According to one of these, the serpent envied Adam his privileges in Paradise. When he saw Adam reclining, whilst attending angels roasted flesh and strained wine for him, he was moved to envy[3]. This reads more like the fanciful invention of a Rabbi than a genuine old tradition. More ancient, in all probability, was the view taken in *Pirke di R. Elieser*, c. 13[4] and elsewhere, because of its affinity with that of the *Vita Adae*. But still more commonly do we meet with the view that the serpent

---

[1] "Urheber von grossen Traditionssammlungen...welche sich der Mischna Jehuda's I an die Seite stellten," Bacher, *Pal. Amoräer*, 1. 89.

The passage alluded to above occurs in *Beresch. Rabba*, c. 19; in c. 20 it is added that, after beguiling Eve, the serpent's hands and feet were cut off by angels.

[2] Cf. the description of the tempter in *Apoc. of Abraham* (p. 194 of this work). This tradition appears again in Aphraates, *Homilies*, ed. Wright, p. 255 (a reference due to Ginzberg, *Monatsschrift f. Geschichte u. Wissenschaft Judenthums*, 43, S. 153).

[3] *Sanhedr.* 59 b, where the teaching is assigned to R. Jehuda b. Thema; in *Aboth di R. Nathan*, c. 1, it is referred to R. Jehuda b. Bathera.

[4] The view according to which the serpent envied Adam his lordship over creation, and his greatness in general.

envied Adam on account of his wife, whom he desired himself to possess. These two ideas are indeed combined in a saying attributed in one place[1] to R. Jose b. Chalastha (second century), but elsewhere cited anonymously, according to which the serpent's plan was to kill Adam and marry Eve, and to be king over all the earth. But in the majority of rabbinical sayings on the motive of the tempter, desire for Eve alone is ascribed to him, and envy of Adam's greatness becomes secondary or vanishes. Thus, in *Sota*, 9 b, the tempter is made to say : " I will kill Adam and take Eve to wife," and in *Bereschith Rabba*, c. 18, it is related that the serpent was filled with desire for Eve on witnessing the life of the man and wife in Paradise. In c. 20 of the same midrash a similar statement to that just cited from *Sota* is ascribed to R. Asi and R. Hoschaia ; and in the latter case the ascription is corroborated by Bacher, thus carrying the saying back to the earliest generation of Amoraim.

It was shown in an earlier chapter that there is some reason to suspect that the original legends which were woven into the Fall-story of Genesis were connected with the origin of the sexual relation. Such a suggestion has been forced, in different ways, upon writers of different ages. It may be of interest to note that the narrative of the first sin was sometimes interpreted in rabbinic literature as symbolical in this sense, as it also was occasionally in Jewish pseudepigraphic writings[2]. The proof that such interpretations contain an echo of ancient Hebrew tradition—a thing perfectly possible in itself—is not forthcoming ; for we possess no connecting links, no evidence of continuity of development from the hypothetical Hebrew legend to the Jewish haggada, necessary to the establishment of such a conclusion. Moreover we have to allow for the fertility of the rabbinical imagination, and also for the fact that the interpretation in question is far from

[1] *Aboth di R. Nathan*, c. 1 (3 a).
[2] *Apocal. of Abraham* (see p. 194) and *Slavonic Book of Baruch* (ed. Bonwetsch, S. 97). " The first thing by which Adam came to fall is the vine; the second sinful lust, which Satanail poured out upon Adam and Eve." This passage, however, may refer to the belief in the intercourse of Adam and Eve with demons ; see below.

universal. The following instances of it, however, may be mentioned.

Edersheim[1] told us that the account of the Fall in *Bereschith Rabba* seemed to him to insinuate a symbolical view of its history, and to assign evil concupiscence as its cause. This tendency is certainly suggested by several passages of that midrash. In c. 20 is a saying attributed to R. Acha, an Amora of the fourth century, which may possibly imply this line of thought. It is to the effect that in Eve's name[2] lies the proof that she was 'the serpent' of Adam, and tempted him as she herself was tempted by the serpent. A little further on (c. 22), the same saying takes the following form: "The serpent was thy serpent, and thou wast Adam's serpent." Now it will presently be shown that the belief that Eve was tempted by the serpent to unchastity with him was widely prevalent in rabbinic and other circles, and probably goes back to pre-Christian times. If then the words quoted above be taken to imply that Eve not only tempted Adam, but tempted him in the same way as that in which she herself had been beguiled by the serpent, the Fall would seem to be represented here as consisting in the fleshly union of Adam and Eve. The inference is possible, however, rather than necessary. A very explicit instance of the particular form of the belief in question which sees in the forbidden fruit the union of Adam and Eve with *each other*, is furnished by a passage cited by Ginzberg[3] from *Pirke di R. Elieser*, c. 21, in which the command to Adam and Eve to abstain from the tree in the middle of the garden is expounded piecemeal, in the light of other texts of scripture, as a prohibition from the marriage relation. This work is, of course, of late date for our purpose, being generally assigned to the seventh or eighth century at the earliest, and is said to betray contact with Mohammedanism. Thus, though some of its haggada is proved, by its kinship with that of such writings as the *Book of Jubilees* and the Enoch literature, to be pre-Christian, the passage to which reference has been made cannot be assumed

---

[1] *Life and Times etc.*, vol. I. p. 165, note 3.
[2] See above, p. 26.
[3] *op. cit.*, 43, S. 224.

VII]   *in Rabbinical Literature*   155

to be necessarily of high antiquity : the more so because it appears to be unique. Indeed the view that the Fall consisted in the union of Adam and Eve is on the whole foreign to the rabbinical way of thinking. There was a widely current haggada to the effect that Adam and Eve enjoyed a period of married life in Eden, and that it was this that made the serpent envious[1]. R. Jochanan b. Chanina is said to have taught that Cain and his sister were born to Adam *before* the Fall, and indeed this view is ascribed to several Rabbis[2]. Moreover the sin of partaking of the forbidden fruit, *i.e.* the fall described in Genesis, is not unfrequently associated in the midrash with abuse of the vine.

A passage to this effect is adduced by Weber[3] from *Bammidbar Rabba*, c. 10, a work assigned by Schürer to the twelfth century, in which it is represented that Eve, when conversing with the serpent, drank wine, and awakened passion in Adam by offering it to him. It is then added : "this is Adam the old, who is the head of all men, for through wine has death been inflicted upon him"; and further, "this is Adam the first; for through the wine which he drank has the world been cursed for his sake, for R. Abin says : Eve mixed wine for Adam and he drank." This may not be an ancient tradition, as R. Abin lived in the fourth century. The same doctrine however is taught elsewhere. Thus in *Sanhedr.* 70 a, we find the saying, ascribed by some to R. Mar Ukba, by others to R. Saccai[4]: "The Holy One, blessed be He! said to Noah, 'Thou shouldst have taken

---

[1] At the end of c. 18 of *Beresch. Rabba*, R. Joshua b. Karcha (Tannaite) is said to have stated, as a reason for including the words "And the serpent was subtil..." within the last verse of Gen. ii., that they serve to show *the sinful motive* for the serpent's attack upon Adam and Eve. The words italicised are what we take to be implied by Wünsche's rendering *wegen welcher Sünde*. The German translation continues: *es sah sie nämlich mit dem Beischlafe beschäftigt und im Folgen dessen bekam es Lust zu ihr*. Cf. also c. 19 (on Gen. iii. 2). The same teaching is ascribed to R. Eleazar b. Azariah, of the mishnic period.

[2] *Sanhedr.* 38 b. The *Book of Jubilees* maintained the opposite doctrine, which was embraced also by Christian writers. See Ginzberg, *op. cit.*

[3] *op. cit.*, S. 220.

[4] See Bacher, *Pal. Amoräer*, Bd. III. S. 643.

156   *The Fall and Original Sin*   [CHAP.

warning from Adam and not indulged in the use of wine as he did[1].'" That the forbidden tree was the vine was a common opinion, both in rabbinical and pseudepigraphic haggada[2]. To cite from the former class of literature, R. Meir (of the second century) is stated to have held this belief, and to have said: "for wine alone brings misfortune into the world[3]." The same opinion is attributed, in *Beresch. Rabba*, c. 19, to R. Ibo.

It cannot, therefore, be maintained that the view according to which the Fall consisted in the natural union of Adam and Eve was other than very exceptional, and probably late, in rabbinic literature, whatever may have been the origin of the material of the Hebrew narrative itself. It is beyond question, however, that various legends concerning the *monstrous* intercourse of Adam and Eve with demons, and especially of Eve with the serpent or Satan, were both widespread and ancient among the Jews; and this is rather the sense in which, as Edersheim observed, the Fall is associated in rabbinic writings with evil concupiscence.

The curious belief just mentioned is of some importance because it supplied Judaism with a doctrine in some respects similar to that of original sin and hereditary corruption, coarse and materialistic as is the conception of human pollution which it contains[4]. Several pseudepigraphic writings,

[1] Cf. the passage cited above, from *Slav. Baruch*, p. 153, note 2, where the Fall is associated with both the sins of drunkenness and lust.

[2] See *Apocal. of Abraham*, 22; *Book of Enoch*, XXXII. 4; *Greek Apocalypse of Baruch* (3 *Apoc. Bar.* of Dr James); *Slav. Baruch* (Bonwetsch, in *Nachr. d. königl. Gesellschaft zu Göttingen*, 1876, S. 97); *Apocalypse of Job* (*Texts and Studies*, vol. V. p. lxii). Ginzberg refers also to Origen, *in Gen.* X. 20, and Epiphanius, *Haer.* XVI., in illustration of the fact that the belief obtained amongst the Gnostics.

[3] *Beracoth*, 40 a.

The nature of the forbidden tree was a matter of discussion among the Rabbis, and different views were maintained. In addition to those already mentioned, some held it was the fig, others the olive (see Weber, S. 220). R. Joshua b. Levi (3rd cent.) declared that the nature of the tree had never been revealed and never would be (Bacher, *Pal. Amoräer*, I. 169). R. Chanin, one of the later Amoraim, held that the knowledge of good and evil came to Adam, not by the tree, but through the removal of his rib (Bacher, *op. cit.*, III. 92).

[4] An eminent German scholar, with singularly perverted ingenuity, has endeavoured to trace the Pauline anthropology to this root.

as will be seen, emphasise the fact that it was Eve only whom the devil tempted, and that the temptation took the form of seduction to unchastity with him. The same notions are insisted upon in rabbinic writings. Meanwhile, an indication of the existence of a story intermediate between those mentioned and those about to be given, deserves notice. In c. 1 of the *Aboth di R. Nathan*, a work whose midrash, allowing for later tampering, probably represents that of a time prior to the general reception of R. Jehuda's mishna[1], 'the evil serpent' is described as saying "if I cannot undo Adam, I will attempt it with Eve." He therefore approaches her and draws her into conversation, during which he shakes the forbidden tree, so that its fruit falls to the ground. It is extremely probable that we have here, in uncompleted form, the same legend as occurs (see p. 197) in the *Apocalypse of Moses*, according to which the tempter, before giving Eve of the tree to eat, infused lust into the fruit, whereby passion was aroused in her. This, however, is not the usual form of the story of Eve's pollution. In several tractates of the Talmud a contamination of the race is spoken of, which is ascribed to the serpent's intercourse with Eve, and to the poison which she derived from him[2]. This stain was removed from Israel by the great redemptive act in the nation's history, the giving of the law at Mt Sinai; but it still remains in the Gentiles. We thus have a Jewish doctrine of inherited corruption, which, derived from Satan, was transmitted by Eve to all her seed. And the doctrine was persistent. Malan supplies a reference to a similar belief in Maimonides,

[1] See Winter u. Wünsche, *Die Jüd. Litteratur*, Bd. 1. S. 619 ff., where a translation of the passage relating the account of the Fall is to be found.

[2] *Sabbath*, 146 a. "Why are the Cuthites contaminated? Because they did not stand at Mt Sinai; for when the serpent had intercourse with Eve, it injected poison into her. The Israelites, who stood at Mt Sinai, have lost this poison; the Gentiles, on the contrary, who did not stand on Mt Sinai, have not lost this poison." This is attributed to R. Jose. R. Abba b. Kahana, another Amora, taught that the poison was not lost during the first three patriarchal generations, because Abraham begat Ishmael, and Isaac begat Esau; but that in the twelve sons of Jacob, because they were without blemish, it disappeared. The same doctrine as is here ascribed to R. Jose is attributed to R. Jochanan in *Jebamoth*, 103 b; and it occurs again in *Aboda Zara*, 22 b.

which, he adds, is told somewhat differently in *Yalkut Schim.* (fol. 8, 25) by R. Elieser. It occurs again in *Neve Schalom*, x. c. 9: "By observing the commandments a man is cleansed from his impurity; and he is purged from the pollution of the old serpent." As to its antiquity, the evidence of other Jewish writings than those of the talmudic period abundantly proves that, in the germ at least, the story was current in the first century A.D. It may be questioned, however, whether it was of purely Jewish origin. The rabbinic writings, as we have seen, frequently speak of the serpent as the instrument used by Samael or Satan. A further instance may be given from *Pirke di R. Elieser*, c. 13, where it is stated that "among all the creatures Samael found none so fitted to do evil as the serpent. The serpent glided like a camel, and Samael mounted it; and so it was, that everything which the serpent did and said was only at the instigation of Samael." This passage has been cited because it presents the familiar story of the devil's use of the serpent in language which is more than usually suggestive of a foreign source. The colouring, in this case, may possibly be Mohammedan[1]. There can be little doubt, however, that the story of the *inquinamentum*, to which the foregoing legend is the necessary preliminary, is ultimately of Iranian derivation. Kohler has pointed out the close resemblance of the Jewish story of the descent of Samael and his selection of the serpent as his instrument for the seduction of Eve and for polluting her with a poison of impurity, to a legend contained in the Bundahesch[2], according to which Ahriman appears in the guise of a serpent and casts poison into man with the aid of Jeh, the personification of menstrual impurity[3].

The legendary event on which the crude and coarse Jewish doctrine of inherited corruption is based, the union, that is, of Eve and the serpent, is often alluded to in rabbinical and other Jewish writings independently of the consequence some-

---

[1] Ginzberg, *op. cit.*, 43, S. 152; Grünbaum, *Semit. Sagenkunde*, S. 61.
[2] *S. B. E.* VI. 6. See also Windischmann, *Zoroast. Studien*, S. 61.
[3] It should be noted that in *Aboth di R. Nathan*, part of Eve's punishment consists in pains etc. connected with the class of things personified by the Iranian 'Jeh.'

VII]   *in Rabbinical Literature*   159

times attributed to it. The Rabbis appear to have taught that Cain was begotten of Eve by Satan. The two passages which Weber cites (S. 219) in proof of this are indeed from works that cannot claim to be regarded as ancient. *Pirke di R. Elieser*, however, contains ancient tradition, as is proved by the similarity of its contents with the legendary matter found in early pseudepigrapha. *Yalkut Schim.* is of much later date—Zunz assigns it to the beginning of the thirteenth century[1]; but this too embodies very ancient haggada, and the passage with which we are here concerned may therefore possibly reflect very early tradition. Moreover there is direct proof that this curious notion as to the parentage of Cain was not an invention of late Rabbis. It was known to several of the early fathers as a belief possessed by Gnostic Sects[2]; and it was therefore, in all probability, of high antiquity; for otherwise it would be difficult to account for the fact of its being so widely spread.

Another class of sayings involving, perhaps, a reference to the view which identified the first sin of Eve with a sin of unchastity, are those which assert the prolonged intercourse of both Adam and Eve with demons. Weber quotes, in illustration of such a belief, from the late mediæval work *Yalkut Schim.* The same passage occurs, however, in the talmudic tractate *Erubin*, and is there attributed to R. Jirmeja b. Eleazar[3], who lived, according to Bacher[4], most probably in the latter half of the third century. This haggadist said: "All those years which Adam spent in alienation from God, he begat evil spirits, demons and fairies." A similar saying is

[1] Weber, *op. cit.*, S. xxx.
[2] See, *e.g.*, the following passage from Epiphanius, *Haer.* XL. 5: ἕτερον δὲ πάλιν μῦθον λέγουσιν οἱ τοιοῦτοι, ὅτι φησίν, ὁ διάβολος ἐλθὼν πρὸς τὴν Εὔαν συνήφθη αὐτῇ ὡς ἀνὴρ γυναικὶ καὶ ἐγέννησεν ἐξ αὐτῆς τόν τε Κάϊν καὶ τὸν Ἀβελ.
When Ginzberg, *op. cit.*, S. 225, attributes the same view to Tertullian on the strength of the passage (*De Patientia*, c. 5): *Nam statim illa semine diaboli concepta malitiae foecunditate iram filium procreavit*, surely he is in error. The context does not at all suggest that *illa* refers to Eve; indeed it can only refer to *impatientia*, in the preceding sentence. And if it were taken to refer to Eve, what would become of Tertullian's latinity?
[3] Hershon, *Rabbinical Commentary on Genesis*, and Bacher, *Die Agada der Pal. Amoräer*, Bd. II. S. 450.
[4] *op. cit.*, Bd. III. S. 583.

attributed, in *Bereschith Rabba*, to R. Simon of the same period[1]. It is shown in another chapter that legends connecting the Fall with the sin of impurity were known to pseudepigraphical writers of the first century A.D.[2]; consequently it will not be rash to agree with Gfrörer, that "the belief that Samael and his host tempted our first parents to unchastity and practised it with them is very old, and reaches right back into the times of Christ[3]"; nor to see, with Thackeray, who cites these words with approval, traces of the same belief in the writings of S. Paul[4].

It would naturally be expected, from all the fancifulness and triviality in their treatment of the details of the Fall-story, that the Rabbis entertained but a light estimate of the first sin itself, and of its consequences for the race. According to Weber's judgment, who, however, is perhaps not wholly free from an unconscious tendency to contrast Judaism unfavourably with Christianity, this was generally the case[5]. And certainly the Fall is asserted by some teachers to have been merely the transgression of a slight command. One of the earlier Amoraim, in fact, went so far as to say it was an event for which we ought to be grateful, since, had it not occurred, we should not be in existence[6].

Nevertheless, there is a vein of seriousness in the rabbinical teaching concerning the fall of man. How far it is exceptional need not here be investigated. Nor will it be necessary to reproduce the passages which have already been collected by

[1] *op. cit.*, Bd. II. S. 450.
[2] See pp. 194, 197, 209, and cf. the Gnostic doctrine described by Irenaeus, *Adv. Haer.* I. 30. 7.
[3] *Jahrhundert des Heils*, Bd. I. S. 398.
[4] *The relation of S. Paul to contemp. Jew. thought*, p. 52 ff. Cf. below, p. 208. See 2 Cor. xi. 2—3, 1 Tim. ii. 13—15; and cf. 4 Macc. xviii. 7—8.
[5] *op. cit.*, S. 221.
[6] The saying is attributed to R. Simon b. Lakisch (3rd cent.); see Bacher, *Pal. Amoräer*, Bd. I. S. 354. It is based on Ps. lxxxii. 6, 7, and therefore does not serve to illustrate the interpretation of the Fall-story discussed in the preceding pages.

Beresch. Rabba (on Gen. iv. 13) understands Cain's speech to imply that his father's transgression, involving the punishment of expulsion from Paradise, was slight indeed in comparison with his own. Finally, Schechter mentions that R. David of Roccamartica wrote a work proving the sinlessness of Adam, for which he was not rebuked.

Weber to show that Adam's disobedience was at least occasionally regarded as a momentous act of deliberate revolt against God. A striking saying, cited by Dr Schechter[1], may, however, be added to Weber's list, which maintains that Adam would not have committed his sin "unless he had first denied the 'Root of all' (or the main principle), viz. the belief in the omnipresence of God."

It was of course universally taught by the Rabbis that our first parents' disobedience brought death upon themselves. The Targum of Pseudo-Jonathan on Gen. iii. 6 says that Eve, when beside the tree, "saw Samael, the angel of death, and was afraid," and repeats the denunciation of death against Adam and Eve much in the words of the Scripture. And such teaching is representative. The difficulty arising out of the fact that Adam did not die in the day on which he ate the forbidden fruit is sometimes explained by the Rabbis, as it is in the *Book of Jubilees*, by taking the day to be a thousand years.

It is more important, however, to ascertain what opinions were held by the Rabbis upon the relation of the mortality of the race to the punishment of Adam and Eve with death. For here we enter again upon the subject of the consequences of the Fall, and approach the doctrine of original guilt. Previous writers, such as Edersheim and Weber, have pointed out the existence of two or three different views in rabbinical literature with regard to the cause of death amongst mankind; but no certain knowledge has yet been attained as to whether these divergent views succeeded one another in time, or whether they coexisted in different schools or in the minds of individual Rabbis. Ginzberg, in one of the series of papers to which reference has several times been made, has argued that the view, according to which every man brings death upon himself by his own sin, was the prevalent teaching in the earliest centuries of our era, but that this gave place to the doctrine that the universal mortality of the race is due to Adam's fall. And this generalisation would seem to be for the most part true. But, in the light of the fact that, already in Ben Sira's

---

[1] *J. Q. R.* I. 54, and *Studies in Judaism*.

day, the first sin was assigned as the cause of death to the race, and that this view was quite general amongst the pseudepigraphists of the first century, whose haggada was very largely identical with that of the Rabbis of the mishnic and talmudic periods, the statement is perhaps too sweeping. It is very probable that the individualistic view was much more generally held in the first and second than in the third and following centuries, and was then rapidly replaced by that which had already obtained a footing in the Christian Church. But that the doctrine which attributes our mortality to Adam was not held by any of the Tannaim is perhaps more than can be proved, though traces of its existence amongst them seem to be extremely rare[1].

The Old Testament view that man is by nature mortal, and that death was predetermined for him by his Creator from the first, a view which some have believed still to survive in Ecclesiasticus, in spite of verse 24 of the twenty-fifth chapter of that book[2], is not frequently met with in rabbinic literature[3]. Death is generally regarded as the consequence of sin, for us as well as for Adam. The question remains, how far is it regarded as in each case the consequence of the individual's sin, and how far as the consequence of the fall of Adam?

It has already been mentioned that the generations of Rabbis nearest the time of Christ seem to have been more inclined to emphasise the individual's responsibility for his death, just as they emphasised his responsibility for his sinfulness. Following the individualistic doctrine of guilt, of which Ezekiel was a foremost preacher, R. Ammi rigidly maintained that "there is no death without sin[4]." Dr Schechter[5] considers that there can hardly be any doubt that this view was held by the authorities of much earlier times than that

---

[1] *Beresch. Rabba*, on Gen. iii. 7, attributes ultimately to Akiba a comparison or illustration in which occur the words: "Even so did God show to the first of mankind how many generations they had ruined." This most probably refers to physical death.
[2] See p. 119.
[3] See Edersheim, *Speaker's Commentary, in loc.*
[4] *Sabbath*, 55 a, where rival traditions are brought together.
[5] *Studies in Judaism*, pp. 260 ff.

of R. Ammi, viz. the third century A.D. He refers to the anxiety frequently betrayed by the Tannaim to explain away the cases in the Old Testament of the children suffering for the parents' sin, and to assign great crimes as the causes of great sufferings.

To illustrate the position maintained by R. Ammi, a legend is narrated in *Tanchuma*[1], according to which "all the pious, being permitted to behold the Shekinah before their death, reproach Adam (as they pass him by at the gate) for having brought death upon them; to which he replies: 'I died with but one sin, but you have committed many; on account of these you have died, not on my account[2].'" Curiously enough, an exactly similar legend is elsewhere appealed to, as will presently be seen, in support of the opposite theory. But there is better evidence that the individualistic view was strongly supported in pre-talmudic times. The direct consequence of such a doctrine would be the sinfulness of the saints and patriarchs; yet even this was definitely maintained by R. Elieser b. Hirkanos: "If the Holy One, blessed be He! should enter into judgment with Abraham, Isaac and Jacob, they would not be able to stand before the proving (or exposure)[3]." This, if we are justified in extracting so much from a sentence of Justin Martyr's, would seem to have been the prevailing Jewish teaching so late as the second century. For that apologist says to Trypho[4]: "And not even will you (Jews) venture to assert that anyone performed all those commandments (Deut. xxvii. 26) exactly; but some kept them more, and some less, than others." Another second century Rabbi, Chanina b. Dosa, has been credited with a saying which, though not all referring to the Fall-story, serves to illustrate the belief in the doctrine that individualism is in every case the cause of death: "It is not the serpent which kills, but the sin in us[5]."

[1] This is cited by Kohler in *Jewish Encyclopaedia*, Art. *Adam*.
[2] Cf. *Test. of Abraham*: see p. 195.
[3] *Arachin*, 17 a.
[4] *Dial. c. Tryph*. c. 95.
[5] The words refer to death from serpent-bites; see *Beracoth*, 33 a, and also *Schemoth Rabba*, c. 3 (on Ex. iv. 3), where it is reproduced in connexion with Moses' fear of the serpent into which his rod was converted.

Again, to return to the discussion in the tractate *Sabbath*, it was objected to R. Ammi's teaching, "no death without sin," that when the angels of service asked God if Moses and Aaron had not kept the whole law, and yet had died like Adam, God answered in the words of Eccles. ix. 2, "All things come alike to all; there is one event to the righteous and to the wicked." But the authority of R. Simeon b. Eleazar is then claimed by Ammi: "Moses and Aaron also died on account of their own sins, as is said in Num. xx. 12, 'therefore, because ye have not believed.'" It is added, "R. Simeon b. Eleazar has, however, said: 'there is also a death without sin, and suffering without guilt.'"

Here we have an instance of the conflict of the two alternative views. The need for making exceptions to R. Ammi's teaching is further evidenced by the saying that four men, Benjamin, Amram, Jesse and Chiliab, were free from actual sin, and died because of the transgression brought about by the serpent's counsel[1]. On the principle of the exception proving the rule, this saying is a witness to the authority of the view which made each man "the Adam of his own soul."

The rival view, that all men owe their mortality to their first father, is found, at least from the time of the Amoraim, existing side by side with this teaching. Schechter remarks that there was never any decision between them[2]. But it would seem that, as Judaism grew older, the individualistic view dwindled in strength and it became more and more generally believed, perhaps through the emphasis on original sin within the Church, that Adam was responsible for the death of his descendants. The change would perhaps also be partly due to growing reverence for the patriarchs and other great Old Testament figures, rendering R. Elieser's earlier insistence on their sinfulness in the sight of God, and the doctrine of absolute individual responsibility upon which it depended, less tenable. But, however this may be, the doctrine that death was due to the original transgression

---

[1] *Baba Bathra*, 17 a. It is also stated here as a tradition of the Rabbis, that "over six had the angel of death no power, viz. Abraham, Isaac, Jacob, Moses, Aaron and Miriam."

[2] *op. cit.*, p. 180.

of Adam was common in the talmudic period. R. Jose (4th cent.) is stated in *Siphra*, 27 a, to have said with regard to Adam, "for whose single transgression he and all his posterity were punished with death[1]." Moses, who was declared by R. Simeon to have brought death upon himself by his unbelief, was held by R. Levi[2], to have died "because of the sin of the first man, who brought death into the world." In *Erubin*, 18 b, Adam is said to have isolated himself from Eve because he saw that his sin was the cause of universal death: a saying which reappears with a modification at the end of c. 21 of *Beresch. Rabba*, where Adam is said to have abstained from begetting children because he saw his posterity would be condemned to Gehenna, until he perceived that, after six and twenty generations, the Israelites would accept the Law. Delitzsch[3] quotes a passage from *Pesikta di R. Cahana*, 118 a, according to which Adam's posterity appeared to him when he ate of the forbidden tree, and he acknowledged to them that he had been the cause of death. It would seem that legends once used to support what was probably the older doctrine with regard to death were actually altered to suit the increasingly prevalent idea of original sin.

Though rabbinic teaching *may*, at the time when Christianity appeared, have sometimes supported the view that death was a consequence of Adam's sin, and though apocalyptic writers certainly did so, it does not appear that the

---

[1] In *Yalkut Schim.* this saying is expanded; referring to *Siphre*, 27 a, and to *Yalkut*, I. 479, a writer in *Journal of Philology*, XVI. pp. 139-40, quotes thus: "R. Jose says: if thou wishest to know the reward of the pious in the world to come, go and learn it from the first Adam, who had only been commanded one single law, which he transgressed; see how many deaths were decreed against him and his generations, and against the generations of his generations, to the end of his generations."

[2] *Debarim Rabba*, 9. (Wünsche, S. 101.) Cf. Bacher, *Pal. Amoräer*, Bd. II. S. 420. See also *Kohel. Rabba*, on v. 13.

[3] *Paulus d. Apostel's Brief an die Römer, u.s.w.*, S. 82. *Pesikta* is a post-talmudic work, and perhaps a century later than *Beresch. Rabba*.

Tholuck, in his work on the Epistle to the Romans, cites the following passages: "But the serpent and the woman led him astray, and caused death to be inflicted upon him and upon all the inhabitants of the earth"; *Chald. Targum* on Eccles. vii. 29. "Jesse lived many days, until the counsel which the serpent gave to Eve was called to mind before God; on account of this counsel all men became subject unto death"; *Targum* on Ruth iv. 22.

manner in which such consequences of the Fall were mediated to the race was ever definitely conceived, even in the talmudic age with which we have here chiefly been dealing. It has been seen, indeed, that the pollution of the serpent received by Eve, was held to have been physically propagated; and so far the Rabbis had a doctrine of inherited corruption of nature. Whether mortality was thus regarded as a physically transmitted inheritance, we cannot easily determine. The idea of the potential existence of the race in Adam, of which S. Augustine made use, for all that a kindred conception was already formulated by the writer of the Epistle to the Hebrews[1], does not appear to have occurred to the ancient Rabbi; or, if it had occurred, does not appear to have been used in connexion with the universal consequences derived from Adam's sin. The nearest approach to the doctrine that the race is included in Adam which can here be cited from at all ancient rabbinic tradition is supplied by the following passage from *Schemoth Rabba*[2]: "What is meant by 'And it is known that it is man (Adam)'? (Exod. xxxi. 1, 2 and Eccl. vi. 10). When the first man was still an unformed mass, God let him see every single righteous man who should some time proceed from him; one hung from his head, another from his hair, the third from his forehead, the fourth from his eyes, the fifth from his nose, the sixth from his mouth, the seventh from his ears, the eighth from his jaws[3]." And even this cannot be regarded as certainly embodying teaching belonging to the mishnic period. In later ages, no doubt, statements concerning the relation of the race to Adam similar to such as we call Augustinian, are to be met with in Jewish books. The Cabbalists certainly, as Dr Schechter says, evolved the whole of ideal humanity from the archetype Adam; and commentators of the modern period and of the middle ages frequently regarded our first parent as the sum of the race[4].

[1] vii. 9, 10.   [2] c. 40. Wünsche, S. 282.
[3] Cf. the saying of R. Chayim Vital, that the souls of two great teachers, Maimonides and Nachmanides, both sprang from the head of Adam (Schechter, *Studies in Judaism*).
[4] The following instances may be given:
"One must not wonder that the sin of Adam and Eve was ascribed to after

We have, however, been unable to discover one instance of the occurrence, in rabbinical literature previous to the close of the talmudic period, of the idea that Adam included in himself, potentially, the whole race, and that his sin was the sin of all mankind.

This idea, dominant in the Western Church since the time of S. Augustine, was used as an expedient for justifying the attribution of guilt to all men for their inborn 'sinfulness.' In the absence of such an expedient among the Rabbis, it may be asked whether it was possible for them, when they taught, as they sometimes did, that men died on account of Adam's sin, to regard mankind as participating in the guilt of that transgression? In other words, did they hold a doctrine of original, or inherited, guilt (*Erbschuld*)? Weber answers this question affirmatively in one place and negatively in another[1]. So far as a conclusion may be drawn from the

generations and sealed for them with the seal of the King. For just on the day in which the first man was created had everything been completed, and he is the completion of the structure and its totality; for on him was the world (i.e. the human world) founded. And when he sinned, the whole world sinned, and we have got to bear his sins...." *Cabbalistic Commentary on the Pentateuch*, by Menahem Rekanati (beginning of 14th century), ed. 1545, Venice; fol. 29, col. 1.

"On account of the sin of Adam, who has caused death to himself and his seed after him to the end of all generations. [It is known from Nature that, when the root is struck and hurt, the branches suffer with it. So are the later generations the branches from the root (Adam).]" Berhai, *Kad ha-gemach*, Venice, 1546, fol. 5: a work written at the end of the 13th century.

For the above two references the author is indebted to the kindness of a German scholar unknown to him; they were received through Prof. Pfleiderer of Berlin.

The following passage is quoted in a work the reference to which has, unfortunately, been lost; its source was there said to be *The Two Tables of the Covenant*, p. 8, col. 2:

"Since the soul of Adam is the root of all souls, and from him all souls were spread out, therefore when death was decreed upon him, it was also decreed upon all that came out of him; for all were by his strength (or, proceeded by his power)."

Tholuck, *Umschreib. Uebersetzung des Briefes Pauli an die Römer*, S. 157, quotes from R. Mosche v. Trana's *Beth Elohim*, f. 105, c. 1 (15th century): "With the same sin with which Adam sinned, sinned the whole world, for he was the whole world."

[1] S. 224 f. "*Es gibt eine Erbschuld, aber keine Erbsünde; der Fall Adams hat dem ganzen Geschlechte den Tod, nicht aber die Sündigkeit im Sinne einer Nothwendigkeit zu sündigen, verursacht.*" Here, apparently, guilt is said to be inherited by Adam's posterity because his punishment of death has passed over to

passages in which Adam's sin is spoken of as the cause of human mortality, it would seem that they only meant to teach that the punishment alone, and not the guilt, of Adam's sin was attached to the race.

It only remains now to inquire whether rabbinical theology knew of any such conception as that of inherited inborn 'sinfulness,' of a state of disharmony or corruption produced once and for all in human nature by the first transgression and transmitted by inheritance to all the human race. This is, of course, what is now generally understood by 'original sin.'

We have seen already that Judaism possessed, apparently from very early times, a coarse physical theory of a pollution attaching to the race in consequence of the sin of Eve. Such a fact serves to show that the idea of inherited and inborn taint of sin, acquired at the very beginning of human history, did not emerge for the first time in the ecclesiastical doctrine of original sin. But it is very doubtful whether this Jewish fancy played at all an important part in the rabbinic doctrine of human sinfulness[1]. The moral nature of man was gener-

them. On S. 249, however, we read: "*Adam's Sünde ist ja nicht die Sünde des Geschlechts, sondern seine eigene. Der Mensch wird nicht zum Sünder vermöge seiner Abstammung von Adam, sondern lediglich durch seine eigene That. Wie kann, wo die Sünde nicht auf das Geschlecht übergeht, die Strafe der Sünde übergehen? Wenn die Sünde und Schuld nicht erblich ist, kann dann die Strafe erblich sein?*" In this passage Weber seems to imply that, inasmuch as mankind was not held, in rabbinical theology, to have participated in Adam's sin, nor by descent from Adam to have inherited a sinful state, a difficulty is encountered when man's subjection to death comes up for explanation. Mankind receive Adam's punishment, but do *not* share or inherit his guilt.

[1] Prof. Stevens, in his work *The Pauline Theology*, collects from Tholuck a few citations which serve to illustrate comparatively modern Jewish teaching, but which are valueless as a guide to rabbinic doctrine at the beginning of the Christian era. The following may be reproduced here:

"If Adam and Eve had not sinned, their descendants would not have been infected with the disposition to sin, and their form would have remained perfect like that of the angels, as the curses (upon them) show, and they would have continued eternally living."

This is quoted from "the mystical commentaries" by R. Shemtob, 13th century, in *Sepher Haemunoth*.

The next passage is from R. Mayer b. Gabbai, *Avodath Hakkodesch*, f. 52: "Adam opened, through his fall, a source of impurity, so that impurity and poison spread themselves throughout the whole world."

Such doctrine as this was most probably borrowed by Jews from the Christian Church.

VII]   *in Rabbinical Literature*   169

ally discussed in terms of the conception of the good and evil *yezers*. And since Weber, in his already often quoted work, *Jüdische Theologie*, maintained that certain rabbinic sayings implied that the *yezer hara* was permanently strengthened in mankind by the sin of Adam, it has become impossible fully to discuss the Jewish doctrine of the Fall without referring to the doctrine of the *yezers*.

With this latter doctrine in general, indeed, we are not here concerned. The only question with regard to it which calls for consideration is, whether it supplied a view of man's moral constitution such as was inconsistent with the explanation of human sinfulness in terms of an inherited propensity to evil introduced once and for all by Adam into our common nature, or whether it was ever actually so blended with the doctrine of the Fall as to furnish a means for expressing the moral consequences of that catastrophe for all subsequent generations of mankind.

The doctrine of the *yezer*, and later, of the two *yezers*, originated and developed, of course, without any connexion with the doctrine of the Fall and its consequences. Its origin, moreover, was exegetical rather than speculative; and the earliest stages of its growth have been noticed in connexion with Ben Sira's doctrine of sin. In the period in which the New Testament was written, the conception of the evil inclination must have been definite and widespread[1], for it had been known to Ben Sira on the one hand, and was a commonplace with the Tannaim on the other. That it was a post-Christian rabbinic production has been abundantly disproved by the recovered fragments of the Hebrew of

---

[1] It was known to the writer of the apocalypse of Ezra. Dr Taylor suggests that the N.T. phrases διαλογισμὸς πονηρός (Matt. xv. 19), παλαιὸς ἄνθρωπος (Eph. iv. 22, 23), κρυπτὸς τῆς καρδίας ἄνθρωπος (1 Peter iii. 4) are probably equivalents of *yezer hara*. Cf. also James i. 13—15. The doctrine of the *yezer* perhaps appears, in Stoic dress, in 4 Macc. ii. 21, where man's inclinations are said to have been implanted by God, though the understanding was put on the throne over them; and in iii. 4, where reason is said to be not the extirpator, but the conqueror, of inclination. Again, in *Testament of Aser*, 1, occurs the passage: δύο ὁδοὺς ἔδωκεν ὁ θεὸς υἱοῖς τῶν ἀνθρώπων καὶ δύο διαβούλια καὶ δύο πράξεις καὶ δύο τόπους καὶ δύο τέλη. Perhaps there is also an allusion to the *yezer* in *Test. of Judah*, 20.

Ecclesiasticus; that it was Hellenic in origin is also disproved by the fact that, in its earliest form, the conception of the evil *yezer* does not appear to have been correlated with the conception of a good *yezer*, so that the doctrine was not at first dualistic, and by the fact that the contrast between the good and the evil inclination, when it arose, was purely ethical, and did not imply a dualistic anthropology or metaphysic, such as many recent theologians consider Judaism to have borrowed from Hellenic thought[1].

It is probable, if not certain, that the idea of the *yezer tob*, or good inclination, did not arise till a considerably later time than that at which the *yezer hara* had become a definite and well-known conception. The earliest rabbinical saying given by Bacher in which it occurs is one attributed to R. Jose the Galilaean, who lived in the earlier part of the second century[2]. It plays always a very inferior part, as compared with the *yezer hara*, in the discussions of the Rabbis on man's moral nature. That both the good and the evil inclination were created by God was taught by R. Nachman b. Chisda[3], who drew the inference from the fact that in Gen. ii. 7, where the creation of man is narrated, the word for 'formed' is written with two *yods*, implying the existence of two natures in man. That the evil *yezer* was the creation of God is taught in other passages also, and seems to have been the general belief[4]. One of the most important of these is of interest because of its close similarity to Ecclus. xxi. 11: "I (God) created the evil *yezer*; but I created also the antidote for it, the torah[5]." The Rabbis do not attempt to explain thoroughly the difficulty involved in regarding God as the creator of man's evil impulse. Perhaps the conception of the good inclination was the result of the pressure of this difficulty; but the introduction of that

---

[1] This is proved in Dr Porter's able examination of the doctrine of the *yezer hara*, and of Weber's very faulty representation of it; *Historical and Critical Contributions to Biblical Science*, New York and London, 1901.

[2] *Die Agada der Tannaiten*, Bd. I. S. 368. It occurs in the passage just cited from the *Testament of Aser*, perhaps, for the first time.

[3] *Beracoth*, 61 a.

[4] See Weber, *op. cit.*, S. 211, Porter, *op. cit.*, p. 117 ff. and a passage cited by Schechter, *J. Q. R.* VII. pp. 195–6.

[5] *Kiddusch*. 30 b.

conception does not really solve the problem. Sometimes the evil *yezer* appears to have been regarded as not essentially evil. R. Samuel b. Nachman understood the divine pronouncement that the creation was very good (Gen. i. 31) to include the evil impulse, and explained that this impulse was essential to the continuance of human life and business[1]. This teaching, however, was exceptional. The general belief was that the *yezer hara* is essentially evil, and yet that, though man is responsible for intensifying it, its existence is due not to man but to God[2].

Consequently it was not supposed that the evil impulse was in any sense a consequence of Adam's sin. At least this was certainly not the general view. Weber gives no instance of such a belief; and Dr Porter, in his recent exhaustive discussion of the doctrine of the *yezer hara*, says: "It does not appear that its rise was traced to Adam's sin." This writer then mentions the passage from *Tanchuma*, to which reference has just been made; but even this does not refer to the Fall, but to the sinfulness of mankind in general, as the cause of the evil nature of the *yezer*. There is one instance, however, of the occurrence of this opinion in rabbinical literature, viz. in the second recension of the *Aboth di R. Nathan*[3], where it is said that the seventh of the ten punishments decreed against Adam was: "There shall be in him the *yezer hara*." This statement, so far as we know, is unique; and, even if it were a genuine saying of R. Nathan, it would only date from the second century. The nearest parallel to it which we have been able to discover is afforded by Raschi's exegesis of Isai. v., where the allegory of the vineyard is applied to Paradise and the history of its two inhabitants. The following fragment may be quoted: "'And

---

[1] *Beresch. Rabba*, c. 9.

[2] In *Tanchuma*, Gen. iii. 22, a late source, it is stated that man, and not God, made the *yezer* evil.

The essentially evil character of the *yezer hara* is implied in passages which represent the patriarchs, David and others, as not having been under its dominion; see, e.g., *Baba Bathra*, 17 a.

[3] c. 41, ed. Schechter. This recension is only to be found in Dr Schechter's edition of the *Aboth di R. Nathan*. The author is indebted, for the reference, to Dr Schechter himself.

gathered out the stones thereof,' *i.e.* the *yezer hara*, until he ate of the tree, and then entered into him the *yezer hara*;... 'but there shall come up briars and thorns,' *i.e.* the *yezer hara* shall prevail in him and in his posterity after him[1]." Here the *yezer* is supposed to have been in man at the first, to have been removed from him in the state of innocence, and to have been implanted in him again after his transgression.

The solitary instance of the occurrence, in literature of the talmudic period or thereabouts, of the belief that the *yezer hara* was implanted as a punishment for the first sin, only serves to prove that as a rule this opinion was not held; it was not a common tradition.

Weber has maintained that a somewhat similar, though quite distinct view, is to be gathered from several passages in the literature with which we are here concerned. According to him, the Fall was supposed by the Rabbis to have increased (permanently) the intensity of the evil impulse which was previously only dormant. Thenceforth it gained a lasting ascendancy in Adam and in his posterity, and could only be resisted with the greatest effort[2]. If this be a true interpretation of the views of the Jewish teachers with regard to the effect of the Fall upon man's moral constitution, it is plain that they held a theory which was equivalent to that of S. Augustine, though expressed in different language. The permanent ascendancy of the evil impulse, brought about once and for all in mankind by the sin of Adam, is practically identical with the corruption of our nature asserted by Christian theology. Weber's statements have been adopted by subsequent writers; and, on the strength of them, a doctrine of inherited taint, conceived in terms of the conception of the evil impulse, has been attributed to S. Paul, who is supposed to imply, in the well-known passage Rom. v. 12 ff., and perhaps elsewhere, the doctrine which Weber regarded as current in rabbinical theology.

---

[1] Raymund Martin, *Pugio Fidei*, ed. Voisin, Paris, 1651, fol. 473. Raschi wrote in the 11th or 12th century, so that the above citation is no certain witness to ancient rabbinical opinion.

[2] *op. cit.*, S. 213, 216, 224.

It is therefore of some importance to examine the chief references on which Weber based his view.

When describing the rabbinic accounts of the unfallen state of man[1], Weber quotes a saying of R. Jose which refers to woman having been the cause of Adam's death and loss of innocence, from which he deduces that the *yezer hara*, though present in Adam from the first, was only a sensuous impulse, in itself morally indifferent; as yet it was but dormant (*ruhte*). After the Fall, however, it is subsequently stated, the *yezer* became more irrepressible, because, when the present condition of man is in question, it is frequently called 'a king[2].'

Now the saying of R. Jose which speaks of Adam's lost innocence does not mention the *yezer hara*, and it is gratuitous to identify innocence in general with non-activity of the *yezer* which is elsewhere said by Rabbis, when not thinking specially of the unfallen nature of Adam, to have been in him from the first. Further, if the *yezer* acquired its might in consequence of the Fall, how came the first sin itself to be committed? And if, as the Rabbis seem generally to have held, the period between Adam's creation and his sin was only a few hours, we can hardly credit them with any definite conception of the unfallen nature of man such as Christian theologians elaborated; certainly they could hardly have conceived that state in terms of ideas such as those of the quiescence or importunity of the *yezer*. In fact there are no rabbinical statements as to the behaviour of Adam's *yezer* before his fall, and it is useless to draw inferences on the point from mere general statements that he was made in the image of God, and was at first pure.

And it would seem to be equally mistaken to infer that, because the evil impulse in man, as he now is, is frequently stated to be very powerful, or to have acquired the ascendancy, this is characteristic of him *as fallen*, and denotes a result of the Fall, unless the distinction between the fallen and the unfallen state is contemplated in the context in which

---

[1] *op. cit.*, S. 213.
[2] S. 216, and 224; see below.

the violence of the *yezer* is described. This condition is wanting, however, in each of the passages of which Weber made use. They one and all describe the evil impulse as it is known by actual experience, and simply assert that it is very powerful. Its supremacy is a matter of observation, not a deduction from any view as to the effects of Adam's sin[1].

On the other hand, "the doctrine that God made man with both good and evil instincts and dispositions, and that it is man, not God, who made the evil prevail, is sometimes expressed, though it cannot be the original form of the doctrine, and never appears to be accepted as a sufficient account of man's moral condition[2]." But when it was taught that man is responsible for the greater power of his evil *yezer*, it is the individual man that is meant; each one, through yielding to his inclination and not seeking with sufficient diligence to overcome it, has caused its increase of

---

[1] The following are three of the chief passages to which Weber refers (S. 224) when emphasising the ascendancy ascribed to the *yezer hara* in connexion with the consequences of the Fall. The others will be found, on perusal, to be equally irrelevant to the conclusion which is extracted from them.
Bammidbar Rabba, c. 15 on x. 2 (Wünsche, S. 402): "Und der König" d. i. der gute Trieb herrsche (sei König) über den bösen Trieb, welcher König genannt wird, wie es heisst, Koh. IX. 4; "Und es kommt über sie ein grosser König und umzingelt sie."
S. 405, "Herr der Welt! du kennst die Macht des bösen Triebes, dass er sehr arg ist."
Koheleth Rabba (IV. 13). Wünsche, S. 64: "Unter dem dürftigen, aber weisen, Jüngling ist der gute Trieb zu verstehen. Warum heisst derselbe aber Jüngling? Weil er im Menschen erst vom dreizehnten Jahre an sich regt.... Und dem alten thörichten König dagegen ist der böse Trieb zu verstehen. Warum heisst derselbe König? Weil ihm alle gehorchen. Warum ist er alt? Weil er mit dem Menschen von seiner Jugend bis zu seinem Alter sich zu schaffen macht."
S. 131. "Oder: 'Eine kleine Stadt' d. i. der Körper, 'die Männer' d. i. seine Glieder 'sind wenig,' 'es kommt ein grosser König' d. i. der böse Trieb, der deshalb gross genannt wird, weil er dreizehn Jahre älter ist, als der gute Trieb, der sich erst in diesem Alter regt, 'er umgiebt sie und legt grosse Bollwerke an' d. i. Verstecke und Irrwege, 'es fand sich ein armer, aber weiser, Mann' d. i. der gute Trieb, der darum arm genannt wird weil er sich nicht bei allen Menschen findet, und die meisten ihm nicht gehorchen."
Part of this last piece of exegesis occurs in *Nedarim*, 32 b (Wünsche, *Bab. Talmud*, II. i. 204).

[2] Porter, *op. cit.*, p. 118.

might. The ascendancy of the evil over the good *yezer* is a universally acquired habit, not a hereditary disease.

Again, talmudic literature insists on a man's capacity to control his evil inclination, mighty as it is. There is no hint that his free-will is diminished in consequence of the sin of his first parents; and herein lies the main difference between the spirit of the teaching of the Synagogue and that of the Church. The Rabbis recognised, of course, the general sinfulness of humanity, but yet maintained the theoretical possibility of sinlessness, and indeed held that in some cases this had actually been attained [1].

In so far, then, as the actual sinfulness of mankind is accounted for in rabbinic literature by the conception of the *yezer hara*, it is explained without reference to the Fall and the heredity of its consequences. The evil impulse was implanted by God in Adam, whose sin it caused [2], and it appears to have been conceived as similarly implanted in every individual child of Adam. The *yezer hara* was not held to have its seat in the body, as distinguished from the soul, in spite of figurative expressions which describe its situation; and therefore, as the Rabbis were not traducianists, it could not have been thought to be propagated, like the original sin, or fault of nature, of Christian theology, by physical inheritance. Indeed various opinions were held as to whether it arose in the individual before or after birth. It was said that the evil inclination is thirteen years older

[1] See above, p. 164. The sinlessness of Reuben, the sons of Eli (!), David and Solomon was maintained by one ingenious Rabbi (see *Sabbath*, 55 b—56 a), and R. Eleazar taught that "he who dwells in the land of Israel abides without iniquity"; but one must not take such doctrines too seriously. A more typical representative of the characteristics of early rabbinic teaching was Akiba, who held sin to be a consequence of free-will (*Sanhedr.* 57), mocked at the idea of one's incapacity for self-mastery (*Kiddusch.* 81 a), and identified Elihu, for his bewailing the frailty of man, with Balaam (*Jerus. Sota*, 5). From *Erubin*, 13 b (see also Kohler, *J. Q. R.* VII. 603), we gather that the school of Hillel took a brighter view of man, with all his shortcomings, than that of the school of Schammai, whose pessimism meets us also in 4 Ezra and other apocalypses of the same period.

[2] The evil *yezer*, after being personified into an external agency, regarded as sitting at the door of the heart, came to be identified sometimes with Satan (*Baba Bathra*, 16 a); and it was asserted (*Joma*, 69 b) to have been the (external) tempter of Adam to his fall.

than the good; after thirteen years the good inclination reveals itself[1]. In the same context it is asked how a man shall free himself from the evil *yezer* 'which is in his bowels'; "for his very conception is due to the *yezer hara*, which strengthens itself till the time comes for him to leave his mother's womb, and at that moment it is already dwelling at the entrance of his heart." Elsewhere the activity of the *yezer* is said to begin after birth; but even the passage just quoted (in abridged form), though strongly suggesting physical transmission of the *yezer*, need not be so interpreted.

It must be concluded, then, that the only consequences of the Fall, for the human race, which were asserted in rabbinic teaching, are death and loss of the various supernatural adornments of Adam's life at its beginning. No diminished freedom of will, no permanent ascendancy of the *yezer hara* established for all generations, were ascribed to the first transgression. Nor do we find any reference to the idea of all the race being in Adam, or identified with Adam, when he sinned. Judaism possessed, indeed, the legend of the pollution of Eve by Satan, and of the taint transmitted by her to her posterity. But this belief, though widespread, does not appear to have served the purpose of an explanation of universal sinfulness. Whether the defilement was understood to be of a moral kind is not made plain; but this fanciful story witnesses to the existence, in rabbinic circles, of a series of ideas which bear some sort of similarity to those which constitute the doctrine of original sin and hereditary infection of nature.

* * * * *

NOTE. The student interested in the curious Jewish fancies concerning the details of the Fall-story will find ancient traditions, having much in common with those collected in the succeeding chapters from ancient apocalyptic writings, in the late works *Sepher-ha-yaschar* (8th—9th cent.), translated in Migne, *Dictionnaire des Apocryphes*, Tome II. 1069 ff., and in the still later *Chronicles of Jerahmeel*, translated in *S. B. E.*, new series, vol. IV.

---

[1] *Aboth di R. Nathan*, 16.

CHAPTER VIII.

THE FALL AND ORIGINAL SIN IN JEWISH PSEUDEPIGRAPHICAL LITERATURE.

THE last class of Jewish writings to be examined for the roots of New Testament and ecclesiastical teaching, with regard to the Fall and to its consequences for the human race, is the pseudepigraphic, which consists mainly of apocalypses. There is no room for doubt that these writings were more nearly akin than those examined in the two preceding chapters, both in tone and in doctrine, to the literature of the New Testament, and of the early Church. The exposition of their teaching with regard to human sinfulness will serve to illustrate the truth of this assertion for some, at least, of them.

It is too remote from the purpose of the present work to attempt a detailed account of what has been thought as to the origin of Jewish apocalyptic literature. A few statements must suffice to differentiate its origin, subject-matter and standpoint from those of other Jewish writings, in so far as this is possible. This class of literature has seemed to certain writers to have roots in Essenism[1]. Some authorities emphasise the possibility that foreign influences stimulated the growth of its characteristic ideas and supplied models for its method. Gunkel has argued that it contains ancient traditional elements of mythical nature, preserved in folk-lore[2]. These

[1] See Porter in Hastings' *Dict. of the Bible*, I. p. 113; Hilgenfeld, *Die Jüdische Apokalyptik*, etc.
[2] *Schöpfung und Chaos*, etc.; see also Bousset, *The Anti-Christ Legend*.

elements, in part at least, have been said to be Babylonian[1]. Other scholars[2] have pointed to Mazdeism for the source of certain apocalyptic ideas. Yet again, in consequence of the opinion that no models, from which apocalyptic writings may have been derived, are known in Persian literature, Greece and Egypt have been thought to have more probably supplied the external conditions which gave shape to some of the characteristics of this class of writings[3]. Possibly there is truth in all these views; but the extent to which foreign influences had been at work in stimulating the flow of apocalyptic literature is as yet uncertainly known. There can be little doubt, however, that although it was not, perhaps, wholly indigenous to Judaism, and not entirely a product of the Jewish native genius, it was a direct outgrowth, in some respects at least, from later prophecy, and a development of tendencies already exhibited in canonical books of the Old Testament. In Isaiah, Ezekiel and Zechariah, for instance, we find passages which, in respect of both subject-matter and treatment, *i.e.* eschatology and visionary revelations, approach the character of the literature distinguished as apocalyptic; and the book of Daniel is an immediate precursor of the whole class of such writings, if not contemporary with some of them.

There is no extant example of this kind of literature, after the close of prophecy, until about the Maccabean age, the events of which are supposed to have been a cause of literary activity in this direction. The felt need of something more akin than official scribism to those elements of prophecy which dealt with the future of Israel, and which should solve pressing difficulties suggested by the apparent non-fulfilment of the prophets' predictions of Israel's destiny, led to that revival of one side of prophecy in which the work of the pseudepigraphical writers may be said largely to consist.

But in offering a forecast of the future, these writers sometimes attempted a review of the divine plan in the past history of the race as a whole, and thus supplied a rough

---

[1] Beer, in Kautzsch's *Pseudepigraphen*, S. 233.
[2] Kohler, *Jew. Quart. Review*, v. 405.
[3] See Torrey, in *Jew. Encyclopaedia*, Art. *Apocalyptic Literature*.

attempt at what might, with a generous stretch of meaning, be called a philosophy of history. In order to include the future, they review the past; and, in doing so, they try to satisfy curiosity more completely than was done by the 'historical' element in the Mosaic Law pure and simple. They profess to disclose the secret things of the distant past as well as of the future, and, amongst them, the history of the first men and the beginnings of sin. They afford a doctrinal interpretation of passages of the Old Testament which were originally founded on mythical legend, whose earlier significance had been forgotten and was now irrecoverable, because the methods of historical criticism and scientific exegesis were foreign to their age. They thus serve to illustrate, more conspicuously, perhaps, than other Jewish writings, how, when doctrinal exegesis of the ancient records commenced, it proceeded from the first upon the wrong tack. For these reasons the pseudepigrapha are of importance to our investigation.

For the purpose of supplying knowledge on such matters as those which have just been named, the apocalyptist would seem to have drawn from the national stock of tradition which the Old Testament had by no means exhausted, owing chiefly to the fact that it rigorously excluded all save such as was, or could be made, most edifying, and lent itself most readily to sacred use. It is not surprising thus to meet with a reappearance of mythical, or rather legendary, material at a date subsequent to that of the latest books included in the canon: of ancient material enriched with newly invented additions and embellishments, as well as with elements borrowed from foreign sources[1]. It is not easy to ascertain, in many cases, which details are probably survivals of ancient myth amongst the larger quantity which are undoubtedly products of the fancy and imagination of the writer or of the circle which he represented. But the expansions of biblical narrative with which we meet in the apocalyptic books are of the nature of haggada[2], and grew

[1] See Beer, *Das Buch der Jubiläen*.
[2] See arts. by Kohler on Pre-Talmudic Haggada in *Jew. Quart. Review*, V. and VII.

180   *The Fall and Original Sin*   [CHAP.

largely out of the same roots as that of the talmudic literature. The pseudepigraphic writings are in fact a branch of haggada. It was once more usual than it appears to be now for writers, especially Jewish writers, sharply to dissociate the apocalyptic from the talmudic literature; to regard the former kind as off the lines of orthodox thought and official teaching, and as devoid of importance in the history of Judaism[1]. It is true, of course, that the pseudepigraphical writings were never sanctioned by the official Judaism of the talmudists; but this is probably due, at least in part, to the fact that these writings were largely adopted by the Christian Church[2]. They form a valuable, and indeed indispensable, guide to the popular religious beliefs of their time, to the 'folk-faith' of the Jewish people; and they express much of the current speculation of provincial, but generally orthodox, Pharisaism. It is an exaggeration to say that they represent a mere fringe, and not at all the dominating thought and speculation of their time.

Many authorities are now able to endorse the words of Schürer[3]: "Der Standpunkt aller dieser Schriften ist im wesentlichen der correct Jüdische."

Assuming, then, that the pseudepigraphical books represented the mind of the more earnest and inwardly religious scribes, the soil in which Christianity most naturally took root, and that they were studied, esteemed and produced within orthodox Pharisaic circles, we have now to collect such passages from them as illustrate the development of Jewish speculation and exegesis on the subject of the Fall and its consequences for mankind. At present these writings will be examined separately and in order, for the teaching which they severally offer, in so far as it is relevant to our

---

[1] As, *e.g.*, Jost (*Geschichte des Judenthums*, Bd. II. S. 218); Grätz; Weber (*Jüd. Theologie*, 1897, S. xv); Montefiore (*Hibbert Lectures*).

[2] Dr Schechter has expressed the doubt whether these writings were so much as heard of by the Rabbis. It is very astonishing that the rabbinical literature should teem with elements of haggada identical in the minutest particulars, however fanciful and grotesque, with such as we meet with in these apocalypses.

[3] *Geschichte des jüdischen Volkes*, Bd. II. S. 612; cf. Baldensperger, *Das Selbstbewusstsein Jesu*; Stanton, *The Christian and the Jewish Messiah*; Torrey, *loc. cit.*, and other English writers.

inquiry. To the classification, according to subject-matter, of the teaching so derived—together with that yielded by the classes of literature previously discussed—another chapter must be devoted, in the hope that, in spite of the repetition so involved, some slight service may thereby be rendered to the student of the history of doctrine.

I. *The (Aethiopic) Book of Enoch.*

The *Book of Enoch* is recognised to be a redaction of several writings of different authorship and date. The portion which is usually called its groundwork, consisting of cc. i—xxxvi., lxxii—civ., is generally assigned to the second century B.C.; and there is considerable agreement that cc. i—xxxvi., the oldest part of this groundwork, date from a time earlier than 167 B.C. The exact analysis of this composite work, and the dating of its several sections, cannot yet be taken as finally settled; but we may safely assume that the most ancient portion of the apparently composite groundwork contains the earliest extant apocalyptic writing[1]. For this reason the *Book of Enoch* is here examined first in order.

(a) *The Groundwork.*

The groundwork, consisting of cc. i—xxxvi., lxii—civ. (save interpolations), is of interest because it contains an elaborate development of the ancient elohim-legend embodied in Gen. vi. 1-4, concerning the descent to earth of the 'sons of God,' and, as will presently be argued, it traces the sinfulness of the world to this event. These celestial beings are not called 'sons of God' in *Enoch*, but 'sons of the heavens,'

[1] It implies the existence of a considerable literature similar in character and earlier in date.

Prof. Charles's mode of division of the whole *Book of Enoch* is here followed as a matter of convenience to English readers, and his translation has been cited throughout this chapter. In this author's *The Book of Enoch*, 1893, guidance will be found to the views of critics who hold different opinions as to the subdivision and date of the constituents of the apocalypse. These questions have been more recently discussed by Beer in Kautzsch's *Pseudepigraphen des A.T.* A new Aethiopic text, and a German translation of the book (to be followed by notes), have recently been supplied by Flemming and Radermacher.

'sons of the holy angels' or 'watchers.' We may compare the rendering ἄγγελοι τοῦ θεοῦ of the LXX. and of Philo (*De Gigant.*): "une modification des expressions de la Gen.," as M. Lods[1] has said, "destinée à la fois à expliquer les termes bibliques et à leur enlever ce qu'ils avaient de choquant pour le judaïsme de l'époque grecque, si jaloux de la transcendence divine."

The object of the watchers in coming to earth was to possess themselves of human wives. These they "taught charms and enchantments, and made them acquainted with the cutting of roots and of woods." The offspring of such unions were giants, which "turned themselves against mankind in order to devour them," so that "the earth complained of the unrighteous ones[2]." The teaching of the arts to men by the angels is described with fuller detail in some (interpolated) verses of c. viii., Azazel taking the most prominent part. A little later we read: "See then what Azazel hath done, how he hath taught all unrighteousness on earth and revealed the secret things of the world which were

---

[1] *Le Livre d'Henoch*, p. 104.

Charles (*in. loc.*) referring to Delitzsch, *New Commentary on Genesis*, where analogy between Gen. vi. 1—4 and the Avesta (*Yasna* IX. 46) is mentioned, seems to believe that the original Hebrew myth of the descent of the sons of God was derived from Persia. This is improbable to the last degree, partly because of the lack of contact with Persia before the time of J, and also because the legend appears, as W. R. Smith believed, to be Semitic and of extreme antiquity. Delitzsch does not suggest a Persian origin. Persian influence may well have directed the development which the old legend received at the hands of the apocalyptic writers, however. Certainly there is a great difference between the treatment which the biblical story receives in *Enoch* (and other apocalyptic writings) and its incidental usage in passages such as Ecclus. xvi. 7, Wisd. xiv. 6, 3 Macc. ii. 4, Bar. iii. 26. Philo's application of it is, of course, quite off the lines of Judaism, and Josephus was doubtless familiar with the developed form of the legend, which, it is interesting to note, he calls a tradition; *Antt.* I. iii. 1, "For many angels of God formed connexions with women, and begat sons that were violent, and despisers of all that was good, on account of the confidence they had in their strength; for the tradition is, that their acts resembled the daring of those whom the Greeks call giants."

[2] c. vi. These seem to be two cycles of tradition interwoven in this and the following chapters: in the one Semjaza is leader of the fallen angels, who bound the others by an oath to join in the sin; in the other Azazel is the chief. Passages of the former kind are considered to be interpolations; see Charles, *in loc.* With c. vi. cf. xv. 3 ff.

wrought in the heavens¹." But human sin is still more definitely ascribed to the fallen angels in the following chapter: "And heal the earth which the angels have defiled, and proclaim the healing of the earth, that I will heal the earth, and that all the children of men shall not perish through all the secret things that the watchers have disclosed and have taught their sons. And the whole earth has been defiled through the teaching of the works of Azazel: to him ascribe all the sin²."

The passages so far referred to in the groundwork imply that the angels descended to earth from lust, their descent presupposing, or being, a moral 'fall.' They further imply that the watchers were the cause of all human corruptness; this corruption of the world being at the same time closely connected with, or mediated through³, the introduction of hidden knowledge and the initiation of progress in arts and science. It is of interest to note that Gen. vi. is here more closely followed than in the *Book of Jubilees* and the *Testaments of the XII Patriarchs*⁴, where a different reason is given. According to the latter of these writings the angels are led astray by the women of earth. This last idea is also apparently implied in a passage in the groundwork of *Enoch*,

---

¹ ix. 6.
² x. 7, 8. Cf. xiii. 2, "because of the oppression which thou hast taught, and because of all the works of blasphemy, oppression and sin which thou hast shown to the children of men."
    Attention must be called to the note of Lods (*op. cit.*, p. 110) on Azazel. He regards cc. vi—viii., in which Azazel was merely one of Semjaza's band, as having been 'retouched' (cf. Charles's view); for in the rest of the book he plays a different *rôle*, being responsible for all human sin because he introduced evil by revealing the mysteries of heaven (not the manufacture of weapons etc., ascribed in viii. 1 to Azazel, but in lxix. 6 to Gadreel). He is elsewhere not associated with the angels who descended through lust, and is spoken of not as having taught the women enchantments, but as having taught mankind generally. In *Yalkut Schim.*, *Beresch.*, 44, Azazel and Semjaza descended for the purpose ascribed to them in *Enoch* vi., but Azazel returned without accomplishing his crime.
³ See esp. xvi. 2, 3: "And now as to the watchers who have sent thee to intercede for them, who had been aforetime in heaven, (say to them,) 'you have been in heaven, and though the hidden things had not yet been revealed to you, you knew worthless mysteries, and these in the hardness of your hearts you have recounted to the women, and through these mysteries women and men work much evil on earth.'"
⁴ See below.

184   *The Fall and Original Sin*   [CHAP.

which, for other reasons, is regarded by Charles as an interpolation in the present text[1].

Another stratum of the groundwork of the *Book of Enoch*, believed by Charles and other critics to have been due to different authors from that of cc. i—xxxvi., consisting of cc. lxxxiii—xc. and dating from the 2nd cent. B.C., lays stress upon the story of the fallen angels. In his first dream-vision Enoch says: "And now the angels of Thy heavens trespass (against Thee) and Thy wrath abideth upon the flesh of men until the great day of judgment[2]." In the second vision "the writer gives a complete history of the world from Adam down to the final judgment and establishment of the Messianic kingdom. After the example of the Book of Daniel men are symbolised by animals;...the fallen watchers by stars[3]." While nothing is said of Adam's sin, it is distinctly taught, though the teaching is conveyed chiefly in figurative dress, that the corruption of the earth which brought down the punishment of the Deluge—the first great world-judgment, was due, not to the sin of man, but to that of the angels who came down[4].

---

[1] xix. 2: "And with their women also who led astray the angels of heaven it will fare in like manner with their friends."
The verse which precedes this is of interest: "Here will stand the angels who have connected themselves with women, and their spirits assuming many different forms have defiled mankind and will lead them astray into sacrificing to demons as gods..."; (1) because of its mention of sacrifice to demons as being introduced by the fallen angels, and the inconsistency of this (see Charles, *in loc.*) with cc. x. xvi.; (2) because of its witness to the belief that the spirits assumed different forms, and not only human bodies (*Test. Reuben*, 5), in order to enter into relation with the human race. M. Lods (*op. cit.* p. 164 f.) refers to *Kiddusch*. 81 a (Weber, S. 243), where Satan is said to have appeared sometimes in the form of a beautiful woman, sometimes in that of a beggar. Cf. *Enoch* lxix. 6; perhaps the identification of the serpent with Satan in late Jewish literature (Wisd. ii. 23 and N. Test.) is a consequence, and particular application, of this new-Hebrew belief.

[2] lxxxiv. 4.

[3] Charles, p. 227. See cc. lxxxvi—lxxxviii.

[4] In xcviii. 4, a chapter which, according to Charles, belongs to yet another distinct layer of the groundwork, occurs a statement which has sometimes been taken to be inconsistent with the prevailing doctrine of this book as to the angels being the cause of sin in the human world: "Even so sin has not been sent upon the earth, but man himself has created it, and into great condemnation will those fall who commit it." But the instigation of the watchers, who showed mankind how to sin, would in any case require voluntary cooperation and acquiescence on

VIII] *in Jewish Pseudepigraphic Writings* 185

These passages are of interest because they reveal a line of fanciful semi-gnostic speculation parallel to, but essentially different from, that which connected the sinfulness and corruption of the world with the transgression of the first parents of the race. Whatever may have been the original meaning of the legend contained in the opening verses of Gen. vi., or that which the Jahvist writer intended them to convey, there can be little doubt that they were used by the writers of the groundwork of *Enoch* in the 2nd century B.C. not only as a biblical account of a fall of angels, but also as an explanation of the entrance of sin into the world, and therefore as the cause of the corruptness of the human race. The view of M. Lods, that the *Book of Enoch* does not seek for an explanation of the origin of evil in its account of the fallen angels[1], cannot here be accepted. Not only are philosophy of history and theodicy problems with which apocalyptic literature in general was largely concerned, but they appear with great prominence in the portions of the *Book of Enoch* which we have been considering. The influence of the watchers is repeatedly connected with the prevalence of human sin, and human sin with divine judgments and the ordering of the world[2]; so that the frequent and copious

the part of those whom they seduced, and this is all that is condemned in the verse before us. Judaism invariably insisted on man's freedom, however it may have regarded sin to have been 'introduced.' In one version of the story of the watchers (see above), the women are regarded as having taken the initiative in wrong-doing.

Thus, whether in the verse ch. c. 4 : "And in those days the angels will descend into the secret places and will gather into one place all those who brought down sin," we read " who brought down sin " (with Charles), or "who aided sin" (with Beer, who follows other MSS.), is unimportant so far as doctrine is concerned.

[1] *op. cit.* p. 103 f.: "L'auteur ne cherche pas dans la chute des anges une explication du mal sur la terre (voyez 98, 4). S'il la raconte, c'est en premier lieu parce qu'il s'intéresse pour eux-mêmes à ces êtres supérieurs, anges et démons, qui occupent une place si envahissante dans les préoccupations de ses contemporains ; mais c'est aussi parce qu'il y trouve un exemple particulièrement saisissant de la justice de Dieu, qu'aucune grandeur ne saurait arrêter."

[2] In lxxx. 2–8 the writer regards the course of nature as dependent on, and modified by, man's sin. The miscarriage of the functions of nature are, however, not attributed, as elsewhere in Jewish literature, to the Fall. Cf. ch. c. 11, which unlike the former passage, is not supposed to be an interpolation : "And He will summon to testify against you cloud and mist and dew and rain ; for they will all be withheld by you from descending upon you, and that because of your sins."

allusions to the ancient legend plainly serve a definite purpose and cannot be looked upon merely as an expression of the writers' interest in demonology for its own sake. The fall of the watchers is said, moreover, in one passage, to have been the cause of the existence of the post-diluvian demons on earth, and is connected therefore with present sin, as well as with that which provoked the Deluge.

It is to be inferred, then, that we are presented in the oldest portions of the *Book of Enoch* with an alternative, perhaps a rival, theory as to the historical origin of human sin, to that which would account for it by Adam and Eve's temptation and transgression. It is noteworthy that the eating of the tree of knowledge is but once alluded to in *Enoch*, and that only incidentally and without any doctrinal intention. In c. xxxii. 3 ff., Enoch narrates that when he came into the garden of righteousness (*i.e.* the earthly Paradise), he saw, amongst other trees, "the tree of wisdom, which imparts great wisdom to those who eat of it. And it is like the carob tree: its fruit is like the clusters of the vine, very beautiful: the fragrance of the tree goes forth and penetrates afar. And I said: 'This tree is beautiful, and how beautiful and attractive is its look!' And the holy angel Rafael, who was with me, answered me and said: 'This is the tree of wisdom, of which thy old father and thy aged mother, who were before thee, have eaten, and they learnt wisdom and their eyes were opened, and they recognised that they were naked, and they were driven out of the garden[1].'" As Dr Charles has remarked on these verses, "Adam's sin is not (here) regarded as the cause of man's fall and destruction in the Deluge." Indeed that sin seems to have been ignored in accounting for the universality of human corruptness. In the above passage the partaking of the tree is not even called a sin; and the garden of Eden, according to this book, "has no connexion with the destinies of mankind." At this date, at least, the exegesis of the Fall-story which later held the field, both in Jewish and in Christian literature, was not of

---

[1] This is the earliest known interpretation of the tree of knowledge. That tree is regarded as imparting wisdom, etc. *when eaten.*

VIII] *in Jewish Pseudepigraphic Writings* 187

exclusive and unequivocal authority even for a Palestinian writer with whom "the old Hebrew standpoint is fairly well-preserved[1]," even if it was known to him at all.

The groundwork of *Enoch* alludes, in a similar incidental manner, to the tree of life of Gen. ii., iii.[2] Enoch finds it on "a mountain range of fire which flamed day and night," magnificent with precious stones. On the seventh mountain was a throne encircled with fragrant trees, supreme amongst which was the tree of life. "It had a fragrance beyond all fragrance: its leaves and blooms and wood wither not for ever: and its fruit is beautiful, and it resembles the dates of a palm." Enoch expresses his wish to know about this tree, whereupon Michael answers: "This high mountain which thou hast seen, whose summit is like the throne of the Lord, is His throne, where the Holy and Great One, the Lord of Glory, the Eternal King, will sit, when He shall come down to visit the earth with goodness. And no mortal is permitted to touch this tree of delicious fragrance till the great day of judgment, when He shall avenge and bring everything to its consummation for ever; this tree, I say, will (then) be given to the righteous and humble. By its fruit life will be given to the elect; it will be transplanted to the north, the holy place, to the temple of the Lord, the Eternal King." In the light of the growing Jewish faith in a future life, the earthly Paradise and the tree of life are transferred to a 'new Jerusalem'; and the fruit of this tree is to confer, not immortality, but long life such as the patriarchs were endowed with[3]. The whole conception of the tree of life is as materialistic as that in Genesis, and is the best guide, on account of the antiquity of the writing in which it occurs, to the Jahvist writer's idea as to the functions and mode of action of the tree which he describes in his Paradise-story. That these details as to Paradise and its two trees should be recorded by the writer of cc. i—xxxvi. of the *Book of Enoch*,

---

[1] Charles, *op. cit.* p. 55.
[2] cc. xxiv., xxv.
[3] xxv. 6: "Then will they rejoice with joy and be glad: they will enter the holy habitation: the fragrance thereof will be in their limbs, and they will live a long life on earth, such as thy fathers have lived."

and yet no allusion whatever made to Adam's sin as involving consequences for the race, although his mind is full of the sinfulness of the ante-diluvian world and its causes, must once more be declared to be remarkable, if not significant and suggestive.

(b) *The Similitudes*, cc. xxxvii—lxx.

In this portion of the apocalypse, much later, apparently, than the groundwork which has been examined, we find the origin of sin traced a stage further back. Evil spirits or satans are distinguished from the watchers or fallen angels, and are supposed to have existed as evil agencies before them. The fall of the watchers, in fact, is represented as due, not to a desire to unite with the daughters of men, but to their becoming subject to the satans[1], a body of evil spirits whose existence is presupposed from the beginning. Thus whereas the older portions of the book, in their use of Azazel (or Semjaza), fall back upon the nature-religion which the prophets had thrust into the back-ground, but which apocalyptists were rousing to new life[2], the Similitudes employ the late-developed doctrine of Satan as more sufficing, and thereby carry the actual origin of evil further back. The story of the watchers is, however, retained as the explanation of the corruption of mankind[3]. In the Similitudes, as in the groundwork, the origin of human sin and the basis for theodicy is still Gen. vi. 1—4, not Gen. ii., iii. At least this is so if we may, with Charles, regard certain sections of cc. xxxvii—lxx. as interpolations, whether from a lost Noah-apocalypse or not[4]. To these alleged interpolations it now remains for us to turn.

[1] liv. 6: "Michael, Gabriel, Rafael and Fanuel will take hold of them (the hosts of Azazel, *v.* 5) on that great day and cast them on that day into a burning furnace, that the Lord of Spirits may take vengeance on them for their unrighteousness in becoming subject to Satan and leading astray those who dwell on the earth."

[2] See Stave, *Einfluss des Parsismus u.s.w.*, S. 268.

[3] *e.g.* lxiv. 2, "These are the angels who descended to the earth, and revealed what was hidden to the children of men and seduced the children of men into committing sin."

[4] The Palestinian Enoch-literature proper would thus seem to know of no

(c) *Interpolations.*

The passages which some critics regard as interpolations in the groundwork have already been examined in treating of that portion of the book. They do but supply minute variations of the legend of the fallen angels.

But some of the extracts from an apocalypse of Noah which have found their way into the book of the Similitudes not only specify more fully the nature of the secret wisdom brought by the watchers[1], and supply a demonology resembling that of the *Secrets of Enoch* rather than that of the rest of the apocalypse in which they have been incorporated[2]; they also refer to the Fall-story of Genesis. It is stated that the third chief among the angels, called Gadreel, "led astray Eve," besides showing to men the weapons of war and death[3]. In the same chapter we read "for man was created exactly like the angels, to the intent that he should continue righteous and pure, and death which destroys everything could not have taken hold of him, but through this their knowledge they are perishing and through this power (of knowledge) it (death) is consuming me[4]." It would thus seem that the lost Noah-apocalypse, from which Charles regards this passage to be taken[5], taught that man was originally immortal as well as innocent, and that death was introduced on account of his acquisition of knowledge and the sin connected therewith. But, once again, no use is made

great sin affecting the race, or calling for a universal judgment, before the period immediately preceding the Deluge. Its world-history, in fact, takes its departure thence. In later apocalyptic writings this point of departure is superseded by the catastrophe of Adam and Eve, and the centre of gravity of the whole problem of sin is shifted to the point with which it ever afterwards remained identified.

[1] *e.g.* lxv. 6–8, lxix. 6–12. This knowledge included sorcery, extraction of metals, manufacture of idols and of implements of war; also writing, for the purpose of "giving confirmation to good faith, with pen and ink."

[2] See Morfill and Charles's edition, p. 21, note to xviii. 3.

[3] lxix. 6. Hilgenfeld, *op. cit.*, S. 159—60, sees in this verse and its context the implication of the idea (which he calls Gnostic), that the devil was father of Cain by Eve. See above, pp. 156 ff.

[4] lxix. 11.

[5] See *op. cit.*, and also Art. *Noah, Book of*, in Hastings' *Dict. of the Bible*, vol. III.

of these statements; and they certainly deal in a very free manner with the story of Gen. iii., from the details of which they deliberately diverge.

Thus the *Book of Enoch* supplies little material for the history of the exegesis of the Paradise-story; but it shows that, even within the circle of Pharisaism, the doctrine of a fall of our first parents affecting the whole race was not the only current explanation of the origin of human sinfulness, if indeed such an explanation was known at all when the earlier portions of the book were written.

II. *The Testaments of the Twelve Patriarchs.*

This work is an example of haggadic midrash which, in all probability, was enriched with additions by an apocalyptic writer before its Christian interpolations were inserted. In its Jewish form it may well have been a product of the second or first century B.C., and therefore contemporary with portions of the composite *Book of Enoch*. Like that work, it contains allusions to the story of the descent of the angels. Thus in *Test. Reuben*, v., we find a curious variant of the usual tradition, making the daughters of men the seducers of the watchers, who changed themselves into men in order to have relations with them. In *Test. Dan.*, v., occurs the passage: "and in every form of wickedness will the spirits of seduction be active among you," which implies the biblical and commoner form of the tradition, regarding the watchers as responsible for the guilt of the unnatural unions. Again in *Test. Naphthali*, iii., we find allusion to the "spirits of seduction," followed by the words: "likewise the watchers changed the natural use, whom the Lord also cursed before the Flood[1]." These allusions point to the prominence of the legend in Jewish thought about sin, though they are not made,

[1] In *Test. Levi*, iii., there is an allusion to the punishment of these watchers.
Besides the other passages cited in this chapter which refer to the legend of the watchers, allusions are also found in the *Testament of Solomon*, xxi., xxvi. (E. Trans. in *Jew. Quart. Rev.* XI.), a writing believed by Conybeare and others to have been the work of a Jew, like the *Tests. of the XII. Patriarchs*, and existing now in the form of a Christian recension. Josephus (*Antt.* I. iii. 1) also refers to the story. Cf. Jude 6; 2 Pet. ii. 4.

in this writing, the basis for conclusions as to the cause or introduction of human sin: a subject with which the work is not at all concerned, though in *Test. Levi*, xviii., Adam's fall seems incidentally to be assigned an important place[1].

III. *The Book of Jubilees.*

The *Book of Jubilees*[2] is not of great importance to the historian of the Jewish doctrine of the Fall. The work is not an apocalypse, but a haggadic commentary on Genesis written by a Pharisee of Palestine. Its date has not been unanimously agreed upon. It has been assigned to the reign of John Hyrcanus[3], and to the first century A.D.[4]; but the majority of critics place it in the latter half of the first century B.C. It is the earliest example of continuous haggadic treatment of O.T. narrative that we possess.

The narratives of Genesis are reproduced in this book with a considerable amount of that fanciful amplification characteristic of all but the very earliest Jewish exegesis. This will be seen, to some extent, from its treatment of the Fall-story.

First, however, the use which this book makes of the narrative of Gen. vi. 1—4 may be briefly noticed. "The angels of God which are called watchers" are said to have descended to earth in order to teach the children of men how to practise justice and righteousness on earth[5]. This appears to be a unique variation of the legend. It approaches to that

---

[1] Bousset, *Die Religion des Judenthums im N.T. Zeitalter*, cites as follows: (The Messiah) "will open the gates of Paradise, and he will remove the sword which threatens Adam, and will give to the saints to eat of the tree of life."
It may be added here that the earliest known occurrence of the doctrine of the two *yezers* is in *Test. Aser*, i.: δύο ὁδοὺς ἔδωκεν ὁ θεὸς υἱοῖς τῶν ἀνθρώπων καὶ δύο διαβούλια....

[2] See Charles, Art. *Apocal. Literature* in *Encyclop. Bibl.*; his translation of the book in *Jew. Quart. Review*, 1893-5; and his edition of *The Book of Jubilees*, 1902; Littmann, in Kautzsch's *Pseudepigraphen*; Rönsch's, Singer's, and Beer's *Das Buch der Jubiläen*.

[3] Kohler, on *Pre-Talmudic Haggada*, *J.Q.R.*, v.

[4] Singer, *op. cit.*

[5] iv. 15.

found in the *Testament of Reuben*, but does not ascribe the initiative in evil to the daughters of men. According to *Jubilees*, it was only later that the watchers began to sin by marrying with the women[1]. This was the cause of 'corruption of the way' of all flesh, man and beast[2], and of the accumulated sin which called down the judgment of the Deluge[3]. Sin after the Deluge, *e.g.* that of the sons of Noah, is ascribed, as in parts of the *Book of Enoch*, to the instigation of the demons (the offspring of the watchers); but the passages[4] in which this is the case are probably interpolations from a lost apocalypse of Noah[5]. It will be obvious that the incident of the watchers is not assigned the same importance in the world's history which it bears in the groundwork of *Enoch*; it is used, as in Genesis, to explain the corruption which immediately preceded the Deluge, a corruption which, it is expressly stated, was afterwards wholly done away[6]; it is not employed to describe the original entrance of sin amongst mankind.

For that purpose the writer rather uses the alternative biblical narrative of the sin in Paradise; and on this account his work is of the greater interest here.

The account which the *Book of Jubilees* gives of the life of the first pair in Eden contains a few peculiar details. We are told, for instance, that Adam and Eve lived in the garden seven years before their transgression[7]. The account of the temptation and sin, given in c. iii., closely follows that of Genesis; the tempter is called simply the serpent, and is not identified with Satan, although Satan is mentioned elsewhere in the book (xxiii. 9). Embellishment, however, appears again when it is stated[8] that, on the day on which

---

[1] iv. 22; v. 1. [2] v. 2 ff.
[3] vii. 21 ff. This, however, is here said to have been only one out of three reasons for the punishment of the Flood.
[4] vii. 26—39; x. 1—15.
[5] This seems certain at least in the case of the former passage mentioned. See Art. *Noah, Book of*, in Hastings' *Dict. of the Bible*, III. 556.
[6] v. 12. "And He made a new and righteous nature for all His creatures, that they should never sin any more in their whole nature, and should be righteous."
[7] iii. 15. [8] iii. 28.

Adam was expelled from the garden of Eden, "the mouths of all beasts and cattle and birds and things which walk and move ceased to speak; for they all talked, one with another, one tongue and one language." The animals also were turned out of Eden along with Adam[1]. It may be noticed that elsewhere in this book[2] the Fall is said to have involved the loss of man's power to speak "the language which was revealed," *i.e.* the Hebrew tongue. The former of these passages is interesting as embodying the belief that the Fall affected the lower animals and the course of nature[3]. This idea is not further developed, however, and nothing is said of any moral consequences resulting from Adam's sin to his posterity. The writer of the book either did not attach much weight to the teaching which represented the first sin as fraught with lasting and universal consequences for mankind, or else he is another witness to the truth of the view that a doctrine of original sin did not arise in Judaism until very near the dawn of the Christian era.

IV. *The Apocalypse of Abraham.*

This writing[4], originally purely Jewish, contains a curious description of the Fall. Its author seems to have been somewhat concerned with the problem of evil and theodicy[5]; and it is to be observed that though his demonology has some resemblance to that of the Enoch-literature[6], he diverges from some of the older apocalyptic writers in making the Fall his starting point for the history of the race. The tempter is

[1] iii. 29.   [2] xii. 25, 26.
[3] See also Chap. X. (below).
The idea that all the animals originally possessed the power of speech was held by Josephus (*Antt.* I. i. 4, "But as all living creatures had one language at that time...") and by Philo, *De Confus. Ling.* 3, *Quaest. et sol. in Gen.* I. 32.

[4] A German translation, by Prof. Bonwetsch, exists in *Studien zur Geschichte der Theologie u. Kirche*, 1897. The date of the apocalypse cannot be accurately fixed.

[5] See *e.g.* the end of the passage, c. xxiii., quoted below.

[6] Bonwetsch (*op. cit.*, S. 66) believes the passage in c. xiv. relating to Azazel, who here, as in the (Aethiopic) *Book of Enoch*, plays the part of chief tempter of mankind, to be based partly on Isai. xiv. 13 ff. and on *Enoch* xcvi. Azazel is represented as banished from heaven, and as having taught the secrets of heaven. From him proceeds all evil. He corresponds here exactly to Satan.

Azazel, who appeared "like a serpent in form, but having hands and feet like a man, and wings at his shoulders." He is not said to have had any relations with Eve such as certain other Jewish writings describe[1]; but it is noteworthy that the Fall, as here depicted, appears to be closely associated or identified with fleshly union[2].

V. Pseudo-Philo.

Cohn[3] regards this work as a specimen of historical haggada which was adopted soon after its composition (*i.e.* after 70 A.D.) in the Christian Church. It may be mentioned here as containing an allusion to the Fall, in which it closely follows the biblical narrative. Adam is led to transgress through Eve, who in turn is tempted by the serpent; and thus "constituta est mors in generationes hominum." The Fall is regarded as the cause of death, but is not connected with human sinfulness.

[1] See above, p. 189, n. 3, and pp. 156 ff.
[2] Cf. below, p. 197, n. 1.
The chapter in which the scene of the Fall is described (xxiii.) may be reproduced here:

"And I saw there (in Eden) a man, tall in stature and fearful in breadth, incomparable in appearance, in embrace with a woman, who also resembled the man in appearance and size. And they were standing under one tree of Eden, and the fruit of this tree looked like a cluster of the vine; and behind the tree was standing one like a serpent in form, but having hands and feet like a man, and wings at his shoulders, six on his right and six on his left; and they held the cluster of the tree in their hands, and they whom I saw embracing lay with one another. And I said: 'Who are these embracing one another, or who is the being betwixt them, or what is this fruit which they are eating, O Mighty, Eternal One?' And he said: 'This is the counsel of man, this is Adam, and these are their desires on earth, this is Eve, but he who is between them is the godless power (*Gottlosigkeit*) of their enterprise in ruin, Azazel himself.' And I said: 'Eternal, Mighty One! Why hast thou granted him such power to ruin the human race in its (his?) works on the earth?' And he said to me: 'Listen, Abraham; those that do evil, and so many as I hated among them that practise it, over them gave I him power and to be loved of them.' And I answered and said: 'O Eternal, Mighty One! Why hast thou willed to cause that evil is desired in the hearts of men, since thou art angry at that which has been willed by thee, with him who deals frowardly with thy decree?'"

[3] *Jew. Quart. Rev.* 1898.
The Latin text of what proved to be portions of this work was edited by Dr James in *Texts and Studies*, vol. II.

The *Assumption of Moses*, probably written early in the first century A.D. by a Pharisee, yields no material, in its present form, that is relevant to our subject. It is said that the latter portion of it, which has been lost, probably dealt with the origin of sin. Indeed Origen, *De Princip.* III. ii. 1, asserts that in this book, as he knew it, the archangel Michael says that the serpent, being inspired by the devil, was the cause of Adam and Eve's transgression. On account of this interpretation of a fragment of the Fall-story the writing just deserves mention here.

The *Psalms of Solomon* are also of no service for our purpose. They contain indeed a passage (ix. 7) in which man's freedom and responsibility are very strongly insisted upon ; but the text at this place is uncertain, and it is a mistake to suppose that the most one-sided insistence on man's self-determination was inconsistent, in a Pharisee, with the possibility of belief in such a doctrine of the Fall as some Jews at least of that day possessed. The passage in question cannot therefore be pressed into a sign of the writer's negative attitude towards a view approaching that contained in the doctrine of Original Sin.

The *Testament of Abraham*, believed by Kohler (*Jew. Quart. Rev.* VII. p. 581) to be a pre-Christian Jewish writing, has something to say of the angel of death, but does not speak of his having any connexion with the fall of man. Death is regarded as universal, but is not here traced to Adam. Kohler believes this angel of death to be the same as Samael, and to have been associated only with physical evil, thus opposing Dr James' view (*Texts and Studies*, II. p. 58), who would identify him with Satan, the introducer of moral evil also. Torrey (*Jew. Encyclopaedia*, Art. *Apocalyptic Literature*) also contends for the purely Jewish origin of this writing, and emphasises the absence in it of any reference to Adam's fall in passages where there was ample occasion for its mention. The souls of men are pictured as passing by Adam, seated on a throne, through the wide and the narrow gate, each by his own merit or fault, but none encumbered by Adam's sin.

VI. *The Books of Adam.*

The pseudepigraphic literature which is associated with the name of Adam may be examined here because, though part of it is undoubtedly of Christian authorship, it is highly probable that two of its most important fragments, at least, have a common Jewish source of pre-Christian date[1]. These

---

[1] See Kautzsch's *Pseudepigraphen des A. T.*, S. 510. This view, it should be mentioned, is dissented from by Dillmann, Schürer and others. See also Hort, in Smith's *Dict. of Christ. Biography*. An Adam-book, however, seems to be alluded to by a Jew at the end of the 2nd century; see *Monatschrift für Geschichte u.*

196   *The Fall and Original Sin*   [CHAP.

two writings are (i) that unhappily named by Tischendorf *The Apocalypse of Moses*, and otherwise called *The Story of the Conversation of Adam*, or simply *The Book of Adam*; (ii) *The Life of Adam and Eve*, edited by Meyer (in the *Abhandlungen d. Königl. Bayerisch. Akademie, philos.-philol. Klasse*, 1876), which is dependent upon the former work, though regarded by its first editor and others as exhibiting no trace of Christian influence.

(a)   *The Apocalypse of Moses*[1].

The *Apocalypse of Moses* contains an account of the Fall, put into the mouth of Eve, which is on the whole true to the biblical narrative, though expanded in the usual style of haggada. The tempter is Satan, and his motive in bringing about the ruin of Adam and Eve is envy. The 'adversary' used the serpent, in whom he saw the wisest of the animals, as his vessel or instrument; but in the account of the temptation this seems momentarily to be forgotten, and Eve is accosted by Satan in the form of an angel. Two traditions are probably here confused and blended into one; for it has already been seen that the tempter of Eve was sometimes said to be a fallen angel, sometimes a speaking serpent, and sometimes a serpent indwelt by Satan[2]. The temptation

Wissenschaft des Judenthums, XLIII. S. 63. Torrey, *loc. cit.*, states that Zunz's assertion that the Talmud knows of an Adam-book is erroneous, but regards it as certain that behind the Adam-literature now existing there lay an ancient *Jewish* collection of legends; so also Kabisch, *Eschatologie des Paulus*, S. 156.

[1] For Greek Text see Tischendorf, *Apocalypses Apocryphae* (an eclectic text). An E. Tr. will be found in *Ante-Nicene Library*, vol. XVI. The E. Tr. by F. C. Conybeare of an Armenian Version, of higher value than the Greek fragments, is published in *Jew. Quart. Rev.* VII. Cf. the translation of Issaverdens, from the Armen. MSS. of S. Lazarus, in *Uncanonical Writings of the Old Testament*, 1901. A German rendering of the Adam-books, and an introduction to them, by Fuchs, will be found in Kautzsch, *op. cit.*

[2] The following is the (abridged) translation of Conybeare:

"The which Satan beheld (to wit) our glory and honour; and having found the serpent, the wisest animal of all which are on the whole earth, he approached him and said unto him" (so far in Armen. only: the Gk. differs): "I desire to reveal unto thee the thought which is in my heart and to unite (with) thee. Thou seest how much worth God has bestowed on man. But we have been dishonoured; let us go and drive him out of the garden, out of which we have been driven because of him. Do thou only become a vessel (tool) unto me, and I will deceive

itself is associated, as elsewhere in similar writings, with sexual passion[1]. Thus, in the Greek, Satan or the serpent, after pledging Eve to give the fruit to her husband as well as to eat it herself, is said to climb the tree and to put upon the fruit "the poison of his wickedness, that is, of his lust (τῆς ἐπιθυμίας αὐτοῦ); for lust is the head (one MS. has 'root and origin') of all sin[2]." In c. xxv. Eve is told she is to pray: "O Lord save me in this present, and henceforth I will not turn me to the same *sinning in my flesh.*"

A few other details of the account are of interest. The serpent, besides receiving the punishment mentioned in Genesis, is deprived of hands and feet, ears, wings and other members[3], because it had allowed itself to "become the vessel of shame." The Fall, moreover, affects Nature generally. One consequence was that, when Eve sinned, all the leaves fell off the trees of the garden, except those of the fig-tree only[4]. The animals, too, lost their fear and reverence for man. The beast which attacked Seth thus addresses Eve: "For when thy mouth was opened to eat of the fruit of the tree, of which God commanded you not to eat of the same, and thou didst eat and transgress the commandment of God, then our nature changed into disobedience to men[5]." Similarly, in the curse on Adam[6], the Greek text adds, as a gloss,

them by thy mouth in order to ensnare them. And instantly the serpent hung himself from and lay along the wall of the garden. Then Satan, having taken the form of an angel, sang the songs of praise. And I looked and saw him on the wall in the form of an angel."

The confusion between Satan as serpent and Satan as angel occurs in all the MSS. There is agreement also as to the cause of Satan's envy; it is the glory and the honour that God had prepared for Adam and Eve, coupled, according to some of the versions, with the remembrance that himself and the animals had been expelled from the garden because of Adam. This last feature is a peculiar embellishment.

[1] Cp. 4 Macc., *Apocal. of Abraham, Slavonic Book of Enoch.* For talmudic parallels see Chap. VII., and Weber, *Jüd. Theologie,* 1897, S. 219. On S. Paul's probable use of this idea, see Thackeray, *The Relation of S. Paul to Contemp. Jew. Thought,* p. 50 ff.

[2] Conybeare's tr. from the Armenian runs thus: "he...drew nigh unto the tree, and took and gave to me of the fruit forthwith; the offspring of his wickedness, that is to say, of desire." Issaverdens has "he gave to me the production of his wickedness, which is lust." This passage occurs in c. xix.

[3] c. xxiv.   [4] c. xx.
[5] c. xi.   [6] c. xxiv.

"and those beasts which thou ruledst shall rise up against thee and rebel, because thou hast not kept my commandment." The darkening of the sun and moon (c. xxxvi.) is not attributed to the Fall, but these heavenly bodies are represented as interceding for Adam[1].

The important question, however, for our purpose, is as to what is the doctrine of this writing concerning the consequences of the first sin for the race: whether or not we find here a doctrine of Original Sin.

As regards the entail of death the answer is plain. In c. x. Eve is said to have wept bitterly and cried: "Woe to me, Woe to me, Woe to me! For if it be unto me to come unto the day of resurrection, all sinners of my progeny will come to curse me, and will say: *Cursed be Eva*, for she has not kept safe the observance of the Lord her God, *and because of this we shall all die with death*[2]." A little later (c. xiv.), Adam, when overtaken with his last sickness, says to Eve: "O Eva, what hast thou done unto me, because thou hast brought upon me wrath exceeding, which also shall be inherited by all the race of my offspring[3]." Perhaps 'wrath' here means only death, as the Greek text reads. It can scarcely be doubted, if the Greek codices are to be trusted, that this apocalypse regards Eve as the cause of her posterity's sinfulness of nature. The passage on which this assertion is based (c. xxxii.) runs thus in the Armenian[4]: "For sin and transgressions have from me originated in the world"; and these words do not necessarily imply more than those of Ben Sira long before: "from a woman was the beginning of sins." But the Greek has: $\pi\hat{a}\sigma a\ \dot{a}\mu a\rho\tau\dot{\iota}a\ \delta\iota'\ \dot{\epsilon}\mu o\hat{v}\ \gamma\acute{\epsilon}\gamma o\nu\epsilon\nu\ \dot{\epsilon}\nu\ \tau\hat{\eta}\ \kappa\tau\dot{\iota}\sigma\epsilon\iota$. These words do not define how the sinfulness derived from Eve was transmitted to her descendants, but $\delta\iota'\ \dot{\epsilon}\mu o\hat{v}$ distinctly implies that she was regarded as

---

[1] The passage however seems to be connected with the tradition embodied in the *Greek Apocalypse of Baruch*, c. ix.

[2] The words italicised occur only in the Armenian.

[3] So the Armenian; the Greek has, in place of the last sentence, "which is death, dominating all our race."

[4] The Armenian text of S. Lazarus, translated by Issaverdens, has: "I am the origin of all sin and iniquity in this world."

its cause. Of course one cannot feel quite certain that the exact shade of meaning of the original apocalypse has been preserved. It is obvious, however, that we have an instance here of that aspect of tradition which emphasises the origin of sin in woman (cf. B. Sira). Eve is held much more responsible than Adam, a point which is emphasised by S. Paul when, and only when, it suits his purpose.

(b) *The Life of Adam.*

This writing seems to have been derived from the same Jewish source as the *Book of Adam*, and has much in common with it.

The envy of the devil, only partially explained in the last apocalypse, is here fully accounted for. Satan narrates to Eve, when telling her the reason for his continued harassing of herself and her husband after their fall, how it was through Adam that he had been cast out of heaven. For when God created Adam, He called upon the angels to adore him as His image. Michael obeyed, and summoned the other angels to do the same. Satan, however, refused; and on being threatened with the wrath of God, said that he would "exalt his throne above the stars of heaven[1]." He was therefore banished with his angels to earth, where he began to envy man his happiness in Paradise[2].

The first and shorter account of the Fall given in the *Apocalypse of Moses* is reproduced in the *Life of Adam*, but no important variations occur. It may therefore here be passed over. The second and more interesting history of the event is omitted altogether. There is no additional light thrown, therefore, on the attitude of the early Adam-legends towards the question of inherited sinfulness.

Both these Adam-books emphasise the first 'glory' of unfallen man.

The later Adam-books, though much less useful for the purpose of arriving at Jewish and pre-Christian teaching as

[1] Part of this story is a haggadic midrash on Isai. xiv. 13. Other versions of it occur.
[2] cc. xii—xvii.

to the Fall, may be briefly noticed at this point. They will serve at least to show the development of some of the ideas contained in the two writings last discussed.

(c) *The Book of Adam and Eve* (Malan), or *The Conflict of Adam and Eve* (Dillmann).

This work may be as old as the fifth or sixth century. It is thoroughly Christian but makes use of old Jewish legend and haggada, and is possibly based on a Jewish original. It does not describe the Fall fully, but contains many allusions to it, and especially to its consequences.

Adam, before his transgression, is described as a 'bright angel[1]'; he and Eve 'were filled with the grace of a bright nature[2],' and had not hearts turned towards earthly things; they were able to behold the angels in heaven[3], and glory rested upon them[4]. All this was lost by the Fall.

The tempter is generally Satan[5], 'who continued not in his first estate, nor kept his faith'; elsewhere he is Satan 'hidden in the serpent[6]'; but in one passage, according to Malan's translation, he is uniquely described as 'the serpent that became Satan[7].' The serpent is said to have been the most exalted of all beasts originally, and the most beautiful[8].

(d) *The Treasure Cave.*

This book has close affinities with the last, and in common with it speaks of the beauty and glory of Adam before the Fall, adding that he was worshipped, when first created, by the angels. The fall of Satan from heaven is described very much as in the Korân; being by nature 'fire and spirit' Satan refused, when called upon, to bow down to 'dust,' and on that account was expelled to earth. There he envied the

---

[1] i. 10.
[2] i. 2, 8, 13, etc.; and see Malan's notes, p. 210.
[3] i. 4 and 8. This is said to be a case of borrowing from *Slav. Enoch*; but the tradition was probably wide-spread.
[4] i. 11.   [5] *e.g.* i. 6, 13, 14, 22.
[6] i. 27.   [7] i. 17.
[8] i. 17.

happy life of Adam and Eve in Paradise, and 'entered into the serpent' in order to tempt them to sin[1].

(e) *The Apocalypse of Adam*, or *The Testament of Adam and Eve*.

According to Renan, the editor of this pseudepigraph[2], we have in it a writing of Gnostic origin. It contains but one or two references to the Fall. In c. iii. we read: "Because thou hast given ear to the serpent, thou and thy children after thee shall be the serpent's food." Further on, Adam, speaking to Seth of the coming deluge, says: "for in consequence of the sin of thy mother Eve they have been made sinners." These words have certainly a Pauline ring.

(f) *History of the Creation and of the Transgression of Adam*[3].

This writing contains an account of Satan's banishment from heaven corresponding to the story referred to above, in the *Life of Adam*, in some points; but Satan here refuses to worship God, not His creature man, who in fact was made after Satan's fall, and on account of his pride[4]. Then Satan, growing envious of man, entered into the serpent, who at first was winged and had a tongue[5]. The serpent was thus used as an instrument for the deception of Eve. He tells her that God himself had not reached the glory of Divinity before He ate of the fruit now offered to Eve—a new embellishment. Eve, on partaking of the fruit, was "bereft of her splendour." A very romantic turn is given in this curious version of the Fall-story to the manner in which Adam yielded to his wife's persuasion. "Better were it for me to die than to be separated and parted from my wife," he exclaimed. After examining the fruit for the space of three hours, his conjugal affection conquered his fear: "I cannot live without my wife!"

[1] See Bezold's German translation, Ss. 3—7.
[2] *Journal Asiat.* Ser. v. Tome ii. pp. 427 ff.
[3] This is from MS. No. 729 of the Armenian Library of S. Lazarus, Venice; an E.T. will be found in Issaverdens' *Uncanonical Writings of the Old Testament* (Venice, 1901), p. 39.
[4] Issaverdens, *op. cit.*, p. 40.
[5] Cf. the accounts in *Apocalypse of Abraham* and *Apocalypse of Moses*, above.

(g) *Fragments of Adam-literature.*

The History of the Expulsion of Adam from the Garden, contained in the same collection in which the last writing occurs[1], states that Satan made a compact with Adam, binding the first father and his posterity to serve him if shown "the light." This is a unique theory of Original Sin, and has a very modern sound.

The narrative, taken also from the same collection, entitled *Concerning the good tidings of Seth*[2], may be mentioned for its version of the story of the angels (Gen vi. 1—4), here interpreted of the relations of the Cainites and Sethites. Cain's descendants were chiefly women, who painted themselves in order to entice the few men, and so deceive the children of Seth, who were men, living piously and not mixing with Cain's descendants. The point most worthy of notice here is that, in spite of its totally different application of the biblical narrative from that met with in the *Enoch-literature* and the *Testaments of the XII. Patriarchs*, this story embodies a variation of the more usual tradition which has already been found to occur elsewhere: the variation, namely, according to which the women were the seducers of the sons of God.

The History of the Repentance of Adam and Eve[3], enumerates the punishments of Adam. Among them are deprivation of 'light,' and of grace, estrangement from God, and equality with the beasts, which were before obedient to and subordinate to man.

VII. *The Greek Apocalypse of Baruch* (3rd *Apoc. of Baruch* of Dr James).

This writing, according to Ryssel[4], probably has a Jewish foundation, though it has been adapted and interpolated by a Christian of the second century.

Part at least of the passage in c. iv. which speaks of the

[1] *op. cit.*, p. 49.   [2] p. 66 ff.
[3] *op. cit.*, p. 76.
[4] In Kautzsch's *Pseudepigraphen*, S. 402.

tree which caused the fall of Adam is a Christian interpolation[1]. The tree is there identified with the vine[2], and is said to have been planted by Samael.

Samael, moreover, figures as the tempter in Eden, and is said to have "put on the vesture of the serpent[3]." In the Slavonic text of the same chapter, according to which the serpent was the tempter, we find another allusion to the belief that the Fall was attended with consequences to the world of Nature. The following is a rendering of Ryssel's German translation: "When the serpent tempted Adam and Eve, and showed them their nakedness, and they wept bitterly over their nakedness, then wept also all creation, the heaven and the sun and the stars, and creation was stirred even to the throne of God; the angels and the powers were moved for the transgression of Adam, but the moon laughed. Therefore God was angry with it and darkened its light[4]...."

[1] Dr James in *Texts and Studies*, vol. v.
[2] Cf. *Apoc. of Abraham*, above, p. 194, n. 2.
[3] c. ix.
[4] Cf. *Apoc. Mosis*, xxxvi.

CHAPTER IX.

THE FALL AND ORIGINAL SIN IN JEWISH PSEUDEPI-GRAPHICAL LITERATURE—(*continued*).

VIII. *The Book of the Secrets of Enoch* (*The Slavonic Book of Enoch*).

THIS pseudepigraph has already engaged our attention in a previous chapter. There, however, it was only the distinctively Alexandrian tendencies of the book with which we were concerned. It remains for us to examine more fully its treatment of the Fall and the problem of human sinfulness.

The value of the testimony of this book to the nature of pre-Christian doctrine on the Fall is impaired by the suspicion which suggests itself, that one of the two recensions of it may perhaps have been expanded with Christian interpolations. Dr Charles, who, in conjunction with Mr Morfill, was the first to edit the book[1], regards the work as practically homogeneous, and as composed in the first half of the first century A.D. Certain of the arguments for this date seem to be a little precarious; and the possibility that some of the resemblances in diction to the New Testament may be due to dependence of the apocalypse on the Scriptures rather than *vice versa*, at least in the case of the longer version A, has not perhaps been sufficiently considered. Dr Charles admits that

---

[1] The *Book of the Secrets of Enoch*, translated and edited by Morfill and Charles, 1896.

CH. IX] *Jewish Pseudepigraphic Writings* 205

the text A is very corrupt and contains interpolations, but takes it for a truer representative of the original than B, which he considers to be a short *résumé* of A. The two versions are certainly not independent writings; but it may well be that, even supposing B to be a condensation of the original Greek text, A is an expansion of it, and is interpolated by a Christian or by a Jew influenced by contact with Christianity. This suspicion is increased when, instead of reading Charles' text, which consists of A corrected by B and other manuscripts, and is therefore eclectic, we study the versions A and B separately, as they have been published, for instance, in the German translation by Bonwetsch[1]. We then find that most (not quite all) of the resemblances to New Testament language are confined to A; we find that in B Adam is scarcely so much as mentioned, whereas in A much is said of him, and he is made responsible for universal human sinfulness in a more thorough sense than is to be met with in any other purely Jewish writing. Egyptian local colouring, however, is evident in both A and B. It is true that other writers go even further than Prof. Charles in asserting the homogeneity and purely Jewish authorship of this book[2].

Without claiming to establish the opposite conclusion, we may here venture to be so far sceptical of that which has hitherto been generally adopted, as to consider the question not yet closed, and meanwhile to follow Bonwetsch's example, and examine the contents of the A and B versions separately, on the possibility that some of the peculiarities of the A manuscript may receive explanation in the future on the supposition of Christian interpolation.

Taking then the A version first, we observe in it some reference to an account of the descent of the angels resembling that contained in the Noachian interpolations of the (Aethiopic) *Book of Enoch*, and differing from the story given

---

[1] *Abhandlungen der Königl. Gesellschaft der Wissenschaft zu Göttingen; philos.-philol. Klasse*, Neue Folge, I.

[2] Torrey, in *Jew. Encyclopaedia*, Art. *Apocalyptic Literature*, states that there are no Christian additions and interpolations; Loisy, in *Revue d'histoire et de littérature relig.* I. p. 32 ff., denies that there is any trace of Christian influence.

in the groundwork of that writing. The watchers, that is to say, are identified with the satans as a class. The corruption of the world, in the period preceding the Deluge, is here again ascribed to them.

"The men took and brought me up into the fifth heaven, and I saw there many hosts not to be counted, called Grigori; and their appearance was like men, and their size was greater than that of giants....... And they (*i.e.* the men) said to me: 'These are the Grigori, who, with their prince Satanail, rejected the holy Lord. And in consequence of these things they are kept in great darkness in the second heaven; and of them there went three to the earth from the throne of God to the place Ermon; and they entered into dealings on the side of Mount Iermon, and they saw the daughters of men, that they were fair, and took unto themselves wives. And they made the earth foul with their deeds. [*Sok.* adds: and the wives of men continue to do evil.] And they acted lawlessly in all times of this age, and wrought confusion, and the giants were born, and the strangely tall men, and there was much wickedness. And on account of this God judged them with a mighty judgment[1].'"

It will be observed that this legend of the descent of the watchers is not used here, as it would seem to be in the *Book of Enoch*, as a starting-point for the history of universal sinfulness. It is referred to incidentally, and the real beginning of human sin is elsewhere traced, as we shall see, to Adam and Eve.

Satanail is not said, in the passage quoted above, to have been leader of the lustful watchers who came down to Hermon. He had previously rebelled against God, with the rank below him, entertaining "the impossible idea, that he should make his throne higher than the clouds over the earth, and should be equal in rank to [God's] power." And so he was hurled from the heights with his angels[2]. His name was changed to Satan after he left the heavens[3]. He now "took thought, as if wishing to make another world, because things

---

[1] xviii. 1 ff. See Charles' note *in loc.*
[2] xxix. 4, 5; cf. *Vita Adae*, above, p. 199.
[3] xxxi. 4.

were subservient to Adam on earth, to rule it and have lordship over it." Moreover "he understood the judgment upon him, and the former sin which he had sinned. And on account of this, he conceived designs against Adam[1]."

The A version of this apocalypse has interesting information as to the unfallen state of Adam and Eve. The tendency to exalt Adam to a position superior in privileges to that of other men, with its humble beginning in Ecclus. xlix. 16, is here almost full-grown. His creation is described in terms which recall the teaching of the Stoics and of Philo[2]. He was placed upon the earth "like an angel, in an honourable, great, and glorious way[3]." Here follow the words of the Almighty: "And I made him a ruler to rule upon the earth, and to have My wisdom. And there was no one like him upon the earth of all My creations. And I gave him a name from the four substances: the East, the West, the North, and the South. And I appointed for him four special stars, and I gave him the name Adam. And I gave him his will, and I showed him the two ways, the light and the darkness. And I said unto him: 'This is good and this is evil'; that I should know whether he has love for Me or hate: that he should appear in his race as loving Me. I knew his nature, he did not know his nature. Therefore his ignorance is a woe to him that he should sin, and I appointed death on account of his sin[4]."

[1] xxxi. 3, 5, 6. We have here more than one reason assigned for the 'envy' of the devil, of which so many pseudepigraphic writings speak.
[2] xxx. 8 ff. See Charles' note. [3] xxx. 11.
[4] The part of this passage which involves the idea that ignorance is in itself evil, has already been noticed, p. 143. The passage is one of considerable interest and importance, containing, as it does, an allusion to the 'two ways,' and to the probation involved in man's endowment with moral faculties, and perhaps at the same time referring to the dual nature of man with his two *yezers*. Man does not sin because of ignorance of right and wrong; he is endowed at the outset with this knowledge of the two ways, and with self-determining will. This line of thought came later to be fused with the conception of the tree of knowledge of good and evil, whence the traditional interpretation of that tree in Christian exegesis. Speculation on this subject, when it began, set out not from the original sense of Gen. ii—iii., which had long been lost and was not recoverable, but from the idea of God's originally endowing man with moral knowledge, prior to his probation by, or participation of, the forbidden fruit, an idea which, perhaps ultimately traceable to such Old Test. passages as Jer. xxi. 8, Deut. xxx. 15, 19,

The latter portion of the passage just cited has led us somewhat away from the topic of the first man's primitive glory. In the following chapter we read that God "made for him the heavens open that he should perceive the angels singing the song of triumph. And there was light without any darkness continually in Paradise[1]." Finally, in xliv. 1, man's creation by God's own hands, and in His image, is strongly emphasised; and in viii. the beauties of Paradise, placed in the third heaven, are graphically described.

The account of the temptation is of interest, brief as it is. Satan is said to have "entered and deceived Eve"; and it is added, "But he did not touch Adam[2]." This passage has been appealed to by Mr Thackeray as a possible illustration of the Jewish tradition according to which "the temptation of Eve by the serpent took the form of a temptation to unchastity." The case for this conclusion, indeed, is much stronger than Mr Thackeray makes it. For the addition, after 'entered,' of "into Paradise," which words are introduced by the manuscript *Sok.* and adopted by the writer referred to, probably misrepresents the meaning of the original. Bonwetsch conjecturally supplies "into the serpent," which is equally on the wrong tack. The verb (*vniide*) is here active; but there is no need to supply any other noun than that which is in the

---

whose meaning is echoed in Ecclus. xv. 17, is developed in such passages as the following: Ecclus. xvii. 6, *Apoc. Baruch*, xix., *Ep. of Barnabas*, xviii. 1, *Didache*, i. 1, *Test. Aser*, i., *Sib. Oracles*, viii. 399, 400, and *Clem. Hom.* v. 7 "I said unto him this is good and this is evil." It was reserved for later exegesis to interpret the tree of knowledge as the means by which such moral knowledge was made accessible to man, whether by eating of it or by the moral probation of abstaining from the temptation. Cf. Charles' note, p. 42, some of whose references have been reproduced here.

According to this passage, the first man sinned, not, of course, from lack of moral knowledge, but from ignorance of his own nature with its inclination to evil. Platonism is here superimposed on the (incipient?) Jewish notion of the two *yezers*, apparently. As was pointed out in Chap. VI., the writer forsakes Alexandrian doctrine for the Palestinian teaching of his time in representing Adam's sin as the cause of his death. It is emphasised, as in Ecclus. etc., that death came "by his wife" (xxx. 18).

[1] xxxi. 2. The account of Adam's life on earth before his fall shows signs of being abridged, as verse 1 contains an obvious lacuna.
In xxxii. 1 A adds: "And Adam was five and a half hours in Paradise."
[2] xxxi. 6.

text, viz. Eve. The verb is frequently used, moreover, in the old Slavonic Bible in the sense of the biblical expression "come in unto," and therefore it is extremely probable that it has such a meaning here[1]. We have, in fact, in this passage, another example of the association of the Fall with the sin of unchastity, and an allusion to the tradition that Satan *seduced* Eve, in the narrower sense of that word.

The words: "But he did not touch Adam," thus receive a natural explanation, and imply, as Thackeray has pointed out, that immunity on the part of Adam from temptation by the serpent to which both Philo and S. Paul seem to allude, and which appears to have been "a subject for discussion in the Jewish schools[2]."

The passage in this book which is by far the most important for our inquiry, is that which deals with the consequences of Adam's sin to his posterity. In c. xl. 1 ff., we read: "And I saw all our forefathers from the beginning with Adam and Eve, and I sighed and wept, and spake of the ruin (caused by) their wickedness: Woe is me for my infirmity and that of my forefathers. And I meditated in my heart and said: 'Blessed is the man who was not born, or, having been born, has never sinned before the face of the Lord, so that he should not come into this place, to bear the yoke of this place[3].'"

---

[1] Mr Morfill has kindly supplied the author with these facts, in confirmation of his suspicion that the verb 'entered' governed 'Eve.'

[2] Thackeray, *op. cit.*, pp. 50-57, where 2 Cor. xi. 2-3, 1 Tim. ii. 13-15 (and, incidentally, other Pauline expressions) are discussed in the light of the above passage and the parallels in Philo, *Leg. Alleg.* III. 20, *Quaest. et Sol. in Gen.* I. 33, *Apoc. Mosis* XIX. etc.

[3] Bonwetsch's translation of this passage, which agrees exactly with that of Morfill, may be cited: "Und ich sah alle Urväter von Ewigkeit mit Adam und Eva, und ich seufzte und weinte und sprach über das Verderben ihrer Gottlosigkeit: wehe mir und meiner Ohnmacht und meiner Urväter! Und ich gedachte in meinem Herzen und sprach: Selig ist der Mensch, welcher nicht geboren ist, oder geboren nicht sündigt vor dem Angesicht des Herrn, damit er nicht komme an diesen Ort, noch bringe (trage) das Joch dieses Orts."

Owing to the kindness of Mr Morfill, the author is able to state that a scrutiny of the language of the original of this passage shows that the translation quoted above gives the only meaning which the passage could bear. The word rendered 'ruin' may mean either physical or moral ruin; that rendered 'infirmity' is the equivalent of *debilitas* or ἀσθένεια. The text, elsewhere corrupt, here seems to be

This passage definitely implies the doctrine of inherited depravity and infirmity, contracted by Adam through his fall, and transmitted to his posterity. Its import seems to have escaped the attention of previous writers; though, if the whole of the longer recension (*A*) of the book be as old as the shorter (*B*), and the date generally assigned to the book as a whole, *i.e.* the first half of the first century A.D., be correct, we have here the earliest occurrence of the idea of inborn infirmity inherited from Adam, and a Jewish doctrine of Original Sin more explicit, and earlier, than the teaching of S. Paul upon the subject. This inference itself makes one, at first, slightly suspicious as to its premisses. Not that such a doctrine of inherited taint was impossible to the pre-Christian Jewish mind: we have already seen how Jewish speculation had supplied all the ingredients of such a theory, and how very nearly it sometimes came to gathering them together in a generalisation identical with that which we especially associate with the name of S. Augustine. Moreover we shall presently see that the writer of 4 Ezra taught an essentially similar doctrine, and it cannot be proved that his teaching was shaped by contact with readers of S. Paul. Further, it may perhaps be maintained that the idea of original sin held by the authors of *The Secrets of Enoch* and 4 Ezra had much more in common with the later doctrine of the Christian Church than had the indefinite teaching of the Apostle himself. There is therefore no reason for denying the possibility that the doctrine of Original Sin, in the sense of inherited bias to evil caused by the Fall, was 'of the Jews.' But the suspicion aroused by the uniqueness of the passage we have just considered is somewhat strengthened when we turn from the version of our book in which it is contained, and with whose contents we have so far been concerned, and look for parallel passages in the shorter version, *B*.

We then discover a complete difference between the two sources; a difference indeed which it is much easier to observe

clear. There appears to be no reason to suspect interpolation. The only question is whether the 'ruin' caused by the wickedness of Adam and Eve could possibly be their own death alone; but the sense of the first sentence surely renders such a supposition impossible.

than to explain. *B* has no allusion to the watchers as a source of corruption of mankind; and though the name of Adam is mentioned incidentally once or twice, nothing whatever is said of his life in Paradise, of his temptation, his sin, or of the consequences of his fall. Such topics are rigorously excluded; and some sentences in *A* which are concerned with them are represented in *B* by words which refer to quite another circle of ideas[1]. The question therefore inevitably arises, whether the curious difference between *B*'s reticence and *A*'s fulness of information as to the first man and his fall is to be explained by postulating omission by *B* of much that was contained in the original Greek text, or addition to *A* of much that never found place in the original. The question is one for the expert in such critical problems, and therefore cannot be dealt with here. But in undertaking to expound the important statements of *The Secrets of Enoch* with regard to the Fall and its consequences, it is desirable that the student's attention be called to the existence of the literary problem connected with this book, a problem which one ventures to consider to be not yet finally and conclusively solved.

The (Syriac) Apocalypse of Baruch.

The remaining two Jewish apocalypses with which we have to deal, those of Baruch and Ezra, and the latter of these two books in a special degree, bring us into a rather different atmosphere than that of the writings dealt with in the preceding chapter. They are more serious, less occupied with ancient legend, and much freer from the grotesque fancies and absurd puerilities which abound in the talmudic writings and in the apocryphal romances both of Jewish and

---

[1] With the important passage in *A*, c. xl. 1 quoted above, compare the parallel verses of *B*. "And when I had seen it, I sighed and wept over the ruin of the godless; and I said in my heart," etc. much as in *A*. These verses, in *B*, are transposed into c. xlii., and follow a description of the guardians of the gates of Hades. The passage shows no signs of having been violently abridged any more than its parallel in *A* suggests subsequent interpolation.

Other examples could easily be cited to show that either *B* deliberately avoids, or *A* deliberately foists in, passages dealing with the first man and the beginning of sin; the one or the other text tampering with the original.

Christian religious literature. And they are somewhat important for the student of Jewish speculation in the first century on the subject of the Fall and Original Sin.

The *Apocalypse of Baruch* is of importance for several reasons. It is generally believed to have been written contemporaneously with much of the New Testament[1]. It seems largely to represent the orthodox Judaism which S. Paul was concerned to controvert; and, as De Faye has said, it is the most rabbinical and accurately theological of all the pseudepigrapha. It has sometimes been considered to have grown out of opposition to the rising influence of Christianity, and to have been concerned, in particular, with combating the teaching as to the cause of human sinfulness which is developed in 4 Ezra, or that which is presented in the Epistles of S. Paul[2].

It is not necessary to adopt here any of the several analyses of this apparently composite book into its different constituents proposed by various critics, nor to discuss separately the teaching of its several hypothetical strata. Even if more certainty attached to the results hitherto reached by criticism than can safely be assumed, the difference between the dates of these elements, and perhaps that between their teaching on the subject here concerned, is not so considerable as to make such a method advantageous.

We may proceed, therefore, to classify the passages which are in any way connected with the development of the doctrine of the Fall.

The legend of the watchers, which has been shown to occupy in some of the earlier pseudepigrapha the place of a history of the origin of human sin and corruption, here

---

[1] See Charles, *The Apocalypse of Baruch*, Introd., for a full account of the literature on this book up to 1896, and Ryssel, in Kautzsch's *Pseudepigraphen*, up to 1900. Most of the recent critics of this work, except Clemen, argue for its composite nature, and regard portions of it as prior to the destruction of Jerusalem.

[2] For fuller information see the works of Charles and Ryssel just referred to. As an example of the subjectivity of literary criticism it may be mentioned that some authorities have considered this apocalypse and 4 Ezra to have been written by the same author, and others have maintained that one of the two books was expressly written to controvert the other.

dwindles into insignificance in comparison with the story of the Fall. The watchers indeed are alluded to in one passage only. Adam is said to have been "a danger to his own soul: even to the angels was he a danger[1]." In the following verses it is added: "For moreover, at that time when he was created, they enjoyed liberty. And some of them descended, and mingled with women. And then those who did so were tormented in chains. But the rest of the multitude of the angels, of which there is no number, restrained themselves[2]." The old legend is evidently familiar to the writer of this portion of the apocalypse, but he nowhere uses it to account for man's depravity, of which he is so deeply conscious.

With regard to the unfallen state of the first man this apocalypse has little to say. But there is an interesting reference to the legend that, before his transgression, the heavens had been open to Adam's vision[3]. The New Jerusalem is said to have been shown "to Adam before he sinned; but when he transgressed the commandment, it was removed from him, as also Paradise." Another passage, which will later have to be studied for its teaching as to the consequences of Adam's sin, indirectly reflects light on its writer's idea of Adam's unfallen state in Paradise, and contains a curious fancy which was afterwards brought into prominence in patristic and scholastic literature. This passage which is

[1] lvi. 10.
[2] Dr Charles remarks on lvi. 10: "This must mean that man's physical nature was a danger to his spiritual; for it was the physical side of man that proved a danger to the angels who fell through lust. Man's physical nature was dangerous; for in it resided the 'evil impulse.'" This apocalypse does not mention the "evil impulse," though its doctrine resembles that of rabbinical writings which have much to say of it. The statement that man "was a danger to his own soul" may be compared with the passage of *Slav. Enoch* quoted on p. 207; while the assertion of danger to the angels reminds us of that version of the story of the descent of the angels which regards the women as having attracted the "sons of God"; it also perhaps helps to understand S. Paul's reason why women should be covered—"because of the angels," 1 Cor. xi. 10.
[3] iv. 3. Cf. *Slav. Enoch*, xxxi. 2; Philo, *Quaest. et Sol. in Gen.* i. 32; *Book of Adam and Eve* (Malan), i. 8; *Pesikta*, 36 b; *Baba Bathra*, 58 a; Ephrem, i. 139 (referred to in Malan, p. 215); *Clem. Homil.* x. 4, xvii. 16. The idea is common to Alexandrian, pseudepigraphic and talmudic Jewish literature, along with Christian. It is the foundation of the doctrine that unfallen man possessed the direct vision of God.

quoted below, implies that before the Fall, not only did man know no grief or trouble, but no such thing as passion; it was by the Fall that "the begetting of children was brought about, and the passion of parents produced[1]." That the introduction of physical death as the universal lot of mankind was a consequence of the first transgression, is frequently asserted in the *Apocalypse of Baruch*. "Therefore the multitude of time that he (Adam) lived did not profit him, but brought death and cut off the years of those who were born from him[2]": "Because when Adam sinned and death was decreed against those who should be born, then the number of those who should be born was numbered, and for that number a place was prepared where the living might dwell and the dead might be guarded[3]." Other passages, attributed by Charles to a different writer, seem to this author to teach that man was originally mortal by nature, but that the Fall introduced premature or 'untimely' death[4]. Thus: "For though Adam first sinned and brought untimely death (*mortem immaturam*) upon all...[5]"; and "For owing to his (Adam's) transgression untimely death came into being...[6]."

It remains to inquire whether the *Apocalypse* teaches any form of a doctrine of original sin, and, in particular, a doctrine of hereditary sinfulness; whether, that is, Adam's transgression implanted an hereditary infection or infirmity in

---

[1] lvi. 6, ff. On the introduction of passion and generation by the Fall cf. Gregory of Nyssa, *De Opif. Hom.* xvii., Augustine *De Civ.* Lib. xiv., Aquinas, Pars I. xcviii. 2, etc.

[2] xvii. 3.

[3] xxiii. 4. These two passages belong to the (hypothetical) stratum which Charles calls B^2. They imply that Adam was conditionally immortal. Note that in xix. 8: "all the time from the day on which death was decreed against those who transgress," it is not those who are to be born of Adam, as in the two preceding passages of the stratum in which this verse also occurs, but those "who transgress," who are to inherit death. Perhaps spiritual death is here rather in view: or we may have a compromise with the common view which attributes death to individual sin, notwithstanding Adam's fall and its necessary consequences.

[4] Thackeray, *op. cit.*, p. 32 n., suggests that 'untimely,' in such passages, is only a standing epithet for death, which seems likely enough.

[5] liv. 15.

[6] lvi. 6. Quia enim cum transgressus est, mors, quae non erat tempore ejus, fuit....

IX] *in Jewish Pseudepigraphic Writings* 215

human nature, thereby making mankind inevitably committed to actual sinfulness, or whether in some more forensic sense he constituted men 'sinners,' without necessarily corrupting their nature so as to weaken their will and power of self-determination, or to burden them with a bias toward evil or an abnormally strong evil impulse.

It is curious that the writer of the *Apocalypse of Baruch* never describes the sinfulness of man in terms of the evil inclination, or evil heart, a conception which plays so large a part, not only in the rabbinical writings, but also in the doctrine of the author of 4 Ezra, as will soon be seen. As Dr Porter remarks: " The principal difference between (these) two writers at this point is, that while Ezra, with a deep sense of sin, feels impelled to go back to the grain of evil seed planted in Adam at the beginning, which explains though it does not really excuse sin, Baruch is satisfied to deal with sin as a fact and with its consequences in a more purely legal spirit[1]."

Another difference which will appear, when the statements of the apocalypses of Baruch and Ezra are compared, is that, whereas the writer of the latter of the two will be found to trace man's propensity towards sin to the original endowment of (unfallen) Adam with the evil impulse, and does not assert this impulse to have been abnormally strengthened once and for all by Adam's sin, Pseudo-Baruch, who insists more strongly upon man's independence of Adam, nevertheless attributes certain derangements of human nature, disposing mankind towards sin, expressly to the Fall. Thus, in a passage which has already been mentioned, we read that when Adam transgressed, "grief was named and anguish prepared, and pain was created, and trouble perfected, and boasting began to be established, and Sheol to demand that it should be renewed in blood, and the begetting of children was brought about, and the passion of parents produced, and the greatness of humanity was humiliated, and goodness languished." It is implied here that human nature suffered some derangement at the Fall. Before then man was passion-

[1] *op. cit.*, p. 153. [2] lvi. 6 ff.

less as well as painless; teaching which it is difficult to reconcile with the current doctrine of the *yezer*.

This mutilation or infection of human nature through Adam's sin differs, of course, from that which was asserted later by the Christian Church. It refers only to one particular quality and does not imply that our nature as a whole was rendered "shattered and unsound." Such other moral changes as are enumerated in the passage before us—the establishment of boasting and the languishing of goodness—are not necessarily to be regarded as consequences of an hereditary alteration in our nature; they simply "began," and are such as might be propagated otherwise than by physical descent, which is not the case, of course, with parental passion.

It is to be concluded then, so far, that the author of this apocalypse taught a partial disturbance of the constitution of our original nature, which he conceives as rather angelic than human, in consequence of Adam's sin. This is a very different thing, however, from moral incapacity, infirmity or thorough corruption, such as other teachers have asserted to have been brought about by the Fall, and to which they trace all man's actual sinfulness. We are not compelled by the passage we have been examining, in fact, to conclude that its writer held such a doctrine of the Fall as would see in that catastrophe the cause of all subsequent sin. Passages awaiting our consideration will make such an inference still less natural, if not impossible.

There are several passages in which it is implied that the corruptness of humanity is due to the imitation of example, or, in technical words, is propagated through the 'social heredity' of environment rather than through the physical heredity of natural descent. Thus: "He that lighted has taken from the light, and there are but few that have imitated him. But those many whom he has lighted have taken from the darkness of Adam, and have not rejoiced in the light of the lamp[1]." This verse is opposed to the doctrine of inborn

[1] xviii. 1, 2. As Charles says, *in loc.*, "the law and Adam are in this passage symbolical names for the opposing powers of light and darkness." We agree also that "the writer does not teach the doctrine of original sin and inherited spiritual incapacities" in this passage, but see here a contrast, not an agreement, as Dr Charles asserts, with the teaching of *Slav. Enoch* (see above, p. 209 f.).

IX] *in Jewish Pseudepigraphic Writings* 217

moral incapacity; it implies that man is left to determine his own spiritual destiny. Much stronger assertions of man's absolute and undiminished responsibility, however, are to be found, and the derivation of his *guilt* from Adam is explicitly denied. "For though Adam first sinned and brought untimely death upon all, yet of those who were born from him each one of them has prepared for his own soul torment to come, and again each of them has chosen for himself glories to come....... Adam is therefore not the cause, save only of his own soul, but each one of us has been the Adam of his own soul[1]." This is as stark a repudiation of what is commonly meant by original sin, *i.e.* the heredity of moral incapacity caused by Adam, as could be expressed. The passage is an explicit assertion of man's ability to fulfil the commandments of God, a capacity in no way prejudiced by the Fall; man's sin consists exclusively 'in the following of Adam.' The words seem to ring with polemic and resentment against a contrary doctrine of which the writer is aware, and with which he has no sympathy[2].

There is one passage in the *Apocalypse of Baruch*, however, in which this prevailing attitude seems to be abandoned, and in which the critics of the book have generally found the doctrine that the fall of Adam involved his posterity in spiritual consequences in spite of themselves. In xlviii. 42, 43 we read: "O Adam, what hast thou done to all those who are born from thee? And what will be said to the first Eve who hearkened to the serpent? For all this multitude are going to corruption, nor is there any numbering of those whom the fire devours[3]."

On reading these verses one may perhaps feel tempted to dispose of the difficulties which they raise by regarding them,

---

[1] liv. 15, 19. That the human heart can be "pure from sins" is implied in ix. 1.

[2] The relation of the teaching of this apocalypse to that of 4 Ezra on original sin is treated below in the discussion of the latter book, and again in Chap. x.

[3] The rendering is that of Prof. Charles, whose Eng. translation has been followed in all the citations in this chapter. Ceriani's Latin translation may also be given: "O quid fecisti Adam omnibus qui a te geniti sunt! Et quid dicetur Evae primae quae serpenti obaudivit! Quia haec tota multitudo ivit ad tormentum, neque est numerus eis quos ignis devorat."

as Dr Charles is inclined to do, as an interpolation[1]. Their teaching, on any view of its precise import, certainly appears, at first sight, to be at variance with that which is so emphatically asserted elsewhere in the book; and, if we adopt the theory of composite authorship, and assign the context in which they occur to a different writer than the author of chap. liv. they are not easily reconcilable even with the presuppositions and statements of the particular section in which they occur[2]. One desires, however, a more objective justification for so summary a course. In this case we can hardly fall back upon the reflection emphasised by Clemen, that discrepancies, even in a work of homogeneous authorship, are to be expected, because apocalyptic writers drew largely from divergent traditions[3]: for it is difficult not to see in the present apocalypse a deliberate polemic against one form of the doctrine of Original Sin; and, if this be so, the author or the general redactor can with difficulty be supposed to have allowed such inconsistency, whencesoever derived, to stand. On the other hand, it is hard to see why an interpolator should meddle only in this chapter, and not elsewhere, when the consequences of the Fall are under discussion. Further, we cannot safely fall back upon the undoubted fact that Jewish writers had not always thought out their doctrine on such subjects so clearly and deliberately as never to express themselves without obvious inconsistency, but frequently stated antithetic aspects of a problem without attempting, and apparently without being sensible of the need of effecting, a reconciliation between them. For, as has been said, in such a writing as this we are justified in expecting the avoidance of language which would seem to militate against a view which it so forcibly advocates and champions. We are brought here, therefore, to an *impasse*. Several ways out of the difficulty can be conceived; but which is the actual key to the problem cannot here be dogmatically decided.

One point may be noticed. Though the passage in question deviates from the general tenour of the teaching

---

[1] p. lxxx.
[2] *e.g.* its doctrine of works and merit.
[3] *Theol. Studien und Kritiken*, 1898. S. 211.

of the apocalypse with regard to the consequences of Adam's sin in implying that spiritual, as well as physical, death is to be traced to that cause, it nevertheless does not imply any doctrine of *inherited infirmity*. The precise manner, in fact, in which such spiritual consequences are mediated to Adam's posterity are not defined. There is no necessary implication of the idea that Adam was virtually the race, and that his sin was therefore potentially ours. If the language of a far later age may be used to interpret Pseudo-Baruch's doctrine here, his teaching is rather to be associated with a theory of imputation. The writer merely extends or amplifies the usual assertion that Adam and Eve involved their posterity in *punishment*. He would seem to mean that, on account of the transgression of its first parents, the race as a whole is (conditionally) subject to spiritual torment, just as it is subject to physical penalties, such as death, spoken of in other places; and the vast majority of individuals, each of whom is elsewhere said to be wholly responsible for his own sins and sinfulness[1], fail—it is not said in consequence of any inherited corruption of their nature—to work out their own salvation by performance of good works, and to procure their justification by devotion to the law. In other words, the writer may be understood to teach, in this passage, that all men are on Adam's account 'children of wrath,' and inherit, or participate in, his punishment even beyond this life; this, and this only, so far as spiritual consequences are concerned, is what Adam "has done to all those who are born" from him, and herein consists the blame that will be attributed to Eve. That the overwhelming majority of mankind are going to spiritual perdition, is not said to be due to the fact that they have inherited an enfeebled nature, from whose influence there is no escape. The statement may even accord with the strong insistence in this book upon individual responsibility and its doctrine of the saving efficacy of good works: men can save themselves from this doom brought down on them by Adam if they will, by blamelessness of life; but they will not. Adam

---

[1] See *e.g.* verse 40, immediately preceding the passage under consideration: "Because each of the inhabitants of the earth knew when he was committing iniquity, and they have not known My law by reason of their pride."

is thus conceived as having made us children of wrath only in the sense that we are on his account *conditionally* liable to future punishment[1].

If this interpretation of the passage xlviii. 42—43, and of the connexion of its teaching with other sides of the doctrine of the apocalypse be admissible, this work then presents no inconsistency with the general trend of rabbinic speculation on the consequences of the Fall, and is not really inconsistent with itself. It serves to illustrate what is the most usual Jewish standpoint with regard to the relation between mankind and Adam[2].

While in this one passage admitting a form of original sin—conditional liability to punishment for imputed sin—it argues, on the whole, for undiminished individual responsibility; and in no case does it sanction a doctrine of hereditary corruption of human nature, though in one particular it approaches such a doctrine.

4 *Ezra (II. Esdras)*.

However the vexed question as to the relative dates of the apocalypses of Baruch and Ezra, or of their component parts, and as to the relations of these pseudepigrapha, the one to the other, may ultimately be decided, there can be little doubt that their attitudes towards the problems of human sinfulness and freedom of will are somewhat sharply

---

[1] That "wrath" was entailed, as well as death, on Adam's posterity in consequence of the Fall, is taught in the passage quoted above, p. 198, from *Apoc. Mosis*, xiv., which resembles the present passage of Baruch so closely as to suggest dependence on one side or the other. Another parallel may be cited to show that the interpretation given above is not inconsistent with Jewish thought: "Adam knew Eve only when he saw in spirit that after twenty-six generations the Israelites would accept the Law; for he had seen that his posterity would be condemned to Gehenna." *Beresch Rabba*, c. 21.

It may be remarked that the writer of the Art. *Baruch, Apocalypse of*, in the *Jew. Encyclopaedia*, gives a similar estimate of its teaching on Original Sin to that which has been suggested above.

[2] Cf. xviii. 1, 2; liv. 14, 15, 19, 21, etc.

Prof. Charles's notes on this subject, and indeed the remarks of many writers, suffer somewhat from lack of necessary discrimination between possible forms of a doctrine of Original Sin, such as those of imputed sin accompanied by arbitrary punishment, and of inherited infirmity or corruption.

IX] *in Jewish Pseudepigraphic Writings* 221

opposed. One cannot indeed infer, from a study of the several passages in these books which deal with such subjects, that the statements of either work were consciously intended to qualify or to correct those of the other; and perhaps, in their treatment of the Fall itself and its consequences, they are in fundamental agreement. But since it is established, upon different grounds, that one of the two works must have been known to the author or authors of the other[1], this possibility becomes a probability. Different opinions are held, however, as to which book preceded and influenced the other; and the complexity of the problem is further increased by the possibility (and indeed the probability, in the case of one of them), that each work is composite in structure[2]. It is very likely, as has here been urged, that the language in which the orthodox Jewish doctrine is expressed in the *Apocalypse of Baruch* (liv. 15, 19) owes its singular and unique pointedness to opposition to existing, and familiarly known, diverse teaching. But this need not imply a knowledge of, and an allusion to, 4 Ezra, rather than contact with Christian thought as moulded by S. Paul, or with a circle of Jewish thought which produced both S. Paul and Pseudo-Ezra. On the other hand, the language of 4 Ezra need not have been determined by particular reference to the standpoint of the *Apocalypse of Baruch*, which is that of the orthodox contemporary Judaism. It may have been influenced by contact with Pauline teaching, or, as is suggested in the able introduction to 4 Ezra by Prof. Gunkel[3], the writer may have been independently led to a similar view, with regard to inherent sinfulness, to that which was arrived at by S. Paul, starting from the same basis of received Jewish teaching. Judaism already possessed, to some extent, a belief in such inherent sinfulness, though this was not, as a rule, attributed to the sin of Adam. And Judaism humbled, as we see it in this book

[1] See Thackeray, Art. 2 *Esdras*, in Hastings' *Dictionary of the Bible*, vol. I., and Ryssel, in Kautzsch's *Pseudepigraphen*, S. 405.
[2] See, *e.g.*, Schürer, *History of the Jewish People*, etc., E.T., Div. II. vol. II.; Charles, *Apocalypse of Baruch*, the Introductions to the two books in Kautzsch, *op. cit.*; also the works of Kabisch and De Faye. Gunkel and others maintain the substantial unity of 4 Ezra.
[3] In Kautzsch's *Pseudepigraphen des A. T.*

of Ezra, almost to despair; Judaism compelled to brood more earnestly and more introspectively than ever before over the world's pain and sin; Judaism tortured with an involuntary doubt in the efficacy and self-sufficiency of the Law without and man's capacity for good works within, is surely a soil from which might grow, naturally and spontaneously, doctrines such as those of a universal fall and of ingrained sinfulness: doctrines which, whether separate, as in Judaism, or interconnected, as in the Christian Church, are but attempts to interpret to the reason the soul's sense of helplessness and sin. What the Christian consciousness did for S. Paul, if indeed it was not already done when he became a Christian, might very well have been done for Pseudo-Ezra by the deepened earnestness and the heightened sense of sin wrought in him, in part, by the recent crisis in his nation's history, and yet more effectually by the internal struggle to retain his national faith, which, in the writer's very attempt to justify it to himself, seems to be sadly confessing its inevitable insufficiency[1]. There is much in common, amidst much difference, between the religious thought of Pseudo-Ezra and that of S. Paul: quite enough to have enabled them independently to reach similar doctrines of human sinfulness by very similar roads. But whether the one who, though breaking in part with Jewish orthodoxy, still remained theologically a Jew, was guided to a somewhat non-Jewish doctrine by his own independent thought, or whether the beliefs and feelings which he shared with S. Paul prepared him for an actual reception of the apostle's deeper teaching with regard to human infirmity and spiritual incapacity, is a question which, though full of interest, is at present far from answerable with finality. In so far as the teaching of these two writers as to sin is really connected with the Fall-story, there is perhaps no difference between them. S. Paul took his premiss from the same tradition as Pseudo-Ezra.

The assertion that Pseudo-Ezra's teaching as to inherent sinfulness approximates, in some respects, rather to that of

[1] Read from this point of view, 4 Ezra is surely one of the most pathetic of books. It also records "the most serious and impassioned struggle with the problem of sin and evil from a Jew of this period." (Porter.)

the Christian Church than to that of the Jewish synagogue, an assertion which has been made more than once in the preceding pages, only requires a perusal of his apocalypse for its proof.

This writer's sense of sin, whether personal, national or universal, colours his book so deeply that it is unnecessary to quote individual passages in which it is especially emphasised[1]. It is with his explanation of the origin of universal sinfulness that we are principally concerned.

This, it can easily be shown, is, in the letter, the same as that usually given in purely Jewish literature. It differs from it rather in the sense of being a marked advance upon it, or a development from it, than in that of being an altogether new production, out of relation to what had gone before.

The earlier apocalyptic writings generally attributed the origin of human sinfulness to the watchers; and its prevalence was sometimes regarded as due in part to the continued instigation of demons, as well as to the influence upon each individual of his hopelessly corrupted human environment. The earliest scribes, if we may judge from the book Ecclesiasticus, saw in Adam and Eve the 'beginning of sin,' but not, in their sin, the source or cause of inherited and universal depravity. The first parents of the race very soon came to be regarded, in all the schools of Jewish thought, as the cause, to their descendants, of physical woes and death; and the Fall was very commonly supposed to have affected for the worse the lower creatures and the course of nature. Now the apocalypse of Ezra completely abandons the legend of the watchers; it contains no allusion to those beings, even in a passage in which the early history of the world, as recorded in the Old Testament, is rapidly passed in review[2]. Sin is traced exclusively to Adam and Eve for its beginning, to man's created nature for its provocative cause, and to his will for its actuality. Satan, his fall and his envy, are likewise never mentioned; and the puerilities of both apocalyptic and

---

[1] See, *e.g.*, iii. 8, 12, 13, 35, 36; iv. 39; vii. 46, 68; viii. 35; in addition to passages mentioned incidentally in the following pages.
[2] iii. 4 ff.

midrashic haggada are conspicuously absent. The writer trusts rather to his own thought than to the more fanciful of traditions.

4 Ezra, in common with all Jewish pseudepigraphic literature of the time, regards Adam as the cause of physical death to all who are born from him[1]: "And unto him thou gavest thy one commandment; which he transgressed, and immediately thou appointedst death for him and in his generations." The book also echoes the belief in cosmical consequences of the Fall[2]: "And when Adam transgressed my statutes, then was decreed that now is done. Then were the entrances of this world made narrow, and sorrowful, and toilsome: they are but few and evil, full of perils, and charged with great toils." Thus far then Pseudo-Ezra is in perfect harmony with current Jewish views as to the Fall. And the agreement goes a step further. For the *Apocalypse of Baruch*, typical of the orthodoxy of that day, in one passage asserts Adam to have been the cause of wrath and punishment to his posterity in the world to come. This passage has already been found to be a source of trouble to the critic, because, unless it is an interpolation, which is not proved, it has hitherto seemed difficult to reconcile with the very rigid insistence of that book on the undiminished freedom and responsibility of the individual to work out his own spiritual destiny. Now in so far as the consequences of the Fall go, the teaching of 4 Ezra does not seem to differ from that of the *Apocalypse of Baruch*. Both apocalypses assert that the punishment for Adam's sin has devolved also upon Adam's posterity, and neither of them maintains that the Fall produced in human nature an inherited spiritual infirmity.

But here the two writings begin to diverge. The *Apocalypse of Baruch* has little to say of inherent infirmity, whence-

---

[1] iii. 7. *Et huic mandasti diligentiam unam tuam; et praeteriuit eam, et statim instituisti in eum mortem et in nationibus ejus* [Syr. (cf. Aeth.) *et in generationes ejus*; Arm. *et omnibus quae ex illo gentes erant*]. In citations from the Latin, Dr James' (Bensly's) text has been used, *Texts and Studies*, vol. III.; English quotations are from the R.V.

[2] vii. 11, 12. Cf. Rom. viii. 20, 22. The earth's sorrow for man's evil, a different idea but one closely associated with S. Paul's words, is described in 4 Ezra x. 9 ff.; also the earth's hope in xi. 46.

soever derived. It is concerned with emphasising, in the strongest manner, the unaltered freedom and capacity of the individual to be blameless and to procure salvation, Adam's transgression and human frailty notwithstanding. Pseudo-Ezra, on the other hand, emphasises human infirmity, but he too does not trace this infirmity to the Fall as its cause. It is the implanted seed of evil ripened into corruption and sinfulness of heart, the disposition apparently transmitted physically from Adam to his posterity, though not created or caused by Adam, on which the writer of 4 Ezra strongly insists. He shifts the centre of gravity of the problem from emphasis on man's freedom to emphasis on man's corruption and infirmity in spite of his remnant of responsibility and self-determination. The difference between his teaching and that characteristic of Judaism generally is, however, one of degree rather than of kind. It is the difference between extreme points of view of the same facts rather than diversity of opinion as to what are the facts to be adjusted. It is the difference between more and less inwardness, and of more and less intellectual desire to trace sin to its ultimate source.

It has been seen that the basis of such ideas concerning the source of sin or of hereditary sinfulness as the talmudists possessed was their doctrine that man was endowed from the first by the Creator Himself with the evil impulse or *yezer hara*. There can be no doubt that Pseudo-Ezra builds upon the same foundation. But his nomenclature is different from that of the rabbinic writings. He does not speak of the evil *yezer* by name[1]; and consequently there is room for inquiry as to which of his expressions (if they are not all synonyms, as is here maintained) is exactly the equivalent for the technical term *yezer hara*, and what is then the relation to the thing signified by that phrase of the other evil dispositions which he attributes to human nature.

That which is by far the most directly and naturally identifiable with the *yezer hara* of synagogue scholasticism is the "grain of evil seed" which "was sown in the heart of

[1] Except in vii. 92, cum eis plasmatum *cogitamentum malum*, where we almost certainly have its Latin equivalent.

Adam from the beginning¹." For it was generally agreed that the evil *yezer* was implanted in Adam by God when He created him; it was not put into him by the tempter, nor did Adam make it himself. Hilgenfeld assumes that the evil seed of which the writer of 4 Ezra speaks was received by Adam through the temptation of the devil²; but this assumption is altogether gratuitous: the book never alludes to the temptation, or the tempter, of Adam, and the creation of the *yezer* by God was a universal belief at the time when 4 Ezra was written. It is safe therefore to identify the 'grain of evil seed,' to which the whole evil history of the world is ultimately traced in this apocalypse, with the God-implanted evil impulse familiar to the reader of rabbinic haggada.

But before arriving at the passage to which allusion has just been made we find that the writer has already spoken of an "evil heart" (*cor malignum*) as existing, not only in the generations of mankind, but in the first Adam, and as existing in him, apparently, when he fell, if not as the immediate cause of his transgression³. Inasmuch as this *cor malignum* was in Adam when he sinned, it seems to be identical with the *granum seminis mali* or *yezer hara*. "It explains Adam's sin, but is not explained by it⁴." It is not a consequence of the Fall, either as an aggravated form of the *yezer* induced by Adam's yielding to its mastery, or as something introduced anew by Adam's sin. According to Dr Charles, however, we are to see in the *cor malignum* a development of the *granum mali seminis*, consequent upon acquiescence in the promptings of the evil impulse, which of itself, being made by God, is not to be supposed to be of the nature of sin though it is the

---

[1] iv. 30, 31. Quoniam granum seminis mali seminatum est in corde Adam ab initio, et quantum impietatis generavit usque nunc et generabit usque cum veniat area. Aestima autem apud te granum mali seminis quantum fructum impietatis generaverit.

[2] *Jüd. Apokalyptik*, S. 230. Kabisch (*Eschatologie des Paulus*, S. 152) has gone further astray in identifying the 'evil seed' with the devil's *inquinamentum* (above p. 156 ff.); Clemen and Charles are in agreement with the position adopted here.

[3] iii. 20, 21. Et non abstulisti ab eis cor malignum, ut faceret lex tua in eis fructum. Cor enim malignum baiolans primus Adam transgressus et victus est, sed et omnes qui ex eo nati sunt.

[4] Porter, *op. cit.*, p. 147.

source of sin. This view is said to be confirmed by the fact that the word *baiolans* (bearing) in the passage just cited is represented in the Syriac and Aethiopic versions by the equivalent for *cum vestivit*[1], implying that when Adam yielded to his inherent 'seed' of evil he established in himself an incipient evil state or disposition, and "clothed himself" with a wicked heart. But even if this be so, the fact remains that the development of the evil seed (or inclination) into the evil heart took place in Adam *before* his great sin; he fell because he already possessed the evil heart. The point in question, whether the evil heart is to be taken as identical with the evil seed, or as a development of it induced by indulgence, thus becomes one of no importance. It is certainly not quite correct to represent Pseudo-Ezra as teaching that "a hereditary tendency to sin was created, and the *cor malignum* developed," *by Adam's sin*[2]. So far as the above statements of 4 Ezra go, the hereditary tendency to sin was implanted in Adam at the first[3], and the *cor malignum* was the cause, and not the effect, of the first transgression.

Not only was Adam overcome in consequence of possessing the *cor malignum*, but "also all that are born of him." "Thus," Pseudo-Ezra continues, "disease (*infirmitas*) was made permanent; and the law was in the heart of the people along with the wickedness of the root (*cum malignitate radicis*); so that the good departed away, and that which was wicked (*malignum*) abode still[4]." The disease or infirmity which is here stated to have been made permanent in the race is not said to have been made so by the Fall; the permanent infirmity seems to be simply the transmitted evil

[1] So Charles asserts, *The Apocalypse of Baruch*, p. 93; see also p. lxx on the doctrine of 4 Ezra with regard to inherited sinfulness.
[2] Dr Charles, *op. cit.*, p. lxx.
[3] Of course, by God, though this is not expressly asserted.
[4] iii. 22. Cf. iii. 26: "in all things doing even as Adam and all his generations had done: for they also bore a wicked heart."

In the passage given above (iii. 22) we observe the contrast between the Law and 'the wickedness of the root.' This is the usual rabbinical contrast of the torah and the *yezer hara*; and thus is confirmed the supposition that 'the wickedness of the root' is yet another synonym for the evil inclination. In iii. 20 it is stated that the *cor malignum* was not removed from the Israelites when the Law was given at Sinai.

inclination, or the universal following of Adam's example in yielding to it. Herein the author of 4 Ezra stops short of the doctrine of S. Augustine; he teaches that man inherits a corrupt heart only in the sense that the evil inclination belongs to his nature as it did to that of Adam before the Fall, and not in the sense that he inherits a nature which became evil only in consequence of Adam's sin. It is true that Pseudo-Ezra seems to regard the evil inclination as having been allowed, through indulgence, to gain in the whole race an abnormal power, or as having established its mastery; but there is no sign that he considers this as having been done once and for all in Adam's sin. Thus it is said: "an evil heart hath grown up (*increvit*) in us, which hath led us astray from these statutes, and hath brought us into corruption and into the ways of death, hath showed us the paths of perdition and removed us far from life; and that, not a few only, but well-nigh all that have been created [1]."

But along with this development of the *yezer* doctrine, which, apparently, is not associated at all with the Fall of Adam and which therefore is theoretically different from the ecclesiastical doctrine of Original Sin, though in practical tendency equivalent to it, we find also in 4 Ezra, as in one passage of the *Apocalypse of Baruch*, an explicit statement that Adam's transgression was attended with spiritual, as well as merely physical, consequences for his posterity. We find, that is to say, a doctrine of Original Sin; though it is not easy to decide with which of the specific varieties of that doctrine, such as differentiated themselves afterwards in the Christian Church, if with any, Pseudo-Ezra's teaching is to be identified.

The influence of Adam's fall upon the spiritual destiny of the race is implied in the reflection that it would have been better if Adam had not been formed, or at least had been restrained from sinning; and it is most definitely affirmed in the statement that his fall, though his act alone, was in some undefined sense our fall also. Thus[2]: "I answered then and said, This is my first and last saying, that it had been better that the earth had not given *thee* Adam: or else when it had

---

[1] vii. 48. [2] vii. 116 ff.

given him, to have restrained him from sinning. For what profit is it for all that are in this present time to live in heaviness, and after death to look for punishment? O thou Adam, what hast thou done? for though it was thou that sinnest, the evil is not fallen on thee alone, but upon all of us that come of thee. For what profit is it unto us, if there be promised us an immortal time, whereas we have done the works that bring death[1]?"

This passage asserts that 'the evil' resulting from Adam's sin fell upon his posterity also (R.V.), or that his deed constituted our fall as well as his (Lat.), though the actual sin was Adam's alone. We might conclude that the meaning was here the same as that which we read in the parallel passage of Baruch; *i.e.* that men were constituted sinners objectively by divine appointment, the punishment of Adam being visited upon his posterity without fault on their part. But the concluding words of the citation seem to imply that this was not quite all that was present to Pseudo-Ezra's mind. Adam has brought the evil upon us, and yet *we* also "have done the works that bring death." These are the two selfsame propositions which are placed side by side by S. Paul in the fifth chapter of the Epistle to the Romans; and here, as there, the link which should connect them is not supplied. In neither place is it explained how Adam's sin made his posterity sinful. Perhaps in neither case had the writer developed or received any definite theory on the point.

There is no doubt, then, that 4 Ezra teaches a doctrine of Original Sin; spiritual consequences were entailed by Adam's fall upon his posterity; but how they were mediated is left an open question. On the other hand, the actual sinfulness of all mankind is taught to be due to the possession of the evil heart or inclination which was in Adam before his sin; and in the passages which embody this side of Pseudo-Ezra's teaching it is nowhere stated that the aggravation of the

---

[1] The Latin of verses 118—119 is as follows: O tu quid fecisti Adam? Si enim tu peccasti, non est factum solius tuus casus sed et nostrum qui ex te advenimus. Quid enim nobis prodest si promissum est nobis immortale tempus, nos vero mortalia opera egimus?

power of the evil impulse is a consequence of the first transgression[1]. The permanent infirmity established in the race would thus appear, from what Pseudo-Ezra says, to be the result of indulgence, by individual members of mankind, of the divinely implanted 'evil disposition,' the natural tendency of the stock. The bias is regarded as so strong, moreover, that only with extreme difficulty can it be resisted[2]; and consequently only few will be saved[3].

And yet man's nature is not so ruined as to leave no room for free-will and responsibility. The aim of the writer is to justify the dealings of God, especially His punishment of the wicked; and this he does by falling back upon the freedom of man's will and the theoretical possibility, however difficult practically, of right determination and of good works. In one passage this freedom is traced to, or identified with, the gift of understanding[4]. It is frequently dwelt upon and emphasised[5]; but it is never so pressed as to conflict with the doctrine of man's infirmity or propensity to evil through his *yezer*, or that of Adam's fall involving his posterity in some of its consequences: doctrines which have been shown to be characteristic of this book.

The relation of the teaching of 4 Ezra to that of the *Apocalypse of Baruch*, on the one hand, and to that of S. Paul, on the other, is difficult to define precisely. The language of each writer is too indefinite to admit of a rigorously systematic theory being extracted from his unconnected, and apparently inconsistent, statements. The same elements

[1] This latter view is attributed to the writer of the apocalypse, however, by Dr Charles (*Apocalypse of Baruch*, pp. 92—3, lxx—lxxi; cf., for similar estimates of the doctrine of 4 Ezra, Rosenthal, *Vier apokr. Bücher*, and Edersheim, *Life and Times* etc., vol. I. p. 167, n. Schiefer, writing in the *Zeitschrift f. wissenschaftl. Theologie*, 1901, on *Das Problem der Sünde im* 4. *Ezrabuch*, says: "Klipp und klar wird hier die Theorie von der Erbsünde ausgesprochen."

[2] vii. 92. Ordo primus, quoniam cum labore multo certati sunt ut vincerent cum eis plasmatum cogitamentum malum, ut non eos seducat a vita ad mortem. Here the *yezer hara* is alluded to; this was 'fashioned together with' each individual.

[3] See, *e.g.*, vii. 140; viii. 1, 3; ix. 16.

[4] vii. 72.

[5] vii. 21—26, 127—131; viii. 56—62; ix. 11.

underlie the doctrine of all, though each of the three writers places the emphasis differently. Baruch, like Pelagius at a later period, champions individual freedom; he is silent about the evil heart, and is legalistic in his attitude towards sin, though admitting that the Fall has somehow been a spiritual catastrophe affecting all generations. Ezra's use of the *yezer* doctrine, like S. Paul's teaching as to the flesh and the spirit, which superficially resembles it, is not definitely brought into relation with the doctrine of Original Sin, which, in some form, is clearly held both by Pseudo-Ezra and S. Paul. Nothing is definitely known as to actual literary relations between any of these three apparently contemporary writers[1]. But we have seen no reason to suppose that, for his doctrine of sin,

[1] Dr Rosenthal, in his *Vier Apokryphische Bücher*, has endeavoured to trace 4 Ezra to the school of R. Elieser B. Hirkanos. Several talmudic students have pronounced his assertion of Jamnian influence being traceable in the work, however, to be very slenderly grounded. There seems indeed to be good talmudic evidence for the fact that R. Elieser insisted strongly upon the universal sinfulness of man (*Sanhedr.* 101 a), and that he taught that even the patriarchs were but imperfectly holy (*Arach.* 17 a: "If the Holy One, blessed be He! should enter into judgment with Abraham, Isaac and Jacob, they would not be able to stand before the proving"). Dr Rosenthal does not support by any evidence, however, his further assertion that R. Elieser derived this universal sinfulness from Adam's fall (*S.* 60). He sees in this doctrine one of the points of contact between the Rabbi in question and Jewish Christians; but the proof which he offers seems to be very far-fetched and precarious. R. Elieser's relations with Jewish Christians, so far as actual evidence exists, appear to be reducible to an incident which he himself records (*Tosefta Chulin*, 2. 24), viz. the meeting in the streets of Sepphoris with Jacob of Kephar Sechariah, and expressing his agreement with a Christian interpretation, which that reputed disciple of Christianity communicated to him, of Deut. xxiii. 18 and Mic. i. 7. This incident is related in Derenbourg's *Histoire de la Palestine*, pp. 357 ff.; Grätz, *Geschichte der Juden*, Bd. IV. S. 53; Bacher, *Die Agada der Tannaiten*, Bd. I. S. 113. The words "from dirt they came and to dirt they shall go forth" (*Baraita Aboda Zara*, 17 a; *Midr. Rabba, Kohel.* I. 8), contained in R. Elieser's reply, are taken by Rosenthal necessarily to imply the doctrine of Original Sin, of which he supposes the Rabbi thus to express his approval. They do not all suggest the idea, however, that the traces of a sinful origin remain and are never lost; and such an interpretation has no relevancy whatever to the passage with which they are associated. The one doctrine at all akin to that of Original Sin which we have any reason to attribute to R. Elieser is therefore that of universal sinfulness without exception of the patriarchs. But this would appear (Justin Martyr, *Dial. c. Tryph.* 95) to have been the prevalent view amongst the Jewish teachers at that day. The representation of the serpent as the instrument of Satan and as inspired by him, ascribed to R. Elieser (*Pirke di R. Elieser*, c. 13), is not a proof of Christian influence (see above p. 158); and,

Pseudo-Ezra was dependent on Christian sources. It is unfair to suppose that religious inwardness was necessarily lacking to a non-Christian Jew; and it is certainly an exaggeration to assert, as has frequently been represented, that Judaism possessed no doctrine of Original Sin.

APPENDIX TO CHAPTER IX.
Incidental Allusions to the Fall in Undoubtedly Christian Apocryphal Writings.

In the *Visio Pauli* c. 45 (Lat. version, ed. James, *Texts and Studies*, vol. II.) occurs an allusion to the Fall as the cause of mortality:

Et tenuit mihi manum et duxit me juxta arborem cognoscende bone et male; et dixit: Haec est arbor per quem mors ingressa est in saeculo et ex ea accipiens a muliere sua Adam manducavit et ingressa est mors in mundo.

The Apocalypse of Sedrach, which seems to be based upon 4 Ezra, and to continue, from a Christian point of view, the discussion in that writing of the origin of evil, contains a passage relevant to our subject. In cc. 3 and 4 the question is asked: if God created all things for man, why his affliction? Placed in Paradise and threatened with death if he ate the forbidden tree, he was led astray by the devil, we are told, and did eat. This, however, was by the will of God. There will also be found here the legend that God ordered the angels to worship Adam, to which reference has previously been made.

The introduction of death at the Fall, both physical and eternal, is mentioned also in *The Acts and Martyrdom of Andrew*: " For the first man through the tree of transgression brought in death."

moreover, the *Pirke* is a late book containing much that R. Elieser probably never taught.

Thus it has neither been proved that R. Elieser held any specifically Christian doctrines nor that he had any connexion with the author of 4 Ezra.

Töttermann, in a small work on R. Elieser, believes that this Rabbi incurred the suspicion of Christian tendencies not without injustice, and that in many ways he was nearer to the Christian than the Pharisaic standpoint.

Friedländer, *Vorchristl. jüd. Gnosticismus*, S. 73 ff. denies that the Jacob mentioned above was a Christian, and asserts him to have been a Gnostic.

"And since the first man, who brought death into the world through the transgression of the tree, had been produced from the spotless earth, it was necessary that the Son of God should be begotten a perfect man from the spotless virgin, that He should restore eternal life, which man had lost through Adam, and should cut off (shut out) the tree of carnal appetite through the tree of the Cross." *Ante-Nicene Library*, vol. XVI. p. 338.

In *Narratio Zosimi* (*Texts and Studies*, vol. II.) the devil is represented (c. 19) as saying that he entered into the serpent as an instrument (σκεῦος), by which to tempt man to disobedience, because man had been made sinless and blessed above the angels.

C. 6 contains the passage: καὶ ἐβόησεν ὁ ἄνθρωπος τοῦ θεοῦ λέγων· Οἴμοι, ὅτι (ἡ) ἱστορία τοῦ 'Αδὰμ (ἐν) ἐμοὶ ἀνεκεφαλαιώθη. ἐκεῖνον γὰρ διὰ τῆς Εὕας ἠπάτησεν ὁ Σατανᾶς....

The Bohairic Account of the Death of Joseph (*Texts and Studies*, vol. IV.) attributes death to the sin of Adam (xxviii. 2, 10, 11, 13, 14; xxxi. 1). Thus, in xxviii. 13: "But because of the transgression of Adam this great trouble has come upon all mankind, and this great necessity of death." Cf. *The Bohairic Account of the Falling Asleep of Mary* (*op. cit.*).

The same point is referred to again in *The History of Joseph the Carpenter*, c. 31: "And our Saviour answered and said: Indeed, the prophecy of my Father upon Adam, for his disobedience, has now been fulfilled." *Ante-Nicene Library*, vol. XVI. p. 76.

The Conflict of S. Peter (Malan's tr. from the Aethiopic, p. 5) has the passage: "For the first man, the old Adam that was born in me, appeared as chief (*or* first); it was the old birth, removed by this death: Adam fell by losing his glory."

In *The Conflict of S. Thomas* (*ibid.* p. 207), the serpent encountered by S. Thomas claims to have been the tempter of Eve and the sender of angels from above (referring to Gen. vi. 1–4). Yet the serpent is not identified with the devil: "I am akin to him who came from the East, and to whom power was given to do what he liked in the earth."

In *The Conflict of S. Andrew* (ibid. p. 105) Satan is distinguished from the devil 'his father.'

The Acts of Philip similarly states that the serpent is the *son* of the wicked one; his father is the devil (*A. N. Library*, vol. XVI. p. 302). The following passage also occurs here:

"Take away from yourselves the wicked disposition, that is, the evil desires, through which the serpent, the wicked dragon, the prince of evil, has produced the pasture of destruction and the death of the soul, since all the desire of the wicked has proceeded from him....... The poison of wickedness is in him."

In the text of this work in Codex Baroccianus there is a passage, quoted in *Texts and Studies*, vol. II. no. 3, p. 158, of which Dr James says: "The drift of this is not very plain: but it seems to be a version of the well-known legend... that the angels were called upon to adore the newly-created Adam, and that certain of them through pride and envy refused to do so. In this passage, their jealousy is materialised and takes the form of the serpent."

In the *Gospel of Nicodemus* (c. 23; ed. Thilo, p. 736), occur the words: ὦ ἀρχιδιάβολε, ἡ τοῦ θανάτου ἀρχή, ἡ ῥίζα τῆς ἁμαρτίας.

Of course this catena is not intended to be exhaustive. The passages are given as samples of the treatment which the story of the Fall continued to receive at the hands of popular writers. They are of no doctrinal interest.

CHAPTER X.

THE GROWTH OF THE DOCTRINE OF THE FALL, AND OF ITS ELEMENTS, IN JEWISH LITERATURE AS A WHOLE.

THE method of treatment adopted in the preceding chapters has been that of examining the various sources, arranged according to such rough classification as was most natural and convenient, for their respective contributions to the history of the Jewish exegesis of the Fall-story and to the building up of the doctrines of the Fall and Original Sin. This plan has perhaps proved serviceable to the student of minutiae, though it may have carried with it the disadvantage of presenting him with the facts without any framework to give them coherence and logical arrangement, and of so rendering it difficult for him "to see the wood for the trees." It is intended therefore, in the present chapter, in spite of the repetition which will necessarily be involved, briefly to collect together the more important facts which have thus been dealt with in their literary context, and to arrange them according, not to source, but to subject-matter; so that some general idea may the more easily be gained as to the historical development of the doctrine of the Fall as a whole, and of its constituent elements in particular. This treatment of the subject, it may be borne in mind, cannot be so objective as that pursued in the previous chapters; for when logical takes the place of historical and literary arrangement, the facts must needs be presented in some kind of perspective, and be woven into some kind of general theory of development; and here begins increased scope for error, because of increased necessity for tentative speculation.

The Fall-stories of Gen. vi. 1—4 *and Gen. iii.*

When we consider the usage, in the various uncanonical books reviewed in the foregoing chapters, of the legend of the descent of the watchers, the idea suggests itself that this, rather than the Paradise-story of Genesis, was the earliest basis for popular Jewish speculation as to the origin of the general sinfulness of the world. The most ancient portion of the literature which has been examined is probably the groundwork of the *Book of Enoch*. This would seem to have been written before Ecclesiasticus, and to embody folk-lore which was then matter of ancient tradition. As has been already observed, the groundwork of *Enoch* uses the legend of the watchers apparently with the full intention of thereby accounting, not necessarily for the first sinful human act, but for the origin of widespread depravity. The fall of the race and the beginning of the unsatisfactory moral condition of humanity as a whole seem there to be traced to the lustful invasion of the world by these fallen celestial visitors. And it is equally noticeable that the Paradise-story, although it is perfectly well known to the earliest Enoch-literature, is completely ignored as a key to the problem of evil, in which so much interest seems to be shown.

Assuming, then, as probable the view, already advocated in a preceding chapter, that the elohim-legend of Gen. vi. at first served the purpose afterwards fulfilled by the Paradise-story, we may next observe that, in passing from the earliest apocalyptic literature down to the latest with which we have here been concerned, there is a gradual change in the emphasis laid upon the legend of the watchers and the narrative of the loss of Eden respectively; the one advancing as the other recedes in importance as regards the doctrinal inferences drawn from them. In the Similitudes of the *Book of Enoch* the story of the angels differs in important respects from that presented in the groundwork of the same book, but is still preferred to the narrative contained in Gen. iii. as a starting-point for the history of the origin and spread of human sin. In the *Testaments of the Twelve Patriarchs* the legend of the watchers is frequently referred to, but is not made the basis for any treatment of the general problem of sin. The *Book of Jubilees*, which is a commentary on Genesis, only uses the story to explain the degeneracy which called forth the Deluge; it rather turns to the Paradise-narrative for an explanation of the evil of the world, though it is the physical and cosmical, more than the moral, consequences of the fall of the first parents upon which it dwells. The book represents, therefore, in this connexion, the same level of development as Ecclesiasticus, which traces death, but not man's present moral state, to the first sin. The same position appears again in *Pseudo-Philo*; and the *Testament of Abraham*, like the Enoch-literature, knows the Fall-story but fails to make doctrinal use of it, even though the oppurtunity to do so lies very close at hand. In the *Apocalypse of Abraham* we seem to meet with a fusion of the streams of folk-lore based respectively on Gen. iii. and Gen. vi. 1—4. The writer makes the former narrative his starting-point for the history of the race, and speaks of the serpent-like tempter; this being, however, is not the serpent pure and simple of the Bible account, but Azazel, who so frequently appears as the central figure of the other group of legends which connected themselves with the opening verses of Gen. vi. Here, perhaps, we get a glimpse of the manner in which the story of Paradise came to possess the significance, for speculation on the problem of human sin, which it afterwards increasingly manifested, and of which, at first, it would seem to have been devoid. It has been noticed, moreover, that the tempter of Eve is elsewhere identified with Satanail or with Gadreel: names which, like Azazel, are also prominent in some accounts of the descent of the watchers and the corruption of mankind by them. There are thus signs of confusion of the two totally distinct biblical stories, which resulted, it would seem, in detaching the idea of the fall of the race from the setting in which it first grew up, and transplanting it to the history of the first temptation and the loss of Paradise. It is noticeable too, that when at first the narrative of Gen. iii. began to be used as a history of a universal fall, the serpent was identified with, or exchanged for, a Satan, and that the motive of envy was ascribed to him; and these points perhaps betray the previous existence of a belief in the fall of the devil or of a class of spirits.

As we pass on to the maturer products of the apocalyptic class of literature we find that the legend of the watchers drops more and more out of sight, whilst the Paradise-story grows more and more both in content and in significance. In the *Slavonic Book of Enoch* the former legend is referred to only as supplying the cause for the Deluge; in the *Apocalypse of Baruch* it is merely alluded to, and no use is made of it; whilst, finally, in 4 Ezra it vanishes altogether.

Development of Doctrine from Gen. iii.

Meanwhile the Fall-story has come to serve for much more than an explanation of human death. Such was the earliest doctrinal purpose to which it was put, though even this usage appears for the first time as late as the time of Ben Sira, and was tardily adopted, it would appear, in rabbinic circles, for generations afterwards. But in the *Book of Jubilees* the fall of Adam is regarded as initiating a stream of cosmical effects[1]; and the derangement of Nature thus brought about assumes more imposing proportions in the apocalypses of Baruch and Ezra and the later midrashic literature. Last of all, spiritual consequences for the whole race are traced to Adam's transgression. If the facts are sufficiently numerous to admit of any generalisation from them that is not wholly precarious, passages referred to in the foregoing chapters would seem to imply that the heredity of a sinful bias or taint of evil (apart from its derivation from Adam) was an idea fairly familiar to Alexandrian writers; whereas the Palestinian school were more inclined to express their thought as to the effects of the first father's sin upon the spiritual condition of his posterity in terms which rather suggest what modern divines would call a theory of imputation. Certainly Alexandrian writers, such as Pseudo-Solomon and Philo, mention particular cases of hereditary sinfulness;

---

[1] The influence of human sin, though not of the fall of Adam, on the course of Nature had already been believed by the writer of the earlier portion of the *Book of Enoch*; see p. 185, n. 2.

and the first definite appearance of the idea that mankind inherit from Adam, and *as a consequence of his transgression*, a moral infirmity of nature, is to be found in the A recension of *Slavonic Enoch*, which there is some reason to believe to have been written in Egypt. It will be remembered that a very similar doctrine of the Fall is implied in the *Apocalypse of Moses*, one of the earliest Adam-books[1]; but inasmuch as we do not possess this work in its original Jewish form, it is impossible to feel quite certain that its teaching on the question of Original Sin, certainly very unusual for an early Jewish book, is really ancient. On the other hand the Fall seems to be regarded by the writer of the *Apocalypse of Baruch* (Syriac) as having brought upon the whole race liability to future punishment, from which it is only possible for the individual to escape through perfect blamelessness of life, and as thus having materially affected the spiritual destiny of all men notwithstanding the fact that everyone is responsible for taking these consequences to himself, and is, in fact, ultimately, "the Adam of his own soul[2]." Pseudo-Ezra's teaching as to the Fall and Original Sin is very similar to this *in so far as it is purely teaching as to the Fall and Original Sin.* But it is so much qualified by his doctrine of the evil heart or *yezer hara*, which, however, as has here been maintained, is not logically connected, or theoretically interwoven, with his speculation on the results of the first transgression, that, as a whole, his treatment of man's moral state is widely divergent from that of his contemporary. While Baruch tries to minimise such effects of the Fall upon man's spiritual state as he admits, by insisting on the individual's undiminished freedom and responsibility, Ezra is full of the sense of human infirmity derived, not by heredity from fallen Adam, but from "the following of Adam" in indulging the evil impulse which is in us at birth as it was in Adam when he came from the hand of God. Our sinfulness is to Adam's as fruit is to seed; but the connexion, for Pseudo-Ezra, is historical, not causal.

We thus find Judaism, at the beginning of the Christian era, in possession of two distinct conceptions of Original Sin:

[1] See p. 198.
[2] For a view identical with this or the foregoing teaching as to Original Sin, see p. 201.

the one, presumably originating from the school of Alexandria, more closely parallel to part of the late Augustinian theory, and stated in terms of the idea of inherited infirmity; the other, so indefinitely formulated that the connecting link between Adam's sin and his posterity's punishment is not expressed, though it seems to be simply the divine appointment, suggesting as the nearest analogy some form of the imputation doctrine prevalent during the Reformation period.

The step from such purely Jewish teaching to that of S. Paul, which is similarly indefinite, will already seem to be but slight. The contents of the following chapter must not be anticipated here: but perhaps it will even now be apparent that the doctrine of Original Sin is not to be looked upon as the creation of S. Paul, any more than it is to be regarded as having its source in the Old Testament.

The stages of the development from the narrative of the third chapter of Genesis to the almost full-grown doctrine of a fall of the race in Adam and the heredity of its consequences, have now been described in so far as the materials render such description possible. Or would it not be more correct to say, that the gulf between the biblical narrative and the ecclesiastical doctrine has been more plainly revealed by means of the literature which has been reviewed? Perhaps there is truth in both these modes of regarding the facts. Certainly there are gaps in the chain which Jewish literature alone does not enable us to fill up. The Adam, the tempter, the consequences of the first sin, of the pseudepigraphic and rabbinical writings are very different from the Adam, the tempter, and the consequences of the first sin which we meet with in the naïve story of Genesis. And the doctrines whose history this work endeavours in part to describe are deduced from the Fall-story as it is told in these Jewish writings, not as it is told in the Hebrew narrative. The question arises again, and presents itself more forcibly than it did at an earlier stage of the inquiry: how did the transition from the Hebrew scenery of the Fall-story to that of its Jewish setting come about? And a similar question might be put with regard to the difference between the account, in Gen. vi., of the descent of the sons of God and the legend of the watchers.

Two views have been suggested, between which future

inquiry must decide. It may be held, with Gunkel for instance, that the more highly embellished form of the legends as they appear in Jewish literature is due to the reappearance of their original characteristics, their ancient mythological dress which was largely stripped off them by their Old Testament editor. On the other hand it may be maintained that the traits ascribed to Adam, and the other figures of the story, in the Jewish period are not survivals from remote antiquity, but new additions; that they are not even derived by exegetical methods from the biblical narrative, but are borrowed, in the first place, from foreign sources, and then read into the old, simple, national folk-lore. Thus the magnified Adam to which the writer of Job seems to refer, and whose first estate is so much glorified in pseudepigraphic and rabbinic literature, and the powerful spirit who, after his fall envied and tempted the first parents to their ruin, would have no connexion whatever, originally, with the corresponding figures in the Hebrew history. This latter view would seem to be much the more probable. In the first place it better explains the divergences and confusions in which the literature on the subject abounds; such, for instance, as the conflicting statements as to the tempter of Eve, who is sometimes the serpent, sometimes the employer of the serpent, and sometimes a Satan replacing the serpent. Secondly, legends of the descent of spirits and their intercourse with mankind, of the fall of angels, of the rivalry between the devil and man, of the wonderful trees such as we meet with in the pseudepigrapha, wholly different from the biblical trees of knowledge and of life, and of various other things involved in the later treatment of the biblical *Urgeschichte*, are known to have existed in Persian, and perhaps other, mythologies to which the Jews, between the Captivity and the Christian era, easily had access[1]. These, however, are points upon which further light may be hoped for, and certainly is desirable.

The development, within Jewish literature, of what may

[1] See on this subject Bousset, *Die Religion des Judenthums im N.T. Zeitalter*, S. 331 ff., 461 ff. etc., and the references there given to papers of Bonwetsch, Grünbaum, and others.

be called constituent elements of the doctrine of the Fall, or of beliefs immediately connected with it, may now be briefly traced.

Adam in the unfallen state.

Two passages contained in post-exilic Old Testament books were mentioned in a previous chapter which testify that, already in their time, ideas about the first man, whencesoever they were derived, such as are not at all suggested by the Jahvist history, were more or less familiar. The writer of Job seems to refer to a belief that the first man possessed extraordinary wisdom and had access to the divine council. Ezekiel's analogy between Adam and the king of Tyre implies that he was familiar with a tradition which represented the first man as one who lived in great outward splendour.

These two attributes, wisdom and splendour, were added to as speculation developed.

Ben Sira observes (xlix. 16) that "above every living thing was the glory of Adam" (Heb.); but this is the whole of his contribution towards the exaltation of the first man. The author of *Wisdom* seems to make little of Adam's sin in comparison with Cain's, which may possibly be due to increasing reverence for the first man; and the same tendency is observable elsewhere in Alexandrian literature. Philo speaks of Adam in the same strain as the Palestinian haggadists.

At the hands of the latter writers the endowments of the first man become greatly multiplied. Adam is represented as of enormous stature[1], as physically perfect and of surpassing beauty[2]. The Adam-books frequently speak of him as endowed with a 'glory[3],' and a 'bright nature' is sometimes attributed to him[4]. Adam was 'a bright angel[5]' or 'like an angel[6].' He was supposed to possess extraordinary powers of perception enabling him to observe the heavenly operations[7];

---

[1] See pp. 134, 149. It will not be necessary in this and the following notes to reproduce the passages referred to; the pages of the present work on which they may be found will be sufficient.

[2] pp. 134, 149.   [3] pp. 199, 200. Cf. p. 149.   [4] p. 200.
[5] *Ibid.*   [6] p. 207.   [7] p. 134.

the New Jerusalem was shown to him, and the heavens were open to his vision¹. Here we perhaps have the foundation of the tradition which has sometimes established itself in Christian doctrine, that unfallen man possessed the direct vision of God. When Adam was first created he found all necessary things prepared for him, and he was supplied with the ministration of angels²; indeed he was even an object of worship to the angels³. He lived in perfect bliss⁴, free from all grief and disease⁵, and possessed a nature undisturbed by concupiscence⁶. He was blessed with superhuman wisdom, and was the father of many arts and inventions⁷.

Of Adam's moral endowments, at the first, comparatively little is expressly stated. Philo seems to imply that he was morally neutral; the *yezer* doctrine, appearing in Ecclesiasticus, and playing a very important part in the treatment accorded to the problem of sin by Pseudo-Ezra and the rabbinical writers, asserts that the impulse toward evil was divinely implanted in Adam from the first, and was the cause of his fall just as it is the incentive to sin in each of his descendants. Here then is a difference between the prevailing Jewish and the later Christian doctrine⁸.

The duration of the unfallen state was a matter of speculation, and various views were held with regard to it. The *Book of Jubilees* states that Adam and Eve lived seven years before their great transgression⁹. More generally the interval is shortened to a few days or a few hours¹⁰, in which case the idea of an 'unfallen state,' typical of what man's life on earth was intended to be, is almost done away with.

Still, most of the endowments which Adam had received at the first are expressly stated to have been taken from him at the Fall¹¹. Philo does not make much of the losses occasioned by the first transgression, barely going beyond the

---

[1] See p. 213, where other references on this point are collected.
[2] pp. 134, 149.   [3] p. 200.   [4] p. 134.
[5] pp. 134, 213.   [6] p. 213.   [7] p. 150.
[8] It may be noted that *The Conflict of Adam and Eve* (Dillmann) says that Adam and Eve, in their unfallen condition, "had not hearts turned to earthly things." See p. 200.
[9] p. 192.   [10] References are collected on p. 151.
[11] See especially the Adam-books.

words of Genesis[1]; but in some of the pseudepigrapha, especially the *Apocalypse of Baruch*[2], and in many passages of rabbinic literature[3], Adam is said to have been deprived of his unique privileges.

The Fall and Death.

The view that universal physical death was the outcome of the Fall is general from the time of Ben Sira. It has been held by some, but perhaps on insufficient grounds, that this writer generally professes the ancient Hebrew belief that death was preordained for man, and natural to him. This question was argued in the chapter on the teaching of Ecclesiasticus, and the opinion was adopted that Ben Sira nowhere so expresses himself as necessarily to imply such a doctrine, but that, on the contrary, he taught that death was a consequence of the Fall. In the Alexandrian School, death is traced to the first sin as its cause; but it would seem to be ethical rather than physical death of which Pseudo-Solomon and Philo speak. Some writers, again, have considered that one of the supposed constituent sources of the (Syriac) *Baruch-apocalypse* deviates from the general view in that it regards the untimeliness or prematureness of death, and not death itself, as occasioned by Adam's sin. This interpretation also seems doubtful. As for the rest of the pseudepigrapha, the (Noachian) interpolations of the *Book of Enoch*, *Pseudo-Philo*, the *Apocalypse of Moses*, the main portion at least of the *Apocalypse of Baruch*, and 4 Ezra all definitely assert that physical death was introduced and caused by the fall of our first parents. This opinion, so general in apocalyptic writers, would seem, however, to have only gradually replaced the individualistic view in the rabbinical schools, if the slenderness of the information at our disposal warrants an inference on the point. The belief was adopted by S. Paul from his contemporaries, and so became general with Christian writers[4].

---

[1] p. 135.   [2] p. 215.   [3] p. 150.
[4] See, in connexion with the summary given above, the passages referred to on pp. 117 f., 123 f., 135 f., 161 f., 189, 194, 198, 214, and in the appendix to Chap. IX.

The Tempter.

The different representations of the tempter met with in the various classes of literature that have been reviewed are not a matter of importance to the essence of the doctrines of the Fall and Original Sin. Inasmuch, however, as they reflect some light on the history of the development of the Fall-story, the scattered references previously given may here be collected together.

The tempter remains simply the serpent in *Jubilees*[1], though Satan is mentioned elsewhere in that book; also in the *Apocalypse of Adam* or *Testament of Adam and Eve*[2], in the (Christian) *Conflict of S. Thomas*[3], in some rabbinical writings[4], and in Josephus[5]. Philo also never refers to a Satanic tempter, but he treats the serpent in allegorical fashion[6].

In another series of passages the serpent is introduced as a means or instrument employed by the devil. This is the case in the *Apocalypse of Moses*, though elsewhere in this book Satan is said to have appeared to Eve in the guise of an angel[7]; in the *Treasure Cave*, where the temptation is closely associated with the expulsion of Satan from heaven because of his refusal to worship the first man, and his envy thereby excited[8]; in the *Conflict of Adam and Eve*, where at the same time the tempter is somewhat strangely described as "the serpent that became Satan[9]"; in the *History of the Creation and of the Transgression of Adam*[10]; in the Greek *Apocalypse of Baruch*, where, however, it is Samael that puts on the vesture of the serpent[11]; in the *Narratio Zosimi*[12], and in rabbinical literature[13].

In yet other cases the serpent is identified completely with Satan, or replaced by him or by some corresponding evil

---

[1] p. 192 f.
[2] p. 201.
[3] p. 233.
[4] p. 152.
[5] p. 136.
[6] *Ibid.*
[7] p. 196.
[8] p. 200.
[9] *Ibid.*
[10] p. 201.
[11] p. 203. In the Slavonic text the serpent is the tempter.
[12] p. 233.
[13] *e.g. Pirke di R. Elieser*, c. 13 (see above, p. 158).

246   *Growth of Jewish doctrine*   [CHAP.

spirit. It is so in the Book of Wisdom ii. 23[1], which probably makes use of the tradition occurring in the *Vita Adae* and elsewhere. Again, in one of the interpolations in the *Book of Enoch*, Gadreel is mentioned as the tempter of Eve[2]; whilst in the *Apocalypse of Abraham* it is Azazel, "like a serpent in form" though with hands, feet and wings, who takes the place of the serpent of Genesis[3]. It would seem that these various representations of the tempter are due to confusion or assimilation of the old Hebrew Fall-story with the (foreign?) legends relating to the fall and envy of the devil, and that of the descent of the watchers: which last was possibly the result of grafting foreign notions upon the story of Gen. vi. 1—4.

It has been observed that the motive ascribed to the tempter, in bringing about the ruin of Adam and Eve, is almost always envy. But the sources differ very considerably as to how the devil's envy was excited. According to one form of the tradition, Satan's jealousy and hostility to man was called forth before his expulsion from heaven, and its occasion was his being summoned to worship Adam, along with the rest of the angels. This legend appears in the *Vita Adae*[4], the *Treasure Cave*[5], the Koran[6], the *Acts of Philip*, the *Apocalypse of Sedrach*[7], and, in modified form, in the *History of the Creation and of the Transgression of Adam*[8]. According to another tradition Satan only envied Adam after his own fall from heaven, and either on account of it or because of the glorious privileges and the happiness which Adam enjoyed in Eden. This is the form which the legend takes in the *Apocalypse of Moses*[9], the *Book of the Secrets of Enoch*[10], and in certain rabbinical writings[11]. In the last-named branch of Jewish literature the prevailing explanation of Satan's action is his desire to possess Eve. One or other

---

[1] See p. 124. Satan is the tempter also in the *Testament of Job*, and in the *Gospel of Nicodemus* and other late apocrypha.
[2] p. 189.   [3] p. 194.   [4] See p. 199.
[5] p. 200.   [6] ed. Sale, pp. 5, 109, etc.
[7] See Appendix to Chap. IX.   [8] p. 201.
[9] p. 196.   [10] c. XXXI., see p. 206.
[11] See pp. 152 ff., especially the reference to *Pirke ai R. Elieser*.

of these various legends as to the devil's envy of man was doubtless present to the mind of the writer of the Book of Wisdom when he spoke of death entering into the world by the envy of the devil. From him, probably, the tradition passed on to the Christian fathers[1].

For other particular points connected with the Fall-story it will suffice to collect here the references to such passages as bear upon them, without further discussion.

On *the Trees of Paradise*, see pp. 154 ff., 186 f., 194, 197, 203; and *Test. of Job* (*Texts and Studies*, v. p. lxii).

On *the Fall as connected with concupiscence*, see pp. 154 ff., 159 f., 189 n. 3, 197, 208 f.: also 4 Macc. xviii. 7—8; Philo, *de Mundi Opif.* 53; *Slav. Baruch*, ed. Bonwetsch; and cf. Thackeray, *op. cit.* pp. 50—57.

On *the Fall as affecting Nature*, see pp. 127, 150 f., 193, 197, 203, 215; cf. p. 271.

[1] *e.g.* Irenaeus, IV. 40. 3; Tertullian, *De Pat.* v.; Methodius, *De Conviv.*; Gregory of Nyssa, *Orat. Catech.*; Augustine, *De Gen. ad litt.* XI. 18.

CHAPTER XI.

S. PAUL'S DOCTRINE OF THE FALL.

THE New Testament writings, with the exception of one or more of the Epistles of S. Paul, contain nothing which serves to throw light upon their authors' beliefs with regard to the origin and mode of propagation of human sinfulness. The Gospels record sayings of our Lord which plainly assert the actual existence of evil in man and imply the absolute universality of human sin[1]. So also do the apostolic writers teach[2]. But such statements as occur in the books of the New Testament, other than those which come from the hand of S. Paul, in reference to the universal presence of sin in mankind are not decisive in favour of any of the possible theories as to the genesis and spread of evil; they are entirely irrelevant to this question. And whilst, from the fact that there is no evidence supplied by these New Testament statements for the existence amongst the evangelists and apostles of such a doctrine of original and inborn sin as afterwards grew up in the Christian Church, it cannot be inferred that they actually did not hold any such theory, yet, on the other hand, it must here be maintained, against the assertions of other writers, that there is nothing in these apostolic statements, or in our Lord's recorded dealings with sinners, whether by word or deed, which *necessarily* implies that the individual's sinfulness is due to anything but his own acts and the habits thereby established,

---

[1] "If ye then, being evil, know how to give good gifts unto your children..." (Matt. vii. 11, Luke xi. 13); "Except a man be born anew, he cannot enter into the Kingdom of God" (John iii. 3).

[2] See, *e.g.*, John ii. 25, 1 John i. 8.

CHAP. XI] *S. Paul's Doctrine of the Fall* 249

or to his voluntary reception of the influences of sinful society around him. S. Paul alone, amongst the first generation of Christian teachers, refers to the original entrance of sin into the human world, and connects, in any way, the sinfulness of the race with the first transgression[1].

In studying the passages in the Pauline Epistles which are concerned with the subject of the present investigation, it is necessary to disabuse our minds entirely of the later theories, whether of the fifth or of the sixteenth century, in terms of which the apostle's statements have been usually interpreted. The historical method leads us to seek the meaning of S. Paul's expressions and assumptions by approaching them from the side of the thought of his contemporaries among Jewish writers. S. Paul's meaning can sometimes *only* be ascertained by studying his ideas in the light of the mental environment of his day; and without such comparative study the most perfect linguistic scholarship may fail entirely to detect the real content of the apostle's speech. This is not, of course, to say that there is one, and one only, key to the apostle's thought; he is far too creative and original a thinker to be wholly explicable in terms of the teaching of his contemporaries, or of the sources of tradition from which he sometimes undoubtedly drew. But such aids to exegesis are certainly indispensable; sometimes their testimony is supreme and decisive.

It is partly with a view to elucidating S. Paul's teaching with regard to the Fall and its consequences that the passages bearing upon this subject in the Jewish apocalyptic literature were so exhaustively collected in foregoing chapters. It is unfortunate that, in the present state of studies connected with the earlier rabbinic writings, much less light can be thrown upon this side of Jewish thought at the time of S. Paul; the literature which we possess is too late to admit of its being used as embodying contemporary teaching, at least for the most part, unless the age of its contents be tested by reference

---

[1] The Apocalypse contains (eschatological) allusions to the tree of life, ii. 7, xxii. 2, 14, and to the 'old serpent,' xii. 9 (on which see above, p. 43, n. 2), but does not deal with the Fall and its consequences.

to such pseudepigraphic writings as are of indisputable antiquity.

There is no doubt that S. Paul's mind was deeply influenced by his rabbinical training. His attitude towards the Old Testament Scriptures, his ideas of the nature of their inspiration, his method of using them for proofs and of interpreting them, his resort to allegory and haggada, all reveal the apostle's early environment. And, more than this, it is beyond doubt that he retained a considerable amount of Jewish, as distinguished from Old Testament, theology. His ideas, for instance, of the first man, the temptation of Eve, the Fall and its results, were derived, as will presently be seen, from the Jewish schools.

With regard to Alexandrian or Hellenic influences there is much less evidence. He would certainly seem to have studied the Book of Wisdom, and indeed to have once at least reproduced in some degree its thought and language. He does not appear, however, to have been indebted to it for any important doctrine; still less can it be shown that he was influenced by Philo. Of the parallels enumerated by Siegfried, none is sufficient to establish direct contact with the Alexandrian's writings. The most important is the resemblance between the Pauline doctrine of the first and the last Adam and the Philonic teaching of the heavenly and the earthly man; but even this does not furnish a conclusive proof of borrowing[1]. The attempt to represent S. Paul's theology as a compound of Hellenism and Pharisaism has been carried by some writers much too far[2], especially in the case of the apostle's doctrine of Sin, which was largely the outcome of his own moral and spiritual experience.

It is chiefly in the sphere of haggada that S. Paul's treatment of the Fall-story reveals the influence of rabbinical, or rather Jewish, speculation. He utilises several ideas which were the common property of Jewish writers of his day, and

---

[1] On the other hand we have no parallel in *ancient* rabbinical literature. For similar ideas in later writings see Taylor, *Sayings of the Jewish Fathers*, 2nd ed., p. 56. See also Thackeray, *op. cit.*, p. 40 ff.

[2] Cf. Bruce, *S. Paul's Conception of Christianity*, p. 132 f., and 217 f. Perhaps Prof. Bruce's protest is a little exaggerated in the other direction.

his treatment of Old Testament history is not always identical with exact exegesis. In the first place, S. Paul's conception of the first man is to some extent an ideal construction. His Adam is a conceptual type, perhaps shaped to a slight extent by the dialectical exigencies of the occasion, and formed by fusing the first man of Gen. iii. with the undifferentiated Adam, or generic man, of Gen ii., who was no longer, strictly speaking, the sum of the race at the moment of his transgression[1]. But this is too small a point to be insisted upon without pedantry.

Secondly, the notion that Eve alone was directly tempted by the serpent or Satan, and the belief that she was tempted to unchastity, appear to have been shared by S. Paul along with the apocalyptic, and perhaps rabbinic, writers of that period. If this be so,—and the matter cannot be argued here[2]—we have very direct testimony to S. Paul's acceptance of some of the popular Jewish speculations as to the Fall.

Again, the narrative of Genesis, if it has here been rightly understood, does not teach that Adam became mortal because of his transgression, nor that his trespass was the cause of death to his descendants: much less does it imply that the first sin made all men sinners, in any sense. Both physical and spiritual death, or at least spiritual consequences of some kind, are attributed, however, as has already been shown, to Adam's sin in early Jewish literature; and it is such Jewish teaching, which the apostle assumes, and which he supposes to need no proof, when he speaks, in Rom. v. 12 ff., of the connexion between Adam and the race as regards sin and death.

There are not many passages in the Pauline Epistles which bear, even indirectly, on the fall of Adam and its consequences for mankind. By far the most important is Romans v. 12—21, where the relation of Adam's sin to the race is described in contrast with the effects which flow from the redemptive work of Christ. The brief allusion to the nature

---

[1] Cf. Beyschlag, *N.T. Theology*, E.T. vol. II. p. 62.
[2] The reader is once more referred to the discussion of this question in Mr Thackeray's work, *The relation of S. Paul to contemporary Jewish Thought*, p. 50 ff.

of the first Adam as contrasted with that of the last Adam, in
1 Cor. xv. 45 ff., is not relevant to the subject, because its
context is not concerned with the problem of Sin. The
account of the immanence of sin in 'the flesh,' the principal
seat of sinful promptings, contained in Rom. vii. 7—25, with
which scattered verses in Rom. viii. and Gal. v. are to be
associated, will call for some consideration, because it touches
upon the psychological side of the problem of the origin
of sin, as distinguished from the historical side which is
brought before us in Rom. v. Finally the expression "by
nature children of wrath," in Eph. ii. 3, which has generally
been expounded in the past as implying a doctrine of Original
Sin, must be briefly noticed. The discussion of human sinfulness contained in the early chapters of the Epistle to the
Romans need not be included, inasmuch as it only aims at
establishing empirically, and by appeal to Scripture, the
observed fact of the universality of actual sin, without endeavouring to explain the absoluteness of such universality by
any theory or doctrine.

It must be borne in mind that although, in the passages
about to be discussed, S. Paul treats of the nature of man, of
his inherent sinfulness, of the historical entrance of sin into
the human race, and of certain consequences which have
followed from that event, he does so in each case somewhat
incidentally.

He does not attempt to supply exhaustive or systematic
instruction with regard to these subjects, after the manner of
the theologian who discusses them for their own sake. He
lays down no dogma, either as to the exact nature, or as
to the cause, of human sinfulness as a subjective state. Sin
and the Fall are spoken of only in so far as they are involved
in the apostle's great doctrine of justification. Both in
Rom. v. 12 ff. and in 1 Cor. xv. 45 ff. Adam is made the
subject of passing consideration only in order to illustrate
the significance of Christ, and the comprehensiveness of His
redemptive work.

And finally, the passages which disclose S. Paul's teaching
on such subjects as human nature, Sin and the Fall, do not
suggest that he had completely developed the various lines of

thought which they contain into a unified and coherent system. The doctrine of each of these passages is incomplete in itself, and their mutual independence is conspicuous.

The passage Rom. v. 12—21 may be considered first. These verses are regarded as constituting one of the most difficult passages in the Bible. The strain which they put upon the exegete's powers does not arise from the profundity of the subject, nor from the intricacy of the argument, as is the case elsewhere in the Epistles of S. Paul. It arises simply from the fact that the indefinite language of the apostle necessarily appears ambiguous to generations which have attempted to advance to precise and definitely formulated views on the subject upon which he touches but incidentally. To ascertain exactly what S. Paul meant with regard to the connexion between Adam's transgression and the universal prevalence of sinfulness and death, in terms of the alternative theories developed in the course of subsequent speculation, is perhaps beyond the limits of possibility. Certainly to assume that it is not so would be to prejudge a question as yet undecided, and therefore possibly to commit an offence against historical method. We must at least be careful not to read into S. Paul's language more than it can legitimately bear, and be prepared to believe, if the facts warrant it, that in all probability none of the several forms of the doctrine of Original Sin which, in the Christian Church, only became differentiated in course of time, was ever distinctly present to the apostle's mind.

The several interpretations of the passage in question may be mentioned, and their inherent advantages and disadvantages briefly pointed out; but as to what S. Paul himself meant by his statements we can perhaps only hope to form a reasonable conviction when we have apprehended certain general characteristics of his thought, and have traced the relation of his teaching to ideas current in his day[1].

[1] Perhaps the fullest discussion of the various interpretations of this passage will be found in Lange's *Commentary on the Epistle to the Romans* (Schaff's ed. E.T.). The treatises of German writers such as Pfleiderer, Hausrath, Weizsäcker, and Beyschlag, on Pauline or New Testament theology, should also be consulted, along with the perhaps more reliable works of Bruce and Stevens on Pauline theology, and the Commentary of Sanday and Headlam.

It is not of much importance to ascertain here whether S. Paul, in Rom. v. 12 ff., uses θάνατος exclusively in the sense of physical death, as is maintained by most writers[1], or whether, after the example of the Book of Wisdom, and as in other places in his own Epistles, the word is endowed also with an ethical meaning. The latter view has been maintained by Toy, Beyschlag and others, but perhaps upon no very convincing grounds. In any case the apostle assumes, as well known, that death is the consequence of Adam's sin; and in doing so he is in accordance with the general tendency amongst contemporary pseudepigraphic writers, though, so far as the scanty light enables us to see, not with that which was most probably the more prevalent view in the rabbinical schools of the time.

Much more important is the relation of the Fall to human sinfulness; and on this S. Paul speaks but briefly, indefinitely and incidentally. He is not concerned expressly with insisting on the solidarity of mankind or with controverting individualism. He is expounding, primarily, the effects of Christ's redemptive work for all; and in order to do so he falls back upon the familiar idea that Adam's sin affected all, as an analogy. In so far as the origin of sin is alluded to in this passage, it is its historical, not its psychological, origin. The question of the existence of evil before its appearance in man is wholly excluded. It is the historical beginning of sinful action in mankind to which S. Paul refers, apart from any metaphysical or psychological questions underlying it; and this beginning of sin he identifies figuratively, and not metaphysically, with the entrance of Sin as a power into the human world. The concrete fact of the beginning of sin is described under the figure of the entrance of Sin. And the apostle then proceeds to allude to the consequences of this event for the race derived from Adam.

Sin, then, in this section of the Epistle, is conceived as a transcendent, objective power, external to man, rather than as an inward or subjective state. The word stands for a hypostatised abstraction, the common quality belonging to all

---

[1] Kabisch, *Eschatologie d. Paulus*, S. 93 f.; Lipsius, *Handkommentar zum N. T.* iii. *in loc.*; Bruce, *op. cit.*, p. 136; Sanday and Headlam, *in loc.*

individual sins, and not, of course, for a metaphysical essence, a 'principle of evil,' whether personal or impersonal. Similarly this external ruling-power, Sin, is represented elsewhere as immanent in the fleshy nature of man, in which it has taken up its abode. Here too we have a figure of speech, descriptive of practical experience and not expressing anthropological doctrine. This immanent sin-power is conceived as 'deceiving[1],' and as playing the *rôle* of the serpent of Eden. It produces sin: the evil which a man does is accomplished by Sin in opposition to his own will[2]. Sin is thus sharply differentiated here from the sinner; it is something distinct from him and from his 'flesh' in which it is conceived as dwelling. It is "a power which makes both the will and the impulses subservient to it." But S. Paul nowhere makes this personified abstraction into a real or objective existence; much less does he identify it with the personal Satan[3]. He gives us, therefore, no metaphysical doctrine of sin.

But we return to the passage in Rom. v. before us.

Sin "entered into the world[4]," S. Paul says, "by one man, and death through sin; and so," *i.e.* through the sin of one and through the causal connexion just asserted to exist between sin and death, "death made its way to all men because all sinned" (καὶ οὕτως εἰς πάντας ἀνθρώπους ὁ θάνατος διῆλθεν, ἐφ' ᾧ πάντες ἥμαρτον). The difficulty of the passage centres in this, its first verse; but its purport cannot be apprehended until these words be taken in connexion with verses 18 and 19, in which the thought, long delayed by parentheses, at last completes itself by means of an anacoluthon. This difficulty consists in the ambiguity of the words 'all sinned,' their connexion with 'so' (οὕτως), and the relation of the whole verse to those which immediately follow. It is assumed here that 'because' is the only satisfactory

[1] Rom. vii. 11.
[2] *Ibid.* verse 17.
[3] Sanday and Headlam, *op. cit.* (1898) p. 145, think that S. Paul would probably have made this identification if the question had been pressed upon him. But are there any passages in which the apostle might have written Satan for Sin, without altering his meaning?
[4] The same phrase is used in Wisdom, and was perhaps a common formula.

rendering of ἐφ' ᾧ; this is now very generally, though not quite universally, recognised[1].

The rendering of S. Augustine and the Vulgate, which would regard ἐφ' ᾧ as grammatically equivalent to *in quo*, is abandoned. It does not follow from this, however, that the sense which would be obtained by such translation is incompatible with the language of the verse, as Pfleiderer asserts in the second edition of his *Paulinismus*. The meaning expressed in the well-known words of Bengel "*omnes peccarunt, Adamo peccante*," and vigorously defended in the first edition of Pfleiderer's work, may still be deduced by mentally supplying ἐν 'Αδάμ after πάντες ἥμαρτον. We are thus led to one of the possible interpretations of the verse.

Before comparing the chief interpretations which have been put upon this passage, however, it may be well to point out that its exegesis involves an answer to two distinct questions. In the first place, does S. Paul imply that death was brought upon all men because they all sinned—in some sense—when Adam sinned, or does he mean that all men die because they all sinned separately and personally? In other words, is it race-solidarity to which the apostle appeals in order to account for universal death, or is it that he maintains what is called an individualistic theory of the connexion between sin and death?

In the second place, supposing the first of these alternative views to be adopted, as will be the case here, the question arises, what is the mediating fact between Adam's sin on the one hand and the individual's sin and death on the other? Is it simply God's appointment; or the seminal existence in Adam of his posterity; or the representation of them by him; or their existence in him, the sum of humanity, in the sense of S. Augustine and mediaeval realism; or inheritance of a sinful state induced by the Fall; or anything else which may have been suggested? The two questions (i) whether S. Paul teaches that the race were made sinners when Adam sinned, (ii) in what way Adam's sin and his posterity's sinfulness are connected, are quite distinct; and the second cannot arise

[1] For other renderings, generally discarded as ungrammatical, see the Commentary of Lange and that of Sanday and Headlam.

XI] *of the Fall* 257

until the first has been settled in one of the two ways possible.

With regard to the former of these questions there is still a hopeless difference of opinion amongst authorities, though perhaps the balance of opinion inclines to the view which we here venture to adopt, according to which the apostle teaches some form or other of the doctrine of Original Sin, in the broadest sense of that phrase, some connexion, that is, between human sinfulness and death and the primary transgression of Adam. There is certainly much to be said in favour of such a view.

In the first place, the whole illustration—and the passage relating to Adam is introduced, it must be repeated, solely as an illustration or analogy—would seem to lose its point if, after all, universal death were due to the actual sins of every single individual. It is the effect of the "one man's" sin on the whole race which is obviously the central point of the analogy between Adam and Christ. Again this interpretation harmonises best with the tense of ἥμαρτον[1], and with the sense of ἁμαρτία in the present passage. The thought of personal, individual sin is quite foreign to the context. Further support is derived from the Apostle's other saying, "In Adam all die." But perhaps the most crucial test of the truth of this interpretation, as against its rival, is furnished by the two verses which immediately follow.

The view which regards the sin of all as connected in v. 12 with the sin of Adam not only harmonises with, but finds support in, the thought which is there expressed. According to these verses, the existence of actual sin during the interval between Adam and Moses is recognised, but is declared to have been insufficient to account for the universal prevalence of death at that time; for without a law to make sin guilty, such sin could not have been imputed to the sinners, and still less could it therefore have been visited with the punishment of death. The inference is that, for this particular period of history, the pre-Mosaic, death was due to

[1] Stevens refers to 2 Cor. v. 15, Rom. iii. 23, Col. iii. 1, etc. for parallel usage of the Aorist by S. Paul.

some other cause than the personal sins of individuals; and this seems to be only reconcileable with the statement that death passed to all "because all sinned," if we take those words to refer to sin regarded as committed once and for all by Adam.

And, on the other hand, there are difficulties in the way of interpreting ἐφ' ᾧ πάντες ἥμαρτον as referring to the actual or personal sins of individuals. The statement, as has often been pointed out, would not be strictly true; there is the very obvious exception of all infants. The verses last alluded to assert that for one period of human history death was not, and could not be, thus due to actual or individual sin. And finally, on such an interpretation the analogy between the first and the second Adam would be partially destroyed. For these reasons it would seem distinctly safer to conclude that S. Paul intended to imply that there was some kind of connexion, other than that of mere order in a series, between the fall of Adam and the sin of each of his descendants.

There is a modified form, however, of the individualistic interpretation of Romans v. 12, which deserves to be mentioned. According to some, S. Paul would seem to teach that Sin indeed entered into the world through Adam's fall, and so gained a footing whence to extend its sway over mankind; but that it actually only acquired its dominion in individual men by means of their voluntary invitation or cooperation. Thus the ruin of the race would not have been brought about had not Adam by his fall admitted sin into the world; nor yet would Adam's transgression have affected any but himself had not his descendants individually fallen in a similar way, thereby appropriating to themselves Adam's condemnation. This view is adopted by Mr Thackeray[1], who is inclined to think that S. Paul reproduces in Romans v. 12 ff. the two antithetic views held by Jewish writers with regard to the connexion between universal death and the Fall.

It is certainly the case that, in some of the apocalyptic books approximately contemporaneous with the writings of S. Paul, we meet with the assertion that death was decreed

---

[1] *op. cit.*, p. 33.

against the race because of Adam's sin, and side by side with this the (apparently) conflicting statement that each individual is responsible for his own ruin, or, as Pseudo-Baruch expresses it, that every man is "the Adam of his own soul." We know, moreover, that it was not uncommon for Rabbis to place two antithetical propositions, such as affirmations of predestination and free will, side by side without reconciliation, as the effective solution of the whole problem. And Weber[1] implies that the teaching of the Synagogue with regard to the connexion between the Fall, sin and death, was capable of being summed up in this way. Such a conclusion, however, is not safe in the absence of proof that the two beliefs which he combines into one were really held together, and were not, as there is some reason to suspect, rather the expressions of the doctrine of different schools, if not of different periods. Still, the insistence of apocalyptic writers, who admit the ruin caused by Adam, upon the responsibility of the individual, together with the probability that in S. Paul's day the doctrine "no death without (individual) sin" was dominant in the rabbinical schools, certainly tends somewhat to diminish the confidence with which we maintain that the Apostle meant to imply, in this difficult passage, that human death and sin were *solely* due to Adam's primary transgression.

These considerations, however, do not appear to have very considerable weight against the exegesis previously supported. However much they suggest that the individualistic theory was common in S. Paul's time, the interpretation of the verse before us to which they point seems incompatible with the meaning of those which follow: verses which present a difficulty in the way of attributing any form of the individualistic theory of the cause of death to S. Paul. In them the Apostle explicitly refers to a period during which death was *not* due to the conscious sins of individuals, or to their deliberate cooperation in perpetuating the state initiated by Adam, and during which, therefore, Adam's trespass must alone have been the cause for which men died.

Assuming, therefore, that S. Paul regarded the Fall as

[1] *op. cit.*, S. 247 ff.

something having a far more momentous result for humanity than that it merely admitted the sin-power into the world but otherwise left men practically as Adam himself was at the first, we may pass on to enumerate the several kinds of 'original sin' which the Apostle has been considered to teach.

First may be mentioned the interpretation, or series of interpretations, obtained by assuming that when S. Paul wrote "for that all sinned," he mentally supplied "in Adam." These omitted words are demanded, so many commentators have urged, in order to define the Apostle's meaning in a sense compatible with the purport of the passage as a whole. The adoption of them certainly makes S. Paul's meaning plain, and gives a consistency to the whole passage which otherwise we have to search for, as it seems to us, in vain. It is true that the two words thus supplied are rather important ones to have been omitted. Many will doubtless think, with Dr Sanday and Mr Headlam[1], that if S. Paul had the words in mind he probably would have written them, since so much hangs upon them. Nor may we suppose, as a way out of the difficulty, that the thought thus unexpressed was so familiar to the writer, and regarded by him as so universally known an assumption, that it scarcely required explicit statement. The *argumentum e silentio* is indeed always precarious; but so far as we know, no authentic instance has been found of the occurrence, in Jewish literature at all near to the age of S. Paul, of the conception that Adam constituted the whole race, or that the race potentially existed in him, and sinned in and with him. That such an idea existed amongst the Jews of that time has indeed frequently been asserted by theologians of note. References, however, are usually not given; and in the rare cases in which they have been offered they have not borne the simple ordeal of verification. Cabbalistic literature, no doubt, supplies abundance of examples of the use of this conception; but that is, of course, quite useless as a guide to the views of writers in the first century. But though the objection raised against Bengel's exegesis of our passage cannot be refuted on this ground, it can perhaps be

---

[1] *op. cit., in loc.*

met upon another. For it is quite plain that a mental interpolation of some kind is necessary, if we are to extract any definite meaning at all from S. Paul's language; and it may be observed that the context, with its unfinished original construction, testifies that the writer's thought was here outstripping his care to give it accurate definition. And failing the words 'in Adam,' to what alternative interpolation must we have recourse? That suggested by Dr Sanday and Mr Headlam, from whose weighty opinion it is here ventured to diverge, is an equally important element to be 'supplied.' Indeed it may be asked whether the idea of inherited sinfulness, as the cause of death to all who came between Adam and Moses, does not call at least as loudly for explicit mention, if S. Paul's full meaning be expressible in terms of it, as that signified by Bengel's addition of 'in Adam'? Would it not be equally novel to the reader, so far as our knowledge of the thought of that age goes, and more remote from the actual language of the verse and its context?

It is more probable then, if we may commit ourselves to an opinion on so difficult and highly disputed a point, that S. Paul meant that it was in Adam that all men sinned, and so brought death upon themselves. It may further be inquired, though again the inquiry will prove difficult to answer, in what sense the Apostle regarded the race as one with Adam, or as included in him.

There is first the possibility that his form of thought was that of the writer of the Epistle to the Hebrews, where he speaks of Levi as existing in the loins of Abraham when the patriarch met Melchisedek, and therefore as paying tithe to him in Abraham[1]. This idea of seminal existence and antenatal participation in an ancestor's act, being used by a writer of the same period, may have been in S. Paul's mind, and have furnished him with an expedient by which to make Adam's trespass the sin of all his posterity likewise. If it was a common notion, it does not seem to have frequently

---

[1] Heb. vii. 9, 10. This passage appears to have been comparatively seldom cited in connexion with Rom. v. 12. Biesenthal calls attention to it, in relation to S. Paul's argument, in his *Das Trostschreiben d. Apostels Paulus an die Hebräer, in loc.*

found expression in literature. We find it actually used by Origen[1] to explain S. Paul's thought, long before S. Augustine borrowed, from a kind of philosophical realism, a different conception to serve the same purpose.

This last is the second of the various ways in which the sinning of the race in Adam may have been conceived by S. Paul. The realism "which makes human nature a certain *quantum* of being and treats descent from Adam as a division of this mass of human nature into parts[2]" is, however, remote from S. Paul's manner of thought. The writer of the Epistle to the Hebrews was somewhat of a Platonist; but this can hardly be asserted of S. Paul.

Much more probable, in the opinion of the present writer, is the suggestion that, in his identification of the race and Adam, S. Paul was using a form of thought occurring by no means exclusively in the particular verse of his writings with which we are here concerned. Stevens has appropriately named it 'mystical realism.' "It is characteristic of Paul's mind," says this writer, "to conceive religious truth under forms which are determined by personal relationship. These relations, especially the two just specified (that of unregenerate humanity to Adam, and of spiritual humanity to Christ), may be termed *mystical* in the sense of being unique, vital and inscrutable; they are *real* in the sense that sinful humanity is conceived as being actually present and participent in Adam's sin...." This mystical realism is a style of thought, a rhetorical mode; it is not a philosophy: the realism is only figurative. S. Paul identifies the race, as sinners, with Adam in the same sense that he identifies the believer with Christ. "The moral defilement of man is *represented* as contracted in and with the sin of Adam[4]."

The sins of all mankind are referred by the Apostle to the first sin, the root of all, not in the sense that all mankind had *actual* participation in that sin; he rather means that all

---

[1] See below, Chap. XII.
[2] Stevens, *The Pauline Theology*, p. 136. The treatment of Rom. v. 12 ff. in this work may be especially commended to the student's notice.
[3] *op. cit.*, p. 32 ff., and elsewhere.
[4] *op. cit.*, p. 37. The italics are the present writer's.

XI]   *of the Fall*   263

sinned in Adam in the same sense that he speaks of believers as being crucified to the world, and having died to sin, when Christ died upon the Cross. Or, again, just as the believer's renewal is conceived by S. Paul as wrought in advance, though of course he did not suppose it actually to be so wrought, so also does he conceive the consequences of Adam's sin as having been wrought simultaneously with it[1].

This attractive interpretation of S. Paul's meaning has the great virtue of explaining his words, which involve so many difficulties when taken, as they generally have been, with too much literalness, as only a particular case of a mode of speech which is characteristic of the apostle. And so long as it is not so far pressed as to lose sight of the undeniable connexion between the apostle's teaching and the somewhat indefinite belief which he inherited from Jewish doctors as to the connexion between the Fall and human sin and death, it would seem to supply the best key to the thought of this difficult passage.

The more weight there is in the reasons which have been advanced for regarding S. Paul as implying the doctrine that all sinned in Adam, and the particular form of that doctrine which was last described, the less support can be given here to the altogether different view, that the apostle held, implicit and unexpressed, the idea of a corruption of human nature caused once and for all by Adam's transgression and inherited by each generation descended from him, and that he so connected the first entrance of sin through the one man with the sinfulness of all men.

Such an interpretation is not to be rejected merely because ἥμαρτον cannot grammatically be rendered *vitiati sunt* or 'became sinful.' But it has several disadvantages as compared with the view which has been previously discussed. It is out of harmony with the objective sense in which ἁμαρτία is used throughout the passage, and which requires a more mystical (some would say a more forensic) sense for the expression "were constituted sinners" in verse 19. The interpretation does not so well preserve the analogy which is being drawn

[1] *op. cit.*, p. 136.

between Adam and Christ. It creates a *tertium quid* between Adam and the death of his posterity which is not suggested by the context, and which is omitted each time the relation of Adam to the race is mentioned; for the 'trespass of one' is several times *immediately* connected with the cause of human death. Again, it is largely open to the main objection lying against the view which takes ἥμαρτον to refer to the actual and personal sins of individuals. For inherited sinful tendencies would still leave room for personal responsibility, and thus universal death would be caused by universal actual sin, a thought precluded in the 13th and 14th verses. The view, in fact, seems to be a compromise between that which is based on the interpolation of ἐν Ἀδάμ, and that which has been designated individualistic. It certainly does not grow necessarily, or even naturally, out of the context itself. In so far as it is imported from elsewhere in S. Paul's Epistles, its further refutation will be involved in the discussion of such passages in the apostle's writings as are assumed to be its source. Meanwhile it may be further remarked that sin whose guilt is diminished by the fact that a bias or tendency towards sinfulness is of necessity inherited is too nearly on the same moral level with sin whose guilt is diminished by ignorance or non-possession of a moral law (as in the pre-Mosaic period) for the one to be considered the cause of death while the other is expressly ruled out as insufficient. If S. Paul meant that death passed to all because all were, by heredity, made personally sinful, it is strange that he should have chosen to write ἐφ' ᾧ πάντες ἥμαρτον. The Aorist aptly describes an act of sin accomplished once and for all in Adam, or the 'mystical' reference of the sins of mankind back to their root as if already then actually committed; it is hardly suitable to describe the past, present and future sinning of men by reason of their inheritance of a sinful tendency from their first father.

It has already been hinted that this interpretation of S. Paul's statements does not receive external support as a current doctrine which S. Paul might be supposed to derive from his contemporaries. The only parallels adduced by Sanday and Headlam from approximately contemporary literature are the passages of 4 Ezra relating to the *cor malignum*. But the *cor malignum* is certainly the *yezer hara* of the Rabbis, regarded by Pseudo-Ezra, as well as by talmudic writers, as inherent in Adam from the first, and as the cause, not the consequence, of his fall. S. Paul, curiously enough, nowhere appears to make use of the current doctrine of the evil *yezer*[1]; certainly not in connexion with the Fall. There would seem to be no evidence that S. Paul held, even in germ, the doctrine of an inherited corruption derived from Adam.

Yet another theory of Original Sin which has been attributed to S. Paul remains to be mentioned. He has been taken to imply that all Adam's race have been "constituted sinners" by imputation; that they have passed into a judicial relation with God such as may be called a state of condemnation. The mediating fact between Adam's sin and all men being sinners would in this case simply be God's appointment.

The injustice attributed to the Almighty by such a view appears, at first sight, to be somewhat mitigated in the kindred 'federal' theory, according to which mankind is involved in the punishment of Adam because he was their representative in a covenant relation with God. In other words, men sinned in Adam not pre-natally, or as potentially contained in him, but in a representative or putative manner. They are regarded and treated by God as sinners because the act of Adam, as representative of the race, bound them also. If S. Paul intended his argument to carry this implication, we should then find the nearest parallel to his meaning in the passage before us in 2 Cor. v. 14, "one died for all, therefore all died," interpreted in terms of the same literalism which lies at the root of the federal theology; or else in the arbitrary visitation of parents' sins upon their children, such as was ascribed to Jehovah in the Old Testament and by the popular Jewish belief of S. Paul's time (cf. S. John ix. 2). This view, which of course would not be mentioned here unless it had been seriously intended for exegesis of S. Paul's statements, is perhaps often held side by side with that of potential sin in Adam, and undistinguished from it. Thus Gifford[2], in

---

[1] See below, p. 271.
[2] *Epistle to the Romans*, p. 117.

defending what is a combination of these two different theories, quotes with approval a passage from Bishop Bull, wherein Adam is represented as one party to a covenant of life which his sin made void, not only for himself, but also for his posterity, so that all his sons, as such, are quite shut out from any promise of immortality: a passage, that is, in which the punishment of Adam's descendants is not ascribed to their inherited depravity, nor to their actual or fictitious participation in their first father's trespass, but simply to the arbitrary visitation of one individual's sin upon others not regarded as in any sense taking part in it.

S. Paul's language in the latter portion of the section of Romans v. which has been discussed above, where a relation of wrath between God and man is spoken of as if set up once and for all, so that all men were "constituted sinners" as it were in anticipation of their actual sinfulness, has led certain recent scholars to consider that the apostle here entertained not merely an objective, but even a forensic or legalistic, conception of sin[1]. One is prevented from subscribing to such an opinion by the reflection that, in his treatment of sin in general, S. Paul was no legalist, and that therefore he could hardly become one upon occasion. Moreover, another interpretation of his language lies to hand, as has been seen, which is both more charitable to the apostle and more reconcilable with his general doctrine and mode of thought. An interpretation of the passage before us, therefore, based upon the supposition that sin is there spoken of purely from the forensic point of view, has no peculiar advantage of its own, though it has its own obvious demerits. And it is only by violence that ἥμαρτον can be made to mean "became legally guilty."

Yet other interpretations, based upon renderings of ἐφ' ᾧ which grammarians will not allow, will be found enumerated in the commentaries; but they need not be reproduced here. It is, of course, quite impossible to arrive at objective certainty as to what S. Paul's exact meaning was. But of those views which have now been discussed, that which regards S. Paul as having clothed the current notion of Adam as the cause of

[1] See Pfleiderer, *Paulinism* (E.T.), 1st ed. vol. I. p. 43 ff.; Weizsäcker, *The Apostolic Age*, E.T. vol. I. p. 148 ff.; Lipsius, *op. cit., in loc.*

human death, and the root of human sin, in the language of his peculiar 'mystical realism,' would seem to be the best grounded. If this be so, his doctrine of the Fall must be regarded as widely different from that which was destined to become general in the Christian Church.

But other passages of his writings still require consideration. The verses which have already been discussed certainly cannot be said *necessarily* to contain the doctrine of inherited inborn taint of sin. They connect mankind's sinfulness with the Fall, but in some entirely undefined way. But it has sometimes been urged that although the doctrine of transmitted depravity cannot be extracted from the fifth chapter of the Epistle to the Romans alone, it is yet forced upon us when that chapter is read in the light of the passage Rom. vii. 7 ff. Here the apostle is supposed to offer teaching as to the psychological origin of sin, as distinguished from the historical origin on which he touches in the former chapter.

It must be stated at the outset that the task of eliciting a psychology of sin from S. Paul's writings is rendered difficult by the fact that he expresses himself in language that is largely popular, figurative and practical, and which makes no pretension to scientific exactness. And the accurate statement by us of the content of his thought is made the more arduous by reason of the inadequacy, as an instrument for precision of expression, of the phraseology still employed in the theological treatment of the subject of sin. Some of its ordinary words are question-begging in regard to problems which emerge when we attempt a rigorous analysis of our familiar traditional conceptions. This, however, is not the opportunity for introducing a reformed vocabulary, and S. Paul's meaning must be presented in terms such as lie to hand[1].

S. Paul speaks of sin existing in a man as 'dead' before the knowledge of the law comes to call it forth into action and to constitute him guilty; yet, strictly speaking, sin that exists prior to law and will-determination is not sin at all. Again, if σὰρξ ἁμαρτίας[2], παθήματα τῶν ἁμαρτιῶν[3], are to be

[1] These questions have been dealt with in the author's work, *The Origin and Propagation of Sin*, pp. 160 ff.
[2] Rom. viii. 3. [3] vii. 5.

translated 'sinful flesh,' 'sinful passions,' it must be borne in mind that the word 'sinful' in these expressions is used rhetorically, as other sides of the apostle's doctrinal teaching very plainly show.

On coming now to examine the passage Rom. vii. 7—25, we find sin there spoken of as an immanent power—Sin—sharply distinguished from the individual in whom it dwells. To this power the sinner is in bondage in spite of himself; he is sold to it as a slave, and is dominated by it. So strongly is this fact expressed, that the dominion of Sin in the flesh and over the will is represented as inevitable. The man's will may be good, but it is absolutely overborne by the irresistible might of Sin in the flesh. But here the apostle speaks figuratively—Sin is a mere personification of an abstraction; and he also describes facts as they present themselves to unreflective practical experience, not as they really are. In Rom. vi. 12 ff., it is distinctly taught that the power Sin can be made subservient to the will. The rule of Sin in our mortal body can be resisted: the surrender of the bodily members to Sin can be withheld: the service of Sin is not inevitable, but voluntary. The will, in fact, is for S. Paul the only ultimate source of sin; although at times, in using the language of practical experience, he sometimes allows expressions to escape him which appear to imply another meaning: expressions which have frequently been seized upon in the interests of rigorous and vigorous system-making.

A man's sinfulness, then, is not accounted for by S. Paul as being due to a *real* Sin-power or agent which dwells within him. Nor is it explained by the supposition of the necessary and inherent sinfulness of the flesh. It is true that the flesh is regarded by S. Paul as the seat or abode of sin when he figuratively speaks of sin as an indwelling power. Not only does he use the expressions 'flesh of sin,' 'passions of sins,' but goes so far as to identify the flesh with the sin-power itself, which he generally represents as only immanent in the flesh. Thus, in Rom. viii. 4—9, the flesh is contrasted with the spirit; its mind (φρόνημα) is 'enmity against God,' and neither is, nor can be, 'subject to the law of God.' In Gal. v. 17—24, again, the flesh is the power 'which lusteth against the spirit,' and various grave sins are called 'works of the flesh.' The link between the idea of an immanent sin-power and the thought of the passages just cited is found in the conception of 'a law in the members' opposed to the 'law of the mind,' or a law of sin opposed to the law of God. There is no doubt that language such as that just quoted would suit well with a metaphysical dualism; and some have not hesitated to attribute such a philosophical position to S. Paul.

There is no reason why S. Paul should not have been familiar with dualism as it existed in Hellenic thought; but that he embraced it or held it is a supposition obviously incompatible with the general tenour of his teaching. The sinfulness of the flesh is for him an unphilosophical description of practical experience and not a doctrine derived from metaphysical speculation; and the truth is expressed in the language of unreflective common sense, not that of psychological analysis. Moreover S. Paul speaks of the flesh as it is actually found, not as it originally and essentially must have been. If human sinfulness is referred back to the flesh as a preceding link in the chain of causation, it is not thereby traced to its ultimate and absolute source. The flesh is 'sinful' simply in the loose sense that it is generally the most conspicuous instrument of the sinful will. The psychological origin of sin is nowhere investigated by the apostle. Consequently his writings, while testifying to the existence of the actual conflict between flesh and spirit as a matter of fact, furnish no explanation of the cause of the conflict, nor do they tell us how the flesh became 'sinful.' It would seem that S. Paul does not regard a man's sinfulness as exclusively the result of habit, or due only to the repetition of sinful acts and to the surrender of the will to inclinations of the flesh or to the motions of an indwelling power of evil. On the contrary, he seems to imply that sin is in man before the consciousness of the law arrives to constitute its guilt. As Ritschl has said[1], S. Paul held that man is not sinful because he commits sins, but commits sins because he is sinful. But why he is sinful the apostle nowhere explains[2]. The tracing of sin back to

[1] *Die Altkatholische Kirche*, S. 64.
[2] In connexion with what is said here see next foot-note.

Adam's fall as its historical beginning does not solve the question; for we still need to ask why did Adam sin, or whether, in the inaccurate language of popular theology, Adam's nature was originally sinful?

The passage 1 Cor. xv. 45—50 has sometimes been appealed to in connexion with the point now under consideration. It does not seem, however, to be very pertinent. That Adam is there represented as by nature 'earthy' ($\chi o\ddot{\iota}\kappa\acute{o}s$), may imply that his body was naturally corruptible, and that he was endowed with human appetites and passions. But it by no means implies that he was by nature 'sinful' in the sense in which that term is referred by S. Paul to 'the flesh.' Nor, on the other hand, can it be assumed that in this passage S. Paul is speaking of Adam's nature as it was corrupted by his sin and then transmitted to his descendants. This is the opinion of some writers, who are driven to such an interpretation because it alone seems to them sufficient to reconcile S. Paul's doctrine of Adam's nature with what they take to be his teaching as to the effects of Adam's fall in Rom. v. 12 ff. But it is a gratuitous assumption that S. Paul did so combine the thoughts of these two passages as to hold a doctrine of inherited corruption; and indeed the passage 1 Cor. xv. 45 ff. has no reference whatever to the question of sin[1].

And it is similarly illegitimate to combine together S. Paul's teaching as to the Fall in Rom. v. and what he writes elsewhere about the sinfulness of the flesh. He nowhere implies that the supremacy of the flesh over the spirit is a consequence of the first transgression. It must be concluded then that strict exegesis fails to find a doctrine of inherited corruption of human nature in S. Paul's theology. And it is noticeable that he says absolutely nothing of an original righteousness, or a sharply defined 'unfallen state.'

Nor will this conclusion need to be revised in the light of

[1] It would rather seem that S. Paul regarded Adam and all mankind as at first simply natural beings, non-moral and therefore sinless, until the spiritual side is awakened by the advent of consciousness of law; then emerges sin, which was before 'dead,' or, as we should say, non-existent. In Rom. vii. this development is described in words that suggest an application of the Fall-story. And perhaps we thus get a deeper insight into the apostle's mind than we do from his treatment of the common tradition underlying Rom. v. 12.

the words (Eph. ii. 3): "we are by nature children of wrath." φύσει does not refer here to heredity, but to the natural state before conversion, apart from the grace of God. There is not necessarily any allusion to a sinfulness which is not the result of personal volition, of habit and sinful intercourse.

The arguments given in the *International Critical Commentary* on the Epistle to the Ephesians by T. K. Abbott seem to be conclusive against such exegesis as would extract from this verse an implication of the doctrine of inherited depravity. Dr Abbott is, of course, by no means alone amongst modern commentators in his opinion as to the meaning of this passage. The reader may also be referred, for instance, to Stevens's remarks upon the verse[1].

It is noteworthy that S. Paul does not express his doctrine of sin in terms of the doctrine of the evil *yezer*. He uses no expression which can be identified with evil inclination. That his contrast between flesh and spirit has little resemblance to the rabbinical contrast of the good and evil *yezers*, has been abundantly established by Dr Porter[2]. Unlike the Rabbis and the author of 4 Ezra, S. Paul seems to have regarded evil as first appearing in the Fall, and therefore in the free-will of Adam: not in an evil inclination implanted in him at first by the Creator.

A few words may be said with regard to a passage in which S. Paul seems to teach that the transgression of Adam was a catastrophe having far-reaching results in the world of Nature. From Rom. viii. 18 ff., it would appear that the apostle regarded the present condition of creation as "neither original nor final." The world was subjected, at a definite time, "to vanity," to a "bondage of corruption" in which it groans and travails; and, like our body, it awaits redemption. The occurrence of this idea in S. Paul's writing is interesting, but it throws no light upon his view as to whether or not the Fall affected the nature of man. It was, of course, not original with him. The apocalyptic writers of his time were familiar with it, and it is met with in the rabbinic traditions which were written down in a later age[3].

* * * * * *

[1] *op. cit.* p. 153 ff.   [2] *op. cit.*   [3] For references see above, p. 247.

The discussion prosecuted in this chapter doubtless raises questions connected with our attitude towards the New Testament writings and the validity of statements directly made in them. The present writer will not need to repeat here what he has already said elsewhere upon this serious topic[1]. But it must be added that, if S. Paul's statements on the connexion between Adam's fall and human sin and death are essentially founded upon, and are largely a reproduction of, the speculations of Jewish writers who preceded him, then they cannot be looked upon as embodying truth, so far as matters of history, science or philosophy are concerned, which was given to the world for the first time through the medium of Christianity. It must be concluded from the foregoing chapters that the doctrines of the Fall and of Original Sin have their beginnings, as doctrines, neither in the Old Testament nor in the New, but rather in the Jewish speculation and the uncanonical literature of the age which intervened between them. It was thence that S. Paul derived, ready-made, his teaching as to the influence of the first man and his sin upon the race. It was therefore thence also, through S. Paul, that the Christian Church derived the main conception out of which the ecclesiastical doctrine of the origin and propagation of human sinfulness was at length elaborated. We are not at all concerned here with S. Paul's teaching on sin in general, derived from his personal experience and finding an echo in the experience of all mankind, but solely with the *form* of that part of it which deals with the consequences of Adam's sin. This, it must be maintained, belongs to the elements which the apostle derived from the common intellectual surroundings of his time, and not to the essential contents of the Christian revelation.

[1] *op. cit.* p. 144 ff.

CHAPTER XII.

THE DOCTRINES OF THE FALL AND ORIGINAL SIN IN THE FATHERS BEFORE AUGUSTINE.

THE concluding words of the last chapter might seem fitly to close an inquiry as to the *sources* of the doctrines of the Fall and Original Sin, especially if the word 'sources' be taken very literally. But this work assumes that the doctrines with whose earlier history it is concerned did not receive definite shape and fulness of content until, during the Pelagian controversy in which they were largely involved, they were systematised by the comprehensive mind of S. Augustine. They underwent, of course, much modification and development in subsequent ages; but with such later growth the present treatise has no concern. The point is that the Christian doctrine of the Fall and of its consequences certainly did not exist in anything like completeness in the mind of S. Paul, whereas it had practically assumed its completeness in that of S. Augustine. For this reason, therefore, it will be necessary to examine in some detail the teaching of the earliest writers within the Church on the subject of human sinfulness, until the elements contributed to the later doctrine by Irenæus, Origen and Tertullian have been respectively estimated and accounted for. So far we shall still, in some sense, be concerned with *sources*. For it will be seen that the fairly definite results of Jewish exegesis and speculation on the Fall, and the theories elaborated by several pseudepigraphic writers, however much of Augustinian thought they anticipated, were not taken over by the earliest ecclesiastical writers, save in so far as these results were indefinitely and incompletely summarised in S. Paul's brief statements about the connexion between man's sinfulness and Adam's sin. The Church rather began the work of elaborating a theory of the origin and propagation of human sin *de novo*. Truly, S. Paul's conception of the solidarity of the race in Adam, once the apostle's writings came to possess canonical authority, was a guiding principle for patristic speculation generally. Of course, too, the Fall-story of Genesis was regarded as a fount of revealed truth: for some time it was the only 'Scripture' the Church possessed upon the subject of the Fall. But it is noteworthy that such elements of doctrine as are not hinted at in the Paradise-narrative of Genesis, and are only vaguely sketched in S. Paul's allusions to the Fall, or are wholly absent from it, but which appear definitely in the doctrine of Original Sin elaborated by the Church, were suggested to their various contributors from wholly new sources, whence had been derived no part of the relatively complete Jewish doctrine on the subject. It will be pointed out in the succeeding pages that, of three main constructors of the doctrine of the Fall before Augustine, namely Irenæus, Origen and Tertullian, each derived his particular contribution of material for the future fabric from reflection on texts, doctrines, speculations or institutions, of which some could not have been, and none of which were, sources of such similar conclusions as had previously been reached by Jewish thought[1]. Inasmuch, then, as the main stream of speculation not only becomes more defined, because flowing through limiting channels, but also becomes enriched, through the addition of tributary rivulets of doctrine arising from new sources, during the period which intervened between the ages of S. Paul and S. Augustine, the task undertaken by this volume has not as yet been accomplished. The course of thought on the Fall and Original Sin within the Church as far as the middle of the third century needs to be traced in some detail. Comparatively little,

[1] This statement needs perhaps to be qualified in some small degree; a detail of quite subsidiary importance may have been borrowed here and there from Jewish thought. Thus Tertullian and Origen may have derived their ideas of the race having been 'poisoned' by the Serpent (see below), from the Jewish legend of the *inquinamentum* mentioned in Chap. VII.

XII] *in the Fathers before Augustine* 275

however, will then require to be said of the teaching of the numerous fathers between Tertullian and Origen on the one hand and Augustine on the other. Such matter scarcely belongs to the scope of the present work; and, moreover, it is already accessible to the student in the books of specialists in the history of Christian doctrine. The more nearly the age of the Pelagian controversy is approached, the less pretext and necessity will there be to discuss here the passages of patristic writings which are relevant to the subject in hand, save in so far as they may be regarded strictly as *sources* of the Augustinian theory of the origin and propagation of human sinfulness.

I. THE APOSTOLIC FATHERS.

The Apostolic Fathers never had occasion to discuss the question of the influence of Adam's sin upon his descendants. The Epistle of Barnabas alludes to the first transgression, but not in connexion with the origin and the nature of sin[1]. Polycarp speaks of the universality of sin, but not of the cause thereof. Ignatius, after S. John, conceives of the world as lying in wickedness, in the might of Satan and under the rule of death[2], or in a state of $\phi\theta o\rho\acute{a}$; but this state is not ascribed to the fall of mankind in its first parent.

II. THE GREEK APOLOGISTS.
Justin Martyr.

It is when we come to Justin Martyr's writings that we first need to weigh the question whether or not an approach towards the doctrine of Original Sin is to be detected. Justin speaks strongly of the universality of sin[3], and of our need of grace; and he alludes to an evil inclination which is in the nature of every man[4]. These things, however, are not deduced from, or connected with, the Fall. When that event is mentioned, Justin would seem to represent it merely as the

---
[1] c. 12.   [2] *Eph.* 19.   [3] *Dial. c. Tryph.*, c. 95.
[4] τὴν ἐν ἑκάστῳ κακὴν πρὸς πάντα καὶ ποικίλην φύσει ἐπιθυμίαν. *Apol.* c. 10.

beginning of sin rather than as the cause of sinfulness; and he does not appear to derive from it any hereditary taint or imputation of guilt. It is by the 'following of Adam' that mankind became corrupted.

Thus:

"But He did it (*i.e. was born and crucified*) for the race of men which, from (the time of) Adam had become subject to death and the deceit of the serpent, each of them having by his own fault committed sin[1]."

And again:

"...the human race, which were created like God, free from suffering and immortal if they should keep His commandment, and were thought worthy by Him to be called His sons, and yet, becoming like Adam and Eve, bring death upon themselves[2];... all are thought worthy to become gods, and to have power to become sons of the Most High, and will be judged and condemned each for himself like Adam and Eve[3]."

There can be little doubt that in these passages the conceptions of race-solidarity, apart from influence of environment, and of heredity, are absent. Justin takes here the individualist view of man's sinfulness and death, which was probably the opinion prevalent amongst the Jewish Rabbis of his day and subsequently became a main tenet of Pelagianism. All men, he seems to imply, have fallen by their own guilt, and because they have all acted like Adam and Eve. It is not that he deliberately adopted this view rather than its alternative; he had simply not worked out a solution of the problem. S. Paul's Epistle to the Romans had perhaps not yet attained the authority which it possessed, soon afterwards, for Irenaeus; at any rate its teaching exerted no influence on that of Justin.

This estimate of Justin's attitude towards the question of human sinfulness is not necessarily in conflict with the

---

[1] ...τοῦ γένους τοῦ τῶν ἀνθρώπων, ὃ ἀπὸ τοῦ Ἀδὰμ ὑπὸ θάνατον καὶ πλάνην τὴν τοῦ ὄφεως ἐπεπτώκει, παρὰ τὴν ἰδίαν αἰτίαν ἑκάστου αὐτῶν πονηρευσαμένου. *Dial.* c. 88.

[2] ὁμοίως τῷ Ἀδὰμ καὶ τῇ Εὔᾳ ἐξομοιούμενοι θάνατον ἑαυτοῖς ἐργάζονται.

[3] *Dial.* c. 124.

passage, sometimes appealed to as implying original sin, in which he asserts that man, being born the child of necessity and ignorance, becomes by baptism the child of choice and knowledge[1]. The loss of right moral feeling, of which Justin speaks elsewhere, is attributed, not to the Fall, but to the influence of evil spirits or to corruption through bad education[2]. The individual's sin appeared to this writer only to have its type, not its cause, in Adam's transgression; and he knew no doctrine of Adam's original state as one differing sharply from that into which every other man is born.

It remains to mention a passage, ascribed to Justin Martyr in Leontius Byzantinus, *Against the Nestorians, Eutychians, etc.*, Bk. II.[3], which runs as follows:

"When God formed man at the beginning, He suspended the things of nature from his will, and made an experiment by means of one commandment. For He ordained that, if he kept this, he should partake of immortal existence; but if he transgressed it, the contrary should be his lot. Man having been thus made, and immediately looking towards transgression, naturally became subject to corruption. Corruption then becoming inherent in nature, it was necessary that He who wished to save should be one who destroyed the efficient cause of corruption. And this could not otherwise be done than by the life which is according to nature being united to that which had received the corruption, and so destroying the corruption, while preserving as immortal for the future that which had received it....[4]"

---

[1] *Apol.* c. 61. See Wendt, *Christl. Lehre v. der menschl. Vollkommenheit*, S. 12; and, on the other side, Schwane, *Dogmengeschichte der vornicän. Zeit*, 2te Aufl., Bd I. S. 309.
[2] *Dial.* c. 93. See Hagenbach, *History of Christian Doctrine*, E. Tr. vol. I. p. 233.
[3] Fragment v., Otto, *Corpus Apologet. Christian.* vol. III. p. 250 ff. The translation given above is from Clark, *Ante-Nic. Library*, vol. II. p. 358.
[4] On the genuineness of this fragment see Hilgenfeld, *Zeitschrift f. wissenschaftl. Theologie*, 1883, S. 26 ff.; and, on the other side, Von Engelhardt, *Das Christenthum Justin's des Märtyrers*, S. 432 ff.

The original of this passage is as follows:

Πλάσας ὁ θεὸς κατ' ἀρχὰς τὸν ἄνθρωπον τῆς γνώμης αὐτοῦ τὰ τῆς φύσεως ἀπηώρησεν ἐντολῇ μιᾷ ποιησάμενος τὴν διάπειραν. φυλάξαντα μὲν γὰρ ταύτην τῆς ἀθανάτου λήξεως πεποίηκεν ἔσεσθαι, παραβάντα δὲ τῆς ἐναντίας. οὕτω γεγονὼς ὁ

278   *The Doctrine of the Fall etc.*   [CHAP.

The 'corruption' here spoken of would seem to be synonymous with mortality. It is therefore only in the sense that Adam brought death upon the race, as well as upon himself, that we have here any doctrine of Original Sin.

Tatian.

Tatian is the first ecclesiastical writer to ascribe consequences other than mere physical death to the fall of the first parents of the race; but his teaching is indefinite if not inconsistent.

This writer's anthropology has affinity, in one respect, with that of Philo[1]. He recognises in man two kinds of spirit: one, called the soul, which is material spirit, and another, more excellent than the soul, which is the image and likeness of God, and is indeed divine, a 'portion of God.'

The soul is not in itself immortal, but mortal; yet, through union with the Spirit, it is possible for it not to die. In the beginning, the Spirit was the constant companion of the soul, the first man being endowed with both[2]. Thus we have a recognition of a primitive, unfallen state, in which the souls of the first parents were capable of immortality and of fellowship with God. This state ceased with the Fall, which is thus described:

"And, when men attached themselves to one who was more subtle than the rest, having regard to his being the first-born, and declared him to be God, though he was resisting the laws of God, then the power of the Logos excluded the beginner of the folly and his adherents from all fellowship with Himself. And so he who was made in the likeness of God, since the more powerful spirit is separated from him, becomes mortal; but that first-begotten one, through his

ἄνθρωπος καὶ πρὸς τὴν παράβασιν εὐθὺς ἐλθὼν τὴν φθορὰν φυσικῶς εἰσεδέξατο. φύσει δὲ τῆς φθορᾶς προσγενομένης ἀναγκαῖον ἦν ὅτι σῶσαι βουλόμενος ἦν τὴν φθοροποιὸν οὐσίαν ἀφανίσας. τοῦτο δὲ οὐκ ἦν ἑτέρως γενέσθαι, εἰ μήπερ ἡ κατὰ φύσιν ζωὴ προσεπλάκη τῷ τὴν φθορὰν δεξαμένῳ, ἀφανίζουσα μὲν τὴν φθοράν, ἀθάνατον δὲ τοῦ λοιποῦ τὸ δεξάμενον διατηροῦσα....

[1] *Leg. Alleg.* I. 13. Harnack, *History of Dogma*, E. T. vol. II. p. 191, n. 4, considers Tatian's anthropology to be related to Gnostic theory.

[2] *Contra Graecos*, cc. 7, 12, 13.

transgression and ignorance becomes a demon; and they who imitate him, *i.e.* his illusions, are become a host of demons, and through their freedom of choice have been given up to their own infatuation[1]."

Thus the first man became mortal through loss of a principle of divine life in consequence of his fall. Similarly Tatian says:

"Now in the beginning the Spirit was a constant companion of the soul, but the Spirit forsook it because it was not willing to follow[2]."

It would thus seem that Tatian held a pronounced doctrine of man's fall from an original superior estate, whereby the *donum superadditum* of the presence of the Holy Spirit or the Logos, involving immortality, was lost. And yet, in the light of other statements of his, it is difficult to ascertain how far Tatian regarded the subsequent generations of mankind as having been affected by their first father's falling under the dominion of evil spirits. The soul is said still to retain a spark of the Spirit; the Spirit still endures with such as live righteously[3]; and the possibility of man's recovering the old relationship of union with the Spirit yet remains[4]. "It becomes us," we are told, "to seek now for what we once had, but have lost, to unite the soul with the Holy Spirit, and to strive after union with God[5]." Thus, as Harnack observes[6], "it is only in appearance that the blessing bestowed in the

---

[1] c. 7. This passage contains a strange fusion of the story of Gen. iii. with some legend of the fall of demons. There are points of contact with the *Enoch-literature*, but many of the details are singular and unique.

[2] c. 13.   [3] *ibid.*

[4] c. 20. Cf. c. 11: "Die to the world, repudiating the madness that is in it, and by apprehending Him lay aside your old nature. We were not created to die, but we die by our own fault. Our free-will has destroyed us; we who were free have become slaves; we have been sold through sin. Nothing evil has been created by God; we ourselves have manifested wickedness, but we who have manifested it are able again to reject it."

[5] c. 15.

[6] *op. cit.* vol. II. p. 191. See also the estimate of the teaching of the Apologists on human sin given on pp. 216, 217. Tatian's doctrine of Sin is also discussed by Wendt, *op. cit.* S. 11 ff.

The translations of passages of Tatian given above are taken from the *Ante-Nicene Library*.

'Spirit' is a *donum superadditum et supernaturale*. For if a proper spontaneous use of freedom infallibly leads to the return of the Spirit, it is evident that the decision and consequently the realisation of man's destination depend on human freedom." Tatian, moreover, by no means makes it clear how far Adam's endowments and losses are ours also.

Theophilus of Antioch.

This apologist's teaching as to the unfallen state of Adam differs from that of Tatian, who attributed to the first men that perfection of divine illumination which it is the purpose of Christianity to restore.

Theophilus assigns to Adam, indeed, a more excellent state than has been enjoyed by subsequent generations of mankind, but one far short of that perfection which is man's ultimate destiny. Perhaps this view was to some extent shaped by the exigencies of the Gnostic controversy. Certainly it evades the Gnostic position, that, if man is naturally mortal and evil, he is no creation of God, as well as the alternative difficulty, that, if man was originally perfect and immortal, he would then have been divine[1]. But however the doctrine may have originated, we find first in Theophilus of Antioch, amongst Christian writers, the idea that Adam was created with "a middle nature," such that a course of advancement or development was needed before perfection could be attained. Thus:

"And God transferred him (Adam) from the earth, out of which he had been produced, into Paradise, giving him means of advancement, in order that, maturing and becoming perfect, and being even declared a god, he might then ascend into heaven in possession of immortality. For man had been made a middle nature, neither wholly mortal nor altogether immortal, but capable of either state."

And a little further on:

"Therefore He made him neither immortal nor mortal, but, as we said before, capable of either state, in order that, if he inclined to immortal things, by keeping the commandment

[1] *Ad Autol.* II. 27.

XII] *in the Fathers before Augustine* 281

of God he might by way of reward obtain immortality from Him, and so become divine[1]." We have still no sign of Christian teaching with regard to the Fall having been moulded by S. Paul's treatment of the subject. The Old Testament is as yet the sole source of inspired truth with regard to the question. But though Theophilus describes the fall of Adam and Eve almost wholly in the language of Genesis, he nevertheless betrays here and there that he has had access to Jewish haggada. Thus, the following citation will serve to show that he was familiar with the notion, met with in several pseudepigraphic writings, that the first transgression affected the animal world; it will also suggest how, perhaps, he represented the solidarity of the race in the consequences of Adam's sin. After stating that the animals were not made evil or venomous at the first[2], for nothing was made evil by God, Theophilus continues:

"But the sin in which man was concerned brought evil upon them. For when man transgressed, they also transgressed with him. For as, if the master of the house acts rightly, the domestics also of necessity conduct themselves well; but if the master sins, the servants also sin with him; so in like manner it came to pass, that in the case of man's sin, he being master, all that was subject to him sinned with him. When, therefore, man shall have made his way back to his natural condition, and no longer does evil, those also shall be restored to their original gentleness[3]."

[1] Μετέθηκε δὲ αὐτὸν ὁ θεὸς ἐκ τῆς γῆς, ἐξ ἧς ἐγεγόνει, εἰς τὸν παράδεισον, διδοὺς αὐτῷ ἀφορμὴν προκοπῆς, ὅπως αὐξάνων καὶ τέλειος γενόμενος, ἔτι δὲ καὶ ἀναδειχθεὶς θεός, οὕτως καὶ εἰς τὸν οὐρανὸν ἀναβῇ....
Οὔτε οὖν ἀθάνατον αὐτὸν ἐποίησεν, οὔτε μὴν θνητόν, ἀλλά, καθὼς ἐπάνω προειρήκαμεν, δεκτικὸν ἀμφοτέρων, ἵνα, εἰ ῥέψῃ ἐπὶ τὰ τῆς ἀθανασίας, τηρήσας τὴν ἐντολὴν τοῦ θεοῦ μισθὸν κομίσηται παρ' αὐτοῦ τὴν ἀθανασίαν, καὶ γένηται θεός. *Ad Autol.* II. cc. 24 and 27.

[2] This assertion may possibly have been suggested by *Wisdom* i. 14. So also may the word μέσος, used to describe Adam's nature, be borrowed from Philo; see above, p. 135. The Apologists seem to have been considerably influenced, as regards their anthropology, by Alexandrian writings; cf. their doctrine of man's higher spirit with that of Philo, and their insistence on immortality, as especially the original endowment or the final goal of man, with the teaching of *Wisdom*.

[3] II. 17. Whatever may be thought of the truthfulness to life of the analogy of which Theophilus here makes use, we can see in it a feeling after the conception of moral solidarity.

In accordance with the idea that Adam was created for development, we find in Theophilus the fancy, which spread to other Fathers, that the first parents of the race were but "infants" in age at the time of their transgression. Their sin was associated with the desire to become wise beyond their years: "And at the same time He wished man, infant as he was, to remain for some time longer simple and sincere[1]."

ATHENAGORAS.

Athenagoras does not allude to the consequences of the Fall. He attributes the sinfulness of the human soul partly to its contact with matter, and partly to the influence of the demons, of whose (present) activity he, along with other Greek apologists, holds a view similar to that of the *Book of Enoch*.

It will have been seen, from what has been said of the Greek Apologists, that they had not advanced very far towards the later ecclesiastical doctrine of Original Sin. They differ in their conceptions of the unfallen state of man, and are very indefinite in their estimation of the consequences for the race of the fall of its first parents. They do not seem to have thought of such a thing as a tainted nature having been thereby imparted to mankind; man's psychological condition, his freedom of will and other moral capacities, are not represented as having suffered change; nor are his natural desires and appetites conceived as in any way sinful in themselves: sin is in the will alone. The sinfulness of Adam's posterity is due to the following of Adam's example in becoming subject to the dominion of evil spirits. Its universality is not associated with the unity and solidarity of the race. The influence of S. Paul had not as yet begun to be felt. But in several interesting details these apologists, especially Tatian and Theophilus, prepared the way for the more systematic writer whose work we have next to examine.

III. IRENAEUS.

Irenaeus builds to some extent upon ideas occurring in the writings of the Greek apologists. His doctrine is founded in

[1] II. 25.

part upon conceptions utilised by his predecessors in their scanty descriptions of Christianity as a plan of redemption from sin ; and it is therefore, so far, a development possessing continuity with what had gone before. Thus, the teaching of Tatian, that the higher spiritual principle in man is not part of his nature, but the indwelling Holy Spirit or a divine effluence, and the loss of this at the Fall was the cause of man's mortality, is sometimes presupposed. Similarly, Irenaeus makes use of the very different, if not irreconcilable idea, met with in Theophilus of Antioch, that the first estate of man was not one of perfection, but one from which, in course of development, perfection was capable of attainment ; and, like Theophilus, he describes Adam, at the time of his sin, as an 'infant[1].'

But in building up a doctrine of the Fall and of Original Sin Irenaeus advances very much further than the Greek apologists. He is the first constructive theologian of the Church. Problems such as those of the constitution of man, the Fall and its consequences, receive in the *Adversus Haereses* a treatment which, in comparison with such as they had received before, would be worthy to be called systematic, if only it were homogeneous and self-consistent ; although, of course, it leaves room for very considerable amplification and for increased explicitness in definition. There is certainly a wide difference, however, as regards fulness and maturity, between the teaching of Irenaeus and that of Justin or of Tatian, concerning the fall of man and original sin. These doctrines begin, in Irenaeus, to assume a position of some importance.

One or two reasons may be given for this advance. In the first place, the necessity of refuting the dualistic solution of the problem of evil attempted in Gnostic systems will perhaps account for the investment of the doctrine of the Fall, in Irenaeus, with an importance which had been conspicuously absent in earlier Christian literature. A sharp demarcation of man's original estate from that in which he is

[1] *Adv. Haer.* iv. 38. 1 (Mass.): οὕτως καὶ ὁ θεὸς αὐτὸς μὲν οἷός τε ἦν παρασχεῖν ἀπ' ἀρχῆς τῷ ἀνθρώπῳ τὸ τέλειον, ὁ δὲ ἄνθρωπος ἀδύνατος λαβεῖν αὐτό· νήπιος γὰρ ἦν.

284   *The Doctrine of the Fall etc.*   [CHAP.

now universally found is, of course, an obvious means of accounting for human sinfulness without ascribing the direct authorship of evil either to God or to a malevolent demiurge. For this line of argument the early chapters of Genesis lay ready to hand as a starting-point. And further, the Epistles of S. Paul had undoubtedly, at the time when Irenaeus wrote, come to be accepted as Scripture, and therefore as a guide to doctrine if not as a source thereof. The fact that Gnostic writers also sometimes appealed to the authority of the Apostle would serve to concentrate the attention of Irenaeus upon the contents of his writings. As a matter of fact, the passages in which S. Paul speaks of Adam in connexion with the sin and death of humanity are quoted by Irenaeus[1], and the apostle's conceptions of Adam's representative character, and of the solidarity of the race with Adam, thence became familiar to the Christian teacher. And thus, with Gnostic error as external impulse, and new scriptural statements as authoritative guide, the rise of a Christian doctrine of the Fall at the precise period represented by Irenaeus may easily be accounted for. New conditions having arisen, a new departure could be made.

Irenaeus accepts the doctrine of man's trichotomous constitution[2]; though, after Tatian, he almost always conceives of the πνεῦμα as not a part of our nature but as something received, under certain conditions, from without, and indeed as identical with the Holy Spirit[3]. Here we have a preparation for the later distinction between the *dona naturalia* and the *dona superaddita* possessed by man: a distinction which is still more nearly approached by Irenaeus when, for the first time amongst Church writers, he differentiates between the image and the likeness of God after which man is said in

---

[1] See iii. 18. 7, iii. 23. 8, etc.

[2] v. 9. 1. Tria sunt, ex quibus perfectus homo constat, carne, anima et spiritu, et altero quidem salvante et figurante, qui est spiritus, altero, quod unitur et formatur, quod est caro; id vero quod inter haec est duo, quod est anima, quae aliquando quidem subsequens spiritum elevatur ab eo, aliquando autem consentiens carni decidit in terrenas concupiscentias.

[3] v. 6. 1. Anima autem et spiritus pars hominum esse possunt, homo autem nequaquam : perfectus autem homo commixtio et adunitio est animae assumentis spiritum Patris et admixta ei carni, quae est plasma secundum imaginem Dei.

Genesis to have been made[1]. This teaching is not always consistently maintained; for not only does Irenaeus in one passage seem to imply that man's πνεῦμα belongs necessarily to his nature[2], but also we find him now identifying man's rationality and freedom of will with the 'likeness,' and now representing these endowments as belonging to man's original and inalienable nature[3]. Nevertheless, the distinction embodies the writer's usual conception of man's constitution. The image of God, then, was possessed by man from the first, and has never been lost. With regard to the likeness of God, it has been shown by Wendt[4], who has been followed by Harnack and others, that the writings of Irenaeus disclose two incompatible lines of doctrine, which run, moreover, through his teaching concerning the Fall and its effects, and consequently also through his treatment of the theology of Redemption or, more correctly speaking, of the mediatorial work of Christ. It has embarrassed many students of this Father to find, on different pages of his writings, statements so diverse as, for instance, the following: that man was made at the first after both image and likeness of God[5]; that both image and likeness were lost through Adam's fall[6]; that the image and likeness were both absent from man when he was first created, and were to be afterwards attained[7]; that man was created after the divine image[8], the likeness being separately received through the Spirit[9], and alone lost by man[10].

These discrepancies receive some explanation when the discordant passages are regarded as illustrations, some of the one, and some of the other, of the two main lines of teaching which Irenaeus has been stated to present.

The one of these is called by Harnack[11] 'apologetic and moralistic,' and is said by him to be 'alone developed with

---

[1] Erbkam, *De S. Irenaei Principiis Ethicis*, points out that Philo uses the terms image and likeness quite differently, the latter being used only to explain the former and not to express a new idea. A distinction similar to that of Irenaeus occurs, however, in *Clem. Hom.* XI. 4: εἰκὼν θεοῦ ὁ ἄνθρωπος.—Τὴν δὲ ὁμοιότητα οὐκέτι πάντες, ἀλλ' ἀγαθῆς ψυχῆς ὁ καθαρὸς νοῦς.

[2] ii. 33. 5.   [3] Cf. iv. 37. 4, with iv. 37. 1, iv. 4. 3, etc.
[4] *Op. cit.*   [5] v. 28. 4.
[6] iii. 18. 1.   [7] iv. 38. 3 and 4.   [8] v. 16. 1.
[9] v. 6. 1.   [10] v. 16. 1.   [11] *Op. cit.* vol. II. p. 268.

286   *The Doctrine of the Fall etc.*   [CHAP.

systematic clearness.' It is based on the doctrine, already encountered in Theophilus of Antioch, that man was originally created imperfect, and was indeed at first incapable of apprehending perfection. Perfection is the destination, not the original endowment, of mankind[1]. The likeness to God (ὁμοίωσις) is realised by the union of man's soul with the Spirit, and consists in the possession of the Spirit and of fellowship with God. It is thus subject to growth, and was not possessed by Adam at the first, save only in the germ.

Consistently with this doctrine of man, Irenaeus ought to teach that the fall of Adam only concerned our first parent himself, or at most that it *retarded the development* of the ὁμοίωσις in subsequent generations. And indeed he sometimes expresses himself, especially when thinking of sin rather than death, as if he adopted the former of these views. Thus he does not regard the race as having been in any degree deprived of communion with God except through their own choice of evil:

"And to as many as continue in their love towards God does He grant communion with Him. But communion with God is life and light, and the enjoyment of all the benefits which He has in store. But on as many as, according to their own choice, depart from God, He inflicts that separation

[1] iv. 38. 1 (Eng. tr. Clark, *Ante-Nicene Library*): "If, however, any one say, 'What then? could not God have exhibited man as perfect from the beginning?' let him know that, inasmuch as God is indeed always the same and unbegotten as respects Himself, all things are possible to Him. But created things must be inferior to Him who created them, from the very fact of their later origin; for it was not possible for things recently created to have been uncreated. But inasmuch as they are not uncreated, for this very reason do they come short of the perfect. Because, as these things are of later date, so are they infantile; so are they unaccustomed to, and unexercised in, perfect discipline. For as it certainly is in the power of a mother to give strong food to her infant, [but she does not do so], as the child is not yet able to receive more substantial nourishment; so also it was possible for God Himself to have made man perfect from the first, but man could not receive this [perfection], being as yet an infant."

Cf. iv. 38. 2, "So, in like manner, God had power at the beginning to grant perfection to man; but as the latter was only recently created, he could not possibly have received it, could he have contained it, or containing it, could he have retained it."

Throughout this chapter the image and likeness of God are conceived as endowments gradually to be attained by man.

from Himself which they have chosen of their own accord. But separation from God is death, and separation from light is darkness; and separation from God consists in the loss of all the benefits which He has in store[1]."

Like the apologists before him, Irenaeus always strongly insists on man's unimpaired freedom; and, in accordance with the line of teaching at present under consideration, he sometimes implies that this freedom, responding to the divine commandments and the reforming influences of Christ, renders man capable of receiving incorruptibility[2]. Consequently it may be concluded, with Wendt, that one side of Irenaeus's doctrine involves the view that "the original destination of mankind was not abrogated by the Fall." Whether the further statement of this writer is equally true, that "the Fall," for Irenaeus, "was intended as a means of leading men to attain this perfection to which they were destined," or, in Harnack's words, Irenaeus "contemplates the Fall as having a teleological significance," is much more doubtful. It cannot be granted that Irenaeus seeks to "palliate" man's fall; nor does it follow that, because he points out how God in mercy used Adam's disobedience and its consequences for educational purposes, these things were not contingencies, but foreordained ends as well as means: which is what is implied in attributing to them 'teleological significance[3]'.

It has now to be shown that Irenaeus also taught a more thorough doctrine of the Fall, scarcely consistent with that previously traced.

It is connected with that side of the anthropological teaching of this writer which attributes possession of the likeness, as well as the image, of God to man at the first.

[1] v. 27. 2, Eng. tr. of Clark, *Ante-Nicene Library*.
Harnack, *loc. cit.*, has collected other passages in illustration of this line of thought, which he calls 'subjective moralism.'
[2] For references see Harnack, *op. cit.* vol. II. p. 271.
[3] Harnack, *op. cit.* pp. 270-1. When this writer says, on the same page: "Here life and death are always the ultimate question to Irenaeus. It is only when he quotes sayings of Paul that he remembers sin in connexion with redemption: and ethical consequences of the Fall are not mentioned in this connexion," he would seem to be seeking unduly to minimise the moral element in the Father's teaching; for are not death and life synonymous, in Irenaeus, for communion with, and separation from, God? See v. 27. 2, quoted above.

288   *The Doctrine of the Fall etc.*   [CHAP.

This likeness is said, in more than one passage, to have been lost at the Fall[1]. We are thus presented with a different conception of man's original state, and one which was in all probability forced upon Irenaeus as a consequence of his doctrine of Recapitulation. Derived ultimately from S. Paul's expression ἀνακεφαλαιώσασθαι applied to Christ in Eph. i. 10, this doctrine teaches that our Lord summed up in Himself all that belonged to human nature as it was destined to be and become, and it includes, or is inextricably interwoven with, the closely allied idea that He repeated what was at the beginning, and restored humanity to what it originally was. It is obvious that the application of such a doctrine to the problems of man's constitution and of the Fall and its consequences necessarily opens out a new train of thought with regard to these subjects. It led Irenaeus away from the position in which he would have found himself in harmony with Theophilus of Antioch, and brought him into agreement rather with Tatian. If Christ restored humanity to what it originally was, humanity could not have been at first imperfect. The image and likeness of God must have been the possession of Adam from the first; and this, it has been seen, was what Irenaeus actually sometimes taught.

Further, inasmuch as the Recapitulation doctrine implies that Christ is the sum and representative of restored humanity, analogy requires that Adam should have similarly been the type and totality of mankind. This again was actually the teaching of Irenaeus; and in its development he was doubtless aided by the Pauline doctrine of the solidarity of the race in Adam. Adam is frequently identified with the race and

---

[1] iii. 18. 1. Sed quando incarnatus est, et homo factus, longam hominum expositionem in seipso recapitulavit, in compendio nobis salutem praestans, ut quod perdideramus in Adam, id est, secundum imaginem et similitudinem esse Dei, hoc in Christo Jesu reciperemus.

v. 16. 2. Ἐν τοῖς πρόσθεν χρόνοις ἐλέγετο μὲν κατ' εἰκόνα θεοῦ γεγονέναι τὸν ἄνθρωπον, οὐκ ἐδείκνυτο δέ· ἔτι γὰρ ἀόρατος ἦν ὁ Λόγος, οὗ κατ' εἰκόνα ὁ ἄνθρωπος ἐγεγόνει· διὰ τοῦτο δὴ καὶ τὴν ὁμοίωσιν ῥᾳδίως ἀπέβαλεν.

In v. 1. 1, we are said to have been 'by nature' (the property) of God, and to have been tyrannised over unjustly by apostasy, and alienated 'contrary to nature.'

v. 2. 1, ...restaurans suo plasmati quod dictum est in principio, factum esse hominem secundum imaginem et similitudinem Dei.

the race with him. We sinned against God in Adam, and through Eve the whole of humanity became liable to death[1]. Passages such as those cited below occur frequently in the parts of his work in which Irenaeus elaborates his doctrine of Recapitulation. In some he quotes from Rom. v. 12 ff.[2] An examination of these passages will show that the identification of the human race with Adam which they assert is of the same kind as that which, if the result arrived at in the foregoing chapter be correct, is to be found in the writings of S. Paul. That is to say, Irenaeus does not conceive of the race as existing seminally in Adam, nor as one with Adam in the sense of philosophical realism. The union or identity of which he speaks is rather what is often called, for want of a better term, mystical; it figuratively and pregnantly expresses a fact in its ideality but does not concern itself with describing the means by which the fact is made an actuality. The doctrine of Redemption implied in the notion of Recapitulation is similarly 'mystical.'

[1] iv. 22. 1. Hic est enim finis humani generis haeredificantis Deum ; uti quemadmodum in initio per primos, omnes in servitutem redacti sumus debito mortis, sic in ultimo per novissimum omnes qui ab initio discipuli, emundati et abluti quae sunt mortis, in vitam veniant Dei.

iii. 22. 4. Eva...inobediens facta, et sibi, et universo generi humano causa facta est mortis; sic et Maria...obediens, et sibi et universo generi humano causa facta est salutis. Cf. v. 19. 1.

v. 16. 3. Quoniam autem per haec, per quae non obedivimus Deo, et non credidimus ejus verbo, per haec eadem obedientiam introduxit, et eam quae esset erga Verbum ejus assensionem, per quae manifeste ipsum ostendit Deum : quem in primo quidem Adam offendimus, non facientes ejus praeceptum ; in secundo autem Adam reconciliati sumus, obedientes usque ad mortem facti. Neque enim alteri cuidam eramus debitores, sed illi, cujus et praeceptum transgressi fueramus ab initio.

v. 34. 2. Dolor autem plagae est, per quam percussus est homo initio in Adam inobediens, hoc est, mors...

v. 21. 1. Omnia ergo recapitulans recapitulatus est, et adversus inimicum nostrum bellum provocans, et elidens eum qui, in initio in Adam captivos duxerat nos.........Propter hoc et Dominus semetipsum Filium Hominis confitetur, principalem hominem illum, ex quo ea quae secundum mulierem est plasmatio facta est, in semetipsum recapitulans : uti quemadmodum per hominem victum descendit in mortem genus nostrum, sic iterum per hominem victorem ascendamus in vitam.

v. 17. 3. Uti quemadmodum per lignum facti sumus debitores Deo, per lignum accipiamus nostri debiti remissionem.

[2] *e.g.* v. 19. 1 ; iii. 18. 7.

The Fall then, with Irenaeus, is the collective deed of the race; provided that such a statement is not interpreted literally or realistically, but is understood to leave the mode in which Adam and his posterity are actually connected together in the first sin entirely undefined, and to express the relation rather by means of figure than by means of theory or concrete fact.

Irenaeus thus prepares the way for later doctrine as to the explicit manner in which we "were all in Adam, and were Adam, when he sinned"; and his language on the subject of human solidarity is interesting as the earliest patristic development of S. Paul's teaching contained in the fifth chapter of his Epistle to the Romans.

But if Irenaeus thus vaguely anticipates one side of the Augustinian theory by insisting on Adam's sin being in some sense ours, he never seems to hint at the other main factor of it, viz. the conception of inherited corruption of nature, which was destined to appear with clear-cut definition in Tertullian. He speaks indeed of death as inherited[1], and it is true that death usually means, with this Father, something more than physical death; but it is not implied here that Adam's act was the productive cause of an ingrained and inherited bias to sinfulness. Other passages as well as the one just referred to have been quoted by Duncker in proof of the view that Irenaeus was the founder of this second element in the Augustinian theory of original sin[2]; but they have been rejected as wholly inadequate for the purpose by most students of Irenaeus, and certainly do not seem to necessitate such a construction as would derive from them the idea of propagation of hereditary moral taint. The mode of production of sin amongst mankind is left an open question. The 'flesh' is never, as in S. Paul, regarded as the seat or occasion of sin; still less is the 'flesh' as disordered by Adam's fall; sin is always traced to the will. Irenaeus maintains the need of baptismal regeneration, but not in connexion with any inborn taint of sin generated by the

---

[1] v. I. 3.
[2] iii. 23. 1, 2; iv. 33. 4; v. 15. 3.

Fall[1]. Sin, again, is universal, and, since the first great transgression, all mankind is in a state of sin; but in the passage where man's apostasy and sonship to the devil is spoken of there is no reference even to solidarity, much less to the precise mode of it specified in the theory of transmitted depravity of nature[2].

It may be concluded then that Irenaeus was the first to initiate the elaboration of the doctrines of the Fall and of Original Sin in the Christian Church, and to insist on the unity of the race with Adam on the lines laid down in S. Paul's brief and incidental treatment of the subject. But, unlike S. Paul, he does not emphasise the subjective aspect of sin as an inherent disease; he is silent about 'evil concupiscence.' Consequently he is not impelled to seek in the Fall an explanation of human infirmity and of man's sinful tendencies. He therefore stops short altogether of a doctrine of inherited corruption; and in this respect he still represents the attitude of the Greek Apologists before him rather than that of the Fathers of the West in the succeeding generations.

IV. The Early Alexandrines.

Clement.

The doctrine of the Fall, which had begun to assume a position of some importance in the writings of Irenaeus, recedes into insignificance in Clement of Alexandria. The teaching of this Father on the subject reverts almost to the plane of development previously attained in the Greek Apologists. Clement was not unfamiliar with the literary work of Irenaeus; but the Paulinism of the latter writer, at least on its anthropological side, obtained no grip on the mind of the Alexandrian. The conception of Adam as representing or including the human race, in which Irenaeus anticipated in an indefinite manner one main element in the Augustinian theory of Original Sin, is wanting in the works of

---

[1] v. 15. 3. Et quoniam in illa plasmatione, quae secundum Adam fuit, in transgressione factus homo, indigebat lavacro regenerationis...
[2] iv. 41. 2.

Clement. The other element of this later theory, inheritance of corrupted nature, a doctrine which arose during Clement's lifetime in the Church of the West, is not only absent from his writings but inconsistent with his theological system; and indeed the traducianist psychology, with which, at its first appearance within the Church, this doctrine was closely connected, is definitely repudiated in the *Stromateis*. Clement believed in the fall of Adam as a fact; but he does not deduce from it any theory of Original Sin.

The question of man's original estate was thrust upon him in a way similar to that in which it had been brought before the notice of Irenaeus and other Church writers. The Gnostic dilemma: if the first man was created perfect, how could he commit sin? elicited from Clement the same answer as had already been given by his predecessors in the anti-Gnostic struggle. Man was not made perfect, but adapted for the attainment of perfection[1]. The distinction between man's original endowment with aptitude for virtue and his developed state of virtue is apparently identified with the distinction, drawn by previous writers, between the image and the likeness of God:

"It is time, then, for us to say that the pious Christian alone is rich and wise, and of noble birth, and thus call and believe him to be God's image, and also His likeness, having become righteous and holy and wise by Jesus Christ, and so far already like God[2]."

[1] *Strom.* Bk vi. cc. 11 (end)-12. "Above all, this ought to be known, that by nature we are adapted for virtue; not so as to be possessed of it from our birth, but so as to be adapted for requiring it. By which consideration is solved the question propounded to us by the heretics, Whether Adam was created perfect or imperfect? Well, if imperfect, how could the work of a perfect God—above all, that work being man—be imperfect? And if perfect, how did he transgress the commandments? For they shall hear from us that he was not perfect in his creation, but adapted to the reception of virtue. For it is of great importance in regard to virtue to be made fit for its attainment. And it is intended that we should be saved by ourselves. This, then, is the nature of the soul, to move of itself. Then, as we are rational, and philosophy being rational, we have some affinity with it. Now an aptitude is a movement towards virtue, not virtue itself. All then, as I said, are naturally constituted for the acquisition of virtue." *Ante-Nicene Library*, XII. pp. 359–60. Cf. *Paed.* I. iii. In *Protrept.* c. x. *Strom.* v. 14, man's mind is said to be an image of the Word, which in turn is the image of God.
[2] *Protrept.* c. xii.

More explicitly he says:
"For is it not thus that some of our writers have understood that man straightway on his creation received what is 'according to the image,' but what is 'according to the likeness' he will receive afterwards on his perfection?"[1]

Adam is again said to have been 'perfect as far as respects his formation,' and in the sense that none of the distinctive characteristics of the idea of man were wanting to him[2].

Clement's account of the Fall is as follows:
"The first man, when in Paradise, sported free, because he was the child of God; but when he succumbed to pleasure (for the serpent allegorically signifies pleasure crawling on its belly, earthly wickedness nourished for fuel to the flames), was as a child seduced by lusts, and grew old in disobedience; and by disobeying his Father, dishonoured God. Such was the influence of pleasure[3]."

In the words that follow in this passage, Adam seems to be vaguely identified with mankind generally, or to be considered as their representative:

"Man, that had been free by reason of simplicity, was found fettered to sins. The Lord then wished to release him from his bonds, and clothing Himself with flesh—O divine mystery!—vanquished the serpent, and enslaved the tyrant death; and, most marvellous of all, man that had been deceived by pleasure, and bound fast to corruption, had his hands unloosed, and was set free. O mystic wonder! The Lord was

---

[1] *Strom.* ii. 22. Cf. the following passage from *Paed.* I. xii. "The view I take is, that He Himself (Christ) formed man of the dust, and regenerated him by water; and made him grow by His Spirit; and trained him by His word to adoption and salvation, directing him by sacred precepts; in order that, transforming earth-born man into a holy and heavenly being by His advent, He might fulfil to the utmost that divine utterance, 'Let us make man in our own image and likeness.' And, in truth, Christ became the perfect realisation of what God spake; and the rest of humanity is conceived as being created merely in His image." *A.-N. Library*, IV. p. 181.

[2] *Strom.* iv. 23.

[3] *Protrept.* xi. (transl. of *A.-N. Library*).

This allegorical interpretation of the serpent is of course borrowed from Philo. The passage should perhaps be read in the light of *Strom.* iii. 17, where Clement, repudiating the Gnostic teaching that marriage is sinful, allows that the first transgression may have consisted in the *premature* union of Adam and Eve.

laid low, and man rose up; and he that fell from Paradise receives as the reward of obedience something greater [than Paradise]—namely heaven itself."

These words represent Clement's nearest approach to the doctrine that our first parents' sin involved posterity in its consequences. Yet it is improbable that they represent Adam's transgression otherwise than as the type of human sin in general[1]. Clement's teaching as to the Fall seems, indeed, to be quite parallel to that of Philo. And this is true as to the connexion of death, as well as of sin, with Adam's transgression. In *Strom*. III. 9 the passage Rom. v. 12—14 is quoted; according to which death entered into the world through the sin of one man, and spread to all men, for that all sinned; but in the same sentence Clement adds that death follows upon birth brought about by generation according to a natural necessity of the divine economy, and that if woman is considered to be the cause of death, for the same reason she may be said to be the source of life, because she gives birth. In thus denying that human mortality is a punishment for the Fall, Clement is a precursor of the teaching of the Antiochenes and of Pelagius[2].

If now Clement did not teach the identity of Adam and the race, or that his sin was also ours, and also did not regard even physical death as a consequence of the first transgression, we should not expect him to hold any form of the doctrine of Original Sin or hereditary guilt; and such is actually the case. He explicitly rejects traducianism[3], and therefore the propagation of inherited taint in the soul itself. In reply to the gnostic Julius Cassianus, who condemned the generation of children as evil, he asks how infants could have fallen under

---

[1] Such is also the view of the author of *The Christian Platonists of Alexandria*. Dr Bigg, citing the words (*Adumb. in Ep. Judae*), 'Sic etiam peccato Adae subjacemus secundum peccati similitudinem,' which also imply that Adam was the type, not the source of sin, expresses a doubt as to whether the context in which they occur is from the hand of Clement; p. 81, n. 1.

[2] Clement teaches, *Strom.* ii. 19, that Adam, through yielding to Eve's persuasion, exchanged an immortal life for mortality, though not for ever. He nowhere implies that other men owe their mortality to Adam.

[3] *Strom*. vi. 16. Ἐπεισκρίνεται δὲ ἡ ψυχὴ καὶ προεισκρίνεται τὸ ἡγεμονικόν, ᾧ διαλογιζόμεθα, οὐ κατὰ τὴν τοῦ σπέρματος καταβολὴν γεννώμενον.

the curse of Adam, who have performed no actions of their own[1].

In the same context he declares that if David was "conceived in sin" (Ps. li.), the sin nevertheless did not attach to himself: ἀλλ' οὐκ αὐτὸς ἐν ἁμαρτίᾳ[2]. Thus, as Neander points out[3], Clement unconsciously combated the doctrine of the North African Church, at that very time first appearing in Tertullian. Tertullian, as will be seen, in spite of his traducianist doctrine of hereditary taint, did not hold the unconditional necessity of infant baptism, and objects to hurrying the age of innocence to the forgiveness of sins. Perhaps he did not regard the inherited stain in the infant as truly of the nature of sin, and considered only actual sin to be washed away in baptism[4]. Clement nowhere alludes to infant baptism; nor indeed does the custom appear to have been established in his day in the Alexandrian Church. The sins forgiven in baptism are always spoken of as actual sins[5]. The things outside the will likely to be taken for the causes of human sin are "the weakness of matter, the involuntary impulses of ignorance, and irrational necessities[6]"; not a fault of nature inherited from Adam. Finally, Clement insists very strongly on the unimpaired freedom of man. Sin is an action, not a substance[7]; it is not brought about through the agency of demons, for then the sinner would be guiltless[8]; the only sinfulness of nature is that which results from a man's having become bad through choosing evil and sinning[8].

[1] *Strom.* iii. 16. λεγέτωσαν ἡμῖν ποῦ ἐπόρνευσεν τὸ γεννηθὲν παιδίον, ἢ πῶς ὑπὸ τὴν τοῦ Ἀδὰμ ὑποπέπτωκεν ἀρὰν τὸ μηδὲν ἐνεργῆσαν.

[2] It may be noted that the two passages Job xiv. 4, 5 (LXX.) and Ps. li. 5, used by Clement to refute the Gnostic idea that sin attaches to the infant through its birth, are appealed to by Origen in support of a doctrine of inborn sinfulness, as will presently be seen.

[3] *Gen. History of the Christian Religion and Church.* E. T., ed. Bohn, vol. II. p. 353.

[4] Cf. Turmel in *Revue d'histoire et de littérature relig.* vi. p. 19.

[5] See Bigg, *op. cit.* p. 81, n. 1, and p. 83, n. 1.

[6] *Strom.* vii. 3. In *Strom.* vii. 16, Clement says: "Though men's actions are ten thousand in number, the sources of sin are but two, ignorance and inability. And both depend on ourselves; inasmuch as we will not learn, nor, on the other hand, restrain lust."

[7] *Strom.* iv. ἀμέλει τὸ ἁμαρτάνειν ἐνεργείᾳ κεῖται οὐκ οὐσίᾳ.   [8] *Strom.* vi. 12.

Though there is a place for faith as a divine gift[1], for grace, right teaching, and the drawing of the Father[2], in effecting man's salvation or τελείωσις, nevertheless the emphasis is more generally thrown upon man's part: "each of us justifies himself"; "the true Gnostic creates himself"; men may "choose to believe or to disbelieve[3]."

The existence of sin in the world receives, then, for Clement of Alexandria, its sufficient explanation in the freedom of man's will. This conception of free-will by no means appears for the first time in Clement's writings; but there is much truth in the statement that the Alexandrines, and Clement in particular, first defined it and made it the foundation of a system[4]. Clement's treatment of the problem of Sin furnishes no link in the chain of development of the doctrine of the Fall, which was based by Irenaeus on conceptions expressed in the Epistles of S. Paul, and which culminated in the great theory of S. Augustine. This Father rather represents the logically completed tendency of the scanty teaching on the question of sin found in the Apologists who preceded Irenaeus; and he unconsciously anticipates, in some respects, an attitude which, after the Pelagian controversy, came to be pronounced unorthodox. Like the Apologists, he held a doctrine of the Fall but no doctrine of Original Sin.

Origen.

Origen would seem to have held, in the earlier part of his life, as individualistic a theory of the universality of sin as did his predecessor Clement. He is equally strong, indeed, in his emphasis upon human freedom; but he feels

---

[1] *Strom.* ii. 4 and 6, v. 13, etc.
[2] τῆς θείας χρῄζομεν χάριτος, διδασκαλίας τε ὀρθῆς, καὶ εὐπαθείας ἁγνῆς, καὶ τῆς τοῦ Πατρὸς πρὸς αὐτὸν ὁλκῆς.
[3] These sayings are collected by Dr Bigg, *op. cit.* p. 81. Similar ones might easily be multiplied: note especially ὁ θεὸς ἡμᾶς ἐξ ἡμῶν αὐτῶν βούλεται σώζεσθαι, *Strom.* vi. 12.
[4] Bigg, *op. cit.* p. 78. See also pp. 284 ff. of that work, where the Alexandrian doctrine of free-will is identified with indifferentism, such as Pelagius afterwards held, and to which Augustine, its strong opponent, had to resort in the case of Adam's sin.

more acutely than did Clement the inherent sinfulness of human nature. Origen's earliest attempt to explain the corrupt state of mankind therefore penetrates more deeply beneath the surface of the problem. But it leaves quite out of account the organic unity of the race; a fact upon which, in its connexion with the universality of sin and death, S. Paul had strongly insisted, and on which, as a basis, Irenaeus had already founded a doctrine of Original Sin.

The idea of the human soul having entered this world in consequence of a moral fall in the celestial sphere occurs in the myth to which Plato resorts, in the *Phaedrus*, in order to describe the soul's history. And of this fancy of Plato, which Philo had previously come near to adopting, Origen makes partial use[1]; indeed he sometimes reads it into texts of Scripture. Souls, he teaches, are fallen celestial spirits. Having become estranged from God in a former state of existence, they were banished to earth and appointed to a corporeal life for their purification and restoration. Thus each human being brings with him, when born into this world, a sinfulness resulting from abuse of free-will in a previous existence.

This theory, destined to find echoes now and again in the thought of subsequent centuries, was first imported into Christian theology by Origen.

It is developed in his early work, the *De Principiis*[2], written before he left Alexandria for Caesarea. His first attempt to account for the universality of sin, therefore, was not based upon previous ecclesiastical teaching, *i.e.* upon the doctrine of Irenaeus, nor upon exegesis of the fifth chapter of S. Paul's Epistle to the Romans; the source of his speculation was the Platonism current in the schools of Alexandria. In this same work Origen declares the Fall-story of Genesis to be allegorical, and its meaning to be mystical[3]. This is

---

[1] It is supplemented by Clement's "vicious theory of the indifferentism of the will." (Bigg, *op. cit.* p. 199.)

[2] See I. v., vi., vii.; II. viii. 3; III. v. 4, etc.

[3] IV. i. 16. Origen also manifests Alexandrian influence in his estimate that Adam's sin was less grave than that of Cain, an opinion expressed in *In Jerem. Hom.* XVI. 4 (Bigg, *op. cit.* p. 205).

consistent; for his theory of a pre-natal fall does not allow of sinfulness being derived in any way from Adam. Equally consistent is his condemnation of the "heretical" doctrine that man is corrupt by *nature*, which would make God the judge, not of actions, but of natural capacities, in His rewards and punishments. The idea that there is accountability without liberty is thus repudiated in the *De Principiis*[1]. Again, it is consistent with the individualistic nature of the doctrine of man's 'fall' contained in the *De Principiis* that this work declines to look upon concupiscence as sin until voluntary consent has carried the natural desire into action[2].

In that stage of the development of his thought on the subject of Sin and the Fall which is represented by the *De Principiis*, Origen must therefore be asserted to have been, to a very large extent, a precursor of Pelagius. This does not apply, of course, to his views as to grace, but only to those concerning the propagation of sin[3].

This attitude towards the various aspects of the problem of Sin, which, whatever else may be said of it, must be avowed to be consistent, does not, however, represent the whole of Origen's thought upon the subject. The idea of the individual's pre-mundane fall, and the tendency to treat the Paradise-story of Genesis as allegory, are still to be met with in his later writings; but along with them we find other teaching with which they are by no means perfectly compatible. It has sometimes been attempted to discover coherency underlying Origen's apparent vacillations and inconsistencies[4]; but these should, perhaps, rather be explained than removed. A theory which derives much probability from its general agreement with such facts as Eusebius has preserved with

---

[1] II. v. 2.

[2] III. ii. 2, 3. Origen says there are certain sins which take their beginning from the natural movements of the body; or, that there are "seeds of sins" from those things which we use agreeably to nature. These seeds of sin, however, are only the occasion of transgression, and are not actually sinful until they are allowed to grow beyond what is proper.

[3] Even in this respect Origen stops short of the position of Pelagius; for he held that each individual comes into the world in a state of sinfulness, and is not, therefore, innocent at birth. But Origen, at this stage, excludes racial solidarity in sin as much as did Pelagius afterwards.

[4] *e.g.* Neander, *op. cit.* vol. II. p. 363.

XII] *in the Fathers before Augustine* 299

reference to the chronological order of Origen's writings has been suggested by Dr Bigg[1] and adopted by Prof. Harnack[2]. According to this theory, the tendency exhibited in some of Origen's works of later date than the *De Principiis*, in which the doctrine of Original Sin is wanting[3], not only to believe in birth-sin but also to explain it in a way different from that employed before, and even in terms of our descent from a historical Adam, is due to the fact that, after his departure from Alexandria, Origen came in contact with the practice of infant baptism at Caesarea: a practice which would naturally lead him to consider the question of birth-sin more deliberately than before[4]. Certainly we find in his works of the Caesarean period frequent references to a stain of sin (*sordes peccati*) attaching to every human being and needing to be washed away in baptism. Thus, when expounding the Law of Purification, Origen finds a reason for its existence by identifying ceremonial uncleanness with impurity to which the guilt of sin attaches: an identification suggested by the well-known fifth verse of the fifty-first Psalm[5].

[1] *op. cit.* p. 202.
[2] *op. cit.* vol. II. p. 365.
[3] Origen's teaching superficially resembles the Kantian doctrine of 'radical evil,' but has no connexion with the ecclesiastical doctrine of Original Sin in any of its various forms.
[4] So far as the evidence goes, the practice of infant baptism existed before the appearance within the Church of any doctrine of a taint inherited by children from fallen Adam. The practice does not seem, therefore, to have been at first connected with, or to have grown out of, a doctrine of Original Sin. On the other hand, the existence of the practice, supported as it was by tradition already ancient at the beginning of the third century, seems to have been a stimulus to the growth of the doctrine, and eventually an argument for its truth.
[5] *In Levit. Hom.* VIII. 3. Nunc vero requiramus etiam illud, quid causae sit quod mulier quae in hoc mundo nascentibus ministerium praebet, non solum cum semen susceperit immunda fieri dicitur, sed et cum peperit. Unde et pro purificatione sua jubetur offerre pullos columbinos, aut turtures pro peccato, ad ostium tabernaculi testimonii, ut repropitiet pro ipsa sacerdos; quasi quae repropitiationem debeat, et purificationem peccati pro eo quod nascenti in hoc mundo homini ministerium praebuit. Sic enim scriptum est: 'Et repropitiabit pro ipsa sacerdos, et mundabitur.' Ego in talibus nihil audeo dicere, sentio tamen occulta in his quaedam mysteria contineri, et esse aliquid latentis arcani, pro quo et mulier quae conceperit ex semine, et pepererit, immunda dicatur, et tanquam peccati rea offerre jubeatur hostiam pro peccato, et ita purificari. Sed et ille ipse qui nascitur, sive virilis, sive feminei sexus sit, pronuntiat de eo Scriptura quia non sit 'mundus a sorde, etiamsi unius diei sit vita ejus.'......Quod si placet

In the passage last cited, as elsewhere, inborn taint is assigned as the reason why baptism is given to infants; unless they needed remission, Origen says, their baptism would be superfluous. It is very doubtful whether this reason for the practice of infant baptism had been given before. Irenaeus had not advanced it; Tertullian, though teaching a hereditary *vitium originis*, was opposed to hastening the baptism of young children because they were not as yet stained with personal sin. The very texts to which Origen appeals for proof of inborn sinful taint had been used by Clement of Alexandria, who does not seem to allude to infant baptism, in proof that sin did not attach to children at their birth; and this Father only knew the idea of birth-sin as a Gnostic tenet. In so far then as Origen appears to have held, in his later years, a doctrine of hereditary taint, he would seem to have derived it, not from ecclesiastical tradition or from his exegesis of S. Paul, but primarily from such Old Testament verses as Job xiv. 4-5, Psalm li. 5, etc., taken in connexion with the Law of Purification on the one hand, and the 'apostolic' custom of infant baptism on the other. Even in commenting on Rom. v. he appeals to this apostolic practice, rather than to S. Paul's statements, in proof of the existence in children of a *sordes peccati*[1].

The exact nature of the 'stain of sin' which defiles every man born into this world is not rigidly defined by Origen. Indeed his expressions with regard to it show that he wavered

audire quid etiam alii sancti de ista nativitate senserint, audi David dicentem: 'In iniquitatibus, inquit, conceptus sum, et in peccatis peperit me mater mea'; ostendens quod quaecunque anima in carne nascitur, iniquitatis et peccati sorde polluitur....Addi his etiam illud potest, ut requiratur, quid causae sit, cum baptisma ecclesiae pro remissione peccatorum detur, secundum ecclesiae observantiam etiam parvulis baptismum dari: cum utique si nihil esset in parvulis, quod ad remissionem deberet et indulgentiam pertinere, gratia baptismi superflua videretur.

[1] *Com. in Rom.* v. Pro hoc et ecclesia ab Apostolis traditionem suscepit, etiam parvulis baptismum dare; sciebant enim illi, quibus mysteriorum secreta commissa sunt divinorum, quod essent in omnibus genuinae sordes peccati, quae per aquam et Spiritum ablui deberent; propter quas etiam corpus ipsum corpus peccati nominatur, non (ut putant aliqui eorum qui animarum transmigrationem in varia corpora introducunt) pro his, quae in alio corpore posita anima deliquerit, sed pro hoc ipso, quod in corpore peccati, et corpore mortis et humilitatis effecta sit.

between attributing a physical and a moral character to birth-pollution. Sometimes he speaks of it as if it were merely a bodily defilement connected with the process of birth[1]; and indeed when the purification of the Virgin Mary and the Child Jesus is discussed, Origen clearly distinguishes between *sordes* and *peccatum*[2].

If *sordes* could always be taken in the sense in which it is used in the passage last quoted, Origen's doctrine of birth-sin would be by no means identical with the later ecclesiastical teaching, according to which such sin carries with it personal guilt. In other words, Origen would then teach no doctrine of Original Guilt. So far he would be in agreement with Clement; but on the other hand, in seeing in birth-sin of any kind a reason for baptising infants, he would have advanced considerably beyond the view of his predecessor in the direction of later doctrine[3].

It is evident, however, from some of the passages cited above, that Origen did not always speak as if the *sordes* inherited by every man were solely a physical pollution. He sometimes speaks of it as requiring 'remission' as well as

[1] *In Levit. Hom.* XII. 4. Omnis qui ingreditur hunc mundum, in quadam contaminatione effici dicitur. Propter quod et Scriptura dicit: 'Nemo mundus a sorde....' Hoc ipso ergo quod in vulva matris est positus, et quod materiam corporis ab origine paterni seminis sumit, in patre et in matre contaminatus dici potest. Aut nescis, quia cum quadraginta dierum factus fuerit puer masculus, offertur ad altare, ut ubi purificetur, tanquam qui pollutus fuerit in ipsa conceptione, vel paterni seminis, vel uteri materni? Omnis ergo homo in patre et in matre pollutus est, solus vero Jesus Dominus meus in hanc generationem mundus ingressus est, in matre non est pollutus. Ingressus est enim corpus incontaminatum. Ipse enim erat, qui et dudum per Salomonem dixerat: 'Magis autem cum essem bonus, veni ad corpus incoinquinatum.'

[2] *In Luc. Hom.* XIV. Nunc vero in eo quod ait, *dies purgationis eorum* (Luke ii. 22), non videtur unum significare, sed alterum, sive plures. Ergo Jesus purgatione indiguit, et immundus fuit, aut aliqua sorde pollutus. Temerarie forsitan videor dicere, sed Scripturarum auctoritate commotus. Vide quid in Job scriptum est: *Nemo mundus a sorde....* Non dixit, *nemo mundus a peccato,* sed *nemo mundus a sorde.* Neque enim idipsum significant sordes atque peccata.... Omnis anima quae humano corpore fuerit induta, habet sordes suas.

[3] See, *e.g.*, the following passage from *In Luc. Hom.* XIV. Parvuli baptizantur in remissionem peccatorum. Quorum peccatorum, vel quo tempore peccaverunt? Aut quomodo potest ulla lavacri in parvulis ratio subsistere, nisi juxta illum sensum de quo paulo ante diximus: *Nullus mundus a sorde...*et quia per baptismi sacramentum nativitatis sordes deponuntur, propterea baptizantur et parvuli.

cleansing away. It passes then into a corruption involving moral guilt, and therefore it must be claimed that, in the period which produced the *Homilies on Leviticus* and the *Commentary on the Epistle to the Romans*, Origen had arrived at a form of the doctrine of Original Sin.

But, birth-sin being admitted to be really of the nature of sin, and to be more than pollution attaching to physical generation, the question of its origin demands an answer. The source of inborn sinfulness might be supplied by Origen's theory of a fall of the soul in a previous existence; and indeed, in disputing with Celsus, Origen closely connects some statements about birth-sin with the notion of an antenatal fall denoted allegorically by Adam's expulsion from Paradise. Thus: "Celsus has not explained how error accompanies the 'becoming,' or product of generation......But the prophets, who have given some wise suggestions on the subject of things produced by generation, tell us that a sacrifice for sin was offered even for new-born infants, as not being free from sin. They say, 'I was shapen in iniquity, and in sin did my mother conceive me'; also, 'They are estranged from the womb.'..."

After also quoting various texts emphasising the vanity of material things, such as Rom. viii. 20, Eccles. i. 2, Ps. xxxix. 5, xliv. 25, etc., Origen continues:

"It is a prophet also who says, 'Thou hast brought us down in a place of affliction'; meaning by the 'place of affliction' this earthly region, to which Adam, that is to say, man, came after he was driven out of paradise for sin[1]."

If Origen resorts here to his earliest theory of the origin of sin in the individual, we have a case of reversion, determined, it may be, by the nature of the adversary against whom his last work was written. For certainly before the date of the *Contra Celsum*, he had adopted the view that our inborn sinfulness was derived from Adam; and that such inborn sinfulness is transmitted not merely through what is now-a-days called 'social heredity' (the fact, that is, that we

---

[1] *Contra Celsum*, VII. 50; Eng. tr. Clark, *Ante-Nicene Library*.

are "the sons and disciples of sinners ")[1], but in virtue of our descent from Adam by generation[2].

In his *Commentary on the Epistle to the Romans*, written apparently between 244 and 249 (which latter date is assigned to the *Contra Celsum*), Origen appears to treat the Fall-story as history, and to teach a doctrine of the Fall and of Original Sin resembling, with allowance for its greater indefiniteness, that which subsequently reached its developed form in S. Augustine. Very little, indeed, is said in this Commentary of original sin in its subjective aspect, of a state of corruption brought about by the Fall; but such a consequence of the first transgression is certainly presupposed, and it is definitely stated that our body is the 'body of sin' because Adam's children were not born till after his disobedience[3].

Origen observes correctly that S. Paul himself has not told us *how* "death passed unto all men[4]." He regards the

[1] *In Rom.* v.
[2] It should be mentioned that in one of his earliest works, the *Commentary on Canticles*, Books I-V., Origen regards the fall of Adam and Eve as involving their posterity in moral consequences. He would seem, from the former of the two passages now to be cited, to have known the Jewish legend, mentioned above in Chap. VII., relating to the pollution of Eve by the serpent:

Cervus quoque amicitiarum quis alius videbitur, nisi ille, qui peremit serpentem illum, qui seduxerat Evam et eloquii sui flatibus peccati in eam venena diffundens, omnem posteritatis sobolem contagio praevaricationis infecerat, et venit solvere inimicitias in carne sua, quas inter Deum et hominem noxius mediator effecerat? *Com. in Cant.* iii.

'Vinea enim Dominus Sabaoth domus Israel est, et domus Juda dilecta novella.' Istae ergo vineae cum primo accedunt ad fidem florere dicuntur; cum vero per religionem operum suorum suavitate adornantur, odorem suum dedisse dicuntur. Non sine causa puto quod non dixerit: odorem dederunt, sed odorem suum; ut ostenderet inesse unicuique animae vim possibilitatis et arbitrii libertatem qua possit agere omne quod bonum est. Sed quia hoc naturae bonum praevaricationis occasione decerptum, vel ad ignominiam, vel lasciviam fuerat inflexum, ubi per gratiam reparatur, et per doctrinam Verbi Dei restituitur, odorem reddit sine dubio illum, quem primus conditor Deus indiderat, sed peccati culpa subtraxerat. *Ibid.* iv.

[3] *In Rom.* v. Corpus ergo peccati est corpus nostrum; quia nec Adam scribitur cognovisse Evam uxorem suam et genuisse Cain, nisi post peccatum. In the sentences which follow, Origen again refers to the law of purification, to the texts from Job xiv. and Ps. li., and to the apostolic tradition that baptism should be administered to infants.

[4] *Ibid.* Quomodo autem in omnes homines pertransierit non ostendit. Videtur ergo mihi in his describere Apostolus velut tyranni alicujus ingressum, qui voluerit regnum legitimi regis invadere.

sin, of which the apostle speaks as 'entering into the world,' as subjective, in that he describes it by the word *contagio*[1]. But there are passages in the *Commentary on Romans* in which a 'Pelagian' explanation of the propagation of sin is offered[2].

Hence it is obvious that Origen taught, in this work, that the first sin was more than the beginning of sin, and that the sinfulness of subsequent generations was caused by the sin of Adam and its transmitted consequences.

When we inquire what were the means by which Origen regarded these consequences to be transmitted, we meet, in the Commentary in question, with the conceptions of (i) the inclusion of the race in Adam, (ii) physical heredity. When Origen interprets the Fall-story allegorically, he regards Adam simply as the type of mankind, after the manner of Philo.[3] But when he uses the narrative as actual history, he employs the two conceptions which have been mentioned, and connects them together by the notion of the race's physical potentiality, or seminal existence, in Adam, its first

---

[1] *In Rom.* v. Peccatum enim pertransiit etiam in justos, et levi quadam eos contagione perstrinxit.

[2] *Ibid.* Dedit ergo Adam peccatoribus formam per inobedientiam, Christus vero e contrario justis formam per obedientiam posuit,...ut qui obedientiae ejus sequuntur exemplum justi constituantur ab ipsa justitia, sicut illi inobedientiae formam sequentes, constituti sunt peccatores.

[3] "For as those whose business it is to defend the doctrine of providence do so by means of arguments which are not to be despised, so also the subjects of Adam and his son will be philosophically dealt with by those who are aware that in the Hebrew language Adam signifies man ; and that in those parts of the narrative which appear to refer to Adam as an individual, Moses is discoursing upon the nature of man in general ($\phi\upsilon\sigma\iota o\lambda o\gamma\epsilon\hat{\iota}$ Μωϋσῆς τὰ περὶ τῆς τοῦ ἀνθρώπου φύσεως). For "in Adam" (as the Scripture says) "all die," and were condemned in the likeness of Adam's transgression, the word of God asserting this not so much of *one particular individual* as of *the whole human race*. For in the connected series of statements which appears to apply as to one particular individual, the curse pronounced upon Adam is regarded as common to all [the members of the race], and what was spoken with reference to the woman is spoken of *every* woman without exception. And the expulsion of the man and woman from Paradise, and their being clothed with tunics of skins (which God, because of the transgression of men, made for those who had sinned), contain a certain secret and mystical doctrine (far transcending that of Plato) of the soul losing its wings, and being borne downwards to earth, until it can lay hold of some stable resting-place." *C. Celsum*, IV. 40 ; Eng. tr. Clark, *Ante-Nicene Library*.

father. He here borrows from the author of the Epistle to the Hebrews that writer's conception of Levi paying tithes to Melchisedek while yet in the loins of Abraham[1]. The bare identity of the race with Adam, without further definition as to mode, occurs in a much earlier work[2]. But the particular idea of race-unity of which Origen makes use, that, namely, of the seminal presence, in Adam, of all his posterity, appears here for the first time. Irenaeus, guided by S. Paul's indefinite and mystical conception of the solidarity of mankind with Adam, had stopped far short of so concrete and definite a notion as this which was suggested by the Epistle to the Hebrews. In this respect Origen makes a new departure in Christian speculation. So does he also in his conception of *sordes peccati*, the probable sources of which have already been mentioned. It is interesting to find, thus early in the Eastern Church, a precursor, in some important points, of S. Augustine: the more so because, though he owes something to S. Paul, he shows no sign of influence from Irenaeus

[1] *In Rom.* v.; Migne, *P.G.* XIV. 1009. Et primo videamus quomodo ' per unum hominem peccatum introivit in hunc mundum, et per peccatum mors.' Fortassis enim requirat aliquis si ante Adam mulier peccavit,...et rursum ante ipsam peccavit serpens......Sed vide in his Apostolum naturae ordinem tenuisse, et ideo quoniam de peccato loquebatur, ex quo mors in omnes homines pertransierat, successionem posteritatis humanae quae hinc morti succubuit ex peccato venienti, non mulieri ascribit, sed viro. Non enim ex muliere posteritas, sed ex viro nominatur...; et ob hoc mortalis posteritas, et corporalis successio, viro potius tanquam auctori, et non mulieri deputatur. Sed ut adhuc evidentius fiat quod dicimus, addemus etiam hoc quod idem Apostolus ad Hebraeos scribit : ' Sed et Levi qui decimas accepit, decimatus est. Adhuc enim in lumbis patris erat cum obviavit ei Melchisedech regresso a caede regum.' Si ergo Levi, qui generatione quarta post Abraham nascitur, in lumbis Abrahae fuisse perhibetur, multo magis omnes homines qui in hoc mundo nascuntur, et nati sunt, in lumbis erant Adae, cum adhuc esset in paradiso ; et omnes homines cum ipso vel in ipso expulsi sunt de paradiso, cum ipse inde depulsus est ; et per ipsum mors, quae ei ex praevaricatione venerat, consequenter et in eos pertransiit qui in lumbis ejus habebantur......Neque ergo ex serpente...neque ex muliere..., sed per Adam ex quo omnes mortales originem ducunt, dicitur introisse peccatum, et per peccatum mors.

[2] *Comm in Joann.* XX. 21. Inspice vero etiam hoc : ' In Adam omnes moriuntur...' et videbis vitam hominis qui est ad imaginem ; cujus vita considerata, intelliges quonam pacto homicida ille interfecerit viventem hominem ; recte dicendus homicida, non quia unum quempiam privatim interfecerit, sed propter universum genus a se interfectum ; unde in Adam omnes moriuntur.

or Tertullian, in his speculation on the Fall and the cause of human sinfulness. And it is the more important to emphasise this side of Origen's teaching because he is generally remembered rather for the very different, if not incompatible, line of thought, expressed in his theory of a pre-mundane fall of man.

CHAPTER XIII.

THE DOCTRINES OF THE FALL AND ORIGINAL SIN IN THE FATHERS BEFORE AUGUSTINE (*continued*).

V. METHODIUS, ATHANASIUS AND CYRIL OF JERUSALEM.

IN Origen's writings, it has been shown, there are to be found two diverse lines of thought with regard to the origin and universal spread of human sin. The one of these, suggested by passages of Holy Scripture and by a traditional Christian practice, anticipates certain fundamental points included in the later orthodox doctrine of Original Sin. The other represents mere speculation inspired by Platonic myth and the allegorical interpretation of Scripture current in the school of Alexandria. Of these two elements, which were incompatible with each other, the former would seem to have made little or no impression upon the teaching of the Eastern Fathers immediately succeeding Origen; and the positive influence of the latter, discernible perhaps in certain notions entertained with regard to man's original estate, was confined to the Cappadocian theology. The negative influence of the great Alexandrian's doctrine of a pre-mundane fall, however, is perhaps traceable in the unwillingness of all subsequent Fathers of the East readily and wholly to accept such definite teaching as to the consequences of the sin of Adam as was now being shaped and propagated in Western Christendom. The attitude towards these speculations of Origen with which we first meet in studying the history of Greek patristic thought on the subject of human sinfulness, is

308   *The Doctrine of the Fall etc.*   [CHAP.

one of reaction; of reaction, not, indeed, in the direction of the doctrine of Tertullian or Augustine, but in the sense of a return to literal interpretation of the Fall-story of Genesis and to the indefinite categories which characterised the thought of Irenaeus, and even earlier Greek writers, with regard to sin.

The most influential teachers of the Eastern Church for a century or so after Origen were Methodius and Athanasius. To these, particularly to the former of them, and also to Cyril of Jerusalem, the concluding remarks of the preceding paragraph are to be taken to apply. These Fathers, though rejecting Origen's speculations in their treatment of the problem of Sin, did not at all develope, so far as definiteness of expression is concerned, that side of his teaching which tended in the direction of later ecclesiastical orthodoxy. Methodius was an avowed and determined opponent of Origen; Athanasius, though educated in Alexandria, gradually threw aside more and more of the influence of Origen which he had there received, and left his great predecessor's speculations on ante-natal sin severely alone. Cyril may be mentioned in this place because he resembles the other two writers about to be discussed in receding from the stage of precision in thought and language with regard to the origin of human sinfulness which had previously been reached by Origen, rather than carrying such thought nearer to the definite and systematic formulation which it was soon elsewhere to receive.

Methodius.

Though an opponent of Origen's Platonism, Methodius was nevertheless himself somewhat of a Platonist. He also leaned much upon the Alexandrian Book of Wisdom, especially in his description of the Fall[1]. His anti-Origenism, which, by

[1] See Bonwetsch, *Methodius von Olympus*, I. *Schriften*, S. 50, 51.
Methodius identifies the serpent of Gen. iii. with Satan, and, in adopting the teaching of Wisdom, according to which envy was the devil's motive in tempting Eve, he embellishes his account after the manner of Jewish haggada. (See Bp. Bull's *Works*, vol. II. p. 297.) He also mentions, after the Alexandrian apocalyptic work *Slavonic Enoch*, that Adam, before the Fall, had vision of the angels and of Wisdom. See Bonwetsch, *op. cit.* S. 75.

XIII] *in the Fathers before Augustine* 309

the way, leads him to abandon the Hellenism of the Book of Wisdom so far as to deny that the body is a fetter to the soul[1], is revealed in his repeated insistence on the fact that Adam was 'in the flesh' when he sinned[2], in his frequent denial that the 'coats of skins' signified human bodies, and in his repudiation of the notion that Paradise was in heaven[3], and that Adam had been banished thence to earth. Sin, Methodius repeatedly affirms, is wrought through the flesh[4]. In the place of this Origenist teaching which he destructively criticises, Methodius gives us little that is positive. He maintains, like the Greek Fathers generally, that since the Fall man's freedom of will is not diminished[5]. He holds indeed that the Fall brought physical consequences to mankind[6], including death—for man was created immortal[7]. In this latter connexion he quotes S. Paul (1 Cor. xv. 22), in a passage in which he uses, and moreover developes, the Recapitulation-doctrine of Irenaeus[8].

From the passages cited below, in illustration of the last statement, it will be seen that Methodius was anxious to

[1] *op. cit.* S. 116, and *passim.*   [2] *Ibid.* S. 75.
[3] *Ibid.* S. 172.   [4] *Ibid.* S. 76, 77; 196.
[5] *Ibid.* S. 46, 177, etc.
[6] *Ibid.* S. 74, etc. In Methodius we find the curious idea that man was banished from the tree of life in order that sin might be killed in him before his resurrection; *Ibid.* S. 136.
[7] *Conviv. dec. virg.* IX. 2.
[8] ταύτῃ γὰρ τὸν ἄνθρωπον ἀνείληφεν ὁ λόγος, ὅπως δὴ δι' αὐτοῦ καταλύσῃ τὴν ἐπ' ὀλέθρῳ γεγονυῖαν καταδίκην, ἡττήσας τὸν ὄφιν, ἥρμοζε γὰρ μὴ δι' ἑτέρου νικηθῆναι τὸν πονηρὸν ἀλλὰ δι' ἐκείνου, ὃν δὴ καὶ ἐκόμπαζεν ἀπατήσας αὐτὸν τετυραννηκέναι, ὅτι μὴ ἄλλως τὴν ἁμαρτίαν λυθῆναι καὶ τὴν κατάκρισιν δυνατὸν ἦν, εἰ μὴ πάλιν ὁ αὐτὸς ἐκεῖνος ἄνθρωπος, δι' ὃν εἴρητο τὸ "γῆ εἶ καὶ εἰς γῆν ἀπελεύσῃ," ἀναπλασθεὶς ἀνέλυσε τὴν ἀπόφασιν τὴν δι' αὐτὸν εἰς πάντας ἐξενηνεγμένην. ὅπως, καθὼς ἐν τῷ Ἀδὰμ πρότερον πάντες ἀποθνήσκουσιν, οὕτω δὴ πάλιν καὶ ἐν τῷ ἀνειληφότι Χριστῷ τὸν Ἀδὰμ πάντες ζωοποιηθῶσιν. *Ibid.* III. 6.
Cf. III. 4. φέρε γὰρ ἡμεῖς ἐπισκεψώμεθα πῶς ὀρθοδόξως ἀνήγαγε τὸν Ἀδὰμ εἰς τὸν Χριστόν, οὐ μόνον τύπον αὐτὸν ἡγούμενος εἶναι καὶ εἰκόνα, ἀλλὰ καὶ αὐτὸ τοῦτο Χριστὸν καὶ αὐτὸν γεγονέναι διὰ τὸ τὸν πρὸ αἰώνων εἰς αὐτὸν ἐγκατασκῆψαι λόγον. ἥρμοζε γὰρ τὸ πρωτόγονον τοῦ θεοῦ καὶ πρῶτον βλάστημα καὶ μονογενὲς τὴν σοφίαν τῷ πρωτοπλάστῳ καὶ πρώτῳ καὶ πρωτογόνῳ τῶν ἀνθρώπων ἀνθρώπῳ κερασθεῖσαν ἐνηνθρωπηκέναι, τοῦτο γὰρ εἶναι τὸν Χριστόν, ἄνθρωπον ἐν ἀκράτῳ θεότητι καὶ τελείᾳ πεπληρωμένον καὶ θεὸν ἐν ἀνθρώπῳ κεχωρημένον· ἦν γὰρ πρεπωδέστατον τὸν πρεσβύτατον τῶν αἰώνων καὶ πρῶτον ἀρχαγγέλων, ἀνθρώποις μέλλοντα συνομιλεῖν, εἰς τὸν πρεσβύτατον καὶ πρῶτον τῶν ἀνθρώπων εἰσοικισθῆναι τὸν Ἀδάμ.

retain the literal or historical sense of Gen. iii. against Origen's allegorical interpretation of the narrative contained in it, and that, to do so, he resorted to a kind of realism such as had already served the purpose of Irenaeus. Adam stood for the whole race in its natural and imperfect state. The same undefined solidarity of mankind with Adam is implied in the words: "the Paradise out of which *we were driven* through the protoplast[1]." Such language does not express any definite theory of our relation to Adam such as is implied, for instance, in Origen's conception of the race's potential (seminal) existence in its first father; it rather recalls the vaguer language of earlier times with its several possible but undifferentiated meanings.

Methodius is equally indefinite in his conception of inherent sinfulness and its cause. "When man had disobeyed," he writes, "sin established its seat in him. Deprived of the divine breath, we have since that time been at the mercy of the passions which the serpent put in us[2]." This is the nearest approach he makes to the doctrine of inherited taint derived from fallen Adam. His doctrine of redemption from a state of φθορά[3] is not expressed in terms of such inherited tendency to evil; φθορά describes an ethical state without specifying anything as to the derivation or mode of diffusion of the state. We cannot discover, in short, in the extant writings of Methodius, any link between the position already reached in the East by Origen and the more highly elaborated theory of Original Sin which is especially associated with the name of S. Augustine.

Athanasius.

In treating of Sin and Redemption, Athanasius, like Methodius, makes use of the predominantly ethical category φθορά, which is indefinite in its significance for anthropological doctrine. This word apparently describes, in the writings of Athanasius, man's "natural" state, of which this Father held an estimate lower than that of his predecessors. The race of

---

[1] Bonwetsch, *op. cit.* S. 170.
[2] Preserved in Eusebius, *Haer.* lxiv. 60.
[3] *Conviv. dec. virg.* III. 7, etc.

XIII] *in the Fathers before Augustine* 311

men, according to his teaching, would not have had from the first, and in virtue of their own nature, the power of "continuing always[1]." Man, indeed, is "mortal by nature[2]," or "corruptible by nature[3]." Mankind might have avoided what was according to nature had they remained good or incorruptible, and might have escaped the state of corruption by retaining the "virtue of (God's) own Word, so that, possessing, as it were, certain reflections of the Word, and becoming rational, they might be capable of continuing in happiness, living the true life, and actually that of the saints in Paradise[4]."

This 'natural state' of man is, of course, quite different from the primitive or unfallen state. The life for which man was destined from the first was, for Athanasius to a much greater extent thàn for the Greek Fathers in general, the outcome of divine grace, or of superadded divine gifts. As a natural[5] being man is quite unable to maintain his proper relation to God, according to the teaching of Athanasius; but in virtue of creation after the divine image (εἰκών) he is enabled to do so.

The Fall is conceived by Athanasius as a lapse of mankind to the 'natural state.' In other words, the Fall is represented as consisting in the loss of what more modern theology has called supernatural endowments[6]. From the first transgression

---

[1] *De Incarn.* 3. ἐν οἷς πρὸ πάντων τῶν ἐπὶ γῆς τὸ ἀνθρώπων γένος ἐλεήσας, καὶ θεωρήσας ὡς οὐχ ἱκανὸν εἴη κατὰ τὸν τῆς ἰδίας γενέσεως λόγον διαμένειν ἀεί......

[2] *Ibid.* 4. Ἔστι μὲν γὰρ κατὰ φύσιν ἄνθρωπος θνητός.

[3] *Ibid.* 5. κατὰ φύσιν φθαρτοί.

These statements in the *De Incarn.* need, however, to be qualified by others occurring elsewhere in the writings of Athanasius, and even in the *De Incarn.* itself. See, on this subject, Harnack, *History of Dogma*, E. T. vol. III. p. 273.

[4] *De Incarn.* 3.

[5] The distinction between the natural and supernatural constituents of man was variously drawn in Athanasius' time; they are not always clearly distinguished by Athanasius himself.

[6] *De Incarn.* 4. Οὕτως μὲν οὖν ὁ θεὸς τὸν ἄνθρωπον πεποίηκε, καὶ μένειν ἠθέλησεν ἐν ἀφθαρσίᾳ· ἄνθρωποι δὲ καταλιγωρήσαντες καὶ ἀποστραφέντες τὴν πρὸς τὸν θεὸν κατανόησιν, λογισάμενοι δὲ καὶ ἐπινοήσαντες ἑαυτοῖς τὴν κακίαν, ὥσπερ ἐν τοῖς πρώτοις ἐλέχθη, ἔσχον τὴν προαπειληθεῖσαν τοῦ θανάτου κατάκρισιν, καὶ λοιπὸν οὐκ ἔτι, ὡς γεγόνασι, διέμενον· ἀλλ' ὡς ἐλογίζοντο, διεφθείροντο· καὶ ὁ θάνατος αὐτῶν ἐκράτει βασιλεύων. Ἡ γὰρ παράβασις τῆς ἐντολῆς εἰς τὸ κατὰ φύσιν αὐτοὺς ἐπέστρεφεν...

Ibid. 7. Εἰ μὲν οὖν μόνον ἦν πλημμέλημα καὶ μὴ φθορᾶς ἐπακολούθησις, καλῶς

312   *The Doctrine of the Fall etc.*   [CHAP.

onwards, mankind have been reduced to the condition of nature above which they were originally raised by the ψυχὴ λογική, which, though in some of its aspects regarded as a natural endowment, is nevertheless rather a superadded gift of grace[1]. In this state of nature, into which Adam fell, all subsequent generations have been born. But this universal fall does not seem to be ascribed definitely to the one great sin of Adam, so that all the race sinned in him or with him, or were constituted sinners in consequence of his transgression and independently of their own actual sins. On the contrary, Athanasius regards the fallen state of the race as a whole as having been brought about gradually[2].

ἂν ἦν ἡ μετάνοια. Εἰ δὲ ἅπαξ προλαβούσης τῆς παραβάσεως, εἰς τὴν κατὰ φύσιν φθορὰν ἐκρατοῦντο οἱ ἄνθρωποι, καὶ τὴν τοῦ κατ' εἰκόνα χάριν ἀφαιρεθέντες ἦσαν, τί ἄλλο ἔδει γενέσθαι;

[1] See *De Incarn.* 3, and cf. *C. Arian.* II. 68. Ὁ Ἀδὰμ πρὸ τῆς παραβάσεως ἔξωθεν ἦν, λαβὼν τὴν χάριν καὶ μὴ συνηρμοσμένην ἔχων αὐτὴν τῷ σώματι.

[2] *De Incarn.* 6. Διὰ δὴ ταῦτα πλεῖον τοῦ θανάτου κρατήσαντος, καὶ τῆς φθορᾶς παραμενούσης κατὰ τῶν ἀνθρώπων, τὸ μὲν τῶν ἀνθρώπων γένος ἐφθείρετο· ὁ δὲ λογικὸς καὶ κατ' εἰκόνα γενόμενος ἄνθρωπος ἠφανίζετο. (Note tenses.)

Ch. 5 of this same treatise also serves as an illustration of the statement asserted above. The following sentences may be cited from it, the translation being that of Robertson in the *Library of Nicene and p. Nicene Fathers*: "For God has not only made us out of nothing; but He gave us freely, by the grace of the Word, a life in correspondence with God. But men, having rejected things eternal, and, by the counsel of the devil, turned to the things of corruption, became the cause of their own corruption in death, being, as I said before, by nature corruptible, but destined, by the grace following from partaking of the Word, to have escaped their natural state, had they remained good. For because of the Word dwelling with them, even their natural corruption did not come near them, as Wisdom also says: "God made man for incorruption, and as an image of His own eternity; but by the envy of the devil death came into the world." But when this was come to pass, men began to die, while corruption thenceforward prevailed against them, gaining even more than its natural power over the whole race, inasmuch as it had, owing to the transgression of the commandment, the threat of the Deity as a further advantage against them. For even in their misdeeds men had not stopped short at any set limits; but gradually pressing forward, have passed on beyond all measure; having, to begin with, been inventors of wickedness and called down upon themselves death and corruption; while later on, having turned aside to wrong and exceeding all lawlessness, and stopping at no one evil but devising all manner of new evils in succession, they have become insatiable in sinning."

This citation embodies, perhaps, all the essential features of Athanasius's teaching as to the Fall. It also serves to suggest that his doctrine of the state of φθορά was, at least in part, derived from Pseudo-Solomon's use of θάνατος in an ethical sense.

XIII] *in the Fathers before Augustine* 313

The transgression of Adam does not seem, therefore, to have been always regarded by Athanasius "as forming a tremendous cleavage" in human history. "That was not the characteristic view of Athanasius," Prof. Harnack says[1]; certainly it is not the view characteristic of the *De Incarnatione*. In other writings of this Father, however, we meet with expressions which bespeak a nearer approach to the later doctrine of Original Sin. Athanasius was by no means 'a Pelagian before Pelagius.' Although his language lacks the precision of that of later, and indeed of some earlier, Fathers, so that it is difficult to ascertain *how*, precisely, he conceived sin to be propagated, or the race to be related to Adam and to be concerned in Adam's sin, he nevertheless is more explicit than, for instance, Methodíus. He certainly held that, in some sense, Adam's sin passed over to us. He taught that Christ's sacrifice was offered "that He might make all men upright and free from the old transgression[2]." In one passage he says that Adam's sin was made to spread over all by the devil[3]; a unique way of expressing the propagation of original sin, and one which embodies only the smaller half of the Augustinian theory on the point. More usually he expresses himself in more general terms, which do not specify the precise mode in which Adam's sin passed to his posterity[4]. If any such mode is implied at all, it is perhaps that of ordinary inheritance by means of physical descent. This certainly appears to be the implication of one or two passages in the writings of Athanasius[5], though it is never very explicitly expressed.

[1] *Op. cit.* p. 274. Perhaps this opinion receives confirmation from the occurrence, in the writings of Athanasius, of statements to the effect that some individual men have existed who were free from sin; see *C. gentes* 2, *C. Arian.* III. 33, and cf. I. 39. But possibly actual sin alone was, in these cases, before the writer's mind.

[2] *De Incarn.* 20; ἐλευθέρους τῆς ἀρχαίας παραβάσεως. In *C. Apollin.* I. 15, he says: "human nature arises in sin and receives the consequences of sin."

[3] *Ibid.* II. 9.

[4] *e.g. C. Arian.* I. 51. τοῦ Ἀδὰμ παραβάντος, εἰς πάντας τοὺς ἀνθρώπους ἔφθασεν ἡ ἁμαρτία; cf. *Expos. in Ps.* xv. 8, "Through Adam's sin were we banished from God's face"; *C. Arian.* II. 60, "All men were lost through his sin"; and see *ibid.* I. 41, *De Trin. et Spiritu Sanct.* 21.

[5] *C. Apoll.* I. 15, cited above; *C. Arian.* II. 14, "Before we were, we were subject to the curse of the law and to corruption." See also *Expos. in Ps.* li.

314   *The Doctrine of the Fall etc.*   [CHAP.

Similar deficiency of explicitness usually attaches to this Father's language as to our solidarity in Adam. Athanasius often speaks as if Adam were, in some sense, the sum of all men: "We all die in Adam[1]"; "God had turned away from human nature because of its transgression of the law in Adam[2]." And once or twice he seems to have expressed this solidarity in terms of the conception of the race's potential inclusion in Adam, the first parent of the race being, as it were, the seed inclosing the race in embryo. Thus he says: "Although Adam alone was formed out of the earth, yet in him were the grounds of the succession of the whole race[3]." Our birth in continuous descent from Adam is also emphasised[4].

These citations will suffice to show that Athanasius held some of the more important ideas essential to the doctrine of Original Sin derived from Adam, but in relatively undeveloped form. His teaching on the subject differs from that later formulated by Augustine chiefly by his lack of emphasis on the subjective or psychological aspect of original sin, and the absence of any identification of it with concupiscence or a disturbance of man's nature[5].

Cyril of Jerusalem.

In connexion with the doctrine of the two Fathers with whom we have last been concerned, a few illustrations may be given of the teaching, with regard to the Fall and its consequences, of another representative of Pre-Augustinian thought in the Eastern Church, who is more naturally associated with Methodius and Athanasius than with either of the two groups of oriental writers which still remain to be mentioned.

---

[1] *C. Arian.* I. 59.
[2] *Expos. in Ps.* lxviii. 18.
[3] *C. Arian.* II. 48. Εἰ γὰρ καὶ ὁ Ἀδὰμ ἐκ τῆς γῆς μόνος ἐπλάσθη, ἀλλ' ἐν αὐτῷ ἦσαν οἱ λόγοι τῆς διαδοχῆς παντὸς τοῦ γένους.
[4] *De decr. Nic. syn.* 8; see also *C. Arian.* IV. 30.
[5] The writer would here acknowledge his indebtedness, in collecting some of the references given above, to the monographs on S. Athanasius and his doctrine published by the German scholars Stäter and Pell.

XIII] *in the Fathers before Augustine* 315

Cyril was less directly concerned with the doctrines here under discussion than even Methodius or Athanasius. His allusions to their subject-matter are yet more fragmentary and more incidental. He clearly recognises one of the universal consequences of Adam's fall:

" And yet one man's sin, even Adam's, had power to bring death into the world; but if by one man's offence death reigned over the world, how shall not life much rather reign by the righteousness of One?...

"If the first man formed out of the earth brought in universal death, shall not He who formed him out of the earth bring in everlasting life, being Himself life[1]?"

This passage only refers to physical death. As regards sin, however, Cyril further recognises that our first parent's transgression was also ours. The universality of sin, upon which he sometimes comments[2], is in one or two places associated with the Fall. Thus, after mentioning Adam's temptation and sin, Cyril writes:

"What then? some will say. We have been seduced and are lost; is there no chance of salvation? We have fallen... We have been blinded...We have been crippled...In a word we are dead[3]."

And again, after speaking of the universality of sin, he says, in connexion with the Fall, " Very great was the wound of our nature[4]."

These passages, however, do not specify by what process, or in what respects, our nature was affected by our first parent's sin. There is likewise no explanation of our solidarity in Adam or in the consequences of his sin, nor any reference to inborn taint. Indeed Cyril of Jerusalem, after the manner of Clement of Alexandria, seems not to recognise any such hereditary bias to evil in man, and he identifies human corruption with personal sin[5]. So also in

---

[1] *Cat.* XIII. 2, Eng. tr. *Library of the Fathers*, Oxford.
[2] *Ibid.* XII. 6 7 etc.
[3] *Ibid.* II. 5.   [4] *Ibid.* XII. 7.
[5] *Ibid.* IV. 19. Ἐλθόντες εἰς τόνδε τὸν κόσμον ἀναμάρτητοι, νῦν ἐκ προαιρέσεως ἁμαρτάνομεν. Cf. XIII. 1.

treating of the sacrament of Baptism, it is only actual or personal sin of whose remission he speaks. He represents our life as beginning in a state of innocence, and our freewill as unimpaired[1]. It may be that he thus intends merely to set aside Origen's speculations as to a fall in a previous state of existence; but in any case his expressions are very unguarded for a writer subsequent to Origen, and seem to imply scanty recognition, on his part, of the tendencies of the thought of his time with regard to inborn sinfulness and the far-reaching consequences of the first transgression.

VI. THE CAPPADOCIANS.

Basil.

Basil's utterances with regard to the Fall and its consequences are neither numerous nor important. They serve, however, to illustrate a stage in the development from the position of Athanasius to that of Gregory of Nyssa, who best represents the tendencies of Cappadocian theology.

Basil's writings witness to the growth, taking place during the period in which he lived, of the doctrine of man's primitive state; also to the permanent incorporation into Christian tradition of the Jewish legend as to 'the envy of the devil.' It was the angelic dignity of unfallen man which, according to this Father's embellishment of the bare statement of the Book of Wisdom, excited Satan's jealousy[2].

The unfallen state of grace, which man has forfeited through sin, is the state also to which redemption is to bring us. Redemption, in fact, is regarded as a rescue from the effects of the Fall. Thus:

"The dispensation of God and our Saviour towards man is the recalling him from the Fall, and his return into the

---

[1] *Ibid.* IV. 21. Αὐτεξούσιός ἐστιν ἡ ψυχή, καὶ ὁ διάβολος τὸ μὲν ὑποβάλλειν δύναται· τὸ δὲ καὶ ἀναγκάσαι παρὰ προαίρεσιν οὐκ ἔχει τὴν ἐξουσίαν.

[2] *Quod Deus non est auctor mali*, 6. Ὁρῶν γὰρ ἑαυτὸν ἐκ τῶν ἀγγέλων καταρριφέντα, οὐκ ἔφερε βλέπειν τὸν γήϊνον ἐπὶ τὴν ἀξίαν τῶν ἀγγέλων διὰ προκοπῆς ἀνυψούμενον. See also a passage of greater fulness, quoted by Bp. Bull, *Works*, vol. II. p. 299, from Basil, ed. Paris, 1638, tom. I. p. 468.

XIII] *in the Fathers before Augustine* 317

friendship of God from that estrangement which sin had caused¹."

Again Basil teaches that the Holy Spirit "renews us and makes us again the image of God; and by the laver of regeneration and the renewing of the Holy Ghost, we are adopted to the Lord, and the new creature again partakes of the Spirit, of which being deprived, it had waxed old. And thus man becomes again the image of God, who had fallen from the divine similitude, and was become like the beasts that perish²."

This passage implies, of course, that Adam's sin affected all his posterity, in that the divine image was lost once and for all by man when Adam fell. Elsewhere Basil states that Adam transmitted death³, and also sin⁴, to mankind; indeed our first parent's transgression is imputed to all and makes all men actual sinners⁵.

Beyond this, however, Basil does not carry us. He never defines more precisely the mode in which our solidarity with

¹ *De Spiritu Sancto*, c. 15. Migne, *P.G.* XXXII. 128. Ἡ τοῦ θεοῦ καὶ Σωτῆρος ἡμῶν περὶ τὸν ἄνθρωπον οἰκονομία ἀνάκλησίς ἐστιν ἀπὸ τῆς ἐκπτώσεως, καὶ ἐπάνοδος εἰς οἰκείωσιν θεοῦ ἀπὸ τῆς διὰ τὴν παρακοὴν γενομένης ἀλλοτριώσεως. Διὰ τοῦτο ἡ μετὰ σαρκὸς ἐπιδημία Χριστοῦ, αἱ τῶν εὐαγγελικῶν πολιτευμάτων ὑποτυπώσεις, τὰ πάθη, ὁ σταυρός, ἡ ταφή, ἡ ἀνάστασις· ὥστε τὸν σωζόμενον ἄνθρωπον διὰ μιμήσεως Χριστοῦ τὴν ἀρχαίαν ἐκείνην υἱοθεσίαν ἀπολαβεῖν. With the teaching here given cf. that of Athanasius, *De Incarn.* cc. 4 and 8.

² *Adv. Eunomium* (quoted by Bull, *op. cit.* p. 329). Ἐν ἁγιασμῷ τοῦ Πνεύματος ἐκλήθημεν, ὡς ὁ ἀπόστολος διδάσκει, τοῦτο ἡμᾶς ἀνακαινοῖ, καὶ πάλιν εἰκόνας ἀναδείκνυσι θεοῦ, διὰ λουτροῦ παλιγγενεσίας, καὶ ἀνακαινώσεως Πνεύματος ἁγίου υἱοθετούμεθα Κυρίῳ· καινὴ πάλιν κτίσις μεταλαμβάνουσα τοῦ Πνεύματος, οὗπερ ἐστερημένη πεπαλαίωτο, εἰκὼν πάλιν θεοῦ ὁ ἄνθρωπος ἐκπεσὼν τῆς ὁμοιότητος τῆς θείας, καὶ παρασυμβληθεὶς κτήνεσιν ἀνόητος καὶ ὁμοιωθεὶς αὐτοῖς.

³ *Sermo de renunt. saeculi*, 7 (M. XXXI. 640). Αὕτη (γαστριμαργία) τὸν Ἀδὰμ θανάτῳ παρέδωκε, καὶ τῷ κόσμῳ συντέλειαν ἐπήγαγε διὰ τὴν τῆς γαστρὸς ἡδονήν.

⁴ *Homil. in famem et sicc.*, c. 7. ὡς γὰρ Ἀδὰμ κακῶς φαγὼν τὴν ἁμαρτίαν παρέπεμψεν.

⁵ *Epist.* CCLXI. 2. Migne, *P.G.* XXXII. 969. Εἰ γὰρ ἄλλο μὲν ἦν τὸ βασιλευόμενον ὑπὸ τοῦ θανάτου, ἄλλο δὲ τὸ παρὰ τοῦ Κυρίου προσληφθέν, οὐκ ἂν μὲν ἐπαύσατο τὰ ἑαυτοῦ ἐνεργῶν ὁ θάνατος· οὐκ ἂν δὲ ἡμέτερον κέρδος ἐγένετο τῆς σαρκὸς τῆς θεοφόρου τὰ πάθη· οὐκ ἀπέκτεινε δὲ τὴν ἁμαρτίαν ἐν τῇ σαρκί· οὐκ ἐζωοποιήθημεν ἐν τῷ Χριστῷ οἱ ἐν τῷ Ἀδὰμ ἀποθανόντες· οὐκ ἀνεπλάσθη τὸ διαπεπτωκός· οὐκ ἀνωρθώθη τὸ κατερραγμένον· οὐ προσῳκειώθη τῷ θεῷ τὸ διὰ τῆς ἀπάτης τοῦ ὄφεως ἀλλοτριωθέν....τίς δὲ χρεία τῆς ἁγίας Παρθένου, εἰ μὴ ἐκ τοῦ φυράματος τοῦ Ἀδὰμ ἔμελλεν ἡ θεοφόρος σὰρξ προσλαμβάνεσθαι.

318 *The Doctrine of the Fall etc.* [CHAP.

Adam is to be conceived, the nature of the 'sin' which he vaguely states to have been 'transmitted,' nor the means by which such transmission was actually effected. As to hereditary taint, or inheritance of a corrupted nature, he appears to be wholly silent.

Gregory of Nazianzus.

Gregory of Nazianzus, like his namesake of Nyssa, shows more of the influence of Origen upon his doctrine of man than does Basil. He identifies the Paradise whence Adam was expelled with the celestial place to which S. Paul was caught up[1], though he definitely repudiates the theory of a pre-mundane fall of souls[2]. Perhaps there is also a trace of Origenism in his use of the Fall-story of Genesis after the manner of an allegory, as if it applied to mankind in general.

This Father sometimes speaks of Adam's sin as having brought punishment or condemnation upon us all[3]. He also calls it 'our' sin, thereby implying some undefined form of the doctrine which was soon to occupy an all-important place in the theology of Augustine[4]. Gregory, in fact, held the doctrine of Original Guilt.

---

[1] *In Psalm.* cxviii. IV. 2.
[2] *Orat.* xxxvii. 15, cited below, p. 321.
[3] *Orat.* xxxix. 16. "Adam closed heaven, like Paradise, to all his descendants."
Orat. xxii. 13. Ἐχρῆν γάρ, ἐπειδὴ θεότης ἤνωται, διαιρεῖσθαι τὴν ἀνθρωπότητα, καὶ περὶ τὸν νοῦν ἀνοηταίνειν τοὺς τἄλλα σοφούς· καὶ μὴ ὅλον με σώζεσθαι, ὅλον πταίσαντα καὶ κατακριθέντα ἐκ τῆς τοῦ πρωτοπλάστου παρακοῆς, καὶ κλοπῆς τοῦ ἀντικειμένου.

Turmel, *op. cit.*, gives the following citations and references:
καὶ οὕτως ὁ νέος Ἀδὰμ τὸν παλαιὸν ἀνασώσηται καὶ λυθῇ τὸ κατάκριμα τῆς σαρκός, σαρκὶ τοῦ θανάτου θανατωθέντος. (*Orat.* xxxix. 13.) "Since those whom the enjoyment of the forbidden tree has condemned (κατέκρινε) have been justified through the passion of Christ." (*Orat.* xxxviii. 4.)

[4] Μὴ βαρυνέσθω δὲ ὁ ζυγός, μηδὲ τῆς πρώτης ἡμῶν ἁμαρτίας τὸ ἐπιτίμιον. *Orat.* xix. 13. Cf. *Orat.* xxxiii. 9 (Migne, *P. G.* XXXVI. 225). ...πάντες δὲ οἱ τοῦ αὐτοῦ Ἀδὰμ μετασχόντες, καὶ ὑπὸ τοῦ ὄφεως παραλογισθέντες, καὶ τῇ ἁμαρτίᾳ θανατωθέντες, καὶ διὰ τοῦ ἐπουρανίου Ἀδὰμ ἀνασωθέντες, καὶ πρὸς τὸ ξύλον τῆς ζωῆς ἐπαναχθέντες διὰ τοῦ ξύλου τῆς ἀτιμίας, ὅθεν ἀποπεπτώκαμεν.
Cf. also *Orat.* xliv. 4 (M. XXXVI. 611). Εἰ μὲν οὖν ἐμείναμεν, ὅπερ ἦμεν, καὶ τὴν ἐντολὴν ἐφυλάξαμεν, ἐγενόμεθα ἂν ὅπερ οὐκ ἦμεν, τῷ ξύλῳ τῆς ζωῆς προσελθόντες, μετὰ τὸ ξύλον τῆς γνώσεως.

XIII] *in the Fathers before Augustine* 319

He is not more definite in his allusions to transmitted sin in the subjective sense of that term, *i.e.* hereditary taint or sinful tendency. Indeed he only seems to hint once or twice at such a conception: and when he does so, fleshly birth is suggested as the means whereby such moral taint is handed down. He quotes the well-known verse of Job (xxv. 4), in which the inherent defilement attaching to every mortal is spoken of[1]: but he does not cite it in connexion with the doctrine of the Fall. He emphasises, however, the Virgin-birth of our Lord, as a means whereby we are freed from " the fetters of our birth[2]." He also regarded infants, dying without baptism, as excluded from the glory of heaven, though not as condemned to suffer pains[3]. The innocence which he ascribes to them may of course be merely innocence of actual sin, and his teaching on this subject may be independent of the presuppositions involved in the doctrine of Original Sin, though it is perhaps more natural to infer that his denial of the glories of heaven to the unbaptised was in some way connected with the doctrine of our condemnation for Adam's sin.

Gregory stops considerably short of the teaching of Augustine, though he was appealed to by the latter Father as a witness to the catholicity of his views. Gregory was far from asserting the total depravity of man or the loss of his free-will; but he held that mankind had become impaired in body and soul, and had passed into a state of condemnation, in consequence of Adam's sin.

Gregory of Nyssa.

Of the three great Cappadocian divines Gregory of Nyssa was the most systematic as a theologian and philosopher. For this reason, perhaps, we find in his writings a somewhat fuller treatment of the doctrine of the Fall, and the use of

[1] *Orat.* xiv. 30 (M. xxxv. 897). καθαρὸς γὰρ ἀπὸ ῥύπου παντελῶς οὐδείς, οὐκ οὖν ἐν γεννητῇ φύσει, ὥσπερ ἠκούσαμεν.
[2] τῶν δεσμῶν τῆς γεννήσεως, *Orat.* xxxviii. 17.
[3] *Orat.* xl. 23.
χείρους δὲ οὗτοι, τῶν ἐξ ἀγνοίας καὶ τυραννίδος ἀποπιπτόντων τῆς δωρεᾶς...τοὺς δὲ μήτε δοξασθήσεσθαι, μήτε κολασθήσεσθαι παρὰ τοῦ δικαίου κριτοῦ, ὡς ἀσφραγίστους μέν, ἀπονήρους δέ, ἀλλὰ παθόντας μᾶλλον τὴν ζημίαν, ἢ δράσαντας.

somewhat more precise language in its exposition, than we meet with in the works of the two theologians last considered. The influence of Origen's speculation on the Fall is distinctly traceable in the anthropology of Gregory of Nyssa. The coats of skin, wherewith Adam and Eve were clothed after their transgression, are explained as denoting mortality, or the bodily consequences of the Fall[1]; and man is not only declared to have been originally immortal[2], but also, as will presently be seen, almost angelic in nature. Further, the Fall bestowed upon us all we share in common with the irrational creatures[3]. As a particular case of such a general consequence, Gregory held that human generation is one result of the fall of man. And this view is not only adopted when he is concerned to uphold the dignity of the state of virginity[4]. It is implied upon other occasions; for he tells us that, had there been no Fall, the human race would have multiplied after the manner of the angels[5]. On the other hand, a contrary opinion finds expression in his writings[6].

But in spite of these opinions, which certainly must be called Semi-Origenistic, Gregory did not accept, in its entirety, the earlier of Origen's theories as to the nature of the Fall. Indeed he repudiated the idea of a pre-existent state and of

---

[1] See *Orat. Catech.* c. 8 (Migne, *P.G.* XLV. 33), where the 'skins' are explained to mean mortality; also *De Anima et Resurr.* (M. XLVI. 148) where they signify birth, generation, gradual growth, age, sickness, as well as death, and are explained as τὸ σχῆμα τῆς ἀλόγου φύσεως, ᾧ πρὸς τὸ πάθος οἰκειωθέντες περιεβλήθημεν. Cf. also *De Virginit.* c. 12, where the coats of skin are identified with τὸ φρόνημα τῆς σαρκός.

This interpretation of the coats of skin, associated above chiefly with the name of Origen, is, however, not in the first instance due to that Father. It is found in Clement of Alexandria, and was used also by the Gnostics. Its source has indeed been thought to be rabbinical. But Origen used it in the interests of his Platonic doctrines of pre-existence and the fall of souls, and it is in this connexion that it chiefly concerns us here.

[2] *Vita Moysis* (M. XLIV. 397; cf. XLV. 33. C).

[3] *De Anima et Resurr.* (M. XLVI. 148). ἐπεὶ οὖν ὅσα ἐκ τῆς ἀλόγου ζωῆς τῇ ἀνθρωπίνῃ κατεμίχθη φύσει οὐ πρότερον ἦν ἐν ἡμῖν πρὶν εἰς πάθος διὰ κακίας πεσεῖν τὸ ἀνθρώπινον.... See, further, M. XLVI. 373, 376.

[4] *De Virginit.* c. 12 (M. XLVI., cf. 377, etc.).
A similar view to this occurs in the *Apocalypse of Baruch*; see above, p. 215.

[5] *De Hom. opif.* cc. 16, 17, etc.

[6] *Orat. Catech.* c. 28 (M. XLV. 73).

XIII] *in the Fathers before Augustine* 321

the entrance of human souls into this world in consequence of their defection from good in another world[1].

Thus Gregory was led to depict the paradisaic state of our first parents as in some sense heavenly, or angelic, though he stopped short of Origen's belief that the human race enjoyed this heaven-like life in another and higher world than this. His Origenistic tendencies are, doubtless, mainly responsible for his undue exaltation of the unfallen state of Adam[2].

It will already be manifest, from the foregoing statements and citations from Gregory's works, that this Father taught that the Fall introduced death into the world for all, and that, in consequence of that catastrophe, the nature of man's body was changed and concupiscence arose.

Passing on to inquire into Gregory's usage of the conception of man's solidarity with Adam, we again, perhaps, find his thought moulded chiefly by Origenistic, or at least Hellenic, speculation. We have seen that this Father's adherence to the traditional and literal interpretation of the early chapters of Genesis was very loose. It must further be pointed out that he often uses 'Adam' as equivalent to 'the race,' or rather to the human nature common to the race[3]. Gregory thus supplies a link between Origen's conception of

[1] See *De Hom. Opif.* cc. 28, 29.
Harnack, *op. cit.* vol. III. p. 277, says: "though Gregory rejected Origen's theories of the pre-existence of souls, the pre-temporal fall, and the world as a place of punishment, regarding them as Hellenic dogmas and therefore mythological, yet he was dominated by the fundamental thought which led Origen to the above view."
It was mentioned above that Gregory of Nazianzus similarly declined to accept completely the theory of Origen. This Father's words may here be quoted: φοβοῦμαι μὴ καὶ ἄτοπός τις εἰσέλθῃ λογισμὸς ὡς τῆς ψυχῆς ἀλλαχοῦ πολιτευσαμένης, εἶτα τῷ σώματι τούτῳ ἐνδεθείσης. Greg. Naz. *Orat.* XXXVII. 15.

[2] *De hom. opif.* c. 17. Ἡ δὲ τῆς ἀναστάσεως χάρις οὐδὲν ἕτερον ἡμῖν ἐπαγγέλλεται, ἢ τὴν εἰς τὸ ἀρχαῖον τῶν πεπτωκότων ἀποκατάστασιν.
Ibid. c. 5. καθαρότης, ἀπάθεια, μακαριότης, κακοῦ παντὸς ἀλλοτρίωσις καὶ ὅσα τοῦ τοιούτου γένους ἐστίν, δι' ὧν μορφοῦται τοῖς ἀνθρώποις ἡ πρὸς τὸ θεῖον ὁμοίωσις.
See also the numerous references to passages on man's first estate given by Hilt, *Des h. Gregor v. Nyssa Lehre v. Menschen.*

[3] See *De hom. opif.* cc. 16, 17, 22. Prof. Harnack, *op. cit.* p. 279, note 1, says, with reference to these passages: "Gregory here carries his speculation still further: God did not first create a single man, but the whole race in a previously fixed number; these collectively composed only one nature. They were really *one*

mankind's physical existence in Adam and the Augustinian realism.

Unlike all the Greek Fathers, with the solitary exception of Origen, Gregory of Nyssa has a definite conception of original sin in the subjective sense, or, in other words, of hereditary moral taint traceable to the Fall as its cause. The heredity of death, a thing now natural to us, is recognised[1], and the sinfulness of our nature is also asserted[2]. Further, Gregory speaks of our *nature*, and not merely of us men as individuals, as having fallen into sin[3]. To partake of Adam's nature is to partake of his fall[4]. Consequently, whenever we find allusions, in this Father's writings, to inborn sin, or to sin as belonging to our nature as it now is[5], we must assume that they presuppose the doctrine of the Fall. Such inborn sin is removed by baptism[6].

The nature of the inborn sin which we all inherit is yet more precisely defined by Gregory. In other words, particular ways in which human nature has been affected by the Fall are distinguished. Some of these have indeed already been incidentally mentioned. Gregory's doctrine of the original

man, divided into a multiplicity. Adam—that means all. In God's prescience the whole of humanity was comprised in the first preparation."

The idea that Adam represented the race appears, as was observed above, in Methodius, whom Gregory seems sometimes closely to have followed. See, *e.g.*, Methodius, *Conviv. dec. virg.* III. 4, 7, 8, and III. 6. οὕτω δὴ πάλιν ἐν τῷ ἀνειληφότι Χριστῷ τὸν 'Αδὰμ πάντες ζωοποιηθῶσιν.

[1] *In Cant. Cantor. Hom.* XII. (M. XLIV. 1021). καταμιχθέντος ἅπαξ τοῦ θανάτου τῇ φύσει, συνδιεξῆλθε ταῖς τῶν τικτομένων διαδοχαῖς ἡ νεκρότης. "Οθεν νεκρὸς ἡμᾶς διεδέξατο βίος.

[2] *Orat. Catech.* c. 8 (M. XLV. 33). Man is here said to have produced sin through free-will, and to have mingled it with our nature, and so to have transformed that nature into a state of vice.

In *De Vita Moysis* (M. XLIV. 336) Gregory says of Christ : τὸν τὴν ἁμαρτητικὴν ἡμῶν φύσιν περιβαλλόμενον.

[3] M. XLIV. 337. Λόγος τίς ἐστιν ἐκ πατρικῆς παραδόσεως τὸ πιστὸν ἔχων, ὅς φησι, πεσούσης ἡμῶν εἰς ἁμαρτίαν τῆς φύσεως μὴ παριδεῖν τὸν θεὸν τὴν πτῶσιν ἀπρονόητον.

[4] M. XLIV. 756. ὁ κοινωνῶν τῆς φύσεως τοῦ 'Αδάμ, κοινωνῶν δὲ καὶ τῆς ἐκπτώσεως.

[5] *e.g. In Psalmos* (M. XLIV. 609); ἡ ἁμαρτία ἡ συναποτικτομένη τῇ φύσει. Cf. the next citation, and *De Beatitud.* (M. XLIV. 1273).

[6] *Orat. Catech.* c. 35 (M. XLV. 89). δι' ὧν ἐκλύεταί πως ὁ ἄνθρωπος τῆς πρὸς τὸ κακὸν συμφυΐας.

XIII] *in the Fathers before Augustine* 323

state involves that concupiscence, which he calls τὸ φρόνημα τῆς σαρκός[1], is necessarily a consequence of the Fall; and this inference he himself expressly draws. Our whole nature has also been weakened, and our understanding darkened[2]. The ideas expressed in the series of passages which have just been cited represent the nearest approach which the thought of the Eastern Church had ever as yet made to the Augustinian theory of Original Sin. And if the homily *In illud*: '*Tunc ipse Filius subjicietur*' etc. be a genuine work of Gregory of Nyssa, which some authorities have doubted, we may quote from this Father still more definite language concerning the transmission of sin through one to the whole race[3].

In any case we have evidence sufficient to show that the essential constituent ideas of Augustine's theory, that of our inclusion in Adam and that of our 'corrupted' nature as derived by physical descent from Adam, were integral elements in Gregory's anthropology. Gregory of Nyssa therefore occupies an interesting place in connexion with the history of the doctrines of the Fall and Original Sin. He was anticipated, of course, in his approach to the Augustinian teaching, by Origen among the Fathers of the East; and he did not perhaps contribute much that was wholly new to the discussion of the problem of human sin. But what Origen taught tentatively, and apparently with a certain amount of vacillation, with regard to hereditary corruption, Gregory had grasped with clearness and firmness. He stood, unlike

---
[1] M. XLVI. 376, B.
[2] *De orat. domin.* 4 (M. XLIV. 1164). ἀσθενὴς ἡ ἀνθρωπίνη φύσις πρὸς τὸ ἀγαθόν ἐστιν, ἅπαξ διὰ κακίας ἐκνευρισθεῖσα. Οὐ γὰρ μετὰ τῆς εὐκολίας, ἧς πρὸς τὸ κακὸν ὁ ἄνθρωπος ἔρχεται, καὶ ἀπὸ τούτου πάλιν ἐπὶ τὸ ἀγαθὸν ἐπανέρχεται.
De Beatitud. 5 (M. XLIV. 1249). Ἐν τούτῳ γὰρ μάλιστα τῷ μέρει πλημμελεῖται ἡμῶν ἡ ζωή, ἐν τῷ μὴ δύνασθαι ἀκριβῶς συνιέναι, τί τὸ φύσει καλὸν καὶ τὸ δι' ἀπάτης τοιοῦτον ὑπονοούμενον.
Cf. *De Vita Moysis* (M. XLIV. 397, B).
[3] M. XLIV. 1312. Δείξας τοίνυν ἐν τοῖς πρὸς αὐτοὺς λόγοις, ὅτι τοῦ πρώτου ἀνθρώπου εἰς γῆν διὰ τῆς ἁμαρτίας ἀναλυθέντος, καὶ διὰ τοῦτο χοϊκοῦ κληθέντος, ἀκόλουθον ἦν κατ' ἐκεῖνον καὶ τοὺς ἐξ ἐκείνου γενέσθαι πάντας χοϊκούς καὶ θνητοὺς τοὺς ἐκ τοῦ τοιούτου φύντας, ἀναγκαίως ἐπήγαγεν καὶ τὴν δευτέραν ἀκολουθίαν, δι' ἧς ἀναστοιχειοῦται πάλιν ἐκ τοῦ θνητοῦ πρὸς ἀθανασίαν ὁ ἄνθρωπος, ὁμοιοτρόπως λέγων, τὸ ἀγαθὸν ἐγγεγενῆσθαι τῇ φύσει ἐξ ἑνὸς εἰς πάντας χεόμενον, ὥσπερ καὶ τὸ κακὸν δι' ἑνὸς εἰς πλῆθος ἐχέθη, τῇ διαδοχῇ τῶν ἐπιγινομένων.

324   *The Doctrine of the Fall etc.*   [CHAP.

Origen, at the threshold of the Augustinian era, and used the categories more akin to those of the great Father of the West. And herein he marks, from the point of view of the historian of the doctrine of Original Sin, a stage of progress in the thought of the Greek Fathers. He witnesses, in fact, to the readiness now existing within the Eastern portion of Christendom to assimilate the more essential features of the theory which was soon to dominate the thought of the Church as a whole with regard to the origin and propagation of human sin[1].

VII. THE ANTIOCHENE SCHOOL.

Under the above heading, a few words may be said with regard to the attitude of the two Fathers Chrysostom and Theodore of Mopsuestia towards the doctrines whose early history is here being investigated. It is true that their writings cannot be searched for what can properly be called *sources* of these doctrines. They serve to illustrate the the growth of the doctrines of the Fall and Original Sin rather in a somewhat negative manner. Chrysostom, indeed, was cited by Augustine as an authority on his side, in his controversy with Julian of Eclanum; but not perhaps very pertinently[2]: whilst Theodore is rather to be called an

---

[1] Two passages should perhaps be mentioned here which have seemed to some writers to imply a denial, on Gregory's part, of the doctrine of Original Sin. The one passage occurs in *De Infantibus qui praem. abrip.* (M. XLVI. 177). Τὸ δὲ ἀπειρόκακον νήπιον μηδεμιᾶς νόσου τῶν τῆς ψυχῆς ὀμμάτων πρὸς τὴν τοῦ φωτὸς μετουσίαν ἐπιπροσθούσης, ἐν τῷ κατὰ φύσιν γίνεται, μὴ δεόμενον τῆς ἐκ τοῦ καθαρθῆναι ὑγιείας, ὅτι μηδὲ τὴν ἀρχὴν τὴν νόσον τῇ ψυχῇ παρεδέξατο. The other is to be found in the *In Bapt. Christi* (M. XLVI. 580). ἀλλὰ τὸν κατεστιγμένον ταῖς ἁμαρτίαις καὶ κακοῖς ἐπιτηδεύμασιν ἐμπαλαιωθέντα χάριτι βασιλικῇ ἐπανάγομεν εἰς τὸ τοῦ βρέφους ἀνεύθυνον.

These passages may possibly refer only to the freedom of infants from actual sin, as Hilt maintains (*Des heil. Gregor von Nyssa Lehre vom Menschen*, S. 120 ff.). But a pre-Augustinian writer, in dealing at different times with subjects touching the fringe of so intricate a matter as original sin, might easily be unintentionally guilty of inconsistency in expression. However these exceptional utterances are to be interpreted, there can be no doubt that Gregory was an upholder of the doctrine of hereditary sinfulness derived from Adam, though possibly he had not so clearly thought out all its far-reaching consequences, as Augustine was soon to do.

[2] *C. Julianum*, I. vi. 24, 26. Augustine quotes Chrysostom as declaring that Adam "condemned the whole human race" (*Ep.* iii. 3). He also quotes, from

XIII] *in the Fathers before Augustine* 325

avowed Pelagian, so far as the doctrine of Sin is in question, than to be quoted as a witness to the catholicity or to the development of the Augustinian theory of the Fall. The Antiochene Fathers, in fact, represent rather, in its logical completion, that side of Eastern thought concerning human sinfulness which emphasised individual responsibility, and not that which, from Origen downwards, approached more or less the position elaborated by S. Augustine in the West.

Chrysostom.

There is little to be found in Chrysostom's writings in favour of a doctrine of Original Sin, save that he recognises that universal mortality was a consequence of Adam's sin[1]. Even in this assertion he makes an advance in the direction of Augustinianism in which at least one Antiochene theologian will not accompany him. But otherwise Chrysostom tends to minimise the results of the first transgression. This is very obvious in his Homilies on the Epistle to the Romans. In his exegesis of Rom. v. 12 ff., he appears to be evidently out of harmony with the thought of the apostle upon whose words he is commenting; and his interpretation of them is sometimes arbitrary and otherwise unsatisfactory. The citations given below will serve to illustrate Chrysostom's misapprehension of S. Paul's meaning, and to show how he shrank from teaching the solidarity of the race in Adam's sin or in its moral consequences. The words of S. Paul, "for that all sinned," Chrysostom took to mean: 'all became mortal[2].'

an address to neophytes, as follows: "Ἔρχεται ἅπαξ ὁ Χριστός, εὗρεν ἡμῶν χειρόγραφον πατρῷον, ὅ τι ἔγραφεν ὁ Ἀδάμ. Ἐκεῖνος τὴν ἀρχὴν εἰσήγαγεν τοῦ χρέους, ἡμεῖς τὸν δανεισμὸν ηὐξήσαμεν ταῖς μεταγενεστέραις ἁμαρτίαις.

This latter passage, like others appealed to by Augustine, is hardly sufficient to furnish him with valuable support.

[1] *Hom. in Gen.* xiii. 4, xv. 4, xvi. 6, etc.

[2] The following passage was appealed to as implying Pelagian ideas by Julian of Eclanum. Τί ποτ᾽ οὖν ἐστι τὸ ζήτημα; τὸ λέγειν διὰ τῆς παρακοῆς τοῦ ἑνὸς ἁμαρτωλοὺς γενέσθαι πολλούς· τὸ μὲν γὰρ ἁμαρτόντος ἐκείνου καὶ γενομένου θνητοῦ, καὶ τοὺς ἐξ αὐτοῦ τοιούτους εἶναι, οὐδὲν ἀπεικός· τὸ δὲ ἐκ τῆς παρακοῆς ἐκείνου ἕτερον ἁμαρτωλὸν γενέσθαι, ποίαν ἂν ἀκολουθίαν σχοίη; εὑρεθήσεται γὰρ οὕτω μηδὲ δίκην ὀφείλων ὁ τοιοῦτος, εἴ γε μὴ οἴκοθεν γέγονεν ἁμαρτωλός. Τί οὖν ἐστιν ἐνταῦθα τὸ ἁμαρτωλοί; ἐμοὶ δοκεῖ τὸ ὑπεύθυνοι κολάσει, καὶ καταδεδικασμένοι θανάτῳ.—*Hom.* x. *In Rom.* v. (Migne, *P.G.* LX. 477).

For further illustration of Chrysostom's exegesis of Rom. v. 12 ff., a few

Chrysostom does not appear to have recognised any doctrine of inherited sinfulness of nature. It is true that, when he speaks of infants as having no sin, his language is capable of being so interpreted as only to assert the absence of personal, or actual, sin. But even then, his expressions would seem to be very unguarded if he really believed in inborn taint of nature. Moreover he nowhere allows that the Fall had any effect upon man's freedom of will, or that concupiscence is of the nature of sin.

Chrysostom wrote before the Pelagian controversy came up, or perhaps he would have expressed himself in words different from some of those which he actually used in discussing human sin. We observe in him, however, apparently as spontaneous tendencies, germs of some of the ideas afterwards to be identified with the heresies of Pelagius, and

sentences may be quoted from the same *Homily*. The Eng. tr. is that of the *Library of the Fathers*, Oxford.

"How then did death come in and prevail? *Through the sin of one.* But what means: *for that all sinned?* This: He having once fallen, even they that had not eaten of the tree did from him, all of them, become mortal...."

"In saying that *till the Law, sin was in the world*, what he seems to me to mean is this: that, after the Law was given, the sin resulting from the transgression of it prevailed, and prevailed too so long as the Law existed. For sin, he says, can have no existence if there be no law. If then it was this sin, he means, from the transgression of the Law that brought forth death, how was it that all before the Law died? For if it is in sin that death has its origin, but where there is no law sin is not imputed, how came death to prevail? From whence it is clear that it was not *this* sin, the transgression, that is, of the Law, but that of Adam's disobedience, which marred all things. Now what is the proof of this? The fact that even before the Law all died."

Here the commentator allows that Adam's disobedience "marred all things." But he does not consider that S. Paul himself made his meaning clear in the passage which he here discusses. For elsewhere, *Hom.* xvi. *on Rom.* xi. 10, while referring to Rom. v. 17, Chrysostom writes thus:

"And the case of Adam, indeed, he does not clear up, but from it he clears up his own, and shows that it was more reasonable that He who died in their behalf should have power over them at His will. For that, when one had sinned, all should be punished, does not seem to be so very reasonable to most men. But that, when One had done right, all should be justified, is at once more reasonable and more suited to God. Yet still he has not solved the difficulty he has raised. For the more obscure that point remained, the more the Jew was put to silence."

Another passage which somewhat minimises the doctrine of the Fall may be found in *Hom. on* 1 *Cor.* xvii. 4.

XIII] *in the Fathers before Augustine* 327

indeed consciously embraced, and defended against the champions of Augustinian views, by his later contemporary, Theodore of Mopsuestia.

Theodore of Mopsuestia. Theodore, who supplies us with the ripest fruits of Antiochene theological thought, shaped a philosophy of man differing in a marked degree from those of previous Fathers, such as Irenaeus, Origen and Gregory of Nyssa[1]. Confining ourselves here to the briefest summary of his views concerning the Fall and its consequences, we may note, in the first place, that he stands out in a somewhat isolated position in that he repudiates the practically universal belief that Adam's transgression was the cause of mortality to all mankind[2].

Theodore asserts our unity with Adam; but this idea is never used by him to explain the universal spread of sin[3]. In

[1] For some account of his system the reader is referred to Harnack, *op. cit.* vol. III. pp. 279 ff.

[2] *In Epist. ad Gal.* ii. 15, 16. Dominus Deus mortales quidem nos secundum praesentem vitam instituit. Resuscitans vero, iterum immortales nos facere promisit et faciet. Nec enim illud contra suam veniens sententiam, ob solum Adae peccatum ira commotus, fecisse videtur—indecens enim id erga Deum existimare; neque secundum quod nos facit immortales, poenitentia ductus id facit, aut quia de his melius postea voluit cogitare. Sed inenarrabili sapientia a primordio illa quae de nobis sunt omnia instituit, sicut et fas est nos sentire de illo, qui bonitate sola nos faciebat et factos tuebatur. Dedit autem nobis praesentem hanc vitam mortalem, ut dixi, ad exercitationem virtutum et doctrinam illorum quae nos conveniunt facere.

Theodore, a little further on, uses the phrases 'naturalis mortalitas,' 'mortalitate naturae.'

The view implied in the foregoing passage is more explicitly stated in the following Latin fragments of Theodore's work on Original Sin:

Migne, *P.G.* LXVI. 1005. Non ait Deus 'mortales eritis,' sed '*morte moriemini*,' prorsus existentibus natura mortalibus inferre mortis experientiam comminatus...non quod tunc mortales fierent, sed quod digni essent qui mortis sententiam per transgressionem referrent.

Ibid. 1011. Certum est enim quia si eum immortalem esse voluisset, ne ipsum quidem intercedens peccatum Dei sententiam commutasset, quia nec diabolum fecit ex immortali mortalem, et quidem cunctorum malorum existentem principium.

[3] *In Epist. B. Pauli Commentarii*, ed. Swete, vol. I. p. 57. τῆς παρούσης ζωῆς ἀρχὴ μὲν τοῖς πᾶσιν ὁ Ἀδάμ. Εἰς δὲ ἄνθρωπος οἱ πάντες ἐσμὲν τῷ λόγῳ τῆς φύσεως, πρὸς γὰρ δὴ τὸ κοινὸν ὡσπερεὶ μέλους τάξιν ὁ καθεὶς ἡμῶν ἐπέχει. So, he adds, will Christ be our founder in our future, immortal, life, and we shall, as it were, be made one in him. Here obviously, we have mysticism, not realism.

the matter of sin, he regards Adam as our type, not our ancestor. The doctrine of Original Sin was repudiated by Theodore, and he denied that baptism removed inherited corruption[1]. This Father is mentioned here only because he represents the opposition which served to give definiteness to the Augustinian doctrine.

VIII. TERTULLIAN.

Since reviewing the doctrine of Irenaeus with regard to the Fall and its effects upon the moral state of mankind, we have been exclusively occupied with the thought, on this subject, of the more important Fathers of the Eastern Church. And we have seen that, in spite of the tendency, natural to the Eastern mind, to emphasise individual responsibility and free-will, nevertheless the belief in the race's solidarity and unity with its first parent, on the one hand, and in the heredity of moral taint derived from fallen Adam, on the other, was discoverable in most of the Greek Fathers from Origen onwards.

We have now to return to the time at which Western or Latin thought began to busy itself with problems connected with the origin and universality of human sinfulness, and attempted to formulate a system of doctrine on this subject.

The beginning was made by Tertullian.

The speculations of this Father on the subject of the propagation of sinfulness are of the highest importance in the history of the doctrine of Original Sin. Tertullian may perhaps be regarded as the founder of the Church's doctrine of hereditary sinfulness of nature derived from Adam. For whilst Origen taught that every man born into the world brought with him some kind of defilement, he did not always identify this taint with sin, and scarcely ever attributed it to Adam's Fall: but Tertullian is very explicit as to both these points. And further, although one line of Origen's teaching tended, hesitatingly, in the direction of Augustinianism, as has been shown above, this Father seems to have exerted extremely little direct influence upon the treatment accorded

---

[1] See Harnack, *loc. cit.*

to the problem of Original Sin by his successors, at least until the time of the Cappadocians; whereas Tertullian's discussion of the problem served, without doubt, to fix once and for all the main lines along which speculation was to proceed within the Latin Churches, and perhaps also to impart an element of precision to the less definite thought of some of the later pre-Augustinian Fathers of the East.

It was, however, the results of Tertullian's reasoning, divorced from the presuppositions which guided him to them, which alone were taken over as permanent doctrine. The theory by which he explained the transmission of inborn corruption, and gave coherence to his views concerning our relation to Adam and our participation in our first father's fall, did not become an integral part of the doctrine of Original Sin which was adopted by the Church.

It would perhaps be fruitless to attempt to estimate what might have been the extent of Tertullian's interest in the problem of Original Sin and of his influence on the thought of subsequent theologians, had his own speculation not been guided by his traducianist theory of the origin of the human soul. But certainly much of the definiteness of his vocabulary, a very important item in any system of doctrine, and probably much of the coherence and distinctness of his thought as to human solidarity in sin, would, in that case, have been wanting. To some extent, at least, it must be supposed that his traducianism was to Tertullian what the Recapitulation-doctrine probably was to Irenaeus, and what the Jewish law of purification and the Christian practice of infant baptism were to Origen; namely, a source of his particular conception of the hereditary consequences to the race of the transgression of its head, and of his particular explanation of the universal sinfulness of mankind.

Inasmuch as we are here primarily concerned with the *sources* of the doctrine of Original Sin, it will be relevant to point out whence Tertullian derived his traducianist psychology.

A word may first of all be said, however, as to this Father's relation to his immediate predecessor, Irenaeus. The latter writer, it will be remembered, had no doctrine of Original Sin in its subjective sense of inborn moral taint or corruption of nature; but he conceived of Adam as in some mystic sense representing and including all his children.

From this conception, it may well be, Tertullian's doctrine took its start. Such a stage of thought would seem to be represented, for instance, in his words: ita omnis anima eo usque in Adam censetur donec in Christo recenseatur[1]. But concreteness was the most characteristic quality of Tertullian's thought; and the vague, mystical language of Irenaeus, modelled probably on the largely rhetorical and symbolical phrases of S. Paul with regard to Adam's relation to the race, is almost always replaced, in the writings of the African lawyer, by terms embodying the bluntest physical realism.

This fact is the consequence of Tertullian having been deeply imbued with the Stoic philosophy, which, more than any other system, prevailed in the Roman world of his time. Though Tertullian frequently declaims with his usual energy against philosophy as the fertile source of heresy, with which Christianity can come to no terms, and professes to deduce his doctrine of the nature of the soul only from what has been revealed,[2] it is nevertheless true that he was himself somewhat of a philosopher, and that he was very largely indebted to current philosophy in the elaboration of his own theological teaching. His relation to Stoicism, in particular, will be made obvious by the following exposition of Tertullian's doctrine of the soul and its mode of origin.

Tertullian taught the corporeality of all existences. "Everything that is, is body[3]." Consequently he held that the soul, and even God Himself, are corporeal. Of the soul he says: Nihil enim, si non corpus[4]; and of God: Quis enim negaverit deum corpus esse, etsi deus spiritus est? Spiritus enim corpus sui generis in sua effigie[5]. The meaning of 'corpus' is not perhaps always quite the same in Tertullian's writings. Sometimes it seems to bear the sense of sub-

---

[1] *De Anima*, 40.
[2] See the early chapters of the *De Anima*.
[3] Omne quod est, corpus est sui generis; nihil est incorporale, nisi quod non est (*De Carne Christi*, 11).
[4] *De Anima*, 7.   [5] *Adv. Prax.* 7.

stantiality, but sometimes it certainly rather appears to signify attenuated materiality; the soul, at any rate, is said to possess the properties of matter. The source of such ideas is undoubtedly the Stoic ontology[1]; though, as has been said, Tertullian professes to derive them from the gospel, and merely to have the philosophers sometimes on his side.

More important for us is Tertullian's view as to the origin of human souls. This, which can be gathered in detail from the citations given below[2], may briefly be summed up as follows. The soul is produced, like the body, by the union of the parents. It does not enter the body after birth, but is produced simultaneously with it. As the parent bodies produce the child's body, so do the parent souls produce in similar way the child's soul.

This traducianist theory of the soul's origin and self-propagation was commonly held by representatives of the Stoic system of philosophy; and it was thence that Tertullian originally learned it. He himself quotes Cleanthes as saying that "family likeness passes from parents to their children not merely in bodily features, but in characteristics of the soul," words which, however, do not necessarily imply traducianism; and he also cites Zeno as "defining the soul to be a spirit

[1] Cf., *e.g.*, Diog. Laert. VII. 56, πᾶν γὰρ τὸ ποιοῦν σῶμά ἐστιν, and Cicero, *Acad.* I. II. 39, Nec vero aut quod efficeret aliquid, aut quod efficeretur posse esse non corpus. Other elements also in Tertullian's doctrine of the soul are identical with Stoic tenets.

In *De Anima*, 5, Tertullian quotes Chrysippus and Cleanthes as teaching the corporeality of the soul. For references to Stoic philosophers who taught traducianism, see below.

[2] *De Anima*, 27. Eng. tr. Clark, *Ante-Nic. Library*. "How, then, is a living being conceived? Is the substance of both body and soul formed together at one and the same time? Or does one of them precede the other in natural formation? We indeed maintain that both are conceived, and formed, and perfected simultaneously, as well as born together; and not a moment's interval occurs in their conception, so that a prior place can be assigned to either."

The discussion of this point is contained in chapter 36, thus:

Anima in utero seminata pariter cum carne, pariter cum ipsa sortitur et sexum, ita pariter ut in causa sexus neutra substantia tenetur. Si enim in seminibus utriusque substantiae, aliquam intercapedinem eorum conceptus admitteret, ut aut caro, aut anima prior seminaretur, esset etiam sexus proprietatum alteri substantiae adscribere per temporalem intercapedinem seminum; ut aut caro animae, aut anima carni insculperet sexum.

generated with the body¹." But the view appears to have been that most generally adopted by the Stoics².

It is obvious that this theory of the corporeality of the soul and of its mode of origin lends itself to support and explain the doctrine of the race's unity with, and inclusion in, its first parent. And such is the most important application to which his traducianism was actually put by Tertullian. In so using it, this Father was led on to formulate, by means of it, a theory of hereditary sinful taint. As Irenaeus had been the first to assert, as a doctrine, that Adam represented and summed up in himself the whole human race, in a mystical sense, so Tertullian was the first to impart a realistic meaning to this doctrine, and also to give to the Church a definite theory of inherited corruption of nature.

Inasmuch as the soul of the child was regarded by Tertullian as derived from the soul of its father, like a shoot (*tradux*) from the parent stock of a tree, it followed that he must look upon every human soul as ultimately a branch (*surculus*) of Adam's soul. And inasmuch as the soul inherits from its parents their spiritual characteristics and qualities, those of Adam must have been transmitted to all his descendants. In fact, *tradux animae tradux peccati*. "Our first parent contained within himself the undeveloped germ of all mankind, and his soul was the fountain-head of all souls; all varieties of individual human nature are but different modifications of that one spiritual substance. Therefore the whole of nature became corrupt in the original father of the race, and sinfulness is propagated together with souls³." This corruption of nature is said to be 'a second nature'; but Tertullian did not regard our corruption to be so complete that no goodness at all resides in the soul, nor any real freedom in the will⁴.

---

[1] *De Anima*, 5, Eng. tr. Clark, *op. cit.*
[2] Rauch, in his essay *Der Einfluss der Stoischen Philosophie auf die Lehrbildung Tertullians*, 1890, S. 37, gives the following references: Plutarch, *De plac. phil.* IV. 2, V. 1; Zeno, cited by Eusebius, *Praep. Evang.* XV. 20, 1; Chrysippus, cited in Diog. Laert. VII. 159; Panaetius, *Cic. Tusc.* I. 32, 79.
[3] Neander's *Church History*, ed. Bohn, vol. II. pp. 346—7.
[4] See *De Anima*, 21. Inesse nobis τὸ αὐτεξούσιον naturaliter; also *ibid.* 41.

XIII] *in the Fathers before Augustine* 333

The following passages give, in Tertullian's own words, the details of the theories whose outlines have been sketched.

"Every soul, then, by reason of its birth, has its nature in Adam until it is born again in Christ; moreover it is unclean all the while that it remains without this regeneration; and because unclean, it is actively sinful, and suffuses even the flesh (flesh by reason of their conjunction) with its own shame[1]."

The sentence preceding this refers to baptism and quotes John iii. 5. Thus the nature of every infant is here, by implication, declared to be actively sinful because possessing Adam's nature.

The source and cause of this inherent uncleanness is thus concisely described:

"Through whom (*i.e.* Satan, the corrupter of the whole world) man being at the beginning beguiled into breaking the commandment of God, and on that account being given over to death, thenceforth made the whole race, infected with his seed, transmitters also of his condemnation[2]."

Of the corruption of nature itself Tertullian says:

"There is, then, besides the evil which supervenes on the soul from the intervention of the evil spirit, an antecedent, and in a certain sense natural, evil which arises from its corrupt origin (*ex originis vitio*). For, as we have said before,

---

[1] *Ibid* 40, E. tr. Clark, *op. cit.* This passage should be remembered when Tertullian's utterance as to the innocence of infancy (*De Baptismo*, 18) is discussed; see below.

[2] *De test. animae*, 3. (Satanam) per quem homo a primordio circumventus, ut praeceptum Dei excederet, et propterea in mortem datus, exinde totum genus de suo semine infectum suae etiam damnationis traducem fecit.

Cf. also: *De resurr. carnis*, 34. Si quidem transgressio, quae perditionis humanae causa est, tam animae instinctu ex concupiscentia quam et carnis actu ex degustatione commissa hominem elogio transgressionis inscripsit, atque exinde merito perditionis implevit.

De Patientia, 5, where Eve, because she was the first to sin, is said to be the "single womb of all sin, pouring down from her spring the various streams of crime."

De Spectac. 2: "When the power of that corrupting and adverse angel in the beginning cast down from his innocency man himself, the work and image of God, the lord of the whole world, he changed, like himself, into perverseness against his Maker, the whole substance of man, made, like himself, for innocency." E. tr. *Library of the Fathers*, Oxford.

the corruption of our nature is another nature (*naturae corruptio alia natura est*) having a god and father of its own, namely the author of that corruption. Still there is a portion of good in the soul, of that original, divine and genuine good, which is its proper nature. For that which is derived from God is rather obscured than extinguished[1]."

Finally, for statements with regard to the mode of the transmission of Adam's nature to his posterity, other than such as have already been given, the reader is referred especially to the *De Anima*[2], and also to the following incidental allusion to the heredity of sin:

"Unbidden, I would, in such ways and at such times as I might have been able, have habitually accounted food as poison, and taken the antidote, hunger; through which to purge the primordial cause of death—a cause transmitted to me also, concurrently with my very generation[3]."

Tertullian does not seem to have spoken definitely of original guilt. Adam's condemnation, his mortality, and his corrupted nature are transmitted; and the state of corruption is described as one of active sinfulness. But though Adam's punishments are represented as shared by his descendants and their souls were potentially in his when he sinned, Tertullian does not explicitly draw out the consequence, if necessary consequence it be, that the race shares the responsibility and guilt of its first father's sin.

It has indeed sometimes been argued that, because Tertullian resisted the practice of hastening the baptism of young children, he did not regard their uncleanness as sinfulness to which guilt attaches. The passage in which this practice is discouraged is well known[4]. As has been pointed out in the

[1] *De Anima*, 41.
[2] Two passages may be cited. Anima (hominis) velut surculus quidam ex matrice Adam in propaginem deducta, et genitalibus feminae foveis commendata cum omni sua paratura pullulabit, tam intellectu quam sensu (c. 19).—A primordio in Adam concreta et configurata corpori anima, ut totius substantiae ita et conditionis istius semen effecit (c. 9). Migne, *P.L.* II. 682, 661.
[3] *De Jejun.* 3, E. tr. Clark, *op. cit.*
[4] *De Bapt.* 18. Quid festinat innocens aetas ad remissionem peccatorum? Tertullian has said, a few lines earlier: "And so, according to the circumstances and disposition, and even age, of each individual, the delay of baptism is preferable; principally, however, in the case of little children." (E. tr. Clark, *op. cit.*)

foregoing pages, several similar passages occur in the writings of Fathers who, like Clement, did not believe in original sin at all, or who, like Gregory of Nazianzus, believed in it thoroughly. Such statements may imply that baptism only removes actual sin, or that the pollution attaching to human nature, whether in consequence of the process of birth (as Origen generally represented it) or in consequence of descent from sinful Adam (as Tertullian taught), though cleansed in baptism, is not really of the nature of sin. The latter view is adopted with regard to Tertullian's teaching by Harnack, Loofs and Turmel[1]. The rigorous and logical application of the consequences of the doctrine of Original Sin to the case of infants was only made late in the development of this doctrine; it was, in fact, part of the work of S. Augustine. Perhaps the Fathers previous to him would have been willing to use the words of Cyprian : " (infanti) remittuntur non propria sed aliena peccata."

It may be concluded, from the passages of Tertullian's writings which have now been examined, that this Father more, perhaps, than any other, prepared the way for S. Augustine. He was the first to formulate the idea of inherited sin or corruption of nature, and to explain the process by which such corruption is handed on from generation to generation. This latter factor in his theory, which served doubtless to give the definiteness and point to Tertullian's teaching as to the consequences of the Fall. was indeed rejected, or, rather, was not adopted, by Augustine or the Church generally. It was therefore mere scaffolding, which served a purpose during the building of the fabric of the doctrine of hereditary sin, but which was afterwards discarded. The results reached by its means were alone permanently preserved. But it may reasonably be doubted whether, without its aid, the definiteness of Augustine's theory would have been attained, and whether, without its implication, his doctrine can be considered self-consistent. These,

---

[1] Harnack, *op. cit.* II. 274; Loofs, *Leitfaden f. seine Vorlesungen über Dogmengeschichte*; Turmel, *op. cit.* Neander, *op. cit.* II. 347, remarks that the *De Bapt.* is an earlier treatise than those in which the doctrine of hereditary sin is unfolded.

however, are questions which we are not here concerned to discuss.

IX. FROM TERTULLIAN TO AUGUSTINE.

The development of doctrine with regard to the Fall and Original Sin in the Western Church after Tertullian is to be looked for in the writings of Cyprian, Hilary and Ambrose.

Cyprian.

Cyprian was not a theologian, and we cannot expect to find in his writings much discussion of the theoretical side of Christian doctrine. His few scattered allusions to the Fall recall the language of Tertullian[1]. He speaks incidentally of the first man's endowment with the Holy Spirit[2], and of the loss of the divine image through sin[3]. But the only passage that is of any importance here is the allusion to original sin and its relation to baptismal regeneration, in the *Epistle to Fidus*[4]: "If then even to the most grievous offenders, and who had before sinned much against God, when they afterwards believe, remission of sins is granted, and no one is debarred from baptism and grace, how much more ought not an infant to be debarred, who being newly born has in no way sinned, except that being born after Adam in the flesh, he has by his first birth contracted the contagion of the old death; who is on this very account more easily admitted to

---

[1] Such are the following: *De Bono Pat.* 19 (Migne, *P.L.* IV. 634). Adam contra coeleste praeceptum cibi lethalis impatiens, in mortem cecidit ; nec acceptam divinitus gratiam patientia custode servavit.

De op. et eleem. 1 (M. IV. 603). Nam, cum Dominus adveniens sanasset illa quae Adam portaverat vulnera, et venena serpentis antiqua curasset, legem dedit sano....

[2] *Ep.* 74.

[3] *De Bon. Pat.* 5. similitudo divina, quam peccato Adam perdiderat.

[4] *Ep.* 59 (Pamel etc.) or 64 (Oxon.). E. tr. *Lib. of Fathers*, Oxford. The following is the original : Si etiam gravissimis delictoribus et in deum multum ante peccantibus, quum postea crediderint, remissio peccatorum datur, et a baptismo atque a gratia nemo prohibetur, quanto magis prohiberi non debet infans, qui recens natus nihil peccavit, nisi quod secundum Adam carnaliter natus contagium mortis antiquae prima nativitate contraxit...qui ad remissionem peccatorum accipiendam hoc ipso facilius accedit, quod illi remittuntur non propria, sed aliena peccata.

receive remission of sins, in that not his own but another's sins are remitted to him."

Cyprian here opposes the influence of his master in urging the baptism of children at the earliest age. He would hasten them to the font in spite of their freedom from actual sin, and in spite of the fact that they cannot be regarded as sinful save in the sense of having contracted the contagion of death through carnal descent from Adam; the very reason why innocents should be baptized early, in fact, is that the sins remitted to them are not their own but another's. This Father is concerned to show that there is no reason why infants should not be baptized, notwithstanding their innocence, rather than to insist on the necessity of their regeneration on account of inherited taint. He cannot be said, therefore, to carry Tertullian's teaching onwards in the direction of Augustinianism.

Hilary of Poitiers.

Hilary, like Cyprian, is a link in the chain of tradition connecting Tertullian and Augustine, without contributing materially to the development of thought on the subject of Sin which intervened between those two teachers.

Hilary was himself influenced by Tertullian. He repudiated, indeed, the traducianism of that writer[1], but retained his doctrine of *vitium originis*[2]. Sin accompanies birth[3] and, though not transmitted with and in the soul, it is conveyed to

---

[1] *Tract. in Ps.* cxviii. *Litt.* 4 (Migne, *P.L.* IX. 527). Igitur, vel quia in terrae hujus solo commoramur, vel quia ex terra instituti conformatique sumus, anima quae alterius originis est, terrae corporis adhaesisse creditur.
De Trinit. X. 20. Cum anima omnis opus Dei est, carnis vero generatio semper ex carne sit.
Ibid. 22. Sed ut per se sibi assumpsit ex Virgine corpus, ita ex se sibi animam assumpsit; quae utique numquam ab homine gignentium originibus praebetur. (M. X. 358, 359.)

[2] *Tract. in Ps.* cxviii. *Litt.* XIV. 20 (M. IX. 599). Cor suum ipse declinat, et ex naturae humanae peccatis in obedientiam Dei inflectit. Natura quidem et origo carnis suae eum detinebat: sed voluntas et religio cor ejus ex eo in quo manebat originis vitio ad justificationum opera declinat.

[3] *Ibid.*, *Litt.* XXII. 6 (M. IX. 641). Scit sub peccati origine et sub peccati lege se esse natum.

338   *The Doctrine of the Fall etc.*   [CHAP.

the soul through its union with the flesh[1]. Hilary abandons Tertullian's theory of the mode of propagation of sin, but he fails to present us with one in its place. He preserves Tertullian's inference whilst rejecting his premiss. And he consequently reverts almost to the indefiniteness of thought which obtained before Tertullian wrote.

And what thus applies to Hilary's treatment of hereditary sin applies equally to his statements as to our unity with Adam. Adam stands for the race, and his sin is theirs; but how or why, Hilary does not define[2].

Hilary thus contributed nothing to the elaboration of the doctrine of the Fall; he merely handed on something of the tradition already established.

Ambrose.

With Ambrose the case is very different. This Father's writings represent a distinct and considerable step onwards towards the fulness of the Augustinian doctrines of the Fall and Original Sin.

Ambrose, in the first place, supplies Augustine with suggestions for his exaltation of the original estate of Adam before the Fall. It has already been shown that the most ancient Jewish haggada, Palestinian and Alexandrian alike,

[1] See, *e.g.*, the following passages :
Comm. in Matt. x. 23 (M. IX. 976). Nam ut corpori anima data est, ita et potestas utrique utendi se ut vellet indulta est; atque ob id lex est proposita voluntati. Sed hoc in illis deprehenditur, qui primi a Deo figurati sunt, in quibus coeptae originis ortus effectus est, non traductus aliunde. Sed ex peccato atque infidelitate primi parentis, sequentibus generationibus coepit esse corporis nostri pater peccatum, mater animae infidelitas; ab his enim ortum per transgressionem primi parentis accepimus.
Ibid. x. 24. Cum ergo innovamur baptismi lavacro per verbi virtutem, ab originis nostrae peccatis atque auctoribus separamur; recisique quadam ex sectione gladii Dei, a patris et matris affectionibus dissidemus: et veterem cum peccatis atque infidelitate sua hominem exuentes, et per Spiritum anima et corpore innovati, necesse est ut ingeniti et vetusti operis consuetudinem oderimus.

[2] *Ibid.* XVIII. 6 (M. IX. 1020). Ovis una homo intelligendus est, et sub homine uno, universitas sentienda est. Sed in unius Adae errore omne hominum genus aberravit; ergo nonaginta novem non errantes, multitudo angelorum coelestium opinanda est....
Tract. in Psalm. lix. 4 (M. IX. 385). Quia ex uno in omnes sententia mortis et vitae labor exiit.

had endowed the life of our first parents in Paradise with celestial privileges; and doubtless such literature, familiar to many of the Fathers, was the original source of the doctrine as to man's state before the Fall which grew up during the first three centuries. It has also been suggested that the Cappadocian Fathers were probably led to their exalted conception of the primitive state by Origen's allegorical interpretation of the Fall-story, by which he supported his speculations as to a previous celestial life of human souls. Certainly the tendency to regard unfallen Adam as almost a heavenly being is conspicuous in the writings of those Fathers, and from them doubtless the like tendency was derived by Ambrose. Moreover Ambrose drank at one of the original founts of such fancies, the writings of Philo[1].

The Fall is said by Ambrose to have involved the loss of the divine image[2].

More important than his teaching as to the Fall itself, in which there is nothing original, is Ambrose's contribution to the doctrine of Original Sin. Consistently with the method

[1] As examples of Ambrose's teaching with regard to Adam's condition in Paradise the following passages may be given:

In Psalm. cxviii. *Serm.* xv. 36 (M. XV. 1422). Adam, cum in Paradiso esset, coelestis erat, post lapsum autem terrenus est factus.

Ibid. iv. 3. Qui ante beatissimus auram carpebat aethere.

De Parad. 42 (M. XIV. 294). Sunt enim qui putant mandatum istud (de manducando et non manducando) convenire caeli et terrae atque omnium Creatori; nequaquam dignum incolis paradisi, eo quod illa vita similis angelorum sit. Et ideo non terrenum et corruptibilem hunc cibum esui fuisse possumus aestimare.

Ambrose's dependence on Philo is shown, as Siegfried has pointed out in his well-known work on Philo, in his distinction between the heavenly and the earthly man, the latter πεπλασμένος and the former κατ' εἰκόνα: *De Parad.* 5 (M. XIV. 275). In hoc Paradiso hominem Deus posuit quem plasmavit. Intellige etiam quia non eum hominem qui secundum imaginem Dei est, posuit, sed eum qui secundum corpus. Incorporalis enim in loco non est. It is still more plainly shown, and in this case acknowledged by Ambrose himself, in his representation of the Fall as a seduction of the reason by means of sensuousness. Siegfried cites *De Parad.* 11. Delectatione (ἡδονῇ) deceptam per sensum (αἴσθησιν) mentem (νοῦν) asseruit Scriptura.

[2] *Hexaemer.* vi. 7 (M. XIV. 258). Secundum hanc imaginem Adam factus est ante peccatum; sed ubi lapsus est, deposuit imaginem coelestis, sumpsit terrestris effigiem. Cf. *In Luc.* x. Angelos tenebrarum, velut latrones, indumentis gratiae salutaris hominem spoliasse...where the unfallen state is regarded as a state of grace as contrasted with a state of nature.

hitherto generally adopted in the present account of patristic teaching, we may endeavour to collect separately, so far as is possible, the passages in the writings of Ambrose which deal respectively with the hereditary sinful state caused by Adam's sin, and the means of its transmission, on the one hand, and those which describe mankind's unity with Adam, and participation in his sin and guilt, on the other.

Ambrose was cited by Augustine as an upholder of hereditary corruption[1]. And indeed this doctrine is frequently asserted in his writings. More, perhaps than any Father before him, Ambrose emphasises the sinful condition of mankind and regards sin rather as a state than an act. In this respect he certainly prepared the way for S. Augustine and doubtless helped that Father to his profound sense of the depravity of human nature.

Ambrose, like the majority of ecclesiastical writers, did not adopt Tertullian's traducianist ideas, which indeed seem to have obtained little hold upon the ancient Church[2]. On the contrary, Ambrose seems definitely to incline to the creationist theory of the origin of souls[3]. His utterances on the subject of inherited taint recall the language of Origen at times[4]. That is to say, they in some cases seem to refer the

[1] In his *De Peccato Originali*, c. xli. (c. 47 in E. tr. of Marcus Dods).
One passage which Augustine quoted is taken from a lost exposition of Isaiah: Omnis enim homo mendax; et nemo sine peccato nisi unus, Deus. Servatum est igitur, ut ex viro et muliere, id est, per illam corporum commixtionem, nemo videatur expers esse delicti. Qui autem expers delicti, expers est etiam hujusmodi conceptionis. This passage seems to connect hereditary sin with concupiscence and generation.
Another passage adduced by S. Austin is the following:
Omnes homines sub peccato nascimur, quorum ipse ortus in vitio est sicut habes lectum, dicente David: Ecce in iniquitatibus conceptus sum, et in delictis peperit me mater mea. Ideo Pauli caro corpus mortis erat, sicut ipse ait: Quis me liberabit de corpore mortis hujus? Christi autem caro damnavit peccatum, quod nascendo non sensit, quod moriendo crucifixit; ut in carne nostra esset justificatio per gratiam, ubi erat ante colluvio per culpam.

[2] Jerome regarded Tertullian, perhaps in part on account of his traducianism, as no 'homo ecclesiae.' The former Father's influence was largely responsible for the decay of traducianist opinion, such as there was, in the West.

[3] See, *e.g.*, *De bono mortis*, 9, *De Parad.* 11, and the explicit statement in *De Noe et arca* IV. 9: Quia ex nullo homine generantur animae.

[4] *e.g. Apol. David*, 11 (M. XIV. 873). Antequam nascamur, maculamur contagio; et ante usuram lucis, originis ipsius excipimus injuriam, in iniquitate concipimur:

pollution of which they speak to the process of birth itself, as if conception were unclean. Possibly, however, the meaning is: no act of conception and birth is free from sin because no parents are free from sin. Though traducianist modes of accounting for the transmission of sinful taint are excluded, Ambrose always seems to regard heredity as the means of its propagation[1].

Ambrose appears, like others before him, to regard the inborn taint, which every man inherits, as something distinct from sin to which guilt attaches, and as something not cleansed away in baptism, which, he asserts, removes the guilt of personal or actual sin. Whereas Cyprian spoke of 'another's sins' being remitted to infants in baptism, Ambrose, in one passage, speaks of Adam's sin as not ours, and as something for which we need fear no punishment[2].

Adam's sin is indeed spoken of very differently in passages soon to be quoted; but here original sin is considered, non expressit, utrum parentum, an nostra. Et in delictis generat unumquemque mater sua : nec hic declaravit, utrum in delictis suis mater pariat; an jam sint et aliqua delicta nascentis. Sed vide, ne utrumque intelligendum sit. Nec conceptus iniquitatis exsors est, quoniam et parentes non carent lapsu. Et si nec unius diei infans sine peccato est, multo magis nec illi materni conceptus dies sine peccato sunt. Concipimur ergo in peccato parentum et in delictis eorum nascimur. Sed et ipse partus habet contagia sua, nec unum tantummodo habet ipsa natura contagium.

The passages of Scripture cited in this context are those to which Origen so frequently appealed.

[1] *In Psalm.* xxxviii. (Migne XIV. 1053) we read: ipsa noxiae conditionis haereditas adstrinxit ad culpam.

[2] *Enarr. in Psalm.* xlviii. n. 8 and 9 (M. XIV. 1158 ff.). Alia est iniquitas nostra, alia calcanei nostri, in quo Adam dente serpentis est vulneratus, et obnoxiam haereditatem successionis humanae suo vulnere dereliquit, ut omnes eo vulnere claudicemus.

Again : Dominus autem qui sua peccata non habuit, nec cognovit proprias iniquitates, ait : *Iniquitas calcanei mei circumdabit me*; hoc est, iniquitas Adae, non mea. Sed ea non potest mihi esse terrori; in die enim judicii nostra in nobis, non alienae iniquitatis flagitia, puniuntur. Unde reor iniquitatem calcanei magis lubricum delinquendi, quam reatum aliquem nostri esse delicti. Meritoque Dominus qui pro nobis universa suscepit : Lavemus, inquit, et pedes, ut calcanei lubricum possumus auferre...et non metuat lubricum haereditatis, qui cupit vestigium tenere virtutis. Iniquitas ergo calcanei nostri praevaricatio est Adae....

The following passage is also of interest here :

Habebat enim primi hominis de successione peccatum...ideo planta ejus abluitur ut haereditaria peccata tollantur; nostra enim propria per baptismum relaxantur—*De Myster.* 32 (M. XVI. 398).

apparently, solely in one aspect, namely as consisting in natural concupiscence; the *iniquitas calcanei* is, in fact, identified here with Adam's sin on the one hand, and with concupiscence or sinful tendency on the other. In this context Ambrose appears to be combating the notion that concupiscence is sin. He is therefore here rather in harmony with Origen, and perhaps with Tertullian and other earlier Fathers, than with the teaching soon to be formulated by Augustine.

Turning now to the solidarity of the race with Adam, we find Ambrose making advances upon previous thought in the direction of S. Augustine's mode of conceiving our participation in Adam's sin. Ambrose teaches, indeed, as plainly as Augustine himself, that we all were Adam, and in Adam, and sinned in Adam[1]. Such statements imply, of course, that Adam's *guilt* is ours also. This is definitely asserted, too, by Ambrose[2]. Such guilt is not merely imputed, according to this Father, as earlier writers seemed to imply, without showing any justification for its imputation. It was actually incurred by us because we sinned in and with Adam. Lastly, we find already stated in Ambrose the idea that Adam's sin is ours because it was not merely the sin of himself as an individual man, but because he was human nature, and therefore the first transgression of the first man was the sin of human nature in general. This idea, in slightly varying forms, dominated Christian thought concerning original sin and its derivation throughout the middle ages[3].

* * * *

[1] *In Luc.* xv. 24 (M. xv. 1762). Fuit Adam et in illo fuimus omnes; periit Adam et in illo omnes perierunt.

Apol. David, 71. Omnes in primo homine peccavimus et per naturae successionem culpae quoque ab uno in omnes transfusa est successio.

De Exc. Pat. ii. 6. Lapsus sum in Adam, de Paradiso ejectus in Adam, mortuus in Adam; quomodo non revocat nisi me in Adam invenerit, ut in illo culpae obnoxium, morti debitum, ita in Christo justificatum.

The following passages occur in the *Commentary on S. Luke*:

Cave ergo ne ante nuderis, sicut Adam ante nudatus est, mandati coelestis custodia destitutus et exutus fidei vestimento et sic lethale vulnus accepit, in quo omne genus occidisset humanum, nisi Samaritanus ille descendens vulnera ejus acerba curasset......Adam atque Eva primi illi nostri ut generis ita erroris parentes.

[2] *De Cain et Abel*, I. 1 (M. XIV. 315). Illa penes auctores non stetit culpa.

[3] Ambrosiaster should be mentioned as a precursor of S. Augustine. The

in the Fathers before Augustine

Ambrose is the last Father to whom we can have recourse for light as to the *sources* of the doctrines of the Fall and Original Sin; for it has been assumed all through this work that, notwithstanding later developments and deviations in the theology of various branches of the Church, these doctrines practically took their permanent and fully matured form in the writings of S. Augustine. The title of the present volume will sufficiently explain the exclusion of S. Augustine's work from its contents. Moreover so many treatises dealing with this great teacher's doctrine of Sin have been supplied by the ablest writers on the history of dogma, that it would be as unnecessary as it would be presumptuous to offer here any minute analysis or description of an intricate system of doctrine, the main outlines of which are familiar to all students of theology.

The main results of the foregoing inquiry into the sources of the patristic doctrine of the Fall may therefore now be summarised.

It has been seen that though Judaism, in the earliest Christian centuries, possessed definite theories of Original Sin, these were not taken over in their Jewish form by the Fathers of the Church. The doctrine of the Fall, as a whole, was deduced afresh[1]. S. Paul was, of course, the connecting link between Jewish and Christian teaching on this point. His doctrine of Adam was derived from the Jewish schools; and it served to mould, to a considerable extent, the subsequent thought of the Fathers. But the ecclesiastical doctrines of the Fall and Original Sin were not *deduced* from S. Paul's brief statements on these subjects; in fact they were not contained therein. Irenaeus, in whom a Christian doctrine of the Fall first appears, seems to have been guided to his view of

following citation from him will serve to illustrate that he shared with Ambrose the preparation for the final elaboration of the Augustinian doctrine.

In Rom. v. 12 (M. XVII. 92). In quo...omnes peccaverunt;...manifestum itaque est in Adam omnes peccasse quasi in massa. Ipse enim per peccatum corruptus, quos genuit omnes nati sunt sub peccato. Ex eo igitur cuncti peccatores, quia ex eo ipso sumus omnes.

[1] Of course many details of non-essential character, relating to the original estate of Adam, the tempter, and particular losses occasioned by the Fall, were borrowed directly from Judaism.

the connexion between the sinful race and its first parent by his doctrine of Recapitulation. The passage Rom. v. 12 ff. was used to confirm the results thus obtained, but does not appear to have been the starting point whence Irenaeus set out.

Immediately later than Irenaeus, we have the practically simultaneous appearance of two definite theories, at once explaining the nature of hereditary taint and the mode of its propagation, and also accounting for the virtual participation of the race in Adam's sin. Tertullian, in the West, seems to have been enabled to furnish the very concrete and definite hypothesis contained in his writings by the traducianist psychology which he borrowed from heathen philosophers. In spite of his own protestations, we must consider Stoicism the main factor in his theory of the propagation of sin from Adam; without this external aid, his ideas as to original sin would probably have been more akin to the much less definite notions of Irenaeus. Origen, in the East, does not set out from S. Paul's Epistle to the Romans, nor yet from the position attained by Irenaeus. Entirely new influences seem to have guided his mind towards the acceptance of a view essentially identical with that later elaborated by Augustine. And these influences again were quite different from those which enabled Tertullian to advance, to so marked an extent, upon Irenaeus. The traditional practice of infant baptism in the Church, and certain Old Testament passages relating to inherent sinfulness and to the impurity attributed by the Law to human birth, appear to have suggested to Origen's mind the idea of hereditary taint of sin attaching to all men; and in casting about for an explanation of this, he would seem to have come upon the truth of racial solidarity as expressed by S. Paul, and to have proceeded to formulate that solidarity in terms of the notion of mankind's potential (seminal) existence in their first father, just as the writer of the Epistle to the Hebrews regarded Levi as existing, and paying tithe, in Abraham.

Such, then, are the sources, in so far as they are avowed in the writings of the pre-Augustinian Fathers, or are to be inferred from them. After Tertullian and Origen but little development was needed, save in the elaboration of details and the thinking out of consequences, to carry speculation with regard to the Fall and Original Sin onward to the point attained by S. Augustine. Such development proceeded uniformly in the West, Tertullian's results being generally accepted, though the means whereby, in the main, they were reached, *i.e.* his traducianist ideas, were rejected. In the East where, it should be noted, the essential ideas of the Augustinian theory had been formulated as early as in the West, development was more interrupted. Teachers in the age subsequent to that of Origen neglected the doctrine of the Fall and Original Sin contained in this Father's later writings, and relapsed into the indefiniteness of thought characteristic of Irenaeus and the Greek apologists. The Cappadocians, however, and Gregory of Nyssa in particular, supply a link between the fully-developed doctrine of Augustine and its germ which had long before appeared in Origen.

Finally, if the results thus summarised be essentially correct, an important conclusion may be drawn which the present writer has ventured to presuppose elsewhere, and has here sought to justify: "that the development of the highly complicated doctrine of Original Sin was less the outcome of strict exegesis than due to the exercise of speculation: speculation working, indeed, on the lines laid down in Scripture, but applied to such material as current science and philosophy were able to afford[1]."

[1] The author's *Hulsean Lectures*, p. 41.

ADDITIONS AND CORRECTIONS.

PAGES 38 AND 49.

SINCE Chapter II. was printed a work has appeared which contains new information relating to Babylonian traditions concerning Paradise or Eden and making it perhaps necessary to qualify the statement made on p. 49: "It may be safely concluded, then, that we possess no Babylonian parallel to the Hebrew Fall-story." The work in question is Pinches' *The Old Testament in the light of the historical records and legends of Assyria and Babylonia*. On pp. 71 and 75 ff. of this book will be found evidence that the tree of Eridu, compared to 'white lapis,' was probably a vine. For instance, we are told that the ideograms composing the word for 'wine' are 'drink of life,' and those composing the word for 'the vine' are 'tree of the drink of life.' What is said on p. 72 ff. makes it overwhelmingly probable that the scenery of the Paradise described in Gen. ii—iii. is derived from Babylonia.

Further, on p. 77 an inscription is mentioned in which it is narrated that certain persons or gods wished to obtain possession of the 'tablets of the gods' containing the secrets of heaven and earth. These persons or gods seem, in the record, to possess themselves of the tablets, and to have broken off branches of 'the cedar beloved of the great gods.' The text afterwards speaks of someone who did not keep the commandment of Samas (the Sun-god) and Rimmon (the wind-god), and continues: "To the place of He[1], Samas, Marduk, and Nin-Edina (Lord of Eden) which (is) the hidden place (?) of heaven and earth, the band (lit. number) of the companions must not approach for deciding the decision; the message of the decision they shall not reveal; their hands (shall not touch?) the cedar tree beloved of the great gods."

---

[1] A stream connected with the paradise at Eridu.

Additions and Corrections 347

One desires, of course, the criticism of experts on this rendering of the inscription to which Dr Pinches refers, before building upon it. But if it has, on the whole, been rightly interpreted, it would seem that Babylonian literature furnishes us with a parallel to the tree of knowledge as well as with a parallel to the tree of life, and also, apparently, with a story akin to the narrative of the Fall.

PAGES 49 AND 92.

For F. Delitzsch *read* Friedrich Delitzsch.

PAGE 211.

Before the title of the Apocalypse of Baruch *insert* IX.

PAGE 220.

Before the title 4 Ezra (2 Esdras) *insert* X.

ERRATA

PAGE 169

Note, line 4. After *yezer hara* read 'or *yezer hatob*'

PAGE 170

Line 10. For *tob* read *hatob*

INDEX OF PASSAGES

OF THE BIBLE, AND OF JEWISH PSEUDEPIGRAPHIC AND RABBINIC WRITINGS.

OLD TESTAMENT.

	PAGE		PAGE
Gen. i. 26	104, 138	Gen. iv. 11	7
27	104	13	160
31	125, 171	16	64
ii. 4 ff.	20, 36 f.	v. 1, 3	104
5	30, 37	vi. 1–4	11, 94, 96, 120, 128, 132, 181 ff. 202, 236 f.
6	37		
7	170	3	15
8	18, 19	5	98 f. 103
9	18, 41	5 ff.	10
10–14	18, 27, 37	12	10
15	18 f. 30	viii. 21	10, 98, 103
17	30, 118, 120	ix. 6	104
22	41	20–27	10
24	26, 41	25	99, 130
25	155	xi. 1–9	10
iii. 1–19	17	6–8	15
3	18	xiii. 10	64
5	15, 40	xviii. 23	99
9	7	xix. 15	99
16	7	xx. 9	99
17	7, 30	xxv. 26	102
17–19	18	xxvi. 10	99
19	118	xxxviii. 21	39
20	17 f. 25 f. 67	Exod. xx. 5	99
21	18	xxxii. 33	99
22	15, 18, 25, 64, 72, 118	xxxiv. 7	99
22–24	18	Levit. xviii. 23	41
24	18	xx. 15, 16	41
iv. 7	7, 10, 97	Num. xiii. 32	30
9	7	xxi. 14	17

Index of Passages

	PAGE		PAGE
Deut. v. 9	100	Psal. lxxxii. 6, 7	160
vii. 10	100	7	91
xxiii. 17	39	xc. 3	91
18	231	ciii. 14	103
xxiv. 16	100	cxxx. 3	101
xxvii. 26	163	cxliii. 2	101
xxix. 29	16	Prov. iii. 18	91
xxx. 15	207	viii. 22 ff.	62
19	207	x. 11	91
xxxi. 21	103	xi. 30	91
Josh. x. 13	17	xiii. 12	91
Jud. ix. 8 ff.	81	14	91
1 Sam. viii. 6	15	xiv. 27	91
12	31	xx. 9	101
2 Sam. i. 18	17	Eccles. i. 2	302
iii. 29	99	vii. 20	101
xii. 1–6	81	29	91
xxi. 5 ff.	99	ix. 2	164
xxiv. 1 ff.	15	xii. 7	91
1 Kings ii. 33	99	Isai. ii. 4	30
viii. 46	101	7–22	16
xvii. 1	99	iii. 1–4	16
2 Kings v. 27	99	v. 1–7	81
xiv. 6	100	1 ff.	171
9–10	81	vii. 17	100
1 Chron. xxi. 1	129	x. 13 ff.	16
xxviii. 9	103	33	16
xxix. 18	103	xi. 6 ff.	33
2 Chron. vi. 36	101	xiv. 12 ff.	16
Job iv. 17	101	13	64, 199
xiv. 4	101	13 ff.	193
4, 5	295, 300	21	100
xv. 7	62	xxii. 7–11	16
7 ff.	61	xxiv. 21	97
14, 15	101	xxviii. 26 ff.	30
xxi. 22	16	xxxvii. 24	16
xxv. 4	101, 319	xliii. 27	91
xxviii. 21	16	27, 28	102
xxxi. 33	91	xlviii. 8	102
xxxiv. 15	91	li. 3	64, 91
xxxviii. 15	16	lxi. 5	31
Psal. viii. 6	104	lxv. 25	91
xxxvi. 1	115	Jer. xiv. 20	100
xxxix. 5	302	xv. 4	100
xliv. 25	302	xvii. 9	102
xlvi. 4	64	xxi. 8	207
li. 5	101, 103, 295, 299, 300	xxii. 28, 30	100
lviii. 3	102	xxiii. 18	61
lxxx.	81	xxvi. 15	100

Index of Passages

	PAGE		PAGE
Jer. xxxi. 29, 30	99	Hos. i. 4	100
33	111	vi. 7	91
xxxii. 18	100	viii. 3, 4	15, 16
Lam. v. 7	100	x. 13	16
Ezek. xvi.	81	xii. 3	102
xvii. 2–10	81	8, 14	16
xviii. 2–4	99	xiv. 7	30
xxviii.	16, 63 f. 81	Joel ii. 3	64, 91
13	91	Amos ix. 8	100
14, 16	63	13	30
xxxi.	63, 81	Obad. 10	100
8	64	Mic. i. 7	231
8, 9	91	vii. 17	91
xxxvi. 26	111	Zech. xiii. 5	31
35	64		

APOCRYPHA.

2 Esdras, *see* 4 Ezra, under *Pseud-epigraphic Writings*		Ecclus. vi. 19	31
		vii. 15	31
Tob. iii. 1–6	182	viii. 5	111, 117
iv. 12	120	x. 12, 13	112
xiv. 4 ff.	15	xiv. 7	119
Wisd. i. 11	124	xv. 11 ff.	117
12 ff.	124 ff.	14 ff.	114
13	124	17	208
14	124 f., 127, 281	xvi. 7	182
ii. 23, 24	104, 124, 125, 128, 184, 246	xvii. 1 ff.	104, 113, 117, 120
		6	208
iii. 1 ff.	124, 126	12	120
16	124	31	116, 117
iv. 10–14	126	xxi. 27	115
19	124	xxiii. 24	111
v. 4	128	xxv. 24	111, 113, 117, 119, 121, 162
14	124		
vii. 1	127, 129	xxvii. 6	116
viii. 19, 20	126	xxx. 25	109
20	129	xxxiii. 14, 15	116
21	130	16	109
ix. 2, 3	104	xxxvii. 3	116
15	126	xl. 11	120
x. 1, 2	128, 130	xli. 3	120
4	130	5	111
xii. 10	140, 144	xliv. 2	120
10, 11	130	18	120
xiv. 6	182	xlvii. 20	111
xv. 11	126	xlix. 16	207, 242
Ecclus. iii. 21–24	109	Bar. iii. 26	182
v. 31	117		

Index of Passages

NEW TESTAMENT.

	PAGE
Matt. vii. 11	248
xv. 19	169
Luke xi. 13	248
John ii. 25	248
iii. 3 ...	248, 333
ix. 2 ...	265
Rom. iii. 23	258
v. 12–21	172, 229, 251–258, 261, 262, 266, 270, 289, 294, 300, 344
13, 14	264
19 ...	263
vi. 12 ff.	268
vii. ...	271
5	267
7–25	252, 267, 268
9–11	136
11	255
viii. ...	252
3	267
4–9	268
18 ff.	271
20	224, 302

	PAGE
Rom. viii. 22	224
1 Cor. xv. 22	309
45 ff.	252, 270
2 Cor. v. 14	265
15	257
xi. 2, 3	209
Gal. v. ...	252
17–24	268
Eph. i. 10	288
ii. 3 ...	252, 271
iv. 22, 23	169
Col. iii. 1	257
1 Tim. ii. 13–15	160, 209
Heb. vii. 9, 10 ...	166, 261
Jas. i. 13–15	169
1 Pet. iii. 4	69
2 Pet. ii. 4	190
1 John i. 8	248
Jude 6	190
Rev. ii. 7	249
xii. 9 ...	43, 249
xxii. 2, 14	38, 249

RABBINICAL WRITINGS (TALMUD TARGUMS AND MIDRASHIM).

Aboda Zara	151, 157, 231
Aboth di R. Nathan	151–153, 157, 158, 171, 176
Arachin	163, 231
Baba Bathra	113, 164, 171, 175, 213
Bammidbar Rabba	155, 174
Beracoth	156, 163, 170
Bereschith Rabba	41, 150–156, 160, 162, 165, 171, 220
Debarim Rabba	165
Erubin	151, 159, 165, 175
Jalkut, see Yalkut Schim	
Jebamoth	40, 157
Joma	175
Kiddusch	170, 175
Koheleth Rabba	165, 174, 231
Nedarim	174

Pesikta	165, 213
Pirke Aboth	108, 113, 149
Pirke di R. Elieser	152, 154, 158, 159, 231, 245, 246
Sabbath	157, 162, 164, 175
Sanhedrin	151, 152, 155, 175, 231
Schemoth Rabba	163, 166
Siphra	165
Siphre	10, 165
Sota	153
(Jerus.)	175
Sukkah	113
Tanchuma	150, 163, 171
Targum Jerus.	10, 63, 149
of Onkelos	10, 63, 149
Tosefta Chulin	231
Yalkut Schim	151, 158, 159, 165

Index of Passages

JEWISH PSEUDEPIGRAPHIC WRITINGS.

	PAGE
Abraham, Apocalypse of, c. 22	156
do. c. 23	193, 194
Testament of	195
Adam, Apocalypse of, c. 3	201
Book of, *see* Apocalypse of Moses	
History of the Creation etc. of	201
History of the Expulsion of	202
History of the Repentance of	202
Life of, cc. 12–17	199
Story of the Conversation of, *see* Apocalypse of Moses	
Adam and Eve, Book of, *see* Conflict of Adam and Eve	
Conflict of, i. 2, 4, 8, 10, 11, 13, 14, 17, 22, 27	200
Testament of, *see* Apocalypse of Adam	
Aser, Testament of	
i.	116, 169, 191, 208
v.	116
Baruch, Apocalypse of (*Greek*)	
iv.	202 f.
ix.	198, 202 f.
Baruch, Apocalypse of (*Syriac*)	
iv. 3	213
ix. 1	217
xvii. 3	214
xviii. 1, 2	216, 220
xix.	208
xix. 8	214
xxiii. 4	119, 214
xlviii. 40	219
42–3	217 ff.
liv. 14	220
15	220, 221
15 ff.	217, 221
19	217, 220
21	220
lvi. 6 ff.	214, 215
10	213
lxx., lxxi.	230
Dan, Testament of, v.	190

	PAGE
Enoch, Book of (*Aethiopic*)	
vi.	182
viii.	183
ix. 6	183
x. 7, 8	183
xiii. 2	183
xv. 3 ff.	182
xvi. 2, 3	183
xix. 2	184
xxiv., xxv.	70, 187
xxv. 6	187
xxxii. 3	14
3 ff.	186
4	156
liv. 6	188
lxiv. 2	188
lxv. 6–8	189
lxix. 6	183, 184, 189
6–12	189
11	189
lxxx. 2–8	185
lxxxiv. 4	184
xcvi.	193
xcviii. 4	184 f.
c. 4, 11	185
Enoch, Book of (*Slavonic*)	
viii.	208
xviii. 1 ff.	206
xxi. 4	206
xxii. 1	151
xxiii. 5	143
xxix. 4, 5	206
xxx. 8 ff.	207
11	207
15, 16	143
18	208
xxxi. 2	208, 213
3, 5, 6	207
4	206
6	208
xxxii. 1, 2	208
xl. 1 ff.	209, 211
xlii.	211
xliv. 1	208

T.   23

354 Index of Passages

Enoch, Book of the Secrets of, see Enoch, Book of (*Slavonic*)	
2 Esdras, *see* 4 Ezra	
Ezra, Apocalypse of, *see* 4 Ezra	
4 Ezra iii. 4 ff.	223
7	224
8	223
12	223
13	223
20	226, 227
21	226
22	227
26	227
35	223
36	223
iv. 30, 31	226
39	223
vii. 11, 12	224
21–26	230
46	223
48	228
68	223
72	230
92	225, 230
116 ff.	228 f.
127–131	230
140	230
viii. 1	230
3	230
35	223
56–62	230
ix. 11	230
16	230
x. 9 ff.	224
xi. 46	224
Job, Apocalypse of	156
Job, Testament of	246, 247
Jubilees, Book of, iii. 15	192
iii. 28	192
29	193
iv. 15	191
Jubilees, Book of, iv. 22	192
v. 1	192
2 ff.	192
12	192
vii. 21 ff.	192
26–39	192
x. 1–15	192
xii. 25, 26	193
Judah, Testament of, xx	169
Levi, Testament of, iii.	190
xviii.	191
3 Maccabees ii. 4	182
iii. 22	140, 144
4 Maccabees ii. 21	144, 169
iii. 4	144
xviii. 7–8	144, 160, 197, 247
Moses, Apocalypse of, *see* pp. 196 ff.	
x.	198
xi.	197
xiv.	198, 220
xix.	197
xx.	197
xxiv.	197
xxv.	197
xxxii.	198
xxxvi.	198, 203
Moses, Assumption of	195
Naphthali, Testament of, iii.	190
Noah, Apocalypse of (passages contained in Book of Enoch)	189, 192
Pseudo-Philo	194
Reuben, Testament of, v.	184, 190
Seth, Concerning the Good Tidings of	202
Sibylline Oracles, Bks. i. and ii.	123
Bk. viii. 399 f.	208
Solomon, Psalms of, ix. 7	195
Testament of, xxi., xxvi.	190
Treasure Cave, The	200 f.
Vita Adae, see Life of Adam.	

INDEX OF AUTHORS.

	PAGE
Abbot, T. K.	271
Abrahams	114
Addis	8, 18
Aeschylus	52–3
Ambrose	336, 338 ff.
Ambrosiaster	342 f.
Aphraates	152
Aquinas	150, 214
Aristobulus	123, 141
Athanasius	310 ff.
Athenaeus	50
Athenagoras	282
Aucher	136
Augustine, S.	150, 151 n. 6, 166, 214 n. 1, 247 n. 1, 256, 262, 296, 323, 324 n. 2, 335, 340
Baader	88
Bacher	109, 146, 148 ff., 155 ff., 159, 160, 165, 170, 231
Baethgen	26
Baldensperger	180
Barton	26, 29, 35, 36, 41, 43, 44, 51, 69 ff., 95
Basil	316 ff.
Baudissin	29, 49, 74
Beer	178, 179, 181, 191
Bengel	256, 260
Bensly	224
Benzinger	31
Berhai	167
Bernard, Canon E. R.	90, 99
Berosus	34, 44
Bertholet	63
Beyschlag	251, 253, 254
Bezold	201

	PAGE
Biesenthal	261
Bigg	294 ff., 299
Böhme	88
Bois	110, 122, 128, 142
Bonwetsch	143, 153, 156, 193, 205, 209, 241, 308, 310
Boscawen	48
Bousset	177, 191, 241
Braun	146
Bretschneider	109, 112, 115, 119
Bruce	250, 253, 254
Bruch	112
Budde	6, 8, 13, 17, 18, 62, 95
Bull, Bp.	150, 266, 308, 316, 317
Carpenter and Harford-Battersby	8, 17
Ceriani	217
Charles	119, 143, 181 ff., 204 ff., 212 ff., 226, 227, 230
Cheyne	18, 29, 57, 63, 79, 115
Chrysippus	331, 332
Chrysostom	324 ff.
Cicero	331
Cleanthes	331
Clemen	5, 11, 12, 20, 90, 91, 95, 99, 102, 212, 218, 226
Clement of Alexandria	291 ff., 297, 300, 315, 320, 335
Clodd	78
Cobb	69, 74
Cohn	194
Cohn and Wendland	132
Coleridge, S. T.	80
Conybeare	190, 196–7
Cornill	63
Cox	54, 74

356 Index of Authors

	PAGE
Critical Review, The	6
Cyprian	335, 336 f.
Cyril of Jerusalem	308, 314 ff.
Dähne	110, 122, 129, 142
Dalman	143
Darmesteter	55, 56, 58
Darwin	78
Davidson	62
Davis	97
Dawson, Sir J. W.	77–8
Deane	130
Delitzsch, Friedr.	49, 92
Delitzsch, Franz	61, 165, 182
Derenbourg	231
Dieckmann	43
Dillmann	13, 60, 64, 78, 82, 95, 195, 200, 243
Dînkart	56
Dods, Marcus	340
Donaldson	69
Dorner	11
Doughty	29
Driver	18
Drummond, J.	110, 122, 138, 142
Duff	8
Duncker	290
Edersheim	110, 112, 114, 115, 120, 142, 145, 148, 154, 156, 161, 162, 230
Eisenmenger	40, 59
Encyclopaedia Biblica	18, 19, 26, 29, 37, 57, 63, 101
Encyclopaedia Britannica	54
Engelhardt	277
Epiphanius	151, 156, 159
Ephrem	151, 213
Erbkam	285
Etheridge	149
Eusebius	32, 43, 95, 151, 298, 310
Ewald	62, 109
Fairbairn	78
Faye, De	212, 221
Fergusson	33, 69, 74
Firdûsi	55, 58
Flemming and Radermacher	181
Forlong	74

	PAGE
Frazer	50, 67, 70
Friedländer	232
Fritzsche	108, 112, 115
Fuchs	196
Gfrörer	110, 142, 160
Gibson	91
Gifford	265
Ginzberg	148, 149, 152, 154, 155, 156, 158, 159, 161
Glaser	27
Goldziher	28, 30, 74
Gomperz	53
Grätz	128, 180, 231
Green	8
Gregory (Great)	151
of Nazianzus	318 f., 321, 335
of Nyssa	214, 247, 316, 319 ff., 327, 345
Grimm	126, 127
Grünbaum	158, 241
Gunkel	6, 8, 14, 16 ff., 31, 37, 38, 40, 43 ff., 61, 63, 64, 67, 86, 177, 221, 241
Hagenbach	277
Hamburger	148, 149
Hardwick	59, 60
Harford-Battersby, see Carpenter	
Harlez, De	56
Harnack	278, 279, 285, 287, 299, 311, 313, 321, 327, 328, 335
Hastings (Dictionary of the Bible)	8, 14, 26, 29, 38, 42, 49, 90 f., 99, 122, 189, 192, 221
Hauck	78
Haupt	38, 40
Hausrath	253
Headlam, see Sanday	
Hegel	8
Herder	8
Herodotus	39
Herriot	110, 122
Hershon	40
Hesiod	52–3
Hilary	336, 337 f.
Hilgenfeld	177, 189, 226, 277
Hilt	320, 324
Höffding	84

Index of Authors

	PAGE
Hoffmann	61
Hofmann, Von	12
Hogarth	38
Holzinger	8, 17, 18, 28
Homer	52
Hommel	27, 42, 45, 49
Horn	57
Hort	87, 195
Ignatius	275
Irenaeus	151, 160, 247, 274, 276, 282 ff., 296, 300, 305, 309, 310, 329 f., 332, 344
Issaverdens	196 ff., 201
James	156, 195, 203, 224, 232, 234
Jastrow, M. (Junr.)	26, 29, 36 ff., 48
Jennings	74, 146
Jensen	38
Jeremias, A.	39, 42, 63
Jerome	340
John of Damascus	151
Josephus	72, 79, 130, 136, 151, 152, 182, 190, 193, 245
Jost	180
Julian of Eclanum	324
Justin Martyr	163, 231, 275 ff.
Kabisch	196, 221, 226, 254
Kant	8, 80
Kautzsch	8, 18, 109, 114, 195, 196, 202, 221
Keane	78
Keary	74
Keil	63
King	31, 42
Kittel	8
Kohler	151, 158, 163, 175, 178, 179, 191, 195
Kohnt	55, 57, 58, 63
König	27, 49
Kraetzschmar	63
Kremer	28
Kropotkin	78
Kuenen	196, 202, 221
Kuhn	47, 52, 85
Lagarde	115
Lajard	58

	PAGE
Lang	78
Lange	253, 256
Lenormant	8, 29, 33, 34, 44, 49, 53, 55, 60, 77
Leontius Byzantinus	277
Lévi	114
Liltmann	191
Lincke	38
Lipsius	254, 266
Lods	182 ff.
Loisy	10, 18, 19, 201, 205
Loofs	335
Lowe	146
Lubbock, Sir J.	78
Luther	151
Mackenzie	78
MᶜCurdy	6, 19
Mähly	74
Maimonides	157
Malan	200, 213, 233
Mangey	134
Margoliouth	113, 114
Martensen	82
Martin, Raymond	146, 172
Maspero	34, 35, 42, 44, 65
Massey	35, 74
Max Müller, F.	59, 78
Max Müller, W.	36, 51, 71, 74
Methodius	247, 308 ff., 322
Meyer	196
Mills	56
Montefiore	8, 110, 147, 148, 180
Morfill	143, 189, 204, 209
Moulton	55
Movers	68
Neander	295, 298, 332, 335
Nestle	110
Nicolas	142
Nöldeke	26, 28
Oehler	98
Oldenberg	55
Origen	133, 195, 262, 274, 295, 296 ff., 310, 318, 320 ff., 325, 344
Orr	78
Osiander	125
Otto	277

23—3

Index of Authors

	PAGE
Panaetius	332
Pelagius	294, 298, 326
Pererius	151
Pfleiderer, O.	253, 256, 266
Pherecydes of Syros	43
Phillips	59
Philo Byblus	32, 33, 95
Philo Judaeus	58, 81, 129, 131 ff., 149, 182, 193, 242 ff., 247, 250, 278, 281, 285, 293 f., 297, 304
Pinches	37, 44, 60, 346
Plato	87, 143, 149, 297, 304
Plutarch	332
Polycarp	275
Porter	103, 114, 116, 138, 143, 148, 170, 171, 174, 177, 215, 222, 226, 271
Preller	32, 52
Rabbi Abba b. Kahana	157
Abin	155
Acha	154
Akiba	149, 162, 175
Ammi	151, 162 f., 164
Asi	153
Chanina	156
Chanina b. Dosa	163
Chayim Vital	166
David of Roccamartica	160
Eleazar b. Azariah	155
(b. Jose)	175
b. Pedath	150
Elieser b. Hirkanos	40, 158, 163, 231
Hoschaia	152, 153
Ibo	156
Jehuda b. Bathera	152
b. Simon	150
b. Thema	152
Jirmeja b. Eleazar	159
Jochanan b. Chanina	155
Jose	150, 157, 165, 170, 173
b. Chalastha	153
Joshua b. Karcha	155
b. Levi	156
Levi	165
Mar Ukba	155
Mayer b. Gabbai	168
Meir	156
Mosche of Trana	167

	PAGE
Rabbi Nachman b. Chisda	170
Saccai	155
Samuel b. Nachman	171
Shemtob	168
Simon	150, 160
b. Eleazar	164, 165
b. Lakisch	160
Räbiger	119
Raschi	171
Rauch	332
Rawlinson	44
Redslob	83
Rekanati, Menahem	167
Renan	32, 33, 201
Renouf	35
Reuss	82
Réville	78, 86
Ritschl	269
Rodkinson	148
Romanes	78
Rönsch	191
Rosenthal	231
Rothe	11
Rousseau	65
Ryle	48
Ryssel	109, 114, 115, 202, 203, 212, 221
Sanday and Headlam	253 ff., 260, 261, 264
Saussaye, De la	44, 87
Sayce	37, 43 ff., 47, 49, 60
Schechter	108, 109, 114, 148, 160 ff., 166, 170, 171, 180
Schiefer	230
Schiller	8
Schiller-Szinessy	146
Schoettgen	146
Schrader	17, 37, 49
Schultz	5, 79, 91, 95, 98
Schultze	84
Schürer	109, 122, 142, 145, 155, 180, 195, 221
Schwane	277
Siegfried	142, 250, 339
Singer	191
Smend	13, 14, 16
Smith, W. Robertson	5, 8, 18, 19, 26 ff., 33, 65, 68, 79, 87, 95, 182

Index of Authors

Socin	18
South, Bp	150
Spiegel	55 ff.
Sprenger	27
Spurrell	8, 10, 23
Squiers	74
Stade	18, 40
Stanton	146, 180
Stave	96, 129, 188
Steffens	88
Stevens	168, 253, 257, 262, 271
Stout	84
Swete	327
Syncellus	151
Tatian	278 ff., 283, 284, 288
Taylor	108, 113 ff., 143, 148, 149, 169, 250
Tennant	79, 85, 267, 272, 345
Tertullian	159, 247, 274, 295, 300, 328 ff., 344
Thackeray	160, 197, 208, 209, 214, 221, 247, 250, 251, 258
Theodore of Mopsuestia	324, 327 f.
Theophilus of Antioch	280 ff., 286, 288
Thilo	234
Tholuck	165, 167
Tiele	55, 56
Tischendorf	196
Torrey	178, 180, 195, 196, 205
Töttermann	232
Toy	16, 19, 20, 62, 72, 109, 110, 254
Trumbull	160
Turmel	295, 318, 335
Tyler	110, 114
Tylor	78, 87
Usener	65
Ussher	151
Wake	74
Weber, F. (Author of *Jüd. Theologie*)	147, 150 f., 155, 156, 159 ff., 167, 180, 184, 197, 259
Weber (Author of *Indische Studien*)	56
Weber, O. (In *Der Alte Orient*)	25
Weinstein	142
Weizsäcker	253, 266
Wellhausen	6, 11, 13 ff., 26
Wendt	277, 279, 285, 287
West	56
Wiedemann	35
Windischmann	55, 57, 158
Winter and Wünsche	157
Worcester	8, 18, 37, 40, 41
Wright	152
Wünsche	148, 155, 165, 166
Zeller	129, 142
Zeno	331, 332
Zimmern	31, 37, 38, 45, 48
Zöckler	77
Zunz	145, 150, 159, 196

INDEX OF SUBJECTS.

	PAGE
Adam as representative or sum of the race 166, 256 ff., 261 ff., 281, 288 ff., 304 ff., 310, 314, 321, 327, 332, 338, 342	
Adam, books of	195 ff.
Adapa	38, 45 f.
Agriculture, *see under* Fall-story	
Allegorical interpretation of Fall-story 80 ff., 136, 255, 297, 302, 318	
Allegory	81
Amoraim 145 and *passim* in Ch. VII.	
Angels, Descent of, *see* Watchers	
,, Fall of 96 f., 183, 185, and *see* Satan, Fall of	
Apocalyptic literature, *see* Pseudepigraphic literature	
Apocalypse of Abraham	193
,, ,, Baruch (Greek)	202
,, ,, ,, (Syriac)	211 ff.
,, ,, Noah	189
Apologists	275 ff., 282
Arabia, Arabs	25, 26 f., 71, 73 f.
Aruru	39
Assumption of Moses	195
Athenagoras	282
Avesta	54 ff.
Azazel 182 and *passim* in Ch. VIII.	
Baal-land	27 f.
Babylonian legends related to Fall-story	36 ff., 346
Baptism in relation to Original Sin 277, 290, 294 f., 299 ff., 316, 319, 322, 328, 334 f., 336 f.	
Beena marriage	26
Buddha, tree of	59

	PAGE
Bundahesch	57, 129, 158
Canaanites, influence on the Hebrews of	31, 75
Death, doctrine concerning, in Old Test.	117 ff.
Ecclus.	119 ff.
Wisdom	123 ff.
Philo	135 ff.
Rabbinic literature	161 ff.
Slav. Enoch	142, 207
Test. of Abraham	195
Apoc. of Moses	198
,, ,, Baruch	214
4 Ezra	224
Christian Pseudepigraphs	232 ff.
Jewish literature as a whole	244
S. Paul	253 ff.
Justin Martyr	276 f.
Tatian	278 f.
Clement of Alexandria	294
Methodius	309
Cyril of Jerusalem	315 f.
Basil	317
Gregory of Nyssa	321
Chrysostom	325 f.
Theodore of Mopsuestia	327
Devil, *see* Satan	
Dona Superaddita	280, 284, 311
Ea	44 f., 75
Eabani, legend of	39 ff., 71, 74
Ecclesiasticus, date, value etc. of	107 f.

Index of Subjects

	PAGE
Eden (Paradise) 18, 26 f., 37 ff., 63, 64 ff., 75, 91, 155, 186 f., 346	
Egyptian legends related to Fall-story	34 ff., 71
Elohim-beings	27, 96
Enoch, Book of (Aethiopic)	181 ff.
„ „ „ (Slavonic)	142 ff., 204 ff.
Eridu	38, 44, 75, 346
2 Esdras *or* 4 Ezra, date, authorship etc. of	220 ff. 231 f.
Etana	48
Eve 112, 117, 119, 143, 144, 153 ff., 157, 176, 189, 198, 201, 274	
„ etymology of	17, 26
Fall, the, effects on Nature of, 127, 150 f., 193, 197, 203, 215, 247, 271, 281	
Fall, theory of pre-mundane or ante-natal, 133, 297 f., 318, 320 f.	
Fall and Original Sin, doctrine of	
in Jahvist writing	11
Old Test.	104 f.
Ecclus.	111 ff.
Wisdom	129 ff.
Philo	136, 140 ff.
3 and 4 Macc.	144
Rabbinic writings 157 f., 161 ff., 167 ff., 176	
Book of Enoch	186
Apoc. of Moses	198 f.
Fragments of Adam-literature	202
Slav. Enoch	209 f.
Apoc. of Baruch	215 ff.
4 Ezra	224 ff., 228 ff.
Jew. literature as a whole	Ch. x.
Gospels and Epistles	248, 271
S. Paul (Rom.)	251 ff.
Justin Martyr	275 ff.
Tatian	278 f.
Theophilus of Antioch	280 ff.
Irenaeus	285 ff., 291
Clement of Alexandria	291 ff.
Origen	296 ff.
Methodius	309 f.
Athanasius	311 ff.
Basil	316 ff.
Gregory of Nazianzus	318 f.
Gregory of Nyssa	320 ff.

	PAGE
Fall and Original Sin, doctrine of	
in Chrysostom	325 ff.
Theodore of Mopsuestia	327 f.
Tertullian	328 ff.
Cyprian	336 f.
Hilary	337 f.
Ambrose	339 ff.
Augustine	343 and *passim*
Fall and Original Sin, growth of doctrine of 238 ff. (*see also* Ch. IV.) 273 ff., 282 ff., 291, 307, 323 f., 328 ff., 338, 343 ff.	
Fall-story, allegorical interpretation of	80 ff., 136, 255
Date of	3 ff.
Exegesis of	8 ff.
'Inspiration' of	85, 87 f.
Literary criticism of	16 ff.
„ style of	6 ff.
Oral tradition of	19 ff.
Original significance of	68 ff., 74 ff.
Use of, in Old Test.	90 ff.
in Pseudepigrapha 236 ff. etc.	
Variants of	61 ff.
Non-historical	77 ff.
In what sense mythical	82 ff.
Contains no doctrine of Original Sin	89
Traces of nomadic Hebrew tradition in	25–30
Its reference to agriculture	30
Its connexion with abuse of the vine	155 f.
Its connexion with the sexual relation 40 ff., 67 f., 69 ff., 144, 153 ff., 156 ff., 189, 193 f., 197, 208, 247, 251	
First man, legend of,	
in Job	61 f.
Ezek.	63 f.
Philo	133 f.
Talmud	149 f.
S. Paul	251
Flesh	102, 268 ff., 290
Gadreel	183, 189 f.
Garden of Eden, *see* Eden	
„ „ God, or the gods	27, 49, 53
Gilgamesh, epic of	38 ff.

Index of Subjects

Gnostic legends or doctrines 159, 278, 283, 292
Golden Age ... ... 50, 53, 65 f.
Good and Evil, meaning of 12 ff., 41
Greek legends, related to the Fall-story ... ... 51 ff.
Guilt, Original, see Original Guilt

Haggada, definition of 109, 145, 148
Haoma 57, 68
Hebrews, early history and religion of... 24
Hereditary sinfulness 102 f., 130, 139 f., 302 f., 304, 317 f., 319 ff., 326, 332 ff., 338
Hesperides, garden of 53
Himā 27
Hindu legend related to Fall-story ... ... 59 f.

Image of God 104, 113, 148 f., 284 f., 287 f., 336, 339
Inborn sin, see Sinfulness, inherent
Indian legend, see Hindu legend
Inspiration of Fall-story, see Fall-story
Iranian legends related to Fall-story ... ... 54 ff., 182
Izdubar, see Gilgamesh

Jahveh, delineation of in J 4 f., 14 ff.
Jahvist Document or Writer (J) 3 ff., 19, 68, 75, 79, 95 f.
Jinn 28
Jubilees, Book of ... 191 ff.

Ladon 53

Maschiana 58
Maschya 58
Matriarchate, see Mother-descent
Mishna ... ... 145 f.
Mother-descent 26

Oannes 44
Original Guilt 167, 301, 318, 334, 342
Original Sin, see Fall and Original Sin
Original state of man
in the Jahvist writing ... ... 9 ff.
Philo ... ... 133 f.

Original state of man
in Rabbinical literature 149 ff.
Adam-literature 200
Slavonic Enoch ... 207 f.
Apoc. of Baruch ... 213 f.
Jewish literature as a whole 242 ff.
S. Paul 270
Justin Martyr 277
Tatian 278
Theophilus of Antioch ... 280
Irenaeus 286
Clement of Alexandria 292 f.
Athanasius 311
Basil 316
Gregory of Nyssa ... 320 f.
Ambrose ... ... 338 f.
Original state, duration of the 151, 243

Pahlavi translation of Avesta ... 56
Pandora ... ... 52 f.
Paradise, see Eden
Paul, S., relation to Jewish or Hellenic thought 250 and passim in Ch. XI; 343
Persian legend, see Iranian legend
Phallicism 68
Phoenician influence on Hebrew culture 31
Phoenician legends related to Fall-story ... ... 32 ff., 53
Prometheus ... 47, 52 f., 62, 85 f.
Psalms of Solomon 195
Pseudepigraphic literature, origin, nature etc. of ... ... 177 ff.
Pseudo-Philo 194

Recapitulation-doctrine 288 ff., 309, 344

Samael 152, 158, 195, 203
Satan 28, 43, 104, 110, 115, 128 f., 143, 152 ff., 184, 188, 192, 197, 200, 232 ff., 237, 255, 275 etc.
Envy of 152 ff., 196, 199, 200, 201, 207, 237, 246 f., 316
Fall of 193, 199, 200, 201, 206, 238, 246
Satanail 206
Seal, Babylonian with supposed representation of the Fall ... 48
Semjaza 182 and passim in Ch. VIII.

Index of Subjects

Serpent, the, *or* serpent 28, 33, 41, 43, 45, 48, 71 ff., 104, 136, 152 ff., 184, 192, 194 ff., 200, 201, 203, 232 ff., 249, 255, 274, 293 etc.
Serpent symbolism ... ... 73 f.
Sin, conception of
   in Jahvist writing 97
   Old Test. ... ... 99 ff.
   Ecclus. 111
   Philo ... ... 137 f.
   Slav. Enoch 143
Sin, universality of
   in Jahvist writing ... 10, 98 f.
   Old Test. ... ... 100 ff.
   4 Ezra 223
   New Test. 248
   Fathers 275, 315
Sinful disposition
Sinfulness, inherent or inborn 97 f., 101 ff., 144, 215, 268 ff., 275, 299 ff., 319, 326, 332 ff., 340 ff.
Sirens 52
Siva 59
Solidarity, organic or moral, of mankind 99 f., 161 ff., 209 f., 215 f., 217 ff., 228 ff., 256 ff., 281, 297, 314, 315, 338, 342
Soma 57
Souls, fall of, *see* Fall, premundane
Stoic Philosophy, the source of traducianism ... ... 330 ff.

Talmud, nature, date etc. of ... 145 f.
Tannaim 145 and *passim* in Ch. VII.
Targums ... ... 145 f.
Tempter, *see esp.* p. 245 ff.; *see also* Gadreel, Satan etc.
Testament of Abraham, nature and date of 195
Testament of XII Patriarchs, nature and date of 190
Tiâmat 43
Traducianism 175, 294, 329 ff., 337, 340
Tree of knowledge 12 ff., 18, 29, 44, 66 ff., 118, 154 ff., 186, 232, 247, 346
Tree of Life 18, 44, 49, 66 ff., 91, 118, 187, 247, 249, 346

Unfallen state, *see* Original state

Vedas ... ... 59 ff.
Vîvanghat (Vivasvant) ... ... 55 ff.

Watchers, legend of the 94 ff., 181 ff., 188, 190 ff., 206 f., 212 f., 223, 236 ff.

Yama ... ... 54 ff.
Yezer or yezer hara 98, 103, 113 ff., 138, 143, 169 ff., 207, 225 ff., 271

Zu ... ... 47 f.

www.ingramcontent.com/pod-product-compliance
Lightning Source LLC
Chambersburg PA
CBHW061422300426
44114CB00014B/1501